The Law and Politics of Unconstitutional Constitutional Amendments in Asia

This book explains how the idea and practice of unconstitutional constitutional amendments are shaped by, and inform, constitutional politics through various social and political actors, and in both formal and informal amendment processes, across Asia.

This is the first book-length study of the law and politics of unconstitutional constitutional amendments in Asia. Comprising ten case studies from across the continent, and four broader, theoretical chapters, the volume provides an interdisciplinary, comparative perspective on the rising phenomenon of unconstitutional constitutional amendments (UCA) across a range of political, legal, and institutional contexts. The volume breaks new ground by venturing beyond the courts to consider UCA not only as a judicial doctrine, but also as a significant feature of political and intellectual discourse.

The book will be a valuable reference for law and political science researchers, as well as for policymakers and NGOs working in related fields. Offering broad coverage of jurisdictions in East Asia, Southeast Asia, and South Asia, it will be useful to scholars and practitioners within Asia as well as to those seeking to better understand the law and politics of the region.

Rehan Abeyratne is Associate Professor of Law and Executive Director of the Centre for Comparative and Transnational Law at the Chinese University of Hong Kong. He is a co-editor of *Towering Judges: A Comparative Study of Constitutional Judges* (2021) as well as the forthcoming *Routledge Handbook of Asian Parliaments*.

Ngoc Son Bui is Associate Professor of Asian Laws at the University of Oxford Faculty of Law. He is the author of *Constitutional Change in the Contemporary Socialist World* (2020) and *Confucian Constitutionalism in East Asia* (Routledge, 2016).

Comparative Constitutional Change

Comparative Constitutional Change has developed into a distinct field of constitutional law. It encompasses the study of constitutions through the way they change and covers a wide scope of topics and methodologies. Books in this series include work on developments in the functions of the constitution, the organization of powers and the protection of rights, as well as research that focuses on formal amendment rules and the relation between constituent and constituted power. The series includes comparative approaches along with books that focus on single jurisdictions, and brings together research monographs and edited collections which allow the expression of different schools of thought. While the focus is primarily on law, where relevant the series may also include political science, historical, philosophical and empirical approaches that explore constitutional change.

Series editors:

Xenophon Contiades is Professor of Public Law, Panteion University, Athens, Greece and Managing Director, Centre for European Constitutional Law, Athens, Greece.

Thomas Fleiner is Emeritus Professor of Law at the University of Fribourg, Switzerland. He teaches and researches in the areas of Federalism, Rule of Law, Multicultural State; Comparative Administrative and Constitutional Law; Political Theory and Philosophy; Swiss Constitutional and Administrative Law; and Legislative Drafting. He has published widely in these and related areas.

Alkmene Fotiadou is Research Associate at the Centre for European Constitutional Law, Athens.

Richard Albert is Professor of Law at the University of Texas at Austin.

Also in the series:

Constitutional Change and Popular Sovereignty
Populism, Politics and the Law in Ireland
Edited by Maria Cahill, Colm Ó Cinnéide, Seán Ó Conaill, and Conor O'Mahony

Accountability and the Law
Rights, Authority and Transparency of Public Power
Edited By Piotr Mikuli and Grzegorz Kuca

Illiberal Constitutionalism in Poland and Hungary
The Deterioration of Democracy, Misuse of Human Rights and Abuse of the Rule of Law
Tímea Drinóczi and Agnieszka Bień-Kacała

Courts and Judicial Activism under Crisis Conditions
Policy Making in a Time of Illiberalism and Emergency Constitutionalism
Edited by Martin Belov

The Law and Politics of Unconstitutional Constitutional Amendments in Asia
Edited by Rehan Abeyratne & Ngoc Son Bui

For more information about this series, please visit: www.routledge.com/Comparative-Constitutional-Change/book-series/COMPCONST

The Law and Politics of Unconstitutional Constitutional Amendments in Asia

Edited by Rehan Abeyratne and Ngoc Son Bui

LONDON AND NEW YORK

First published 2022
by Routledge
2 Park Square, Milton Park, Abingdon, Oxon OX14 4RN

and by Routledge
605 Third Avenue, New York, NY 10158

Routledge is an imprint of the Taylor & Francis Group, an informa business

© 2022 selection and editorial matter, Rehan Abeyratne and Ngoc Son Bui; individual chapters, the contributors

The right of Rehan Abeyratne and Ngoc Son Bui to be identified as the authors of the editorial material, and of the authors for their individual chapters, has been asserted in accordance with sections 77 and 78 of the Copyright, Designs and Patents Act 1988.

All rights reserved. No part of this book may be reprinted or reproduced or utilised in any form or by any electronic, mechanical, or other means, now known or hereafter invented, including photocopying and recording, or in any information storage or retrieval system, without permission in writing from the publishers.

Trademark notice: Product or corporate names may be trademarks or registered trademarks, and are used only for identification and explanation without intent to infringe.

British Library Cataloguing-in-Publication Data
A catalogue record for this book is available from the British Library

Library of Congress Cataloging-in-Publication Data
Names: Abeyratne, Rehan, editor. | Bùi, Ngọc Sơn, editor.
Title: The law and politics of unconstitutional constitutional amendments
in Asia / Rehan Abeyratne & Ngoc Son Bui.
Description: Abingdon, Oxon ; New York, NY : Routledge, 2021. | Series:
Comparative constitutional change | Includes bibliographical references and index.
Identifiers: LCCN 2021027992 (print) | LCCN 2021027993 (ebook) | ISBN
9780367562595 (hardback) | ISBN 9780367562625 (paperback) | ISBN
9781003097099 (ebook)
Subjects: LCSH: Constitutional amendments--Asia. | Constitutional law--Asia. | Constitutional amendments--Political aspects--Asia. | Constitutional amendments--Social aspects--Asia. | Judicial review--Asia.
Classification: LCC KNC524 .L39 2021 (print) | LCC KNC524 (ebook) | DDC
342.503--dc23
LC record available at https://lccn.loc.gov/2021027992
LC ebook record available at https://lccn.loc.gov/2021027993

ISBN: 978-0-367-56259-5 (hbk)
ISBN: 978-0-367-56262-5 (pbk)
ISBN: 978-1-003-09709-9 (ebk)

DOI: 10.4324/9781003097099

Typeset in Galliard
by Deanta Global Publishing Services, Chennai, India

Rehan Abeyratne: For Eila and Ahana
Bui Ngoc Son: For Fifi and Fifa

Contents

List of contributors ix
Acknowledgments xi

Introduction 1

1 Unconstitutional constitutional amendments as constitutional politics 3
REHAN ABEYRATNE AND NGOC SON BUI

PART I
Discursive model 21

2 The politics of unconstitutional constitutional amendments in Japan: The case of the pacifist Article 9 23
KOICHI NAKANO

3 "State form" in the theory and practice of constitutional change in modern China 46
RYAN MITCHELL

4 Unconstitutional constitution in Vietnamese discourse 67
NGOC SON BUI

PART II
Denotive model 85

5 The law and politics of unconstitutional constitutional amendments in Malaysia 87
HP LEE AND YVONNE TEW

6 Amending constitutional standards of parliamentary piety in Pakistan? Political and judicial debates 111
MATTHEW J NELSON

7 Limiting constituent power? Unconstitutional constitutional amendments and time-bound constitution making in Nepal 133
MARA MALAGODI

PART III
Decisive model 151

8 Beyond unconstitutionality: The public oversight of constitutional revision in Taiwan 153
JIUNN-RONG YEH

9 Thailand's unamendability: Politics of two democracies 169
KHEMTHONG TONSAKULRUNGRUANG

10 Constitutional politics over (un)constitutional amendments: The Indian experience 189
SURYA DEVA

11 The politics of unconstitutional amendments in Bangladesh 210
RIDWANUL HOQUE

PART IV
Commentaries 229

12 The power of judicial nullification in Asia and the world 231
RICHARD ALBERT

13 Is the "basic structure doctrine" a basic structure doctrine? 244
ANDREW HARDING

14 Eternity clauses as tools for exclusionary constitutional projects 257
SILVIA SUTEU

15 Why there?: Explanatory theories and institutional features behind unconstitutional constitutional amendments in Asia 274
YANIV ROZNAI

Index 297

Contributors

Rehan Abeyratne is Associate Professor of Law and Executive Director of the Centre for Comparative and Transnational Law at the Chinese University of Hong Kong

Richard Albert is William Stamps Farish Professor in Law, Professor of Government, and Director of Constitutional Studies at the University of Texas at Austin

Ngoc Son Bui is Associate Professor of Asian Laws at the University of Oxford Faculty of Law

Surya Deva is Professor at Macquarie Law School, Macquarie University, Australia

Andrew Harding is Visiting Research Professor at the National University of Singapore Faculty of Law

Ridwanul Hoque is Professor of Law at the University of Dhaka, Bangladesh, and University Fellow at the Charles Darwin University, Australia

Hoong Phun (HP) Lee is Emeritus Professor of Law at Monash University, Australia

Mara Malagodi is Assistant Professor of Law at the Chinese University of Hong Kong

Ryan Mitchell is Assistant Professor of Law at the Chinese University of Hong Kong

Koichi Nakano is Professor of Political Science at the Faculty of Liberal Arts, Sophia University, Japan

Matthew J Nelson is Professor of Politics at the School of Oriental and African Studies (SOAS), University of London

Yaniv Roznai is Associate Professor at the Harry Radzyner Law School, Reichman University (IDC Herzilya), Israel

Silvia Suteu is Lecturer in Public Law at the University College London (UCL) Faculty of Laws

Yvonne Tew is Professor of Law at the Georgetown University Law Center, USA

Khemthong Tonsakulrungruang is Lecturer in the Faculty of Political Science at Chulalongkorn University, Thailand

Jiunn-rong Yeh is National University of Taiwan Chair Professor at the National University of Taiwan College of Law

Acknowledgments

We are grateful to the Comparative Constitutional Research Forum within the Centre for Comparative and Transnational Law at CUHK LAW for holding a virtual symposium in November 2020 from which this book emerged. We thank our authors for their rich and diverse contributions and for their patience through the editing process. We are grateful to the editors of the Routledge Series on Comparative Constitutional Change, especially Richard Albert, for including this volume within the series. Finally, we thank the editors at Routledge for their hard work in finalizing the manuscript for publication.

Introduction

1 Unconstitutional constitutional amendments as constitutional politics

Rehan Abeyratne and Ngoc Son Bui

1.1 Background and aims

Constitutional amendments are central to the study of comparative constitutionalism. Amendment rules and processes, as well as their effects on the constitutional order, have been the subject of much scholarship. Of particular interest to constitutional scholars in recent years are the theory and practice of unconstitutional constitutional amendments (UCA).[1] The notion of UCA has diffused globally from its political foundations in France and the United States, to its doctrinal origins in Germany, to its practical application across the globe, including in Argentina, Austria, Greece, Hungary, Portugal, South Africa, South Korea, Switzerland, and Tanzania.[2]

Constitutions may place both explicit and implicit limits on amendments. Article 79(3) of the German Constitution, for instance, makes the following provisions unamendable: the democracy principle (provided in Article 20), the federal structure, and the principle of human dignity (provided in Article 1).[3] Such explicit limitations in the constitutional text are sometimes referred to as eternity clauses – they ensure that fundamental principles endure for as long as the constitution itself. More controversial, through increasingly common, are implicit limits on constitutional amendments. Implied limitations are usually declared by courts. Through a heightened form of judicial review, judges may find that constitutional amendments violate core constitutional principles such

---

1 See Yaniv Roznai, *Unconstitutional Constitutional Amendments: The Limits of Amendment Powers* (OUP 2017); Richard Albert, Malkhaz Nakashidze and Tarik Olcay, 'The Formalist Resistance to Unconstitutional Constitutional Amendments' (2019) 70 Hastings Law Journal 639; David Landau and Rosalind Dixon, 'Constraining Constitutional Change' (2015) 50 Wake Forest Law Review 859–90; Po Jen Yap, 'The Conundrum of Unconstitutional Constitutional Amendments' (2015) 4 Global Constitutionalism 114–36.
2 Richard Albert, 'Constitutional Amendment and Dismemberment' (2018) 43 Yale Journal of International Law 1, 15.
3 Monika Polzin, 'Constitutional Identity, Unconstitutional Amendments and the Idea of Constituent Power: The Development of the Doctrine of Constitutional Identity in German Constitutional Law' (2016) 14 International Journal of Constitutional Law 411.

DOI: 10.4324/9781003097099-1

as the separation of powers or judicial independence. This is what transpired in the Indian Supreme Court's landmark *Kesavananda* judgment (1973), which held that amendments could not violate the Constitution's "basic structure" and inspired many other apex and constitutional courts to follow suit. Indeed, courts around the world have held certain constitutional amendments as unconstitutional on the grounds that the impugned amendments altered fundamental aspects of the existing constitution.[4]

As a result of the global spread of UCA, there is a great deal of comparative constitutional scholarship in this area. The scholarship generally covers one or more of the following dimensions: theory, constitutional design, and judicial review. At a theoretical level, UCA, particularly in its implicit form, poses a conundrum for the classic distinction between constituent and constituent power. The distinction was first articulated by the Enlightenment French theorist Emmanuel Joseph Sièyes, who distinguished between an all-powerful *constituent* power that creates the constitution and a lesser, *constituted* power, which is created by, and operates under, the constitution.[5] Building on this insight more than one hundred years later, the German theorist Carl Schmitt argued that a constitution's core identity – representing the fundamental decisions of the constituent power – could not be destroyed or removed by amendments.[6]

Constitutional amendments do not fit neatly in this framework. On one hand, they may amend the very rules and processes under which the constituted power operates. Constitutional amendments may, for instance, alter executive term limits, legislative voting roles, or judicial appointment processes. On the other hand, the amendment power is often vested in one or more branches of the constituted power – usually the legislature and/or executive – and so it would be odd to view it as on par with the constituent power, which is often (though misleadingly) thought to reside in "the people."[7] So, paradoxically, the amendment power appears be neither part of the constituent power, nor part of the constituted power. One way around this paradox is to argue, as Yaniv Roznai has, that the amendment power is "sui-generis," a "secondary constituent power" that sits between the two poles.[8] For Roznai, the amendment power operates in a fiduciary arrangement with the constituent power, serving as its "trustee" that is subject to procedural and substantive limits.[9] Thus, an amendment may

---

4 Albert (n 2) 15–20.
5 Emmanuel Joseph Sièyes, 'What is the Third Estate?' in Oliver W Lembcke and Florian Weber (eds), *Emmanuel Joseph Sièyes: The Essential Political Writings* (Brill 2014).
6 Carl Schmitt, *Constitutional Theory* (Jeffrey Seitzer tr, Duke University Press 2008).
7 Albert (n 2) 11–13. See also, Gary Jeffrey Jacobsohn and Yaniv Roznai, *Constitutional Revolution* (OUP 2020) 17–22 (showing how constitutional revolutions may happen incrementally and/or through constitutional amendments, rather than simply through extraordinary moments of popular sovereignty).
8 Roznai (n 1) 110–13.
9 ibid 118–20.

justifiably be considered unconstitutional if it violates these fiduciary terms. Roznai's influential account has spawned several responses, both supportive and critical.[10]

Another thorny theoretical issue that implicates UCA is how to deal both descriptively and normatively with constitutional amendments that are amendments in name only. These are amendments that fundamentally reshape or shift the existing constitutional order. Richard Albert refers to such amendments as constitutional dismemberments. They are aimed not at correcting or clarifying an existing constitution, but instead seek "deliberately to disassemble one or more of a constitution's elemental parts."[11] While Albert's terminology and application is value neutral – applying to both progressive changes like the Civil War Amendments in the United States and regressive amendments like the Public Spending Cap Amendment in Brazil[12] – it helpfully theorizes and gives a name to especially consequential amendments, even if those amendments are formally treated like ordinary amendments. The normative implications that flow from an amendment being treated as a dismemberment are substantial. For if an amendment has the effect of creating a new constitutional settlement, the constitutionality of future amendments should be measured against that new settlement, and not the original (or previous) constitutional order.[13]

The second dimension of scholarship on constitutional amendments and UCA focuses on constitutional design. Much recent discussion has been on "tiered" or "multi-track" amendment rules, in which constitutional designers vary the requirements for formal amendment based on the type of provision at issue.[14] For instance, while routine changes are subject to less rigorous rules, changes to fundamental provisions or values are placed on a higher tier and must pass more onerous requirements. Such differentiation among constitutional provisions serves an important expressive function,[15] as core constitutional values are marked as such by being placed in a higher amendment tier. But tiering also

---

10 See, for example, Ali Acar, 'On Yaniv Roznai's Theory of Substantive Unamendability' (2017) 13 European Constitutional LR 836; Adrienne Stone, 'Unconstitutional Constitutional Amendments: Between Contradiction and Necessity' (2018) 12(3) ICL Journal 357.
11 Albert (n 2) 4.
12 ibid 4–5, 40–2.
13 See Po Jen Yap and Rehan Abeyratne, 'Judicial Self-Dealing and Unconstitutional Constitutional Amendments in South Asia' (2021) 19(1) International Journal of Constitutional Law 127.
14 Rosalind Dixon and David Landau, 'Tiered Constitutional Design' (2018) 86 *George Washington LR* 438; Richard Albert, *Constitutional Amendments: Making, Breaking, and Changing Constitutions* (OUP 2019) 177–82.
15 Richard Albert, 'Constitutional Handcuffs' (2010) 42 Arizona State LJ 663, 699–700.

serves a practical purpose, particularly in guarding against abusive constitutionalism.[16] As Rosalind Dixon and David Landau put it,

> [T]iering can combine the best of … [rigid and flexible] constitutionalism. Because most provisions can be changed easily, the constitution can be updated as needs arise. At the same time, enhanced protection of a core set of provisions may help defend against particularly destabilizing forms of constitutional change.[17]

Some parts of a constitution, however, are explicitly immune from constitutional amendment. Such eternity clauses represent the highest level on a tiered or multi-track design. As they cannot be amended, these provisions have especial symbolic or expressive value.[18] They also may be the product of hard-won political bargains – certain parties may not agree to ratify or support a constitution unless their interests are explicitly entrenched beyond the scope of amendment. Article V of the US Constitution, which insulated certain slavery-related provisions from amendment until a certain date and further made it practically impossible to deprive states of equal representation in the Senate, fits this description.[19] As Silvia Suteu argues, though, in post-conflict or post-authoritarian situations, such political compromises may forestall the development of liberal constitutionalism in the long run and may entrench exclusionary majoritarianism at the expense of minority interests.[20]

The third dimension of scholarship in this area concerns UCA as a judicial doctrine. As Roznai has shown, implicit unamendability, as expressed in basic structure or UCA doctrines, has spread from the Indian Supreme Court to courts around the world including in Taiwan, Bangladesh, Kenya, Belize, and Colombia.[21] At a normative level, scholars generally cabin their support for judicial interventions on UCA grounds to situations in which the amendment at issue grossly infringes upon core constitutional provisions. Thus, courts should only strike down amendments that are "manifestly unreasonable"[22] or constitute a "disproportionate violation."[23] Within these limits, courts can play a useful countermajoritarian role in checking the excesses of elected leaders. But when courts

---

16 David Landau, 'Abusive Constitutionalism' (2013) 47 UC Davis LR 189 (referring to the erosion of liberal democratic values by authoritarian governments using lawful mechanisms like constitutional amendments).
17 Dixon and Landau (n 14) at 441.
18 Richard Albert, 'The Expressive Function of Constitutional Amendment Rules' (2013) 59 McGill LJ 225, 228–9.
19 ibid 245.
20 Silvia Suteu, 'Eternity Clauses in Post-Conflict and Post-Authoritarian Constitution-Making' (2017) 6 Global Constitutionalism 63; Silvia Suteu, *Eternity Clauses in Democratic Constitutionalism* (OUP 2021).
21 Roznai (n 1) 47–69.
22 Yap (n 1) 116.
23 Roznai (n 1) 220–1.

are responsible for determining the content and scope of UCA enforcement, rule of law and democracy-related concerns inevitably arise. As Richard Albert put it,

> [I]f the Court takes the broadest reading of democracy, an unamendable rule protecting "democracy" risks swallowing up the entire constitution, bringing all constitutional amendments within the purview of a court's power of judicial review and accordingly its power to invalidate any constitutional amendment.[24]

Such broad policing of the amendment power may bring instability to the constitutional system or turn a democracy into a "juristocracy."[25]

At a contextual level, the doctrine has been defended as a useful tool to protect against abusive constitutional amendments, particularly in new or fragile democracies, but it has also been criticized for aggrandizing judicial power beyond permissible limits. David Landau has defended the use of UCA in Colombia, *inter alia*, to prevent President Uribe from seeking a third term in office, which he was able to do given the low bar to constitutional amendments in that country.[26] By contrast, the Indian Supreme Court's judgment in the *Fourth Judges Case* invalidating the National Judicial Appointments Commission (NJAC) has been heavily criticized.[27] The Court struck down a constitutional amendment and related legislation that would have vested the judicial appointment power in a multimember, multi-institutional commission.[28] As a result, the Court entrenched the deeply flawed and corrupt "collegium" system of judicial appointments, in which the appointment power is vested in a group of judges.

While these debates are important, and we seek to engage with them, this volume aims to expand academic research on unconstitutional constitutional amendments in two ways: substantive and jurisdictional. First, while existing scholarship has focused on the three dimensions discussed above, this volume explores a fourth dimension: constitutional politics. Politics refers to "the control, allocation, use of important resources and the values and ideas underlying these activities."[29] Constitutional politics, therefore, involves the control, allocation, use of public power, and the fundamental values and ideas underlying these activities.

Second, this volume focuses on Asian jurisdictions that have been understudied in the existing scholarship on unconstitutional constitutional amendments. To be sure, the basic structure doctrine in India has been extensively

---

24 Albert (n 14) 171.
25 Ran Hirschl, *Towards Juristocracy* (HUP 2004).
26 Landau (n 16) 199–203.
27 See, for example, Rehan Abeyratne, 'Upholding Judicial Supremacy: The NJAC Judgment in Comparative Perspective' (2017) 49 George Washington International LR 569.
28 *Supreme Court Advocates-on-Record Association v Union of India*, (2016) 4 SCC 1.
29 Ben Kerkvliet, *Speaking Out in Vietnam: Public Political Criticism in a Communist Party–Ruled Nation* (Cornell University Press 2019) 8.

studied.[30] In addition, there are several studies on this topic in other Asian jurisdictions, such as Taiwan[31] and Malaysia.[32] However, the existing scholarship has focused on individual Asian jurisdictions and has largely considered issues of design or judicial review of constitutional unamendability. Several other Asian jurisdictions such as China, Japan, Thailand, and Vietnam have been largely overlooked in the scholarship on unconstitutional constitutional amendments. Moreover, there are no book length treatments of which we are aware on unconstitutional constitutional amendments in Asia generally and on their politics particularly. This volume seeks to fill this scholarly gap by investigating the political aspects of constitutional unamendability in a range of Asian jurisdictions from a comparative perspective.

The politics of unconstitutional constitutional amendment involves the following aspects: diverse *political regimes* including democratic, socialist, and hybrid; diverse political *activities* including political discourse and mobilization; diverse *forums* including legislative, judicial, and popular; diverse social and political *actors* including judges, politicians, lawyers, scholars, activists, political parties, and social movement actors; and the diverse *triggers*, including formal amendments, informal amendments, amendment proposals, and constitutional replacements.

1.2 Typology of Asian cases

The ten case studies in this book could be organized in several ways. Geographically, the volume has broad coverage of the three main Asian sub-regions: East Asia (China, Japan, Taiwan), Southeast Asia (Malaysia, Thailand, Vietnam), and South Asia (Bangladesh, India, Nepal, Pakistan). But more interesting for our purposes is the spectrum on which these cases fall as to their treatment of UCA as a theory and doctrine. Depending on how UCA is used, we develop a three-part typology of our cases: discursive, denotive, and decisive. Each of these is an ideal type. Though none captures the full complexity and dynamism with which constitutional actors have wrestled with UCA, each captures a significant mode of engagement with the concept in three or more of our case studies.

In the *discursive* model, UCA is not adopted in the courtroom but informs public and intellectual discussion. Japan, China, and Vietnam fall within this model.

---

30 See, for example, Sudhir Krishnaswamy, *Democracy and Constitutionalism in India: A Study of the Basic Structure Doctrine* (OUP 2010).
31 See, for example, David S Law and Hsiang-Yang Hsieh, 'Judicial Review of Constitutional Amendments: Taiwan' in David S Law (ed) *Constitutionalism in Context* (CUP Forthcoming), <https://ssrn.com/abstract=3359520> accessed 10 March 2021.
32 See, for example, Wilson Tze Vern Tay, 'Basic Structure Revisited: The Case of Semenyih Jaya and the Defence of Fundamental Constitutional Principles in Malaysia' (2019) 13 Asian Journal of Comparative Law 113.

In Chapter 2, Koichi Nakano analyzes the political processes in Japan that led to informal constitutional amendments through the Abe government's interpretation in July 2014. In the Japanese case, informal amendments might be considered unconstitutional on normative, substantive, and procedural grounds; for instance, if they surpassed the limitations of informal amendments, breached the principles of constitutionalism, violated constitutional pacifism, or exercised arbitrary power. Civil society, the bar, and former judges argued that the informal constitutional amendments are unconstitutional. This chapter explores the dynamics of this public constitutional activism surrounding these informal constitutional amendments.

In Chapter 3, Ryan Mitchell explores the discursive dynamics of Chinese constitutional fundamentals referred to in the People's Republic of China as *guoti* (fundamental form of state). *Guoti* has ideational and institutional aspects of constitutional cores. Its ideational aspects (liberal, socialist…) vary depending on the historical context. The same can be said of its institutional manifestations (rights, party leadership…). The chapter also explores the constitutional discourse on *guoti* surrounding the 2018 constitutional amendments. The idea was used in critical discussions on this topic. For example, it informed different ideational justifications of term limit entrenchment. Some justifications of term limit abolition are instrumental, necessity-based (continuity of reform), while other justifications of term limit entrenchment are normative and value-based. Second, *guoti* was constitutionalized through the 2018 amendments. For example, the chapter discusses the migration of party leadership (a core of Chinese socialist polity) from the Preamble to Article 1 of the Constitution. In addition, the 2018 amendments constitutionalize another core concept within *guoti*: socialism with Chinese characteristics. Third, the newly entrenched constitutional *guoti* has important implications for post-2018 constitutional discourse. Mitchell further argues that aspects of constitutionalized *guoti* seem beyond revision or even questioning.

In Chapter 4, Bui Ngoc Son explores an academic paper criticizing Vietnam's 2013 Constitution as an "unconstitutional constitution." The paper was penned by Hoàng Xuân Phú, a Vietnamese mathematician. Hoàng argues that Vietnam's 2013 Constitution is an unconstitutional constitution because some new provisions in the constitution violate fundamental principles established in preceding provisions. This chapter explores Hoàng's account of an unconstitutional constitution, while situating it within the broader national constitutional debates in Vietnam and comparative scholarship on unconstitutional constitutional amendments and unconstitutional constitutions. It argues that Hoàng's account of an unconstitutional constitution is a political, critical, and normative discourse on Vietnam's Constitution. Hoàng's arguments echo the arguments justifying the doctrine of unconstitutional constitutional amendments and the doctrine of unconstitutional constitutions in comparative scholarship. The Vietnamese case suggests that "unconstitutional constitutions" is not solely a judicial doctrine but can be a political theory which informs public constitutional discourse.

The second, *denotive* model involves UCA as part of judicial rhetoric and reference. Malaysia, Pakistan, and Nepal are grouped within this model. While the courts in these countries have not invalidated constitutional amendments, judges have invoked variants of UCA doctrine in their judgments and have, therefore, affected the politics around thorny constitutional issues.

In Chapter 5, HP Lee and Yvonne Tew chart the "rising trajectory" of Malaysian constitutional jurisprudence from the country's independence in 1957 to the present day. Central to their analysis are three recent cases – *Semenyih Jaya*,[33] *Indira Gandhi*,[34] and *Alma Nudo*.[35] The first two cases witnessed the migration of the basic structure doctrine (BSD) from India to the Malaysian Federal Court. These judgments protected the judicial power against incursions from land assessors and the *Syariah* courts, respectively. They interpreted the Constitution as vesting judicial power only in the courts, and held that this power cannot be reduced or moved elsewhere. The basic structure doctrine was firmly entrenched in *Alma Nudo*. Building on the two previous judgments, Chief Justice Richard Malanjum declared that

> while the Federal Constitution does not specifically explicate the doctrine of basic structure, what the doctrine signifies is that a parliamentary enactment is open to scrutiny not only for clear-cut violation of the [Constitution] but also for violation of the doctrine or principles that constitute the constitutional foundations.[36]

However, as Lee and Tew point out, none of these judgments actually struck down a constitutional amendment, leaving the future path of the BSD uncertain. Indeed, the recent *Maria Chin* judgment, issued by a divided Federal Court, cast doubt on the applicability of the BSD in Malaysia,[37] though Lee and Tew argue that reports of its death are "greatly exaggerated."[38]

In Chapter 6, Matthew Nelson discusses the functional equivalent of basic structure review – the "salient features" doctrine – as it has developed in the context of Islamic features in Pakistan's Constitution. Nelson focuses on Article 62(1)(f) of the Constitution which, among other things, requires those standing for elections to Parliament as well as sitting parliamentarians to be *ameen* (trustworthy in a Quranic sense). The Pakistan Supreme Court has interpreted this provision broadly to disqualify several members of Parliament who had been found guilty of dishonesty by lower courts. The Supreme Court even disqualified

---

33 *Semenyih Jaya Sdn Bhd v Pentadbir Tanah Daerah Hulu Langat* [2017] 3 Malayan LJ 561.
34 *Indira Gandhi Mutho v Pengarah Jabatan Agama Islam Perak and Others* [2018] 1 Malayan LJ 545.
35 *Alma Nudo Atenza v Public Prosecutor* [2019] 4 Malayan LJ 1.
36 ibid [73].
37 *Maria Chin Abdullah v Director-General of Immigration* [2021] 2 Current LJ 579.
38 See HP Lee and Yvonne Tew, Chapter 5 in this volume.

Prime Minister Nawaz Sharif on this basis.[39] With this institutional conflict emerging between the Parliament and the Court, Nelson explores the likelihood of Parliament repealing this provision by constitutional amendment and whether the Supreme Court, asserting its own power, would find that amendment unconstitutional. The Court in 2015 declared that constitutional amendments violating salient features should be annulled,[40] but as in Malaysia, it remains to be seen whether, and in which context, the Court will actually exercise this power.

In Chapter 7, Mara Malagodi explores the unique case of Nepal's Constituent Assembly. Nepal went through a long transitional period as its 1990 Constitution, which established a constitutional monarchy and parliamentary government, was destabilized by a ten-year Maoist insurgency. As Malagodi explains, in 2005, the Maoist and mainstream parties agreed to repeal the 1990 constitution, leading to the adoption of an Interim Constitution in 2007. The government also formed a Constituent Assembly (CA) to draft a permanent constitution, but it was beset by delays. After the CA's term was extended three times, the Supreme Court ruled that any further extensions would violate the Interim Constitution. When the government failed to meet that deadline and sought to amend the term of the CA again, the Supreme Court issued an order that effectively prevented any further extensions. As a result, Nepal was left without a functioning legislature for more than a year, and a new Constituent Assembly had to be formed. Malagodi explores the thorny theoretical issue of judicial intervention in the CA's exercise of constituent power – conventionally thought to be beyond the pale of judicial review – within the complex politics of transitional Nepal. She concludes that this bold assertion of judicial power contributed to the Supreme Court being weakened in several respects under the permanent 2015 Constitution.

The third, *decisive* model involves judiciaries striking down constitutional amendments on UCA grounds.[41] Taiwan, Thailand, India, and Bangladesh exemplify this model. While the legal aspects of the relevant judgments have been analyzed in detail in past scholarship, the chapters in this volume place these judgments in their broader political context.

In Chapter 8, Jiunn Rong Yeh discusses Judicial Interpretation No. 499 issued by Taiwan's Constitutional Court in 1999, which declared constitutional amendments passed by the National Assembly as unconstitutional. The amendments

---

39 *Imran Ahmed Khan Niazi v Mian Muhammad Nawaz Sharif*, PLD 2017 SC 692.
40 *District Bar Association Rawalpindi v Federation of Pakistan*, PLD 2015 SC 401.
41 Joel Colón-Ríos has presented a related typology, which includes two models of UCA review within a broader spectrum of judicial review. One model, "strong basic structure review," is equivalent to our "decisive model" – it applies to jurisdictions in which courts can strike down constitutional amendments. A second model, "weak basic structure review," permits judges to strike down amendments, but allows "the people," through a constituent assembly, to have the final word on the validity of such amendments. This model, as Colon-Rios notes, is practiced in Latin America. It is not, to our knowledge, present in Asia. See Joel I Colón-Ríos, 'A New Typology of Judicial Review of Legislation' (2014) 3(2) Global Constitutionalism 143.

dealt with parliamentary reform, provincial elections, and basic national policies. The chapter explores three political imperatives for the court's ruling on the unamendability (incremental constitutional reform, the status of the National Assembly, and the presidential election) and situates the Court as a political institution within the broader social and institutional dynamics. In particular, civil society mobilized to the Court to nullify the amendment. The chapter concludes that the Court functioned as an instrument for the people to exercise oversight on constitutional amendments.

In Chapter 9, Khemthong Tonsakulrungruang explores the Thai Constitutional Court's four decisions in 2013–14 on the constitutionality of proposed amendments to the 2007 Constitution. In contrast to the normative underpinnings of the doctrine of unconstitutional constitutional amendments, this chapter reveals that judicial rules on unamendability of amendments may undermine democracy in Thailand. It demonstrates that the proposed amendments sought to challenge the authoritarian features of the 2007 Constitution, which was barred by the court's decisions. Therefore, Tonsakulrungruang argues that judicial decisions on unconstitutional constitutional amendments in Thailand entrenched authoritarianism.

Perhaps the most widely known case of UCA is in India, where the *Kesavananda* judgment (1973) inaugurated the modern trend towards courts defining the scope of implicit unamendability and striking down amendments that violate the Constitution's "basic structure." Surya Deva, in Chapter 10, reviews the history and evolution of the basic structure doctrine within the context of two strands of politics. The first strand he calls the "politics of supremacy," which involved a dispute between the political branches and the judiciary on who has the final word on constitutional meaning. Deva refers to the second strand as the "politics of legitimacy," which is contested between dominant political coalitions and members of the public who believe majoritarian politics must abide by constitutional rules. Deva defends BSD as a necessary tool to prevent against majoritarian excesses, particularly in the current context of democratic erosion and the concentration of power in the Modi regime. He calls for a reconceptualization of BSD "as part of a wider constitutional mechanism of checks and balances, rather than as a judicial *brahmastra* (a weapon with no defences) against the legislature and/or the executive."[42] He further argues that BSD should be applicable against the judiciary, to guard against judicial misuse of the doctrine.

A similar story emerges in Bangladesh. Ridwanul Hoque in Chapter 11 recounts how the Appellate Division of the Bangladesh Supreme Court (SCAD) recognized the basic structure doctrine in *Anwar Hossain Chowdhury* (1989) and has used the doctrine in increasingly divisive matters of constitutional law and politics. Hoque's analysis focuses on the politics surrounding the 8th and 15th Amendments to the Bangladesh Constitution. Hoque argues that while both amendments were framed as non-partisan improvements to the constitutional

---

42 Surya Deva, Chapter 10 in this volume.

order, they were both driven – as he argues most constitutional amendments in Bangladesh are driven – by narrow party politics aimed at the consolidation and perpetuation of power. Because of the majoritarian nature of these amendments, they are often exclusionary, resulting in SCAD judgments that implicitly favor one political regime or coalition over the others. A major outcome of the 15th Amendment and the judgment in the 13th Amendment Case that led to it, according to Hoque, is that the Awami League led by Prime Minister Sheikh Hasina now presides over a country that is democratic in name only.

The final four chapters of this volume offer broad theoretical and comparative reflections on the law and politics of UCA. In Chapter 12, Richard Albert situates the judicial nullification power, as it has developed in Asia, within the global context, both to uncover the conceptual roots of this power across borders and regions, as well as to bring Asian cases into a wider conversation. He describes six forms of judicial nullification – procedural irregularity, subject-rule mismatch, temporal limitations, codified unamendability, interpretive unamendability, and supranational constitutional restrictions – and illustrates how each operates using examples from Asia and beyond.

Andrew Harding, in Chapter 13, interrogates the breadth of the basic structure doctrine. He asks whether we should conceive of BSD as a necessary consequence of constitutionalism, particularly when a constitution sets forth a democratic form of government, or whether it is a contingent doctrine, emerging from the constitutional history of a particular society. In making the case for the contingent view, Harding cautions against unwarranted or excessive uses of the doctrine. He argues that an unamendable basic structure is not always implied by the facts of constitution-making or entrenchment; that it should not be implied if constitutional provisions are protected by a referendum requirement; that the actual content of the doctrine varies by context; and that the BSD, in principle, should not apply to unwritten or unentrenched constitutions.

In Chapter 14, Silvia Suteu highlights the majoritarian, exclusionary tendencies of eternity clauses and UCA judicial doctrines. She argues that the potential of these mechanisms to forestall democracy and exclude minorities is greater in fraught constitutional contexts – societies that are divided, fragile, and affected by conflict. In Thailand, for instance, she notes that by making the monarchical system of government unamendable, successive Thai constitutions have constricted possible avenues for democratic change, leading to multiple political breakdowns and constitutional crises. In Nepal, Suteu shows how the 2015 Constitution entrenched a majoritarian, ethnocultural conception of citizenship as well as a federal structure that disadvantages minorities, particularly the Madhesi community, which may be detrimental to the country's stability and democratic governance.

Finally, in Chapter 15, Yaniv Roznai seeks to explain why UCA has been adopted across Asia. He deploys the following theories – Edward Crowin's higher law, John Hart Ely's democracy and distrust, Tom Ginsburg's political insurance, and Ran Hirschl's hegemonic preservation – and explains how each is apposite in certain political and historical contexts. Roznai argues that institutional factors affect the adoption *vel non* of UCA doctrines. These include the flexibility of the amendment process, party or executive dominance, the political-democratic amendment culture, and the existence and effectiveness of supra-national institutions. Roznai illustrates these features with reference to the case studies in the volume, as well as the case of Israel, where the Knesset plays the dual role of constituent power and national legislature and is dominated by the government. He concludes that in such a context there is greater justification for the judiciary to play a role in limiting the amendment power.

1.3 UCA as constitutional politics

The animating idea of this volume is that UCA forms part of, and is influenced by, constitutional politics. The book seeks to explore and explain how and why the idea of unconstitutional constitutional amendments informs political activities through diverse forums, by various social and political actors, through both formal and informal constitutional amendment processes in Asia. Thus, the volume aims to consider not only constitutional design and judicial review, but also intellectual and political debates on unamendability.

Why constitutional politics in the context of UCA? Elsewhere, one of us suggested four reasons: (1) the political nature of the constituent power; (2) the political nature of foundational constitutional questions; (3) the political nature of constitutional disagreements; and (4) consequently the political protection of constitutional unamendability.[43] First, the constituent power is not a legal aggregate entity but a politically constructed one. Second, unconstitutional constitutional amendments often touch on fundamental questions of a polity. These questions are not merely legalistic. These are also political questions as they deal with political ideals and ideas, political systems, political institutions, and they may inform political activities and behaviors. Third, the questions of unconstitutional constitutional amendments may generate higher level political disagreements. Constitutional questions often create disagreements, but the fundamental questions concerning the basic structure and identity of the constitutional order may be more controversial and, hence, induce greater disagreement. Fourth, the protection of constitutional unamendability is not merely a legal or judicial concern, but also a political one. As questions of unconstitutional constitutional amendments are foundational political questions which generate reasonable political disagreements, it is myopic to think that UCA is or should be limited to the courts. Tackling such questions often involves political and social actors beyond courts including citizens, legislators, activists, and political parties.[44]

---

43 Bui Ngoc Son, 'Politics of Unconstitutional Constitutional Amendments: The Case of Thailand' in Henning Glaser (ed) *Identity and Change – The Basic Structure in Asian Constitutional Orders* (Nomos Forthcoming) <https://ssrn.com/abstract=3515859> accessed 10 March 2021.
44 ibid.

Consider first the discursive model of UCA in China and Vietnam. Unamendability in the socialist single-party regimes of China and Vietnam is not a judicial doctrine. Courts in these counties do not have the constitutional review power due to the socialist principle of democratic centralism, which subordinates courts to the supreme legislature. Rather, unamendability is a part of political discourse. Without judicial review, the ideas of constitutional *guoti* and unconstitutional constitution are only debated in academic or popular forums by intellectual actors triggered by the process of formal constitutional amendment (China) and replacement (Vietnam). Unamendability is also not a design issue in China and Vietnam as their socialist constitutions do not have eternity clauses. However, unamendability is not necessarily associated with constitutional review and design: it can be entrenched through political construction. Political construction of unamendability can be procedural and substantive. Richard Albert's concept of "constructive unamendability" captures the procedural aspect: "[a] constitutional rule is constructively unamendable when the codified thresholds required to amend it are so onerous that reformers cannot realistically (though theoretically) satisfy the standard."[45] The substantive aspect of political construction of unamendability is that the existing political reality renders content in the constitution unamendable although amendments are textually plausible. The cases of China and Vietnam fall into this substantive aspect. Every provision in their constitutions is theoretically amendable. However, as the Communist Party remains the single dominant party in these countries, it is practically impossible to amend the core socialist commitments that the party attempts to pursue. These include commitments such as the vanguard role of the communist party itself, the construction of socialism, and the principle of democratic centralism. Such commitments may also rise to the level of constitutional conventions – deeply entrenched practices that over time have come to be seen as unamendable.[46]

The discursive model of UCA in Japan also includes several political aspects although it is different from those of China and Vietnam. Unlike the two socialist countries, Japan is a constitutional democracy with judicial review. However, Japan's Supreme Court has been conservative and rarely exercised its judicial review power.[47] Rather, the government has enjoyed the power of constitutional interpretation (through its Cabinet Legislation Bureau), and the Court tends to avoid making judgments on the government's interpretations.[48] Therefore, public

---

45 Albert (n 14) 158.
46 See Gert Jan Geertjes and Jerfi Uzman, 'Conventions of Unamendability: Covert Constitutional Unamendability in (Two) Politically Enforced Constitutions' in Richard Albert and Bertil Emrah Oder (eds), *An Unamendable Constitution? Unamendability in Constitutional Democracies* (Springer 2018); Richard Albert, 'Amending Constitutional Amendment Rules' (2015) 13 International Journal of Constitutional Law 655, 672–7.
47 See Koichi Nakano, Chapter 2 in this volume. See also, David S Law, 'The Anatomy of a Conservative Court: Judicial Review in Japan' (2009) 87 Texas LR 1545.
48 See Nakano, Chapter 2 in this volume.

intellectuals and civil society organizations have challenged the government's constitutional interpretations (a form of informal constitutional amendments[49]) as unconstitutional through public debate and social mobilization alongside litigation. Japan's basic protection of freedom of speech and association enables the wider public to debate the constitutionality of the government's interpretations. The same cannot be said of China and Vietnam.

The implication of the discursive model in China, Vietnam, and Japan is that UCA is not necessarily a doctrine used by courts: it can be a critical political theory that informs public debate on the (un)constitutionality of constitutional change. In addition, the discursive model shows that the idea of UCA is dynamic because it is not fixed by constitutional texts but presented, circulated, debated, and (de)legitimatized in the public.

The denotive model, by contrast, sees courts enter the constitutional politics of UCA without claiming the last word on the validity of specific amendments. In Malaysia and Pakistan, courts have recognized the basic structure doctrine or salient features doctrine, respectively, and given content to those doctrines.[50] The Federal Court of Malaysia held that judicial review, separation of powers, rule of law, and protection of minorities fall within the unamendable basic structure.[51] The Supreme Court of Pakistan, meanwhile, held that the following salient features cannot be amended: "[F]ederalism, parliamentary democracy and Islamic provisions including independence of judiciary."[52] The Court subsequently ruled that a "parliamentary form of government blended with Islamic provisions" constitutes part of the basic structure.[53]

But why have these courts adopted and given substance to these UCA doctrines if they do not actually enforce them? One reason might be that, in these fragile democracies, courts are hesitant to intervene too forcefully because they might face political reprisals. In Malaysia, the judiciary appears to be treading cautiously, waiting for opportune moments to enhance their constitutional authority vis-à-vis the government.[54] This strategic account makes sense within Malaysian constitutional politics, where one political alliance (Barisan National) has ruled for almost the entire post-independence period.[55] It also fits with the type of case in which the Federal Court has advanced the BSD: those concerning the scope and singularity of judicial power.[56] On these issues, the Court is arguably at its most authoritative, given that it sits atop the judiciary. Moreover, from an

---

49 Craig Martin, 'The Legitimacy of Informal Constitutional Amendment and the "Reinterpretation" of Japan's War Powers' (2017) 40 (2) Fordham International LJ 427.
50 See Lee and Tew, Chapter 5; Matthew Nelson, Chapter 6 in this volume.
51 *Indira Gandhi* (n 34) [42], [90].
52 *Mahmood Khan Achakzai v Federation of Pakistan*, PLD 1997 SC 426.
53 Nelson, Chapter 6; *District Bar Association Rawalpindi v Federation of Pakistan*, PLD 2015 SC 401.
54 See Yvonne Tew, *Constitutional Statecraft in Asian Courts* (OUP 2020) 8–10.
55 ibid 1–2.
56 Lee and Tew, Chapter 5.

institutional perspective, these cases present the highest stakes, where the Court not only must protect its terrain, but may also wish to signal that further incursions on judicial power will not be tolerated.

A strategic motivation may apply in Pakistan too, though in a slightly different form. As Nelson explains, judicial independence has been subject to frontal assaults, most notably in 2007 when General (President) Musharraf tried to sack Chief Justice Chaudhry.[57] Though Chaudhry successfully challenged this removal attempt at the Supreme Court, Musharraf later declared a state of emergency, suspended the Constitution, and removed several judges (including Chaudhry) from their posts. Chaudhry was later reinstated as Chief Justice, but the institutional battle between the government and the Supreme Court has continued.[58] Given this recent history, Supreme Court justices may wish to avoid direct confrontations with the political branches and, hence, have avoided striking down constitutional amendments on salient features grounds.

Another reason for the Pakistan Supreme Court's reticence in this context is the institutional culture of the Court. As Nelson informs us, "[A]ll of my respondents felt that basic structure jurisprudence in Pakistan was now more closely tied to historically specific personalities and the politically contingent patterns of judicial activism (or reticence) attached to them."[59] His respondents specifically mentioned the personality of the Chief Justice as significant in determining the future trajectory of the salient features doctrine. This idiosyncratic, personality-driven style of judicial decision-making has been noted in other studies of South Asian constitutionalism.[60] In addition to rule of law and coherence-based concerns that may arise from this approach,[61] it also makes the future path of the law very difficult to predict. By contrast, on a strategic account, we would expect these courts to eventually strike down constitutional amendments when the constitutional politics are conducive and the institutional stakes are sufficiently high.

The final denotive case is Nepal. By refusing to extend the first Constituent Assembly's term indefinitely – on the grounds that extensions would violate Nepal's 2007 Interim Constitution – the Supreme Court may have stepped on a political landmine. The 2015 Constitution, unlike the Interim Constitution, contains an eternity clause; namely, the Constitution "shall not be amended in way that contravenes with self-rule of Nepal, sovereignty, territorial integrity and sovereignty vested in people."[62] While this clause might be enforced through

---

57 See Sadaf Aziz, *The Constitution of Pakistan* (Hart 2018) 138–42.
58 See Nelson, Chapter 6.
59 ibid.
60 See, for example, Anuj Bhuwania, *Courting the People: Public Interest Litigation in Post-Emergency India* (CUP 2017); Rehan Abeyratne, 'Ordinary Wrongs as Constitutional Rights: The Public Law Model of Torts in South Asia' (2018) 54 Texas International LJ 1.
61 Abeyratne (n 60) 30–3; Chintan Chandrachud, 'Constitutional Interpretation' in Sujit Choudhry, Madhav Khosla and Pratap Bhanu Mehta (eds), *Oxford Handbook of the Indian Constitution* (OUP 2016) 86–92.
62 Constitution of Nepal 2015, art 274(1).

litigation, the principles therein are not amendable to judicial review. Unlike, say, judicial independence or the separation of powers, sovereignty and territorial integrity are subjects usually confined to the political domain. Moreover, as Malagodi argues, the 2015 Constitution weakens the Supreme Court in several ways. Judicial review may only be conducted by a single Constitutional Bench, which is likely to slow down an already backlogged docket; judges can be impeached and removed more easily from office; and judicial appointments must be confirmed by a Parliamentary Hearings Committee, which may politicize the process.[63] Finally, the 2015 Constitution, which emerged from the Court-mandated second Constituent Assembly, has proved unpopular with several minority groups, who are likely to blame the Court for their predicament under the current constitutional order.[64] Thus, the Supreme Court of Nepal, partly as a result of its UCA-related interventions into the Constituent Assembly, finds itself today on shaky institutional grounds and enjoys limited public support.

We turn now to the decisive model of UCA. The four cases here – Taiwan, Thailand, India, and Bangladesh – illustrate the political contingency behind judicial decisions to strike down constitutional amendments. Consider Taiwan. Its Constitutional Court was able to decide on the unconstitutionality of the amendment largely thanks to the island's transitional democracy. Taiwan's democratic transition transformed the dormant Council of Grand Justices into an active constitutional court, which made the institution an attractive and trusted forum to decide major issues of constitutional reform.[65] In addition, democratization helped to generate a vibrant civil society which employed the judicial platform in the struggle to consolidate Taiwan's young democracy.[66] Therefore, the court is not the only actor engaged in UCA.[67] Civil society was also a major social and political force in defending unamendable constitutional essentials.

Meanwhile, Thailand was a fragile democracy when the country's Constitutional Court ruled that the proposed amendments in 2013–14 were unconstitutional.[68] As Thailand's democracy was not stable, the court was more vulnerable to political influences. Tonsakulrungruang observes that

> The Constitutional Court was equipped with the ultimate power to intervene in politics … Moreover, at a personal level, anti-Thaksin figures were

---

63 Mara Malagodi, Chapter 7 in this volume.
64 ibid.
65 See Jiunn-Rong Yeh, Chapter 8 in this volume.
66 Jiunn-Rong Yeh and Wen-Chen Chang, 'The Emergence of East Asian Constitutionalism: Features in Comparison' (2011) 59 American Journal of Comparative Law 813.
67 For details on the legal and judicial aspects of the case, see David K Huang and Nigel N Li, 'Unconstitutional Constitutional Amendment in Taiwan: A Retrospective Analysis of Judicial Yuan Interpretation No. 499 (2000)' (2020) 15 University of Pennsylvania Asian LR 421.
68 On fragile democracies and the politicization of the courts, see Po Jen Yap, *Courts and Democracies in* Asia (CUP 2017) 125–34.

recruited onto the bench. As a result, the Constitutional Court represented the interests of the minority to suppress Thaksin and his political allies.[69]

In this context of judicial politicization, when the Court decided to strike down the Yingluck Shinawatra government's amendment proposals which arguably aimed to dismantle authoritarian legacies,[70] it appears to have been representing the political interests of the anti-Thaksin actors.

These accounts depict two poles of the normative spectrum of UCA judicial enforcement. At the positive end, UCA can be used to protect and consolidate a democracy as it was in Taiwan. Its judicial use was supported by the broader public (including civil society organizations). The normative weight of positive unamendability is connected to values associated with liberal constitutionalism. At the negative end, UCA can be used to undermine the existing democracy as in Thailand. Its judicial use was supported by some political factions, but not by the broader public. The instrumental weight of negative unamendability rests on justifications associated with authoritarianism.

The two South Asian cases in this group – India and Bangladesh – fall somewhere in the middle of the UCA normative spectrum. In India, Surya Deva defends the Supreme Court's use of basic structure review as part of a "wider system of checks and balances in times of serious democratic deficits in all institutions of governance."[71] Deva argues that India faces such deficits today, as Prime Minister Narendra Modi's government has adopted a centralized and quasi-authoritarian mode of decision-making, sidelining political opponents, diminishing the freedoms of speech and press, and politicizing erstwhile independent institutions.[72] In 2019, the Modi government also used executive orders and ordinary legislation to effectively change the constitutional status of Jammu and Kashmir under Article 370 of the Constitution. Thus, for the BSD to be effective in today's political context, Deva contends that it must be expanded. The Supreme Court should not only be able to strike down formal amendments, but also laws or orders that have the effect of amending the Constitution. However, the Supreme Court cannot be trusted to wield this great power with appropriate care and forbearance. In the *Fourth Judges* case, as Deva explains, the Court struck down a constitutional amendment and related legislation that would have created a National Judicial Appointments Commission.[73] The Court's reasoning suggested that any judicial appointment procedure that did not confer primacy on judges in the decision-making process would be a violation of judicial

---

69 Khemthong Tonsakulrungruang, 'Entrenching the Minority: The Constitutional Court in Thailand's Political Conflict' (2017) 26 (2) Washington International LJ 264–5.
70 Khemthong Tonsakulrungruang, Chapter 9 in this volume.
71 Surya Deva, Chapter 10 in this volume.
72 See also Tarunabh Khaitan, 'Killing a Constitution with a Thousand Cuts: Executive Aggrandizement and Party-State Fusion in India' (2020) 14(1) Law & Ethics of Human Rights 49.
73 *Supreme Court Advocates-on-Record Association* (n 28).

independence under the BSD. This logic is both faulty and self-serving,[74] leading Deva to propose that the BSD should also apply to the judiciary, to prevent it from becoming an unaccountable, "supra-constitutional institution."[75]

Meanwhile, in Bangladesh, Ridwanul Hoque charts how the Supreme Court's Appellate Division (SCAD) put the country on a trajectory towards one-party rule. Hoque highlights the SCAD's short order on 10 May 2011, which held that the non-partisan caretaker government (NPCTG) was unconstitutional.[76] The NPCTG was established in 1996 to conduct free and fair elections in Bangladesh, which had hitherto experienced periods of military rule and constitutional crisis. Though the NPCTG had been manipulated by the Bangladesh Nationalist Party when it was in power, Hoque argues that it was a crucial institution in the preservation of this fragile democracy. In 2011, the Awami League (AL) had an absolutely majority in parliament and moved quickly to enact the 15th Amendment to the Bangladesh Constitution, which abolished the NPCTG system. Though the 15th Amendment purported to introduce democracy-enhancing reforms, such as entrenching the BSD within the text of the Constitution and making fundamental rights unamendable, it was rushed through Parliament without public consultation or input from the opposition political parties. Hoque, therefore, argues that the 15th Amendment was exclusionary, and has resulted in the AL consolidating power through elections that have not been fair or competitive.

Both Deva and Hoque, then, see UCA as a potentially positive, democracy-enhancing doctrine. However, their chapters are cautionary tales of how, in practice, dominant political parties have been able to undermine democracy in India and Bangladesh with little judicial resistance or, in the case of Bangladesh, even unwitting judicial assistance. While neither of these judiciaries adopt UCA for "abusive" ends as those described in the Thailand case,[77] their recent uses *vel non* of the basic structure doctrine do not make for optimistic reading if one hoped for the courts to intervene to preserve core elements of liberal constitutionalism.

In sum, we hope that readers will gain new insights from the detailed case studies and broader reflections in the chapters to follow, and that this volume will lead to further scholarship on the law and politics of constitutional amendments – and constitutionalism generally – across Asia.

---

74 See Abeyratne (n 27).
75 ibid.
76 Ridwanul Hoque, Chapter 11 in this volume.
77 Tonsakulrungruang, Chapter 9; Landau (n 16).

Part I
Discursive model

2 The politics of unconstitutional constitutional amendments in Japan
The case of the pacifist Article 9

Koichi Nakano

2.1 Introduction

This chapter provides an analysis of the political process that led to an unconstitutional informal constitutional amendment by the executive in Japan that lifted the ban on the exercise of collective self-defense through the government reinterpretation of Article 9 of the Constitution of Japan (Postwar Constitution) in July 2014 and the subsequent enactment of the security legislation in September 2015. Article 9 renounces war as a sovereign right of Japan, and though the text of the constitution has never been amended, and the overwhelming majority of the constitutional law scholars, legal professionals, as well as the general public, deemed the new government interpretation and the security legislation that followed to be unconstitutional, Prime Minister Shinzo Abe's government pushed through this *de facto* constitutional amendment and maintains that Japan can now exercise "limited" collective self-defense.

2.2 Questions of constitutionality and constitutionalism in Japan

The Postwar Constitution grants courts the power to conduct judicial review on the constitutionality of the laws and government actions in Article 81 ("The Supreme Court is the court of last resort with power to determine the constitutionality of any law, order, regulation or official act.") Constitutional reviews may be divided into two types: "Concrete review requires review in a particular case where the law has already been applied or is about to be applied. Abstract review determines the constitutionality of a statute or government practice without any reference to a specific case," and the Japanese Supreme Court, like its US counterpart, may only hear concrete cases.[1]

Furthermore, in general, the Japanese courts followed the US Ashwander rules for judicial self-restraint and avoiding constitutional questions, and when they did

---

1 Tom Ginsburg, 'Comparative Constitutional Review', 2–3 (US Institute of Peace Report 2012) https://www.usip.org/sites/default/files/ROL/TG_Memo_on_Constitutional_Review%20for%202011_v4.pdf accessed 10 April 2021.

DOI: 10.4324/9781003097099-2

take a position on the constitutionality of laws, it was often in order to protect the individual rights of the citizens that are guaranteed in the Constitution rather than to assert the supremacy of the Constitution over the laws that contradict it.[2] In reality, Japan has had a highly conservative and passive judiciary that is extremely reluctant to get engaged in judicial review that will have it involved in taking positions against the executive or the legislative branches of the state on what it considers to be "political questions." As we note in some detail below, the role of the *a priori* arbiter of the questions of the constitutionality of the laws and government actions has been filled by the Cabinet Legislation Bureau (CLB) in postwar Japan.

The Japanese debate over the constitutionality of laws and government actions dates back to the promulgation of the Constitution of the Empire of Japan (Meiji Constitution) in 1889, in time for the opening of the Imperial Diet the following year. The Meiji Constitution, East Asia's first modern constitution, was a product of compromise and ambiguity. On the one hand, the emperor was supposed to govern "according to the provisions of the present Constitution" – thereby committing the Empire of Japan to be a constitutional monarchy. On the other hand, the Constitution was granted to the imperial subjects by the emperor who was declared to be "sacred and inviolable" (Article 3) in the same Constitution. Moreover, the Constitution provided, "The Empire of Japan shall be reigned over and governed by a line of Emperors unbroken for ages eternal" (Article 1).

As a result, the promulgation of the Meiji Constitution did not unequivocally and irreversibly place constitutional constraints on imperial rule. There were two particular points of contention. First, the ministers of state, including the prime minister, were appointed by and were responsible to the emperor, not the Imperial Diet (Article 55). Second, the emperor was the supreme commander of the Army and the Navy (Article 12).

This ambiguity, combined with the absence of any system of constitutional adjudication, had the effect of pitting the proponents of democratically elected party government, who rallied under the banner of "constitutionalism" and "constitutional government," against the conservative oligarchs and military leaders, who sought to preserve their power to govern in the name of the emperor, particularly from the Taishō period (1912–26) onwards.

The advocates of representative democracy and constitutional government scored some important victories in what is known as Taishō Democracy, but the militarists who abused Article 12 usurped power by imposing their vision of *Kokutai* (National Body) – the principle of imperial rule as the super-constitutional constitution – by attacking the progressive constitutional theorists and scholars for lèse-majesté in the mid-1930s. The Meiji Constitution became more or less meaningless as the militarists and their collaborators brought the Japanese Empire down the path of a devastating war in Asia and Pacific.

---

2 Nobuyoshi Ashibe (with Kazuyuki Takahashi), *Kempō [Constitution]* (7th edn, Iwanami Shoten 2019), 389–94.

Postwar Japan represents a curious case in which its postwar tradition of pacifism that is enshrined in Article 9 of the Constitution has been incrementally modified informally but has remained formally unamendable for over 70 years for reasons that have nothing to do with court protection. Needless to say, not all informal constitutional amendments through government reinterpretation are considered to be unconstitutional, though some have been contested by critics. It was not until the Abe government's lifting of the ban on the exercise of collective self-defense that *de facto* constitutional amendment through the executive's reinterpretation of the constitution has been condemned so widely as unconstitutional, and has even revived a widespread opposition movement under the banner of constitutionalism against unrestrained, arbitrary rule.

2.3 Article 9 controversy during the Cold War

The political controversy over Article 9 is as old as the Constitution of Japan, which took effect in May 1947 under the US occupation. The Postwar Constitution was formally an amendment of the Meiji Constitution, but with three radically different "pillars" supporting the whole structure: (1) popular sovereignty (with the emperor relegated to being "the symbol of the State and of the unity of the People, deriving his position from the will of the people with whom resides sovereign power" (Article 1)), (2) fundamental human rights, and (3) pacifism.

At the time of the promulgation of the Postwar Constitution, the political bosses from the prewar period, including Nobusuke Kishi (Shinzō Abe's grandfather) and Ichirō Hatoyama, were still purged from public office, and as soon as they were de-purged as the occupation drew to a close in 1952, they advocated the need for a wholesale revision of the constitution, which they criticized as an illegitimate imposition on Japan during their forced absence from the political scene. The argument of these reactionary advocates of constitutional revision was that an independent Japan needed an independent constitution. The anger of the revisionists was particularly targeted against Article 9, which stipulates as follows.

> Aspiring sincerely to an international peace based on justice and order, the Japanese people forever renounce war as a sovereign right of the nation and the threat or use of force as means of settling international disputes.
>
> In order to accomplish the aim of the preceding paragraph, land, sea, and air forces, as well as other war potential, will never be maintained. The right of belligerency of the state will not be recognized.

The dominant postwar constitutional theory, however, has been the "limitation of constitutional amendment" doctrine that argues that (1) the principle of popular sovereignty, (2) the principle of individual dignity and human rights, and (3) the principle of international peace should be considered to be beyond the realm of any legitimate constitutional amendment, though this does not mean that specific articles of human rights or the second paragraph of Article 9 cannot be amended.[3]

To date, after more than 70s years since its adoption, the Constitution of Japan has never been formally amended – making it the longest surviving constitution in active use without a single amendment in the world. It is certainly a "rigid" constitution with comparatively high hurdles for a formal amendment. Article 96 of the Postwar Constitution stipulates that

> Amendments to this Constitution shall be initiated by the Diet, through a concurring vote of two-thirds or more of all the members of each House and shall thereupon be submitted to the people for ratification, which shall require the affirmative vote of a majority of all votes cast thereon, at a special referendum or at such election as the Diet shall specify.

It has been pointed out by Kenneth Mori McElwain and Christian G. Winkler, however, that the Constitution of Japan is not uncommonly hard to amend, but that it has never been formally amended rather because (1) it is short and vague on matters that concern political institutions, leaving it to the laws to determine the specifics (thereby rendering constitutional amendment unnecessary in the first place), and (2) it is a very progressive constitution with regard to civil rights and liberties.[4]

Despite the sweeping constitutional ban on war and war potential, the reality of the Japanese defense posture was rather more complex from the very beginning. At the time when the San Francisco Peace Treaty was signed to return sovereignty back to Japan, the US and Japan also signed the Security Treaty thereby placing Japan firmly under the US military umbrella during the Cold War. Moreover, under American pressure, Japan established the Police Reserve already in 1950, which was then reorganized as National Safety Force in 1952, and finally, as the Self-Defense Force (SDF) in 1954.

Political and scholarly contestation over its constitutionality accompanied the SDF from the moment of its founding, but the Japanese courts refused to rule over the issue while the government sought to justify it by arguing that Article 9 does not amount to a renunciation of Japan's right for individual self-defense, and contended that Japan can legitimately exercise it (1) when Japan is under military attack and invaded, (2) when there is no other means to get rid of the invading forces, and (3) as long as the exercise of force is limited to what is minimally necessary.[5]

---

3 Ashibe, op. cit., 409–11.
4 Kenneth Mori McElwain and Christian G. Winkler, 'What's Unique about the Japanese Constitution? A Comparative and Historical Analysis' (2015) 41 Journal of Japanese Studies 249.
5 Minutes, 71st session of the Diet, House of Representatives, Cabinet Committee, No. 32, 21 June 1973, 17. https://kokkai.ndl.go.jp/#/detailPDF?minId=107104889X03219730621&page=17&spkNum=239&current=1 accessed 10 April 2021.

In terms of the institutional setup of the Japanese judicial system, these moves have been enabled by the passive, even conservative, nature of the Japanese courts that has been assisted by the existence of an active and authoritative CLB, an important organ in the executive branch that conducts *a priori* checks on the legality and constitutionality of bills and ordinances and that was initially modelled after the French Conseil d'État.[6] The conservative political leaders of Japan relied on the CLB to construct legal arguments to interpret and reinterpret the Article 9, and the Supreme Court would tacitly endorse the government position by avoiding judgments on the constitutionality of government policies and legislations.

In the famous Sunagawa Case of 1959, when the constitutionality of the US–Japan Security Treaty was at stake after the Tokyo district court ruled it to be unconstitutional, the Supreme Court overturned the verdict, and instead argued that such a political question falls outside the scope of the constitutional review by the courts unless it is "extremely clearly unconstitutional and void at a glance."[7]

On the issue of collective self-defense, the government settled on its official interpretation of the Constitution, provided for it by the CLB, which the Kakuei Tanaka Cabinet submitted to the Diet in 1972 that (1) as a sovereign state, Japan owns the right of collective self-defense as defined by international law, but (2) the pacifist principle that underlies the Constitution does not allow for unlimited exercise of force for self-defense but only what is minimally necessary to protect the lives and rights of the citizens from foreign military attack, and thus (3) the exercise of collective self-defense in order to prevent military attack on another country is not allowed by the Constitution.[8]

This government interpretation of Article 9 – that Japan, as a sovereign state, may minimally exercise its right of individual self-defense when attacked and when diplomatic means to end the invasion fails, can be a signatory to the US–Japan Security Treaty, and it retains but is constitutionally unable to exercise its right of collective self-defense – continued to be challenged by the opposition over the postwar decades. But as the conservative Liberal Democratic Party (LDP) sought successfully to shelve these divisive issues by focusing on the economic reconstruction and growth and stay in power, a growing consensus emerged over this compromise position.

According to the annual opinion polls over the constitution conducted by *Asahi Shimbun* newspaper, public opinion was equally divided between the proponents of the revision of Article 9 and the defenders of the Article 9 with 31% in favor of revision and 32% opposed in 1952.[9] The latter saw a large increase

---

6 Iwao Satō, 'Iken Shinsasei to Naikaku Hōseikyoku' ['Constitutional Review System and the Cabinet Legislation Bureau'] (2005) 56 Shakai Kagaku Kenkyū [Social Science Research] 81–108.
7 Supreme Court of Japan (16 December 1959) vol. 13 no. 1, 3225.
8 Cabinet Legislation Bureau, written answer submitted to the House of Councilors, Audit Committee, 14 October 1972.
9 *Asahi* newspaper (3 March 1952) 1.

in support by November 1957 with 32% in favor of revision of Article 9 and as many as 52% opposed to it.[10] By 1962, only 26% were in favor of revising Article 9 whereas 61% opposed,[11] and by 1978, a mere 15% were in favor of revision compared to 71% against.[12]

In the context of the Cold War, Japanese politics was characterized by a bipolar system pitting the conservative LDP against the progressive Japan Socialist Party (JSP). The US that initially implemented an ambitious set of democratization and demilitarization reforms in the immediate postwar had since reset its priorities to the pursuit of the so-called "Reverse Course" policies that sought to undo them as it set its eye on fighting the communist threat in East Asia. Kishi became a useful anti-communist collaborator for the US but was forced to step down from the premiership amidst huge protests against the revision of the US–Japan Security Treaty that he oversaw in 1960.

The popular backlash against the reactionary policies of Kishi strengthened the position of the moderates within the LDP, who thereafter emphasized economic reconstruction and growth while shelving controversial and divisive issues of constitution revision and security policy. As a result, the LDP succeeded in establishing itself as a "super catch-all party" that dominated the party system and ruled for 38 consecutive years until 1993. The LDP continued to have a minority stream within that strongly advocated the revision of the constitution, but as the cause was largely sidelined even with the party, there was no way that the conditions for the amendment as stipulated in Article 96 could be met.

Politically, the postwar pacifist principle that Article 9 symbolized became so entrenched that it practically became unamendable.

2.4 The neoliberal turn of constitution reform debate

Article 9, however, came under close scrutiny almost as soon as the Cold War came to an end. Less than a year after the Berlin Wall fell in November 1989, Iraq invaded Kuwait and the Gulf War broke out. Japan received renewed pressure from the US and the western countries to take a more active part in the international security arrangement, and it responded by eventually enacting the Peacekeeping Operation (PKO) Law in 1992. At the time, Japan was at the height of the so-called Bubble Economy, and a new kind of argument for constitution revision, including the revision of Article 9, started to be advocated by the neoliberal conservatives, many of whom left the LDP, as part of their wider reform package of bureaucracy, electoral system, and regulatory frameworks.

The best known of these figures was the highly influential Ichirō Ozawa, a former power broker in the LDP, who argued in his best-selling book for the revision of Article 9 by adding a third paragraph:

---

10 *Asahi* newspaper (27 November 1957) 5.
11 *Asahi* newspaper, evening edn (17 August 1962) 3.
12 *Asahi* newspaper (1 November 1978) 1.

3. Paragraph 2 should not be interpreted as prohibiting the maintenance of a Self-Defense Force for peace-building activities; the maintenance of a United Nations reserve force for action under United Nations command when requested; and action by the United Nations reserve force under United Nations command.[13]

In fact, in relation to the focus of this paper – the unconstitutional amendment of Article 9 through a change in government interpretation rather than through the formal revision of the text of the constitution – the most important development that took place in this period, in retrospect, was a key argument that Ozawa started to advocate while he was still the chairman of the LDP, trying to navigate the controversial Japanese response to the Gulf War. As Ozawa's proposal for a formal addition to the Article 9 shows, he took the view that Article 9 (and its second paragraph more specifically) does not prohibit Japan's participation in UN-sanctioned peace-building activities, and that this could be done by either formally revising the constitution or by merely changing the government interpretation of the existing constitutional text.

This put Ozawa and his followers onto a collision course with the CLB, which consists of career bureaucrats and which has conventionally been entrusted with the provision of the official government interpretation of the constitution and laws with a certain degree of autonomy as legal experts from the political leadership of the day. Ozawa took issue and contended that the democratically elected politicians should be in charge of providing and answering for the official government interpretation of the constitution.

Similarly, Morihiro Hosokawa, who became the first non-LDP prime minister in 38 years in 1993, advocated a "new theory of constitution revision" that dismissed both the anti-revision camp and the pro-revision camp of the Cold War era as outdated, and included references to such proposals for revision as a new clause that allows for the participation of SDF in UN-led PKOs in the policy platform of the Japan New Party that he launched in 1992.[14] The document argued that "it is impossible to establish the new ideal of the state that the people seek while avoiding the debate over the constitution as a taboo" and also that "our theory of constitution revision is entirely different from the common pro-revision position that aims at pushing back the clock to prewar Japan." In addition to the expanded role of the SDF, Hosokawa also contended that constitutional amendment was necessary for the sake of the reform of Japan's system of governance to include such items as "the establishment of the autonomy of the legislature and the reinforcement of the leadership of the cabinet," "clarification of the different

---

13 Ichirō Ozawa, *Blueprint for a New Japan – The Rethinking of a New Nation* (Kōdansha 1994) 110.
14 Japan New Party, 'Seisaku Taikō' [Policy Platform] in Tōdai Hō/Kabashima Ikuo Zemi (eds), *'Shintō' Zenkiroku* vol 1 (Bokutakusha 1998) 164–8.

roles of the two chambers of the Parliament," and "the expansion of the subjects of national referenda."

Having fallen from power for the first time in 38 years, the LDP, too, further modified its position on the constitution as it crawled back to power in a previously unthinkable coalition with its erstwhile archrival Japan Socialist Party. In a document called the "new manifesto" issued in 1995, when the LDP was supporting a Socialist prime minister, it was announced that the party

> will debate with the public what a constitution suited to the new era ushering in the 21st century may look like, on the basis of such various principles as pacifism and the respect of basic human rights that are already consolidated.[15]

Some in the LDP were still fixated on the revision of Article 9 as their ultimate goal, but the trend was to attempt to push for a "forward-looking" type of discussion towards an eventual revision of the constitution.

Similarly, significant rethinking took place in the progressive camp as well. A simple refusal and opposition to the revision of the constitution (and Article 9 in particular) was seen as untenable by some liberals as their position was attacked as hypocritical and unrealistic "pacifism-in-one-country" or as "negative pacifism" as Japan faced a growing call for greater "international contribution" in the post-Cold War era.

Thus, Japan saw a considerable transformation in the constitutional amendment debate from the end of the Cold War, from one that pitted those who opposed the revision of Article 9 against those who held a reactionary view that Japan should make its "autonomous" constitution by revising Article 9 and remilitarizing head on, to a new period of rather less focused discussion about all kinds of possible ideas for constitutional reforms that were heavily informed by a neoliberal reformist ethos.

On the one hand, this change had the effect of popularizing and legitimizing the notion that Japan was in a need of revising the constitution to meet the challenges of the post-Cold War era. On the other hand, the vibrant debate lacked a focal point and thus lacked a sense of urgency and feasibility. This was strange and ironic. While the expectation was created that any self-respecting political leader must have an idea for constitutional amendment, in reality the prospect for any revision of the constitution was remote at best since there was no shared sense of need or urgency. The issue became merely a symbol to flaunt the reformist credo of a politician or a party as the Japanese political system was going through a neoliberal transformation through a series of political and administrative reforms, including the introduction of the first-past-the-post system and the centralization of power in the hands of the prime minister and his staff.

The centrist Kōmeitō, too, proposed the institution of a system of national referendum, local decentralization, and the right to a good environment as

---

15 *Asahi* newspaper (4 March 1995) 2.

possible items for a constitution revision, and the leaders of the Democratic Party of Japan (DPJ), which replaced the Japan Socialist Party as the main opposition party over time, emphasized that the party was neither for nor against the revision of the constitution, but was in favor of a future-oriented discussion about the constitution. Reflecting the mood of the time, some of the proposals that were advocated included the direct, popular election of the prime minister, a system for the national referendum, and the introduction of the right to a good environment.

The media and public opinion also went through significant transformation. The conservative *Yomiuri* newspaper published its own proposals for constitution revision in 1991 and followed it up with further proposals in 2000 and 2004.[16] *Yomiuri* boasts the largest circulation in Japan (and indeed the world) as well as close ties with the political class, so its influence on the public opinion as well as on the political parties was not negligible.

By the mid-1990s, various opinion polls showed that those who were in favor of constitution revision outnumbered those opposed. In the liberal-leaning *Asahi* newspaper poll of 1997, the percentage of respondents who thought that there was a need to revise the constitution surpassed their opponents for the first time with 46% to 39%.[17] However, popular support for Article 9 remained high all this while, and in the same poll from 1997, only 20% of the respondents expressed their approval for the revision of Article 9 against 69% who opposed such a revision.

The spread of the feeling that it was about time that Japan revised its Constitution, however, was utilized to focus the debate increasingly on Article 9. In 2000, the Research Commission on the Constitution was established for the first time in the Diet. In the same year, the *Nikkei* newspaper, the business daily, argued in its editorial that "if the constitution was to be revised, it's now time to discuss which concrete point to amend in what way," and thus shifted its position in favor of the constitutional amendment, including Article 9.[18]

The business sector followed suit. The Japan Association of Corporate Executives published its aggressive opinion in favor of constitution revision in 2003,[19] and Keidanren (Japan Business Federation)[20] and the Japan Chamber of Commerce and Industry[21] published their reports in 2005. The Keidanren

---

16 *Yomiuri* newspaper website https://info.yomiuri.co.jp/media/yomiuri/feature/kaiseishian.html accessed 10 April 2021.
17 *Asahi* newspaper (26 April 1997) 1.
18 *Nikkei* newspaper (3 May 2000) 2.
19 Japan Association of Corporate Executives, *Kempō Mondai Chōsakai Ikensho* [Constitution Issue Research Group Report] April 2003 https://www.doyukai.or.jp/policyproposals/articles/2002/pdf/030421.pdf accessed 10 April 2021.
20 Keidanren, *Wagakuni no Kihon Mondai o Kangaeru* [Considering the Basic Issues of Our Country] 18 January 2005 https://www.keidanren.or.jp/japanese/policy/2005/002/honbun.html#part4 accessed 10 April 2021.
21 JCCI, *Kempō Mondai ni Kansuru Kondankai Hōkokusho* [Report of the Commission on Constitution Issues] 16 June 2005. https://web.archive.org/web/20060628060457/http://www.jcci.or.jp/nissyo/iken/050616kenpouhoukoku.pdf accessed 10 April 2021.

report focused on the revision of Article 9 to provide a clear constitutional basis for the Self-Defense Force and for the exercise of collective self-defense and on Article 96 to make it easier to revise the constitution. These arguments were based on the growing big-business consensus that it was imperative to liberate the SDF from the shackles of Article 9 and to strengthen the US–Japan security alliance in order for the Japanese government to provide necessary protection for the international interest of the Japanese corporations under the global economic order.

2.5 US-dependent security "normalization"

The background of this renewed focus on the revision of Article 9 from the late 1990s and the early 2000s was the growing consensus among the US–Japan alliance managers that the Japanese SDF needed to be increasingly integrated into the US military strategy in East Asia and beyond in order to cope with the challenges presented by the changing security environment in the post-Cold War era.

Almost as soon as the conservative LDP regained the premiership in its unlikely coalition with the Socialists, Prime Minister Ryūtaro Hashimoto met with President Bill Clinton and issued the US–Japan Joint Declaration on Security— Alliance for the 21st Century in 1996. The goal of the joint declaration was to redefine the US–Japan relations in the post-Cold War world with a clearer focus on its character as a military alliance. Its scope was also to be expanded from the Far East to the Asia-Pacific region and beyond. While confirming the continuous US presence in Japan and the region, greater integration of the Japanese SDF with the US forces was to be sought.

A major concern at the time was the nuclear and missile development programs of North Korea, and the joint declaration was quickly followed by the revising of the Guidelines for US–Japan Defense Cooperation, the alliance manual, as it were, in 1997, with a particular focus on the so-called "situation in areas surrounding Japan" – a crisis in the Korean peninsula to be specific. The LDP government further enacted the Situation in Surrounding Areas Law to provide the legal basis for a possible operationalization of the US–Japan military alliance outside of Japan, in the surrounding areas.

The pressure for the transformation of the US–Japan military alliance did not end there, however. In 2000, an influential special report published under the auspices of the Institute for National Strategic Studies, National Defense University of the US Department of Defense, by a bipartisan study group led by Richard L. Armitage and Joseph S. Nye, unambiguously singled out Article 9 as an obstacle to the further strengthening of US–Japan relations: "Japan's prohibition against collective self-defense is a constraint on alliance cooperation. Lifting this prohibition would allow for closer and more efficient security cooperation." The global ambition of the alliance relationship was also captured in the passage that stated that "we see the special relationship between the United States and Great Britain as a model for the alliance."[22]

A further boost to this line of reasoning by the US–Japan alliance managers resulted from the shocking terrorist attacks in the US on September 11th, 2001. The Japanese government led by Prime Minister Junichirō Koizumi, who boasted a strong personal tie with US President George W. Bush, embarked on a series of Emergency Legislations, starting with the Counter-Terrorism Special Measures Law in November 2001 that enabled the Japanese SDF to provide "rear area support in non-combat zones" for the US and its allies, including most notably refueling missions in the Indian Ocean. Koizumi also enacted the Iraq Special Measures Law in 2003 to enable the SDF to take part in humanitarian reconstruction and peace-keeping missions in non-combat areas.

The move was followed by further Emergency Legislations in 2003 and 2004. In 2003, three sets of emergency laws were passed, including the Armed Attack Situation Law, which defined the various armed attack situations (including the situation in which armed attack is anticipated) and laid down the responsibilities of the state, local authorities, and designated public organizations (e.g. infrastructure). They were complemented by another seven emergency legislations, including the Protection of People Law in 2004. These laws set out the powers, responsibilities, and procedures for the state and other public authorities to evacuate the citizens, but also to facilitate the military operations of the US military as well as the Japanese SDF in armed attack situations. It bears noting that these Emergency Legislations were opposed by the smaller, leftist opposition parties, which questioned the constitutionality of the bills, but supported by the main opposition, the Democratic Party of Japan.

These laws were clear indication of the accelerating trend of Japan's integration with the US military strategy since the late 1990s. It was as if the demands and priorities of the US–Japan security alliance took precedence over the Japanese Constitution and its pacifist tradition. Tellingly in 2005, Koizumi stated at a joint press conference with Bush that

> There is no such thing as U.S.-Japan relationship too close. Some people maintain that maybe we would pay more attention to other issues, probably it would be better to strengthen the relationship with other countries. I do not side with such views. The U.S.-Japan relationship, the closer, more intimate it is, it is easier for us to behave and establish better relations with China, with South Korea, and other nations in Asia.[23]

---

22 INSS Special Report, 11 October 2000 http://armitageint.wpengine.com/wp-content/uploads/2018/06/ArmNye-Oct-2000-Report.pdf accessed 10 April 2021.
23 https://georgewbush-whitehouse.archives.gov/news/releases/2005/11/text/20051116-5.html accessed 10 April 2021.

Reflecting these political developments, in the *Asahi* newspaper poll of 2005, 56% of the respondents agreed that the revision of the constitution was necessary against 33% who did not think it necessary.[24] More specifically on Article 9, 51% replied that there was no need for revision, while 36% said that it should be revised.

In 2005, the LDP published its first proposal for a new constitution.[25] It proposed to remove the second paragraph of Article 9 altogether and inserted instead a direct reference to the maintenance of a Self-Defense Military. It also sought to lower the bar for the revision of the constitution to a simple majority in both houses for a national referendum (as opposed to the required two-third majority in both houses) by revising Article 96. Article 20 that stipulates the separation of state and religion was also targeted for revision to allow for the prime minister to make official visits to the Yasukuni Shrine – which is unconstitutional under the postwar Constitution.

In the same year, on the occasion of the 50th anniversary of its founding, the LDP adopted a new party platform that advocated "the enactment of a new constitution," "proud and ambitious Japanese," and "small government" among other things, and specifically stated that "we shall strive for the formation of a national consensus in order to enact a new constitution on the basis of an independent national awareness."[26] Koizumi was then succeeded by Abe, who went on to revise the Basic Law on Education to include the "love of country" as a goal of education, upgraded the Defense Agency into a full-fledged Ministry of Defense, and enacted the National Referendum Law and set up the Commission on the Constitution in both houses of the Diet – thereby making it procedurally possible to initiate the formal process of constitution revision.

Abe's single-minded pursuit of "a beautiful country" – his focus on the revisionist agenda that centered around his ambition to revise the Constitution – quickly hit a wall, however. Public opinion was far more concerned about the bread-and-butter issues, namely, the widening gap between the rich and the poor that the Koizumi structural reform agenda left behind, the issue of missing pension records, and the various ministerial scandals, which Abe neglected at his peril. After merely a year in office, he suffered a landslide defeat at the hands of the rival DPJ in the Upper House election and was forced to resign citing ill health.

Now that the DPJ was in its ascendance, it had no interest in joining in the cross-partisan debate over constitutional amendment that would only assist the LDP to cling to power. The Commission on the Constitution did not function at all, and the tide for the constitution revision waned. In the *Asahi* poll

---

24 *Asahi* newspaper (3 May 2005) 1.
25 LDP, *Shinkempō Sōan* [New Draft Constitution], November 2005 http://www.kenpoukai gi.gr.jp/seitoutou/051028jimin-sinkenpousouan.pdf accessed 10 April 2021.
26 LDP, *Shinkōryō* [New Party Platform] 22 November 2005. https://www.jimin.jp/aboutus/declaration/ accessed 10 April 2021.

of 2008, only 23% of the respondents said that they were in favor of revising Article 9 against 66% who opposed it.[27]

2.6 "Taking Japan back"

The constitutional reform debate completely faded away while the DPJ was in power and the LDP was in the political wilderness for three years between summer 2009 and winter 2012, but two crucial developments took place under the surface.

On the one hand, through the vagaries of party realignment that unfolded in the post-Cold War era, Ozawa was by then a central figure in the DPJ government with huge influence on its policy stance. As was touched upon earlier, ever since he was still in the LDP, Ozawa took the view that Article 9 did not prohibit Japan's participation in UN-sanctioned collective security arrangement, including a role in its peace-building and -keeping operations, and also that it was wrong for the official government interpretation of the constitution to be determined by the CLB, which has been shielded from political control by the elected politicians. The latter view was very much part of Ozawa's strong belief in the virtue of a strong political leadership in the British-style majoritarian democracy – the largely unrestrained exercise of power subject only to the check provided by the prospect of a regular change of government in a two-party system based on the first-past-the-post electoral system.

In fact, Ozawa has been a remarkably consistent promoter of these views as he led or belonged to different political parties through the 1990s and the 2000s. He also consistently disagreed with the lifting of the ban on the exercise of collective self-defense under US pressure. Between 1998 and 2000, Ozawa led the Liberal Party into a coalition with the LDP, and during that time, he advocated that the government change its interpretation of Article 9 to allow for Japan's fuller participation in UN operations, while he opposed the position that Article 9 permitted the exercise of collective self-defense. He also unsuccessfully tried to force the LDP to agree to ban the CLB representing the official government interpretation of the constitution and the laws in the parliamentary exchanges.

After having left the coalition government with the LDP, Ozawa took his party and joined the DPJ in 2003 and became its leader in 2006. As a matter of fact, he was the mastermind behind the electoral success that propelled the DPJ to power in 2009, even though by then he ceded the top post to be its chairman in response to the allegation of campaign finance irregularities that was dogging him and the party. As the very powerful chairman of the ruling DPJ, Ozawa sought to legally ban the CLB chief from representing the government's official legal and constitutional interpretation in the Diet, but stopping short of new legislation, he still managed to sideline the CLB and a cabinet minister was assigned

---

27 *Asahi* newspaper (3 May 2008) 1.

that role in the DPJ government for as long as Ozawa retained strong influence in the party.

What is absolutely crucial, in retrospect, is the precedent that this move created in placing the CLB under the political control of the ruling party. Even though the issue of the official government interpretation of the constitution (and of Article 9, in particular) did not surface during the DPJ government, the CLB was no longer as autonomous as it has been in the postwar period. This was to be abused by Abe upon return to power.

On the other hand, deprived of access to pork barrel politics, the LDP drifted further to the right while in opposition as ideological extremism took over as the party was freed from the burden of responsibility in office.

Only five years after the LDP revised its party platform for the first time in 50 years, it once again revised it to place on the top of its fundamental policy ideas that "We shall aim at the enactment of a new constitution that would show Japan at its most Japanese and would allow it to contribute to the world."[28]

Furthermore, as it revised also its proposal for constitution revision, the SDF was to be renamed the National Defense Military, the emperor would be designated as the head of state, and family members were to be obligated to mutually support one another – all these reactionary ideological positions that were rejected as the LDP put together its proposal in 2005 were now adopted. In fact, as the revised proposal was so clearly ignoring the basic principles of constitutionalism and respect for human rights that Yōichi Masuzoe, who was responsible for the 2005 proposal, wrote on his blog that he was astounded to see that "it appears that people who don't even know the basics of a constitution wrote it."[29]

In other words, the neoliberal reformist approach to the issue of constitution revision receded to the background as the reactionary, revisionist view became dominant in the LDP, and it was precisely at that juncture that the DPJ government imploded and the LDP regained power with Abe as the prime minister supported by an overwhelming two-thirds majority in the Lower House. Ironically for Ozawa, because his much-cherished vision of a competitive two-party system was now in ruins, there was no remaining brake on the winner-takes-all system that the years of neoliberal political and administrative reforms have left behind, and Abe faced no serious opposition to speak of in the entire political system.

Previously, Abe sought to change the interpretation of Article 9 to enable the exercise of collective self-defense when he was in power in 2006 but was unsuccessful as his premiership was short-lived and he stepped down in a year. He picked up the issue again soon after he returned to power in December 2012, however. It can be said that Abe had a two-pronged strategy – expanding the

28 LDP, *Heisei 22-nen (2010-nen) Kōryō* [2010 Party Platform] 24 January 2010 https://www.jimin.jp/aboutus/declaration/ accessed 10 April 2021.
29 Yōichi Masuzoe, 'Jimintō Kempō Kaisei Dainiji Sōan no Mondaiten' [Problems with the LDP's Second Draft Constitution] (Masuzoe Yoichi Official Website, 3 May 2019) https://ameblo.jp/shintomasuzoe/entry-12458730623.html accessed 10 April 2021.

scope of what Japan may do through the changes of the interpretation of the constitution while also seeking to formally revise the text of the constitution.

Initially, Abe toyed with the idea of revising first Article 96 of the Constitution, but he immediately faced a rather strong public reaction. The opposition to the move was led by a group of constitutional law scholars, political scientists, and other academics that included but also went beyond the familiar defenders of Article 9, called the Article 96 Association.[30] The Association was headed by Japan's foremost constitutional law scholar, Yōichi Higuchi, and a range of the nation's top constitutional experts, including Setsu Kobayashi, the most prominent advocate of the revision of Article 9 previously.

In its founding statement issued on May 23rd, 2013,[31] the Article 96 Association pointed out that the LDP was seeking to lower the constitutional hurdle to instigate the national referendum for the amendment of the Constitution to a simple majority in both houses of the Diet with an eye to more easily amending fundamental principles of the Constitution that are embodied in the preamble, Article 9, and Article 13, among others, that stipulate respect for the people as individuals and their basic rights and liberties. According to the statement that was drafted by Higuchi and signed by its members, the attempted revision of Article 96 was not merely a technical problem, but a grave issue that concerned the very principle of constitutionalism that centers around the role of the constitution as a brake on power.

The gerrymandering that has been left by the ruling parties, in spite of several court rulings that deemed the existing state of affairs unconstitutional, meant that there was serious doubt as to whether incumbent members of the Diet were constitutionally qualified to debate the amendment of the Constitution, the statement argued. Moreover, Article 96 requires thorough debate and deliberation by the legitimately elected members of the Diet before asking the Japanese people to make a decision that is conferred upon "this and future generations in trust" (Article 97). For the majority party to abuse its inflated majority in the Diet to ram through an amendment of Article 96 is tantamount to a challenge against the raison d'être of the Constitution. It was contended that this move jeopardized the legitimate exercise of the amendment of power of the Constitution by the people.

In the event, in face of strong public opposition in the run-up to the Upper House election in July 2013, Abe quickly gave up on the idea of formally amending Article 96 first to make other formal amendment easier and more feasible, and instead, opted for the informal and backdoor route to constitutional amendment. It was also exactly then that Deputy Prime Minister Tarō Asō caused a controversy by stating in a meeting that "we should learn from the Nazis" on how to

---

30 This author is a member of the Article 96 Association.
31 Reprinted in Asaho Mizushima, '"96-jō no Kai" Hassoku: Rikken Shugi no Teichaku e Mukete' (*Chokugen*, 27 May 2013) http://www.asaho.com/jpn/bkno/2013/0527.html accessed 7 April 2021.

revise the Constitution without a big fuss. Thus, Abe took control over the CLB the following month.

According to postwar convention, the appointment of the head of the CLB was entrusted in the hands of the bureaucrats. The CLB itself does not recruit fresh college graduates, but it consists of bureaucrats who were transferred to it in mid-career. As a rule, CLB cadre originally from either the Ministries of Home Affairs, Finance, Justice, or Trade and Industry took turns in assuming the top position. The term of the CLB head was also unrelated to the term of a cabinet or prime minister. As such, it was not a politically appointed position.

Having come to power for the second time, when the opposition was all but wiped out from the Diet, Abe took a step further than Ozawa had ever managed to do and appointed a diplomat, Ichirō Komatsu, from the Ministry of Foreign Affairs, with no previous experience in the CLB and with no expertise in domestic law. The point, for Abe, was that Komatsu was a known advocate for lifting the ban on the exercise of collective self-defense. In February 2013, Abe also revived an *ad hoc* government council on security legislation that he initially set up during his first stint in power (but which had been left inactive since) with the exact same members – all of whom were known proponents of the exercise of collective self-defense. Moreover, the council merely operated in a "private" advisory capacity to the prime minister because it did not have any legal basis. Komatsu served in the secretariat of this government council previously, and now they were both placed in positions to lead the change of the government interpretation of Article 9.

On an issue as important as this, the government would normally set up a government council of experts, which is both founded on a legal basis (and therefore becomes an "official" council) and composed of a broader range of views on the controversy. Here, Abe handpicked a new head for the CLB, breaking postwar conventions, with an eye on imposing his own interpretation of the constitution that is seen as not only unorthodox but simply unconstitutional by a vast majority of constitutional law experts. Thus, it was not only the conclusion that Abe was seeking to reach but also his means to get there that set off the alarm bell with respect to constitutionalism and the rule of law.

In an attempt to further reinforce Japan's military alliance with the US, Abe also established Japan's National Security Council (NSC) in December 2013. It was supposed to work closely with its original American counterpart, and enacted the much-criticized State Secrets Law, which was widely seen as a serious blow to press freedom and the principle of open and accountable government with little check on government abuses.

In further concerning developments, in January 2014, the Abe government officially modified the school textbook authorization standards (in Japan, the school textbooks need government panel approval) so as to require the inclusion of reference to the Japanese government position on issues of modern and contemporary history in the texts. Also, in the same month, the newly appointed president of the Japanese public broadcaster, NHK, stated in his first press conference following government nomination: "We cannot say 'left' when the government says 'right.'" This statement indicates that he did not grasp the basic concept of press freedom.[32] In April 2014, the government replaced the so-called "Three Principles on Arms Exports and Their Related Policy Guidelines" that put severe limits on arms and arms-related exports with a new "Three Principles on Transfer of Defense Equipment and Technology" which, as the name shows, was intended to lift the ban and facilitate arms export of Japanese companies.

On April 18th, much of the same group of scholars as the Article 96 Association launched a new Constitutional Democracy Association (CDA) in order to counter the "aggressive campaign to transform the fundamental principles underlying Japan's Constitution and democratic politics" by the Abe government, including its attempt to lift the constitutional ban on the exercise of collective self-defense through a change of the government interpretation of the same, unamended text.[33]

In its founding statement, the CDA noted that "The various restraints imposed in a constitutional democracy serve to protect the people from the reckless actions of the government of the day that may show little regard for individual dignity and freedom," but that, steeped in a sense of its own omnipotence after two national election victories, the Abe administration

> has justified as "political leadership" its attempts to impose a partisan orientation upon organizations—including the Bank of Japan, CLB, NHK and other broadcasters, research and educational institutions—that ought to play an important role in imposing checks and restraints upon the exercise of the majority will.

The CDA further noted,

> Abe is attempting to change the existing interpretation of the Constitution by cabinet decision so as to approve Japan's right to collective self-defense, effectively rendering Article 9 of Japan's Constitution meaningless. If the Abe administration is allowed to do as it pleases, the issue of revising Article 96 will be raised again, and the Constitution may no longer be able to restrict the reach of government.

It added,

> What is essential now is that we first return to a politics rooted in the Constitution, setting aside differences over specific policies. This means a revival of constitutional government, with its rules limiting the reach of

---

32 *Asahi* newspaper (26 January 2014) 3.
33 This author is a member of Constitutional Democracy Association as well. See 'Save Constitutional Democracy Japan 2014: Prospectus' (*Rikken Demokurashū no Kai*, 18 April 2014) https://constitutionaldemocracyjapan.tumblr.com/setsuritsushyushi accessed 7 April 2021.

whatever party happens to hold a parliamentary majority, and specification of the areas into which government may not intrude. This also means reviving the Diet's functions as not merely the site of majority-based decision-making, but also of substantive debate and administrative oversight.

The CDA concluded that it intends on joining and expanding the civic opposition against arbitrary, unaccountable government "in order to restore constitutional democracy to Japan."

As was expected, the prime minister's council on security legislation issued its report the following month to recommend the change of the government interpretation of the Constitution in order to lift the ban on the exercise of the right of collective self-defense.[34] The panel argued that the security environment surrounding Japan has changed dramatically and an adherence to an old-fashioned interpretation of the Constitution that only granted the exercise of individual self-defense for the country was both unnecessary and dangerous. According to the report, the first paragraph of Article 9 should be interpreted "as not prohibiting the use of force for the purpose of self-defense, nor imposing any constitutional restriction on activities that are consistent with international law, such as participation in U.N. PKOs etc. and collective security measures." Similarly, paragraph 2 of Article 9 should be reinterpreted in such a way to include the exercise of the right of collective self-defense within the limit of the right of self-defense at the minimum extent that is necessary and constitutional, it contended.

The most significant conclusion of the report was, thus, to recommend that the government lift the ban on the exercise of collective self-defense by replacing the existing three conditions for the exercise of individual self-defense with the following:

> When a foreign country that is in a close relationship with Japan comes under an armed attack and if such a situation has the potential to significantly affect the security of Japan, Japan should be able to participate in operations to repel such an attack by using force to the minimum extent necessary, having obtained an explicit request or consent from the country under attack, and thus to make contribution to the maintenance and restoration of international peace and security even if Japan itself is not directly attacked.

Thus, the 1972 government interpretation of Article 9 as banning collective self-defense was thus reversed after over four decades.

In a press conference on June 9th, the CDA presented its criticism of the government's move from the standpoint of constitutionalism, the security risks involved, the fallacy of the notion of a "limited" collective self-defense, and

---

34 Anzen Hoshō no Hōteki Kiban no Saikōchiku ni Kansuru Kondankai [Panel on the Reconstruction of the Legal Basis for National Security], *Report*, 15 May 2014. https://www.kantei.go.jp/jp/singi/anzenhosyou2/dai7/houkoku.pdf accessed 10 April 2021.

international cooperation.[35] As its opposition to Abe's rejection of constitutionalism and the rule of law, which the CDA described as "an exceedingly reckless act that moves well beyond the realm of constitutional interpretation. It is better described as a full attack on Japan's Constitution," the CDA put forward the following arguments:

> For the more than half-century since the end of the Second World War, the Constitution has been interpreted to permit the SDF's exclusive dedication to self-defense under Article 9 and to prohibit voluntary attacks upon another country except in response to an act of foreign aggression. Changing this longstanding constitutional interpretation by the decision of a single Cabinet far exceeds the realm of decisions that should be made by the Cabinet, which owes an obligation to respect and to uphold the Constitution.
>
> Prime Minister Abe has extolled "the rule of law," together with liberalism and basic human rights, as the fundamental values of the democratic order to which Japan belongs, and criticizes countries still partially subject to the "rule of man." However, if Abe succeeds in changing the existing constitutional interpretation of Article 9, the "rule of law" will be reduced to the arbitrary use of authority by the current administration—in other words, "the rule of man."
>
> The exercise of collective self-defense has never been conceived of as something authorized by the Constitution. The announced intention of the Abe government signifies a change to a fundamental principle of the Constitution. If such a major change is truly to be undertaken, then a sincere appeal to the citizens of Japan, careful national deliberation, and legitimate procedures for the revision of Article 9 must all be essential preconditions.

Nevertheless, on July 1st, 2014, both the National Security Council and the Cabinet approved this new interpretation of the Constitution that enabled lifting the ban on collective self-defense and vowed to enact new security legislation on the basis of the new government interpretation. In May 2015, the government submitted security bills to do precisely that. The bills triggered growing public criticisms and protests, and the demonstrations continued to gain in size and frequency not only in front of the Diet building in Tokyo, but across the country even after they passed through the Lower House in July.

An important moment in the popular protests against the security legislation took place on June 4th, 2015, at a meeting of the Commission on the Constitution of the House of Representatives.[36] The subject of the discussion that day was the

---

35 'Statement on the Report of the Advisory Panel on the Reconstruction of the Legal Basis for Security and the Press Conference Held by Prime Minister Abe' (*Rikken Demokurashī no Kai*, 9 June 2014). https://constitutionaldemocracyjapan.tumblr.com/activities accessed 7 April 2021.
36 Minutes, 189th session of the Diet, House of Representatives, Commission on the Constitution, No. 3, 4 June 2015. https://kokkai.ndl.go.jp/#/detail?minId=118904183X00320 150604&current=1 accessed 7 April 2021.

stability and preservation of the constitution, including constitutionalism, the limitation to constitutional amendment, and constitutional review. Three prominent constitutional law scholars were invited as witnesses, Yasuo Hasebe, Setsu Kobayashi, and Eiji Sasada (Hasebe and Kobayashi are central members of CDA). Following their testimonies, a member of the opposition asked for their views on the constitutionality of the security legislation. All three witnesses, including Hasebe, who was nominated by the ruling parties, unambiguously replied that they considered it to be unconstitutional. The moment was captured and repeatedly aired on television and on the internet, and thus, greatly enhanced popular mobilization for the protests and demonstrations.

Hasebe stated that lifting the ban on the exercise of collective self-defense was unconstitutional as it cannot be explained in the framework of the logic of the decade-long government interpretation of the Constitution, and thus, seriously disturbs the stability of the constitution. He further added that the exercise of collective self-defense would make it impossible to draw a line between the exercise of military power by a foreign military and the activities of the SDF. Kobayashi concurred with Hasebe, and argued that the exercise of collective self-defense, the act of waging war overseas in order to assist a friendly power, is a violation of Article 9, particularly its second paragraph. Finally, Sasada also agreed and stated that the limitation of legitimate interpretation of Article 9 was shown in the 1972 interpretation that the LDP government and the CLB crafted together, and the exercise of collective self-defense must be considered unconstitutional.

Over the summer, the security legislation ignited an historic protest movement from civil society that included scholars, the youth, labor unions, and concerned mothers, among others. The CDA was joined by a new, if partially overlapping, group of academics in the opposition to the security legislation in June 2015 with the establishment of the Association of Scholars Opposed to the Security-Related Bills (the Association of Scholars). It included some key members of the CAD, but was led by an education studies scholar, Manabu Satō, with a much broader range of top academics, many of whom were colleagues of Satō's from the Science Council of Japan, the country's national academy.[37] In its founding statement, the Association of Scholars denounced the security bills as a clear violation of Article 9 that would enable Japan's SDF to cooperate and take part in overseas military activities in another country.[38] Mindful of Japan's history as an aggressor – and of the fact that the professors sent their students to fight overseas during wartime – the statement sounded the alarm that the arbitrary change of the decades-long government interpretation created the possibility of Japan taking part in a war of aggression waged by the United States. By the time the bills were rammed through the Diet, some 14,120 scholars and 30,957 citizens signed the statement, and over 140 universities nationwide and allied scholarly groups were taking part in the protest movement.

37 This author is also a member of the Association of Scholars.
38 'Appeal' (Association of Scholars, 12 June 2015) http://anti-security-related-bill.jp accessed 7 April 2021.

In an *Asahi* newspaper survey that was conducted with 209 constitutional law scholars in June, out of 122 who responded 104 considered the lifting of the ban on collective self-defense to be unconstitutional (with another 15 noting that it was possibly unconstitutional). Moreover, 116 responded that the Cabinet decision to reinterpret the Constitution in July 2014 was inappropriate (with a mere 6 offering no answer). Similarly, in an NHK survey of an even larger number of constitutional law and other law scholars, 377 out of the 422 respondents deemed the security bills to be either unconstitutional or likely to be unconstitutional.

The Japan Federation of Bar Associations (JFBA) also took a clear stance against the security legislation following the passage of a "resolution opposing the approval of exercising the right to collective self-defense" on May 31st, 2013.[39] The central argument of the JFBA resolution is as follows:

> The JFBA believes that the government's interpretation, which has been established as being that, "the use of the right to collective self-defense is not permissible when Japan is not under direct attack" should not be changed or meddled with so easily by Ministers of State or by members of the Diet, on whom the obligations to respect and uphold the Constitution are imposed as stipulated in Article 99 of the Constitution. Moreover, any change in the interpretation of the Constitution by way of laws which are inferior to the Constitution should simply never be allowed because this would go against the principles of Constitutionalism wherein the Constitution i) takes precedence over any law or other act of government which are contrary to the provisions of the Constitution, and disallows such laws to have legal force or validity (Article 98 of Constitution), and ii) limits the power of the government and the Diet.[40]

Even among more conservative legal professionals, four former Supreme Court justices and five former directors of the CLB publicly expressed their view that lifting the ban on collective self-defense through a reinterpretation of the Constitution was unconstitutional. A representative view from these top legal professionals was expressed by Kunio Hamada, former Supreme Court Justice, at the public hearing in the run-up to the final vote on the security legislation at the House of Councilors on September 15th, 2015.[41] He noted the crucial role played by the CLB in postwar Japan in providing constitutional stability in the

---

39 '64th JFBA General Meeting Resolution Opposing the Approval of Exercising the Right to Collective Self-Defense' (JFBA, 31 May 2013). https://www.nichibenren.or.jp/en/document/statements/130531.html accessed 7 April 2021.
40 Article 99 "The Emperor or the Regent as well as Ministers of State, members of the Diet, judges, and all other public officials have the obligation to respect and uphold this Constitution." (Constitution of Japan.)
41 Minutes, 189th session of the Diet, House of Councilors, Public Hearing, Special Committee on the Peace and Security Legislation, No. 1, 15 September 2015. https://kokkai.ndl.go.jp/#/detail?minId=118913930X00120150915&current=1 accessed 7 April 2021.

absence of an active Supreme Court. The fact that the Cabinet simply took away its autonomy and imposed a new interpretation on it meant that the constitutionality of the legislation was highly dubious, particularly because the arguments that were put forth by the government to justify the new interpretation relied on some of the arguments cited from the Sunagawa verdict and the 1972 government interpretation, neither of which had to do with, much less approved the constitutionality of, the exercise of collective self-defense. Various opinion polls indicated also that a large majority of the general public considered collective self-defense unconstitutional as well.

Nevertheless, the big businesses as well as *Yomiuri*, *Nikkei*, and *Sankei* newspapers, and of course, the US supported the bills, and they were finally enacted on September 19th, 2015, as the government rammed them through the Upper House.

2.7 Concluding remarks

The controversy over the informal amendment of Article 9 of the Constitution of Japan that lifted the ban on the exercise of collective self-defense presents a curious case in the debate over unconstitutional constitutional amendments. The change is widely seen as unconstitutional by constitutional scholars, legal professionals, and the general public, but not because of the inherent unamendability of Article 9 or judicial activism in the Japanese Supreme Court. In fact, even mainstream scholarly proponents of the doctrine of limitations of amendment to the Constitution of Japan take the view that the second paragraph of Article 9 may be a legitimate subject of an amendment. The passive and conservative Supreme Court has long adhered to an extreme version of the political questions doctrine, has opted to eschew controversial political issues, including Article 9, and has thus tacitly condoned the government's near free hand on these matters.

Rather, the move is considered unconstitutional because it has surpassed the limits of informal constitutional amendment. Strong popular support for Article 9 has rendered it politically and practically unamendable in formal terms, and the government has therefore resorted to informally amending it through the change of the interpretation of the constitutional text. Not all informal constitutional amendment is considered unconstitutional or illegitimate. This particular case of informal amendment has been denounced and resisted as unconstitutional – and a clear breach of the principle of constitutionalism – by a large coalition of constitutional law experts and civic activists,[42] and while some object to the informal amendment on substantive grounds that are based on the belief that pacifism is an unamendable feature of the Postwar Constitution, the mainstream criticism comes from a procedural perspective against the exercise of arbitrary power, reviving a tradition that dates back to the Taishō era in prewar Japan.

---

42 Noboru Yanase, 'Debates over Constitutionalism in Recent Japanese Constitutional Scholarship' (2016) 19 Social Science Japan Journal 193–202.

Prime Minister Abe, who persistently sought to formally amend the Constitution even after the enactment of the security legislation, resigned in September 2020 amidst the coronavirus pandemic, having failed to accomplish his lifelong dream that would have finally cemented his informal amendment of Article 9. Ironically, shortly after Abe stepped down, for the first time since 2015, an *Asahi* newspaper poll in November 2020 found more respondents in support of the security laws than those who opposed them – no doubt a reflection of the rising tension between the US and Japan on one hand and China on the other hand.[43] It seems fair, however, to say that the broad consensus of scholars and legal professionals on the unconstitutionality of the security legislation that lifted the ban on the exercise of collective self-defense remains intact, and that the LDP government shall continue to face strong criticism for having rammed through laws that are unconstitutional using unconstitutional means.

---

43 *Asahi* newspaper (17 November, 2020) 4.

3 "State form" in the theory and practice of constitutional change in modern China

Ryan Mitchell

3.1 Introduction

Since the early years of the 20th century, Chinese scholars and political leaders have at times debated claims regarding an inherent, pre-legal order of the Chinese society and state. Most often, this idea has been associated with the term *guoti* 國體 (literally "state form").[1] In its usage today, *guoti* conveys two highly distinct concepts. On one hand, it can colloquially stand for the general idea of a sort of "national dignity" or "honor." On the other hand, it is used in legal contexts to refer to the aforementioned basic "pre-legal order" or structure of the state.[2]

During the late imperial era, the term had already been used in (antecedents of) both contexts interchangeably – a natural conclusion of the premise that the Emperor's sacred person was largely synonymous with the polity, and thus failures of deference violated both imperial dignity and state order.[3] After the abolition of the monarchy and the founding of the Republic of China in 1912, however, *guoti* became clearly associated with a distinction, drawn from Meiji Japanese discourse, between *zhengti* 政體 (Jp. *Seitai*, form of government) and *guoti* 國體 (Jp. *Kokutai*, [fundamental] form of the state).[4] This dichotomy has

---

1 See, for example, Wang Hongbin, '"Zhengti" "Guoti" Ciyu zhi Shanbian yu Jindai Shehui Sichao zhi Bianqian [The Change of the Meaning of Regime and State System with the Evolution of Modern Social Thought]' (2014) 5 Anhui Shixue 49; Lin Laifan, 'Guoti Gainianshi: Kuaguo Yizhi yu Yanbian [History of State Form as a Concept: Transnational Transplants and Evolution]' (2013) 3 Zhongguo Shehui Kexue 65; Fan Xianzheng, '"Guoti" yu "Zhengti" zai Jindai Zhongguo de Yanbian yu Fenhua [The Evolution and Differentiation of "Guoti" and "Zhengti" in Modern China]' (2014) 3 Xueshu Yanjiu 40.
2 See, for example, Lin, *supra* note 1. The original connotations of *guoti* related to the dignity of the polity are still preserved today in colloquial uses, but not in legal doctrines or scholarship. As to the former dimension, "stateliness" may better translate its erstwhile implications than "state form" does.
3 See Li Yumin, 'Wanqing Shiqi Guoti Guan de Bianhua Shitan [Evaluating Transformations of the *Guoti* Perspective in the Late Qing Era],' 6 Renwen Zazhi 71 (2013).
4 See, for example, Lin (n 1); *see also* Chen Duanhong, 'Lun Xianfa Zuowei Guojia de Genbenfa yu Gaofa [On the Constitution as Fundamental Law and Superior Law] (2008)' 20(4) Zhongwai Faxue 485.

DOI: 10.4324/9781003097099-3

been maintained ever since, and continues to structure Chinese debates over the concept of *guoti* even today.[5]

In both China and Japan, as in a number of other jurisdictions worldwide,[6] the question of republican versus monarchical state form was the main focal point for early 20th century discussions of a fundamental constitutional structure. In many of its uses since, however, the *zhengti/guoti* dichotomy has come to more closely resemble the conservative German state theorist Carl Schmitt's distinction between a "relative constitution" and the "absolute constitution," the latter referring, once again, to the pre-legal inherent structure of a polity (or its core values) that cannot be (legitimately) altered by positive law enactments or judgments.[7] This resemblance has, of course, been noted and explored by Chinese constitutional scholars.[8]

For comparative constitutional scholars, attention to the notion of *guoti* opens up a unique perspective on questions of constitutional change and amendment, informed by a discursive world highly distinct from that of Anglo-American-style "judicial constitutionalism."[9] The concept's history suggests that the formal norms of written constitutions can be relativized based on prevailing ideas about political ontology and structure. Conversely, those underlying political or social structures may themselves lie beyond the reach of positive law. Importantly, extensive contestation is possible as to the actual specific content of any such pre-legal *guoti* – the idea has been invoked to justify liberal, socialist, and also authoritarian political projects.

3.2 Post-imperial public law

3.2.1 The question of state form

The term *guoti* was already ancient by the Qing era. However, it was not until the Qing's last years, particularly after the decision in 1902 to create a "modern" public law edifice for the empire, that the term derived influences from its Japanese equivalent *kokutai* with the various meanings the latter was provided by Meiji jurists.[10] *Kokutai* was used in Japan to refer to an essential state structure not

---

5 ibid.
6 See Yaniv Roznai, *Unconstitutional Constitutional Amendments: The Limits of Amendment Powers* (OUP 2017) 36 (discussing, *inter alia*, constitutional protections of an unalterable "republican federal form" of government in Brazil's 1891 Constitution).
7 See Carl Schmitt, *Constitutional Theory* (Duke University Press 2008) [1928] 59–66.
8 See, for example, Chen, *supra* note 5; Gao Quanxi, 'Zhengzhi Xianfaxue: Zhengzhi Xianfa Lilun, Yihuo Zhengzhi Lixianzhuyi? [Political Constitutionalism: Political Constitutional Theory or Political Constitutional Governance?],' 5 Qinghua Daxue Xuebao (Zhexue Shehuixue Ban) (2015); see also Ryan Mitchell, 'Chinese Receptions of Carl Schmitt Since 1929' (2020) 8(1) Penn State Journal of Law and International Affairs 181, 245.
9 ibid.
10 See Lin (n 1); see also Carol Gluck, *Japan's Modern Myths: Ideology in the Late Meiji Period* (Princeton University Press 1985).

capable of being (legitimately) transformed despite changes to the "form of government" (i.e. the concrete operations of the state's administrative authority).[11] Above all, the institution of the Emperor himself was supposed to stand above forms such as parliamentary democracy, codified legislation, and administrative bureaucracies. This in turn drew heavily on earlier German discourse, such as *Staatsformenlehre* (doctrine of state forms) that included the "monarchical state" as a perfectly valid form of constitutional organization based on a given people's culture, political traditions, and *Volksgeist* [national spirit].[12]

Advocates of "state form" would agree with the public law theorist Johann Caspar Bluntschli that: "The naturally-ordered *Staatsform* corresponds in every age to the unique properties and stage of development of the people, that live in the [given] State."[13] Official efforts to reconcile Western constitutional law with notions of China's inherent *Staatsform* soon bore fruit in the form of China's first written constitution, the 1908 Constitutional Outline by Imperial Order.[14] This provisional framework, promulgated in the last months of the Qing Emperor Guangxu's (nominal) reign, was a belated response to a movement aiming for the comprehensive political restructuring of the government along the lines of Japan's Meiji imperial state.[15]

The resulting Outline embodied modest reformism, seeking to legally formalize government without abandoning the basic premises of imperial rule. For the first time in Chinese history, it legally defined limitations to the institutional role and powers of the Emperor.[16] At the same time, it was issued in the Emperor's own voice, as an expression of his sovereign authority.[17] This duality is reflected in the document's structure, divided into two sections: 14 provisions on the "Great Powers of His Majesty," and then 9 on "Rights and Obligations of Subjects."

Following the Meiji model, the very first provision of the Constitutional Outline held that "The Great Qing Emperor rules the Great Qing Empire, for all generations, and must be eternally respected." This assertion of imperial *auctoritas* (symbolic legitimacy) did not detract from the fact that its *potestas* (actual ruling

---

11 See Fan (n 1).
12 Johann Caspar Bluntschli, *Allgemeines Staatsrecht, Bd. I, Book II* (J.G. Cotta 1857) 66–76.
13 ibid.
14 Zhang Jian, '"Qinding Xianfa Dagang" yu Qingmo Zhengzhi Boyi [The "Constitutional Outline by Imperial Order" and the Political Struggle of the Late Qing Period],' 6 Shixue Yuekan 48–57 (2007); Xiaowei Zheng, *The Politics of Rights and the 1911 Revolution in China* (Stanford University Press 2018).
15 See, for example, Han Dayuan, 'Lun Riben Mingzhi Xianfa Dui "Qinding Xianfa Dagang" de Yingxiang-wei Qinding Xianfa Dagang Banbu 100 Zhounian er Zuo [On the Influence of Japan's Meiji Constitution on the "Constitutional Outline by Imperial Order": Written on the Occasion of the 100th Anniversary of the Publication of the "Constitutional Outline by Imperial Order"],' 3 Zhengfa Luntan: Zhongguo Zhengfa Daxue Xuebo 19–37 (2009).
16 Ma Ling, 'Junquan Cong Nali Kaishi Rangbu?–Laizi "Qinding Xianfa Dagang" de Qishi [When Did Autocratic Power Begin to Yield?–Enlightenment from the "Constitutional Outline by Imperial Order"]' (2008) 4 Faxuejia 8–15.
17 ibid.

power) was significantly diluted.[18] The Emperor retained "the power to compose, review and issue laws ... although they are decided upon by the legislature[.]"[19] As in the German Imperial Constitution of 1871 and the Meiji Constitution of 1889, all legislation (including constitutional amendment) under the Outline clearly required the Emperor's endorsement (albeit without an explicit veto), but was not to be initiated by him – it was reserved to the legislature, which would draft, debate, revise, and finalize all draft laws.[20] Any future full Constitution would thus have to be the product of Imperial-Legislative compromise. At the same time, it was also clearly established in this first written constitutional text in China that the basic character of the polity as a monarchical state was beyond amendment.

The 1908 Outline was harshly criticized by supporters of republican government for its attempt to reconcile an imperial *guoti* with mere gestures towards separation of powers.[21] Though it has often, not without reason, been seen as an essentially conservative attempt by the Qing court to stave off more radical change,[22] some Chinese legal scholars have more recently come to see the Outline as a true watershed, during which "monarchical power began to yield ground."[23] The constitutional law scholar Gao Quanxi, in particular, has argued that events such as the Qing court's eventual buckling to social pressure in deciding to pass the Outline and other legal reforms played a role in the development of modern China's "unwritten constitution" analogous to that of the Glorious Revolution in British constitutional history.[24] This is a view with implications for present-day Chinese constitutionalism, as for Gao the debates and drafts characterizing Chinese attempts at instituting constitutional government between 1908 and 1949[25] were not simply superseded by the establishment of the new People's Republic of China government; rather, the functioning and development of the latter has followed an "inner logic" deriving from the discursive background and social context against which it arose.[26]

---

18 On the division between *auctoritas* and *potestas*, *cf.* Giorgio Agamben, *State of Exception* (University of Chicago Press 2005).
19 Constitutional Outline by Imperial Order, Provision I.III.
20 ibid.
21 Zhang (n 14).
22 Li Zhiyuan, '"Qinding Xianfa Dagang" yu Jiang Ji "Zhonghua Minguo Xianfa" zhi Bijiao [Comparison of the "Constitutional Outline by Imperial Order" with the Jiang Era "Constitution of the Republic of China"]' (2005) 1 Tianfu Xinlun 160–1 (comparison of Republican constitutional developments with the "Outline" was at times deployed in the mode of mockery and critique based on its perceived backwardness).
23 See, for example, Ma, (n 16).
24 See Gao Quanxi, Wei Zhang, and Tian Feilong, *Inception: From Hundred Days Reform to Xinhai Revolution* in *The Road to the Rule of Law in Modern China* (Springer 2015) 1–18; Gao Quanxi, 'Religious Analysis of Law' (2006) 11 Tsinghua Law Review.
25 Albert HY Chen, 'The Discourse of Political Constitutionalism in Contemporary China: Gao Quanxi's Studies on China's Political Constitution' (2014) 14(2) China Review 183–214.
26 ibid.

3.2.2 Identifying the pouvoir constituant

When the Qing fell in 1912, Sun Yat-sen and his revolutionary Tongmenghui/Guomindang organization were prepared to take up leadership of a new regime. In practice, however, they were marginalized by the military apparatus under Yuan Shikai, who in bargaining to support the revolutionary movement took for himself the newly created position of "Provisional President" (*linshi da zongtong* 临时大总统).[27] This new position was one of several entirely new offices and institutions created under the 1912 Provisional Constitution of the Republic of China, which also established a "Senate"[28] that was to be both responsible for electing the Provisional President[29] and (theoretically) capable of impeaching him.[30]

The judiciary under the 1912 Provisional Constitution was, like that under the 1908 Outline, subject to Executive appointment but also intended to operate independently[31] and not to be susceptible to arbitrary removal.[32] As in the 1908 Outline, no general power of judicial review was conferred upon the judiciary; the issues of constitutional enforcement in case of violation, and even of who should be entrusted with constitutional interpretation, were not broached. One major change was introduced at the level of concepts, however: for the first time, sovereignty/*zhuquan* in the sense derived from Western and Japanese legal texts was introduced into the constitutional framework of the state. Article 2 of the Provisional Constitution reads "The sovereignty of the Republic of China belongs to the people."[33]

The process for drafting and implementing a permanent Constitution, meanwhile, was now provided for in Article 54, which assigned this role to the full National Assembly. As for the Provisional Constitution itself, it could be amended based on a proposal by submitted by either two-thirds of the newly created Senate or by the Provisional President, and only approved based on a Senate session quorum of four-fifths, with at least three-fourths voting in favor of the proposed amendment.[34] The amendment of particular features of the provisional constitutional arrangement was thus placed in a category of lesser importance, and greater flexibility, than the adoption of an entirely new constitutional system (indeed a full written constitution would not be put into legal effect until 35 years later).

---

27 Stephen R MacKinnon, *Power and Politics in Late Imperial China: Yuan Shi-kai in Beijing and Tianjin, 1901–1908* (University of California Press 1980).
28 Philip C Huang, *Code, Custom, and Legal Practice in China: The Qing and the Republic Compared* (Stanford University Press 2001); Provisional Constitution of the Republic of China, Article 4 (1912) (hereafter Provisional Constitution).
29 Provisional Constitution, arts 11–18.
30 ibid.
31 Provisional Constitution, ch VI.
32 ibid.
33 Provisional Constitution, art 2 (中華民國之主權屬於國民全體).
34 Provisional Constitution, art 54 (1912).

The topic of amendment was also included in the constitutional drafts that were produced during the period of validity of the Provisional Constitution. One such draft, composed under the direction of the Minister of Justice Wang Chonghui, created a much more detailed separation of powers scheme modeled on that of the United States, and included an article detailing a rather different amendment process: amendments could be adopted by a two-thirds super-majority of a session of at least two-thirds of both legislative houses, at which point the amendment would be submitted to the Assemblies of all of China's Provinces, as well as to the as-yet-nonexistent Assemblies of the vast minority-populated frontier territories Mongolia, Tibet, and Qinghai. Only if the draft amendment received two-thirds approval from these regional legislatures (who could also comment on, but not modify, proposed amendments), would it pass into effect.[35]

Wang's proposed Constitution was never adopted, however. Conflict between Yuan Shikai and the Guomindang swiftly led to the latter's exclusion from the Beijing-based regime and Yuan's attempt to consolidate full personal control over the new government, still operating under the roughly sketched Provisional Constitution. Yuan then decided in 1915 to launch a transition back to an imperial system with himself as the new Emperor. As his regnal title, he chose Hongxian 鴻憲, or "Great Constitution."[36] In the course of this attempted imperial restoration, Yuan drew on the Meiji example to argue that China had always had an inherently monarchical *guoti*, and that this could not simply be discarded in order to pursue Western trends.[37] The process of imperial restoration that Yuan undertook was associated with a state-directed public debate process, centered on the "Question of *Guoti*" – in this case, the notion that the institution of Emperor was an essential characteristic of Chinese society that should now be restored.[38]

However, Yuan misjudged his own and monarchy's level of popular support. Even many former advocates of constitutional monarchy, such as the activist/political theorist Liang Qichao, became harsh critics. Liang argued that "once a polity has gone through the stage of republican government, the former sacredness attached to the position of the monarch has been broken off and cannot be continued."[39] On the other hand, he also pragmatically asserted that "it is deluded ... to discuss *guoti* in terms of likes or dislikes ... I have always focused on *zhengti* [form of government] rather than *guoti* [state form], and opposed those who talk about some other *guoti* than the one currently in place." Thus, Liang could justify his opposition to republicanism during the imperial era, and

---

35 'Wang Chonghui Xianfa Cao'an [Draft Constitution of Wang Chonghui],' 2(11) Fazheng Zazhi 219 (1913).
36 See MacKinnon (n 27).
37 See, e.g. Zhou Zixian, 'Luntan: Zhongguo Guoti Lun [Discussion Forum: The Theory of China's *Guoti*]' (1915) 1(9) Jiayin 21.
38 Discussed in Gao Quanxi, Zhang Wei, and Tian Feilong, *Xiandai Zhongguo Zou Xiang Fazhi zhi Lu [The Road to the Rule of Law in Modern China]* (Springer 2012).
39 Liang Qichao, 'Yi Zai! Suowei Guotizhe [Bizarre! This So-Called *Guoti*]' (1915) 1 Xiehebao 3–4.

to imperial restoration during the Republic: *guoti* was beyond the scope of "artificial" efforts at change in either direction.[40] This was ironically quite close to Yuan's own arguments, albeit opposite in its implications. In any case, political realities were not on Yuan's side. Regional uprisings centered in Southern China forced Yuan to abdicate by early 1916. Thenceforth, no future invocation of *guoti* premised on monarchy or derogating sovereignty away from the people would be seriously presented as legitimate.

3.3 Theorizing constitutional change

3.3.1 *The politics of transition*

Even after Yuan's departure, most of China would continue to be ruled by various warlord factions for more than a decade. The "question of the *guoti*" would however resurface amidst debates over China's political structure during the republican era (1912–49). Already during this period, some of China's leading legal theorists took up the question of constitutional change in a more universal sense. Among the most important contributions were those by Xu Daolin, John C.H. Wu, and Zhang Junmai each of whom sought to put China's national process of constitution-formation in dialogue with those of other states, including the United Kingdom, United States, Weimar Germany, and Japan.

Xu built on the theories of Imperial German and Weimar jurists such as Paul Laband, Georg Jellinek, Rudolf Smend, and Carl Schmitt to describe a typology of forms of change that could occur within constitutional systems.[41] Broadly speaking, he divided all such changes into those of a "formal" or a "material" character, and he further emphasized the distinction between individual text-based norms of a given state's Constitution and the "holistic meaning" (*Sinnzusammenhang*) of that Constitution; a change, even a violation of written norms, could be legitimate if consistent with the latter.[42] Such practice, legitimate but regarded as inconsistent with existing constitutional text, could lead to a "silent constitutional transformation" and eventually (but not necessarily) formal constitutional amendment. On the other hand, a formal constitutional norm (including amendments) could also be regarded as "impossible" to operationalize due to its inconsistency with the holistic constitutional meaning, and thus rendered *de facto* inoperative.[43]

A similar theoretical approach combined with a sense of *Realpolitik* characterized the work of John C.H. Wu, who was the lead drafter of the so-called "5-5" Constitution draft of 1936. In his draft, prepared during a time of maximum Guomindang dominance in domestic politics but considerable turmoil over internal political divisions and Japanese invasion, Wu assigned the functions of

---

40 ibid.
41 Hsü Dau-lin [Xu Daolin], *Die Verfassungswandlung* (Walter de Gruyter 1932).
42 ibid at 173.
43 ibid.

determining constitutional meaning not to the judiciary but to two of the political branches of the five power government – constitutional interpretations were to be provided by the Judicial Yuan, but initiated by the Control Yuan (a national supervision body unique to China's "five power" constitutional system).[44] Both of these branches of government seemed, given the circumstances of the time, almost certain to remain under far more direct GMD authority than would the judiciary. Constitutional amendment, meanwhile, would still be reserved to the more popular/democratic National Assembly, which could pass amendments by a two-thirds majority at a session meeting at least a three-fourths quorum requirement. However, a new requirement was also added that amendments would have to be proposed at least one year before the opening of the relevant National Assembly session at which they would be considered.[45] This prolongation of the amendment process would, theoretically, stabilize the precarious constitutional order against political adventurism either by individuals or competing factions.

A decade later, a more detailed and comprehensive attempt to preserve "overall constitutional meaning" characterized the efforts of Zhang Junmai, who led the drafting of the Republic of China's 1946 Constitution. During a period of highly uncertain and combustible cooperation between the Guomindang and its rival, the Communist Party, Zhang coordinated the drafting of a Constitution intended for a unity government between the two sides, including basic norms that could be regarded as representing their points of consensus. This search for overlap between rival parties was concretized into Chapter XIII of the ROC Constitution, on "Fundamental National Policies" (*jiben guoce* 基本國策).[46] Though brief, it contained a set of highly important commitments that had been agreed upon (in principle) during negotiations between both the GMD and CPC. It included provisions on the national economy and social security, as well as national defense, education, border regions, and diplomacy. In each of these areas, a set of basic commitments was articulated that comprised the shared policy agenda of China's various rival parties, at greater or lesser degrees of specificity. Social welfare rights were now constitutionalized. So too was a commitment to peaceful foreign policy and recognition of the United Nations Charter, along with defense of China's territorial sovereignty and the interests of overseas Chinese. Though their relation with the rest of the constitutional text was ill-defined, these "Fundamental National Policies" could be seen as a *de facto* "core" of the Constitution beyond future amendment – as the political unity of the rival parties was premised upon precisely these points of consensus.[47]

The 1946 Constitution was adopted by the ROC, but renewed civil war between the GMD and CPC parties led to the latter's disavowal of the Constitution, and the former's nullification of it by means of emergency legislation. The CPC thus

---

44 Draft Constitution of the Republic of China (hereafter Draft Constitution), art 140 (1936).
45 Draft Constitution, art 146.
46 Constitution of the Republic of China (hereafter ROC Constitution), ch XIII (1946).
47 *Cf.* 'Lun Jiben Guoce [On the Fundamental National Policies],' Li Bao, 2 December 1946.

had to create its own constitutional system as it approached victory in the conflict. In laying out the requirements for dealing with constitutional law in light of the Marxist theory of base and superstructure, Mao Zedong turned again to the notion of *guoti*. For Mao, *guoti* now served to encapsulate not only the republican form of government and the vesting of popular sovereignty with the People, but also the dominance of the proletariat within the polity as the true "factual" representative of the state's unity.[48] As Mao defined it:

> This *guoti* issue has been bandied about for decades since the Late Qing period, without being really clarified. In fact, it simply refers to the question of the place of social classes within the state ... Meanwhile the issue of *zhengti* (form of government) is the question of which form of political structure ... is used by a certain social class to oppose enemies and defend its organs of political authority.[49]

In other words, for Mao, China's *guoti* was one in which the proletariat would exercise dictatorship over other classes. However, the specific formal features of government, by which this ultimate authority was to be exercised, were up for debate. The subsequent plan to place the highest legislative authority with a mixed body not limited to (albeit dominated by) the CPC was the key reflection of the ideological platform of "New Democracy."[50] New Democracy stood for the view that all "progressive" forces in society should unite, with workers and peasants leading sympathetic members of other groups to establish a more just and representative political system.[51] This notion was supposed to be compatible with the "People's Democratic Dictatorship" exercised by the Party on behalf of China's workers and peasants as the main components of "the people."

3.3.2 Constitution and mobilization

The Republic of China's 1946 Constitution was officially abandoned by the CPC before the official founding of the People's Republic of China, being specifically superseded by the decisions of a new Chinese People's Political Consultative Conference convened by the Chinese Communist Party on September 21st 1949.[52] As the 1946 Conference managed by the ROC had been, the 1949 CPPCC was orchestrated with the majority of committees and discussions led by the ruling party, now the CPC, and with delegations from minority parties and socially

---

48 Mao Zedong, 'On New Democracy,' (1940), in *Selected Works of Mao Tse-tung Vol. 2* (Foreign Languages Press 1965).
49 ibid
50 ibid
51 ibid.
52 See Chen, (n 5); *cf.* Donald Gasper, 'The Chinese National People's Congress,' in *Communist Legislatures in Comparative Perspective* (Springer 1982) 160–90.

prominent individuals intended to foster a clearly subordinated democratic complement to top-level plans for the *de facto* constitutional convention.[53]

The 1949 CPPCC developed the "Common Program of the Chinese People's Political Consultative Conference" (Common Program) as a constitutional document establishing the basic parameters of the newly established PRC state. Under the system instituted, the CPPCC would act as a national legislature responsible for the passage of state laws, while the central government would have authority to issue and implement more specific administrative regulations. As part of its legislative and consultative duties, the CPPCC went on to convene a number of Small Discussion Groups on key issues, among which were discussions producing advisory opinions on the boundaries between the political subjects "the people" (*renmin* 人民) and "the citizen" (*gongmin* 公民).[54] The latter concept, the groups held, was to be defined in terms of legally conferred rights and duties that should be defined in legal instruments, while the former was essentially "a social and political concept."[55] Inherent in this distinction was recognition of the tension between a national population conceived of as rights-bearing individuals versus one conceived of as a unified, active political subject (represented in this capacity by the Party).[56]

Both due to Soviet suggestions and to prevailing opinion within the CPC, the decision was reached to hold national elections for membership in a new, dedicated national legislature, and then to draft and pass the new Constitution. The resulting 1954 Constitution created the basic structure of PRC government that still exists today, including both supremacy of the newly formed National People's Congress (NPC) and a lack of Anglo-American-style separation of powers.[57]

This Soviet-influenced Constitution had 106 Articles, which established the basic structure of the PRC state system as it continues to exist today. It also established basic institutions of judicial administration, including the Ministry of Justice, and followed earlier Chinese constitutions in calling for "independent" exercise of the judicial function,[58] but like those documents, it did not clearly specify protections for that independence. Further, the 1954 Constitution followed the model of the Soviet Union and its satellite states in asserting in its Preamble, but refusing to formally institutionalize or identify in its main text, the

---

53 ibid.
54 Glenn D Tiffert, 'Epistrophy: Chinese Constitutionalism and the 1950s,' in Michael W Dowdle and Stephanie Balme (eds.), *Building Constitutionalism in China* (Springer 2009) 59–76.
55 ibid.
56 ibid; see also Joshua A Fogel and Peter G Zarrow (eds.), *Imagining the People: Chinese Intellectuals and the Concept of Citizenship, 1890–1920* (Routledge 1997).
57 Cai Dingjian, 'Constitutional Supervision and Interpretation in the People's Republic of China' (1995) 9(2) Journal of Chinese Law 219.
58 Constitution of the People's Republic of China (hereafter 1954 Constitution), Article 78 (1954).

"leading" role of the Communist Party respective to the state.[59] The Preamble to the 1954 Constitution attested to both the "indestructible friendship" of the PRC and the Soviet Union (along with other socialist states) and the need for a gradual process of transition from New Democracy (with its above-noted "bourgeois" elements) to socialism.[60] Finally, in an innovation upon its models, the 1954 Constitution also created the new office of "Chairman of the People's Republic of China," aka State Chairman (*Guojia Zhuxi*) or (in more recent translations) President.[61]

The 1954 Constitution assigned amendment to the new NPC, operating as the notional representative of popular sovereignty. A two-thirds majority of the NPC would be required to pass any future constitutional amendment (or to replace the Constitution as a whole). By 1957, however, ideological conflict and elite politics had resulted in increasingly radical campaigns such as the "Anti-Rightist Movement," which targeted white-collar professionals, especially those in law and the judiciary, as counter-revolutionary elements. Even basic attempts to realize the provisions of the existing 1954 Constitution (for example, by passing basic legislation setting forth liabilities for the purposes of civil litigation) were put on hold as ideological struggle became the Party's priority.[62] Notably, legal scholars who had called for a more liberal constitutional system were prominent targets for criticism and political condemnation.[63]

This situation persisted through the subsequent era dominated by ideological campaigns including the Great Leap Forward (1958–62) and, most significantly, the Cultural Revolution (1966–76). During the Cultural Revolution era, legal professionals, legal studies, the judiciary, and law itself were officially renounced in favor of proletarian activism and "struggle."[64] The Ministry of Justice was shut throughout this period, and many of those with legal expertise were subjected to intense pressure. Towards the very end of the period, however, a new Constitution was promulgated in 1975 in the attempt to "lock in" some of the basic policies that had been favored by the leftist ruling clique. This Constitution of 29 Articles eliminated major parts of the state structure, including the office of the President. Meanwhile, it enshrined class struggle and the "dictatorship of the proletariat,"

---

59 1954 Constitution, Preamble.
60 *Cf.* Jiang Shigong, 'Ruhe Tansuo Zhongguo de Xianzheng Daolu?–Cong Falü Diguo dao Duoyuanzhuyi Fazhi Gongheguo [How to Investigate China's Road to Constitutionalism?–From Law's Empire to the Pluralist Legal Republic],' 18(2) *Wenhua Zongheng* 57 (2014).
61 1954 Constitution, Article 27; *cf.* Jiang Dengqin, 'Guifan yu Xianshi zhi Jian: Zi 1982 Nian Xianfa yilai Guojia Zhuxi Zhidu de Fazhan [Between Norms and Facts: The Development of the State Chairman System Since the 1982 Constitution],' Zhongguo Xianfa Niankan (2011).
62 ibid.
63 See, for example, Jiao Shizhao, 'Bo Chen Tiqiang Guanyu Xianfa Zhiding bu Minzhu de Miulun [Refuting the Fallacious Statements of Chen Tiqiang that the Constitutional Drafting was Undemocratic],' People's Daily, 9 September 1957.
64 Young-tsu Wong, 'The Fate of Liberalism in Revolutionary China: Chu Anping and His Circle, 1946–1950' (1993) 19(4) Modern China 457–90.

and, though enumerating fewer rights than its predecessors, did claim to protect an ideologically important set of "Four Big Freedoms" (四大自由 *sida ziyou*): the freedom to speak out, to air views freely, to hold great debates, and to write big-character posters (*dazibao*).[65] The 1975 Constitution included a reference to the power of the NPC to amend the Constitution but did not specify the requirements for doing so.[66]

The end of the Cultural Revolution led, over the course of a few years, to the dramatic reversal of policies that would henceforth be referred to as the era of Reform and Opening-Up. This reversal also entailed a process of intra-Party debate and competition. Under Hua Guofeng, the new 1978 Constitution was issued that returned to key features of the 1950s. Amendment power was however still assigned to the NPC, without its procedures being specified. General dissatisfaction with the slow pace of reform under Hua and shifting factional politics led to Deng Xiaoping subsequently coming into power as *de facto* Party leader in 1978.[67] Once in power, Deng and his allies promoted legal reform paired with an advocacy of clear boundaries.

These limits were embodied in "Four Cardinal Principles," which served to make clear(er) the division between areas in which free debate would be permitted and those, particularly those concerning the fundamental socialist character of the PRC, the primacy of the Communist Party, and the continuity of its commitment to Marxism-Leninism and Mao Zedong Thought, where speech, advocacy, and political discourse would be restricted.[68] These basic commitments, written into the Charter of the Communist Party, are today still referred to as "the foundation on which to build the country" and as limits on any future projects of constitutional revision.[69]

3.4 Constitutional change in a socialist *Rechtsstaat*

3.4.1 The 1982 Constitution and its evolution

Following Deng Xiaoping's rise to power in 1978, he made clear his commitment to dramatically changing the PRC's approach to law, stating, e.g. that

---

65 Constitution of the People's Republic of China (hereafter 1975 Constitution), Article 13 (1975).
66 1975 Constitution, Article 17.
67 Ezra F Vogel, *Deng Xiaoping and the Transformation of China* (HUP 2011).
68 These Four Cardinal Principles were: "the principle of upholding the socialist path; the principle of upholding the people's democratic dictatorship; the principle of upholding the leadership of the Communist Party of China; and the principle of upholding Mao Zedong Thought and Marxism-Leninism." Carlos Wing-Hung Lo, 'Socialist Legal Theory in Deng Xiaoping's China' (1997) 11 Columbia Journal of Asian Law 469.
69 *Cf.* Larry Catá Backer, 'Central Planning versus Markets Marxism: Their Differences and Consequences for the International Ordering of State, Law, Politics, and Economy' (2016) 32 Connecticut Journal of International Law 1.

> In order to ensure people's democracy, we have to strengthen the legal system. We must make our democracy ordered and legalized, so that this order and law are not changed due to the change in leaders, or changed due to changes in the opinions and attention of leaders.[70]

Such formulae, as is apparent, brought constitutional development within the framework of the Four Cardinal Principles, viewing it as a means to realize and ensure, rather than to challenge or fundamentally transform, the "people's democracy" represented in the state system dominated by the Communist Party.

The turn to "reform" prompted wide-ranging discussions over the "rule of law" (法治 *fazhi*) in China's socialist system.[71] Though some hardliners argued Party power should simply be unconstrained, the more dominant mainstream view held that law should be used instrumentally as an important complement to and stabilizing factor contributing to the success of Party rule.[72] This view influenced constitutional developments. At an expanded meeting of the Politburo in August 1980, Deng made a report detailing the process he envisioned for drafting a new Constitution to replace that of 1978. As he wrote:

> Our Constitution should be made more complete and precise so as to really ensure the people's right to manage the state organs at all levels as well as the various enterprises and institutions, to guarantee to our people the full enjoyment of their rights as citizens, to enable the different nationalities to exercise genuine regional autonomy, to improve the multi-level system of people's congresses, and so on. The principle of preventing the over-concentration of power will also be reflected in the revised Constitution.[73]

The subsequent drafting process resulted in the 1982 Constitution, which featured 138 Articles largely rehabilitated from its 1954 predecessor, a few isolated elements drawn from the intervening two later drafts, and a handful of innovations. Substantive civil and political rights continued to be recognized in the document, and Article 57 asserted that (again, as in 1954) the National People's Congress would be the "highest organ of state power." Article 62 delineated in unprecedented detail the functional supremacy of the NPC over other branches. Article 11 set the basis for economic liberalization by asserting that, while the

---

70 Deng Xiaoping, 'Jiefang Sixiang, Shishi Qiu Shi, Tuanjie Yizhi Xianqian Kan ["Emancipating the Mind, Seeking the Truth from Facts, and Unifying to Face the Future"],' Speech of 13 December 1978.
71 See discussion in Samuli Seppänen, *Ideological Conflict and the Rule of Law in Contemporary China: Useful Paradoxes* (CUP 2016).
72 Li Buyun, Wang Dexiang, and Chen Chunlong, 'Lun Yi Fa Zhi Guo [On Ruling the Country According to Law],' in *Fazhi yu Renzhi Wenti Taolunji* [*Collected Essays on the Rule of Law and the Rule of Man*] (Shehui Kexue Wenxian Chubanshe, 1980) 37, 41.
73 Deng Xiaoping, 'On the Reform of the System of Party and State Leadership,' speech of 18 August 1980, available at: cpcchina.chinadaily.com.cn/fastfacts/2010-10/18/content_11425374.htm

state sector must still dominate the economy, there is a "complementary" role for private economic activity. Finally, Article 5 made clear that "all state organs, the armed forces, all political parties and public organizations and institutions must abide by the Constitution and the law," and that "[n]o organization or individual is privileged to be beyond the Constitution or the law." The position of State Chairman, abolished during the Cultural Revolution, was also reinstated.[74]

Article 1 of the 1982 Constitution, meanwhile, holds that: "The People's Republic of China is a socialist state under the people's democratic dictatorship led by the working class and based on the alliance of workers and peasants." Soon after its adoption, Peng Zhen, the Party's lead official coordinating "Political-Legal Work," described this Article as defining "the essence of the state: the *guoti*[.]"[75] This was, of course, basically continuous with Mao Zedong's invocation of the same concept four decades earlier, before the founding of the PRC.[76] The concept had up until this point, however, never been turned into a detailed or coherent legal doctrine. What actual limits did the "state form" as defined in Article 1 impose upon the practical structure of government (i.e. *zhengti*) – more concretely, must it in practice limit either the Constitution's inherent legal authority or the potential scope of its future amendments?

The first of these questions received a fairly decisive answer after an initial process of contestation. Like all of its predecessors, the 1982 Constitution was not explicitly endowed with actionable/judiciable status, nor was there any mechanism specified for the use of the Constitution to regulate government action. However, legal scholars and professionals did increasingly promote the idea that, like constitutions in the Anglo-American tradition (including many of those adapted by civil law countries influenced by this tradition), the 1982 Constitution should indeed be treated as a jurisdiction-creating document allowing courts to rule on cases in which individuals allege serious state violations of citizens' rights. The famous *Qi Yuling* case of 2001 featured an opinion by the Supreme People's Court stating that infringements of basic rights provided for in the 1982 Constitution (specifically, the "right to an education") could indeed by directly adjudicated in Chinese courts.[77] This opinion represented a high watermark for the liberalization of Chinese constitutionalism, with extensive writing by liberal legal scholars and practitioners defining a vision in which China could follow the model of constitutional litigation in the United States.[78] If it were

---

74 Constitution of the People's Republic of China (hereafter PRC Constitution), Article 79–84 (1982).
75 See Lin (n 1).
76 See (n 46–9) and accompanying text.
77 Robert J Morris, 'China's Marbury: Qi Yuling v. Chen Xiaoqi—The Once and Future Trial of Both Education and Constitutionalization' (2009) 2 Tsinghua China LR 273.
78 ibid; see also Shen Kui, 'Is It the Beginning of the Era of the Rule of the Constitution?—Reinterpreting China's First Constitutional Case' (2003) 12 Pacific Rim Law and Policy Journal 199; Zhu Guobin, 'Constitutional Review in China: An Unaccomplished Project or a Mirage' (2009) 43 Suffolk University LR 625: Yu Xingzhong, 'Western Constitutional Ideas and Constitutional Discourse in China, 1978–2005,' in Dowdle and Balme (n 54).

possible for the Supreme People's Court to interpret the Constitution in particular cases, then the *de facto* transformation pioneered in Anglo-American judicial review practice would also perhaps be possible in China. The *Qi Yuling* decision, however, was explicitly revoked by the Supreme People's Court seven years later. Ever since, it has been generally accepted that the 1982 Constitution is unlikely to be treated by Chinese courts as directly judiciable, and that constitutional interpretation under the auspices of the National People's Congress Standing Committee (mostly by reviewing draft legislation before it is promulgated) is the key site for the application of constitutional norms.

Much the same approach, meanwhile, had long since been embodied in the 1982 Constitution's procedures for constitutional amendments as articulated in Article 64, which now required that:

> Amendments to the Constitution are to be proposed by the Standing Committee of the National People's Congress or by more than one-fifth of the deputies to the National People's Congress and adopted by a vote of more than two-thirds of all the deputies to the Congress.[79]

The assignation of amendment power to the NPCSC, a smaller body more tightly connected with Party leadership and the notional supervision of the Central Committee and Politburo, was seemingly intended to ensure that constitutional amendment (or replacement) would become a regular and "normal" feature of Party-directed legislation rather than an occasional and erratic process only activated in exceptional moments of transition, as had been the case before 1982.

3.4.2 *Invocations of* guoti *in the reform-era discourse of constitutional amendment*

In keeping with the status of the 1982 Constitution as a nominally supreme legal authority that is nonetheless not directly justiciable by the court system, amendments to the document are, under Article 64, treated like any other piece of major legislation. Although this has definitely prevented expansion of the Constitution's contents by means of judicial interpretation, it has at the same time allowed considerable flexibility as regards changes introduced in the legislature.

After its adoption, the 1982 Constitution was amended four times prior to its most recent, fifth round of amendments in 2018. The first amendments were passed in 1988, adding language protecting private economic activity and the transfer of land. Five years later, the amendments of 1993 provided additional clarification of the connection between the PRC state and market economies. In 1999, again, amendments largely focused on emphasizing the protection of rights underlying individual and private economic activity. These amendments of 1999 also represented the first time that the phrase *fazhi* 法治 was included in the constitutional

---

79 PRC Constitution, art 64.

text. Then, in 2004, a set of more general normative amendments were passed to incorporate into the Constitution new language referring to the ideological orthodoxy of Deng Xiaoping Theory and Jiang Zemin's "Three Represents" theory, while also adding language committing to the protection of "private property" and of "human rights."[80] Notably, each of these four rounds of amendments could be interpreted as potentially challenging traditional interpretations of Article 1's definition of China as a "socialist state ... led by the working class."

The question of how to reconcile this constitutional amendment process with China's *guoti* was raised as early as the 1980s, from different angles. On the one hand, some scholars sought to argue for limits to possible constitutional amendment, in part by citing the role of the Preamble of the PRC Constitution, defining the Communist Party's function of political leadership and the nature of the state, as keys to the overall meaning of the constitutional text.[81] Indeed, the earliest positive citations of Carl Schmitt's legal thought in the PRC seem to have been in connection with the premise of a special status for the Preamble that would set outer limits to the scope of possible change to all subordinate constitutional norms.[82] The view that the Preamble of the Constitution sets limits to its amendment was discussed by legal scholars, but achieved neither consensus in academic circles nor explicit state endorsement (though it has remained influential).[83]

Meanwhile, another notion of constitutional amendment also built upon the presumption of a core of "higher" constitutional norms, albeit running in the opposite direction. This was the notion of so-called "benign constitutional violation" (*liangxing weixian* 良性违宪), which would comprise the passing of legislation that, while technically in violation of the constitutional text, nonetheless was consistent with "essential" constitutional norms or values and served to promote broadly agreed-upon goals such as economic liberalization.[84] This concept was promoted by some liberal scholars who viewed the lack of explicit legal safeguards for private property and enterprise (until the passage of the constitutional amendments of 1988–2004) as hampering the essential "Reform" agenda underlying the post-1982 constitutional order. Like the doctrine of a special status for the Preamble, this notion also did not gain official recognition nor did it achieve general consensus among legal academics. Nonetheless, it can be seen as another chapter in the invocation of the same basic idea of a "higher" constitutional order that stands beyond the reach of particular constitutional norms to limit or alter. Indeed, the presumption underlying the "benign constitutional violation"

---

80 PRC Constitution, Articles 22 and 24 (1982) (as amended in 2004).
81 See Dong Fanyu, 'Guanyu Xianfa Xuyan ji qi Falü Xiaoli [On the Constitutional Preamble and its Legal Effect]' (1987) 22 Zhengfa Luntan 9.
82 ibid.
83 See, for example, Ning Kaihui, 'Lun Xianfa Xuyan de Jiazhi Gouzao [On the Construction of Values by the Constitution's Preamble],' Huanan Ligong Daxue (PhD Thesis) (2019).
84 See, for example, Zhang Qingbo, 'Shi Yi Jiben Quanli Xianding "Liangxing Weixian" [Attempting to Limit "Benign Constitutional Violation" on the Basis of Fundamental Rights],' 4 Dongfang Faxue 57 (2014).

doctrine was that such "violations" (e.g. legislation creating private property rights technically conflicting with existing constitutional norms) would eventually be worked into revisions of the constitutional text.[85] In that sense, it could be argued that the 1988–2004 amendments did reflect a pattern whereby changes to the Constitution's text both followed and contributed to broader legislative agendas such as the gradual promotion of private economic rights or property ownership.

The idea of *guoti* has framed several recent debates about the fundamental character of the PRC Constitution and the extent to which its "essence" differs from its non-essential characteristics. Expressing a minority view, Gao Quanxi has built upon the discourse of the Nanjing era to argue that the agent of China's essentially republican *guoti* is the National People's Congress, which builds on a long history of attempts to create a representative legislature embodying the will of the popular sovereign. The gradual move from "exceptional" to "normal" constitutional politics coincides with the move from Party-led governance to an order in which the titular supreme state institution, the NPC, actually takes up the lead role in governing the state.[86]

Much more common, however, are invocations of *guoti* that build upon Mao's and Peng Zhen's uses of the concept. Thus, for example, Zhou Yezhong and Pang Yuanfu note that there is "ambiguity" between the oft-cited concepts of "the character of the state" (*guojia xingzhi*), "the essence of the state" (*guojia benzhi*), and "state form" (*guoti*). However, citing Peng Zhen's statement noted above, the two Wuhan-based constitutional scholars argue that *guoti* basically encapsulates the point that the dictatorship of the proletarian class is the core feature of the PRC state system and is also inextricably intertwined with the Communist Party's "necessary" and "inevitable" leading role in the process of gradually constructing a Chinese *Rechtsstaat* (*fazhiguo*).[87] Such views represent the dominant interpretation of *guoti* in today's PRC.

The PKU constitutional scholar Chen Duanhong argues in more detail that the Communist Party acts as the embodiment of the people's will and *pouvoir constituant*,[88] but also shares this role with four other essential norms (or "fundamental laws": *genben fa* 根本法) that together form China's true *guoti* 国体: (1) "the leadership of the Communist Party," (2) "socialism," (3) "democratic

---

85 Yu Zhong, 'Xiuxian de Zhongguo Yujing: Guanyu Sige Xianfa Xiuzheng An de Shizheng Yanjiu [The Chinese Discursive Sphere of Constitutional Law: An Empirical Study of Four Constitutional Amendments]' (2010) 4 Lilun yu Gaige 122.
86 See Gao (n 24).
87 Zhou Yezhong and Pang Yuanfu, 'Lun Dang Lingdao Fazhi Zhongguo Jianshe de Biranxing yu Biyaoxing [On the Necessary and Inevitable Character of Communist Party Leadership in Constructing a Chinese *Rechtsstaat*]' (2016) 22(1) Fazhi yu Shehui Fazhan 30.
88 Chen Duanhong, 'Xianfaxue de Zhishi Jiebei: Zhengzhi Xuezhe he Xianfa Xuezhe Youguanyu Zhixianquan de Duihua [The Boundary of Knowledge in Constitutional Law: A Dialogue on Constituent Power Between a Political Theorist and a Constitutional Theorist]' (2010) 3 Kaifang Shidai 87–103 (noting that "Schmitt tells us that the People continue to exist, without organization or shape, right alongside the Constitution").

centralism," (4) "modernization," and (5) "protection of basic rights."[89] The order of these norms is not accidental. Individual rights are not to be ignored, but come after Party leadership, the commitment to socialist political economy, the authority of the "democratic" organs of NPC-led governance, and the basic program of state-led modernization.

In Chen's view, Carl Schmitt's thought provides "the most systematic model of political constitutionalism," suited for the articulation of an "absolute Constitution" that is to be considered separate and apart from individual acts of legislation or the possibility of amendment.[90] He has also applied these ideas to the constitutional relationship between Beijing and the Hong Kong and Macau Special Administrative Regions (SARs); here, too, the task is to separate the "absolute" constitutional norms defining the meaning of texts such as the Hong Kong Basic Law from the "relative" or merely "governmental" acts that do not have to do with basic issues of what Schmitt called the "the constitution as a normative unity[.]"[91]

The different points of view regarding the *guoti* issue have also influenced the most recent set of constitutional amendments passed in March 2018, during which the commitment to Party leadership was migrated from the Preamble into the main body of the Constitution. Indeed, some constitutional scholars have explicitly characterized the 2018 amendments as "deepening the public's understanding of China's *guoti*, and thus acting as a 'reconstruction' of China's *guoti* [*woguo guoti de chonggou*]."[92] More pointedly, the 2018 amendments can also be interpreted as having *de facto* refuted arguments like those of Gao, who has sought to locate the embodiment of *pouvoir constituant* in the NPC as the legislative representative of the Chinese people. Countervailing arguments like those of Xiao Jinming of Shandong University attribute to Communist Party leadership the character of *guoti*, while the NPC and its function as the supreme legislative organ of government is relegated to the lesser category of *zhengti*.[93] In this view, legislative sovereignty is indeed a feature of the *form of government* established under the PRC Constitution, but this cannot detract from the *state form* of proletarian/Party leadership.

Among the changes introduced by the 2018 amendments, the abolition of term limits for the positions of State Chairman and Vice-Chairman attracted

---

89 Chen (n 5).
90 Chen Duanhong, 'Xianfaxue Yanjiu zhong de Zhengzhi Luoji [Political Logic in the Study of Constitutional Theory],' Zhongguo Xianfa Niankan 196–9 (2013).
91 Chen Duanhong, 'Lun Gang Ao Jibenfa de Xianfa Xingzhi [On the Constitutional Nature of The Hong Kong and Macau Basic Laws]' (2020) 32(1) Zhongwai Faxue 4; *cf.* Schmitt, *Constitutional Theory* (n 7) 65.
92 Fan Jinxue, '2018 Nian Xiuxian yu Zhongguo Xin Xianfa Zhixu de Chonggou [The 2018 Constitutional Amendments and the Restructuring of China's New Constitutional Order]' (2018) 33(3) Faxue Luntan 16.
93 Xiao Jinming, 'Xin Zhongguo Xianfa Zhengzhi Fazhan de Huigu yu Zhanwang [Retrospective and Prognosis for the Development of Constitutional Politics in New China]' (2018) 33(3) Faxue Luntan 5.

particular attention both domestically and abroad. Previously, the notion of a strengthened "Executive" position had occasionally been advocated based on different rationales both by statist conservatives and by a few liberal constitutional scholars – the latter having raised the idea that long-term continuity for an individual leader might help in promoting consistent progress on reform goals rather than their reevaluation after each ten-year leadership turnover.[94] In advance of the amendments' adoption in 2018, however, some scholars raised bold arguments that constraining individual power and reinforcing collective leadership had been at the "core" of the 1982 Constitution and that there were thus certain "objective" limits on amendment of the term limit provisions.[95] The concept of constitutional structure could thus be invoked in an effort to limit amendments tending towards centralization of power in the hands of a single authority figure. However, structural arguments could also point in the other direction: the idea that the Constitution established a "trinity" of powers (those of Party General Secretary, State Chairman, and Central Military Commission Chairman) intended to overlap in a single individual[96] Following the promulgation of the 2018 amendments, of course, arguments over this topic are seldom heard in mainstream settings – the abolition of formal term limits has already been effectively decided.

Yet debate over the content of China's *guoti* continues, within the limits imposed by political circumspection. A particularly pertinent question that remains to be addressed is whether the Constitution's characterizations of China's economic system – a key element of both the 1982 text and all but the most recent set of amendments – are genuinely prescriptive, and if so, how. This topic was raised by Chen Duanhong in the second of his five "fundamental laws," which asserted that as socialism was part of China's *guoti*, no legislation could be permitted to alter the basically socialist character of the political system.[97] Taking the exact opposite approach, however, are scholars who assert that key aspects of China's economic order have a constitutional status that requires protection *against* state interference. For example, Shan Feiyue and Xu Kaiyuan of the Shandong University Law School cite Carl Schmitt to argue that "specific [social] institutions can be given special protection within constitutional order," and accordingly "[the provisions on] 'socialist market economy' demand that the

---

94 Zhang Qianfan, 'A Constitution Without Constitutionalism? The Paths of Constitutional Development in China' (2010) 8(4) International Journal of Constitutional Law 8.4 950, 956 ("The apparently democratic limitation on terms coupled with the authoritarian mode of governance, in essence, helps to maximize the short-term incentive for abusing power while it is within one's grasp").
95 Han Dayuan, 'Renqi Zhi Zai Woguo Xianfa Zhong de Guifan Yiyi [The Normative Significance of Term Limits in China's Constitution]' (2017) 11 Faxue 3.
96 See, for example, Fan (n 92) 20; *cf.* Jiang Shigong, 'Minzhu, Ruhe Shi Hao [Democracy: Which Way Is Best],' Dushu (2009); Di Zhiyong, 'Guojia Zhuxi, Yuanshouzhi yu Xianfa Weiji' (2015) 27 Zhongwai Faxue 2.
97 Chen (n 5).

autonomy of market actors is not deprived in a long term, over-broad, or essential manner."[98] Clearly, the constitutional text itself does not suffice to inform its interpreters whether they should, like Chen, emphasize the importance of Party leadership and the "socialist" side of "socialist market economy" or, like Shan and Xu, emphasize the "market" side and its autonomy. Both advocates of liberalization and those seeking to preserve a robust role for the state (and Party) can thus continue seeking to marshal notions of *guoti* and fundamental order in defense of their views.

3.5 Conclusion

It is, of course, ironic that a concept originally used to preserve the *dignitas* of the Chinese Emperor is now most often applied to assert the unalterable character of Communist Party rule. The invocation of *guoti* today to define limits to possible constitutional change suggests that notions of "organ sovereignty" [*Organsouveränität*] – i.e. the nominal deference to popular sovereignty while in fact locating this authority as an intrinsic characteristic of a body not necessarily identical with public will[99] – will continue to characterize PRC political constitutionalism.

There is no explicitly defined doctrine limiting the potential scope of constitutional amendment. However, it is possible to read the sections of the Constitution that have been associated with China's *guoti* – that is, those regarding the political leading role of the proletariat and thus the Communist Party as its representative – as *de facto* imposing such limits shaping the future course of China's constitutional order. The 2018 Constitutional Amendments themselves, with the migration of Communist Party leadership from the Preamble to the main text and the strengthening of the position of State Chairman, may also be interpreted as affirming this view. They did not however address the more fundamental problem of determining the status of the constitutional text in relation to extraneous sources of authority such as Party regulations or directives, or even ordinary legislation. Moreover, they strongly suggest that any move towards *judicial* resolution of such questions would, in itself, be incompatible with China's *guoti*.[100]

Party leadership, limits on judicial oversight, and the preservation of territorial integrity all seem to likely to continue being treated as aspects of state

---

98 Shan Feiyue and Xu Kaiyuan, '"Shehuizhuyi Shichang Jingji" de Xianfa Neihan yu Fa Zhixu Yiyi [The Constitutional Content and Significance for Legal Order of the 'Socialist Market Economy]' (2020) Dongnan Xueshu 2.
99 See, for example, Hermann Heller, *Die Souveränität* (1927) in Hermann Heller, *Gesammelte Schriften, Bd. II* (Mohr 1992) [1971] 75–6.
100 There is thus an opposite significance of *guoti* discourse in China as compared with "unamendability" in jurisdictions where it is enforced by judges, and thus may contribute to a "power imbalance" favoring the judiciary as opposed to political branches of government. See Roznai (n 6) 194 (discussing India's "Basic Structure Doctrine").

structure firmly beyond the reach of legislation or constitutional amendment. What remains to be seen, however, is which other aspects of state policy, if any, are ultimately accorded a similar "core" status. If *guoti* is viewed less as a fixed doctrine and more as a mode of constitutional discourse, it seems highly likely that the argumentative tools it offers will continue to inform future significant public debates.

4 Unconstitutional constitution in Vietnamese discourse

Ngoc Son Bui

4.1 Introduction

In 2011, the Vietnamese National Assembly adopted a plan to amend the 1992 Constitution. The amendment process culminated in the enactment of a new constitution on November 28, 2013, which effectively replaced the 1992 charter.[1] After its adoption, state media praised the Constitution as the nation's great achievement,[2] while criticisms of the constitution were published in unofficial platforms.[3] Among the critical views, Professor Hoàng Xuân Phú penned a 25-page paper castigating the 2013 Constitution as an "unconstitutional constitution," published on his personal webpage.[4] This chapter explores this paper from a comparative perspective.

Professor Hoàng's paper is unique in Vietnamese constitutional discourse. It is perhaps the first and only account of Vietnam's constitution as an unconstitutional constitution. The authorship of the paper is also special. Professor Hoàng is a mathematician, not a legal scholar, let alone a constitutional scholar. It is quite unusual for a professor of mathematics to produce an extensive treatment on constitutional law. However, this is understandable in the Vietnamese context. Vietnamese constitutional debate in 2013 involved a range of national intellectuals beyond legal academics. More generally, Vietnamese national intellectuals

---

1 Tiến Dũng – Nam Phương, 'Quốc Hội Thông Qua Hiến Pháp Sửa Đổi' ['The National Assembly Passed The Amended Constitution'], (Vnexpress, 28 November 2013), Https://Vnexpress.Net/Quoc-Hoi-Thong-Qua-Hien-Phap-Sua-Doi-2916328.Html
2 TTXVN, 'Hiến Pháp: Thể Hiện Ý Đảng, Lòng Dân Và Sự Đồng Thuận Của Cả Hệ Thống Chính Trị' ['The Constitution Demonstrates The Party's Will, The Popularity And The Consensus Of The Whole Political System'], (Tuyên Giáo, 25 December, 2013], Http://Tuyengiao.Vn/Tuyen-Truyen/Hien-Phap-The-Hien-Y-Dang-Long-Dan-Va-Su-Dong-Thuan-Cua-Ca-He-Thong-Chinh-Tri-59813
3 Đỗ Kim Thêm, 'Với Hiến Pháp Mới, Việt Nam Ít Hy Vọng Thay Đổi' ['With The New Constitution, Vietnam Has Little Hope For Change'], (Cùng Viết Hiến Pháp, December 5, 2013), Https://Hienphap.Wordpress.Com/2013/12/05/Voi-Hien-Phap-Moi-Viet-Nam-It-Hy-Vong-Thay-Doi-Do-Kim-Them/
4 Hoàng Xuân Phú, 'Hiến Pháp Vi Hiến' ['Unconstitutional Constitution'], (Hoàng Xuân Phú, 04 September, 2014), Http://Hpsc.Iwr.Uni-Heidelberg.De/Hxphu/Index.Php?Page=Readwriting&W=Hienphapvihien-20140904

DOI: 10.4324/9781003097099-4

regardless of their academic background have often engaged in debating national affairs. This may be in part because the Vietnamese culture expects public intellectuals to contribute to public affairs.

Professor Hoàng argues that Vietnam's 2013 Constitution is an unconstitutional constitution because some subsequent provisions in the Constitution violate fundamental principles established in other preceding provisions. This chapter explores Professor Hoàng's account of an unconstitutional constitution, while situating it within the broader national constitutional debates in Vietnam and comparative scholarship on unconstitutional constitutional amendments and unconstitutional constitutions. It argues that Professor Hoàng's account of an unconstitutional constitution is a political, critical, and normative discourse on Vietnam's Constitution. First, his account is not a judicial doctrine but a *political* discourse of a public intellectual on unconstitutional constitutions. The discourse is informed and motivated by political events, particularly the preceding, broader, national constitutional debate, and the adoption of the new constitution. Second, his discourse is *critical* in the sense that it is an intellectual interpretation of some principles of Vietnam's 2013 Constitution in line with liberal constitutionalism and international law. It also relies on comparative analysis to castigate other provisions in the socialist Constitution of Vietnam as unconstitutional. Third, the discourse is *normative* as it calls for constitutional amendments to make the Constitution constitutional by incorporating liberal and universal norms.

Professor Hoàng's arguments echo the arguments justifying the doctrine of unconstitutional constitutional amendments and the doctrine of unconstitutional constitutions in comparative scholarship. The implication of this chapter is that the unconstitutional constitution is not necessarily a judicial doctrine but can be a political theory which may inform public constitutional discourse. In addition, comparative inquiry into unconstitutional constitutions and amendments can be extended to public discourse, beyond courtrooms and constitutional texts.

4.2 Unamendability and unconstitutional constitution

Recent comparative scholarship has moved from the doctrine of unconstitutional constitutional amendments[5] to the doctrine of unconstitutional constitutions and even unconstitutional constituent power.[6] Richard Albert has explored four different conceptions of an unconstitutional constitution in Canada, Mexico, South Africa, and the United States.[7] He argued that "despite their unconstitutionality in different senses of the concept, each constitution is nonetheless rooted in

---

5 Yaniv Roznai, *Unconstitutional Constitutional Amendments: The Limits of Amendment Powers* (OUP 2017).
6 Kim Lane Scheppele, 'Unconstitutional Constituent Power,' in Rogers M. Smith and Richard R. Beeman (eds), *Modern Constitutions* (University of Pennsylvania Press 2020).
7 Richard Albert, 'Four Unconstitutional Constitutions and Their Democratic Foundations' (2017) 50 (2) Cornell International Law Journal 169.

democratic foundations. The strength of these foundations, however, varies as to each."[8] Albert's account focused on procedural aspects of unconstitutionality within democratic constitutions.

David Landau, Rosalind Dixon, and Yaniv Roznai, in a recent paper, turned to the substantive dimensions of unconstitutional constitution.[9] Their inquiry is based on a 2015 case from Honduras where the Supreme Court ruled term limits provisions in the original 1982 constitution as unconstitutional.[10] They demonstrate that:

> The Court focused on the parts of Articles 239 and 42 punishing attempts to change the term limit, holding that these articles were in tension with fundamental rights of freedom of expression found elsewhere in the Honduran Constitution and in regional and international human rights instruments, and which themselves were linked to the political rights of voters and candidates.[11]

The Honduran Court's theory of unconstitutional constitution rests on the collision between some parts of the constitution with other fundamental parts of the existing constitution and with international human rights law.[12] Landau, Dixon, and Roznai conclude:

> some judicial review of original constitutional texts can be justified by using the same arguments currently used to justify the unconstitutional constitutional amendment doctrine. This may mean that the Honduran decision is not an isolated occurrence, but instead the harbinger of a broader trend, which we predict global constitutionalism will see more of.[13]

Professor Hoàng's discourse of "unconstitutional constitution" resonates to some extent with the Honduran Court's theory of an unconstitutional constitution. He also argues that some parts of Vietnam's Constitution are unconstitutional because they collide with other fundamental parts of the same document and with international human rights law. However, Professor Hoàng's account is not a judicial doctrine but a political account of Vietnam's Constitution as an unconstitutional constitution. So, why does it matter? It matters in both a

---

8 ibid 172.
9 David Landau, Rosalind Dixon, and Yaniv Roznai, 'From an Unconstitutional Constitutional Amendment to An Unconstitutional Constitution? Lessons from Honduras' (2019) 8 Global Constitutionalism 40.
10 ibid 42.
11 ibid 52.
12 ibid 53.
13 ibid 69. See also, Po Jen Yap and Rehan Abeyratne, 'Judicial Self-Dealing and Unconstitutional Constitutional Amendments in South Asia' (2021) 19(1) International Journal of Constitutional Law 127.

70 *Ngoc Son Bui*

national and a comparative sense. Nationally, his account helps better understand the sources of constitutional dynamics in Vietnam. It reveals the dissonance within Vietnam's constitution and between it and transnational constitutional norms. This constitutional cacophony creates the space for dynamics of constitutional discourse in the country. Comparatively, Professor Hoàng's account suggests that the unconstitutional constitution is not necessarily a judicial doctrine but can be a political theory which may inform the constitutional public discourse of intellectuals, citizens, legislators, and government officers.

4.3 Background

4.3.1 Vietnamese constitutional debates

Under the leadership of the Communist Party, Vietnam enacted five constitutions in 1946, 1959, 1980, 1992, and 2013, respectively. Originally, the government had a plan to amend the 1992 constitution, but the process ended up with the enactment of a new constitution in 2013.

The 2013 constitution-making process is the most participatory in Vietnam's post-colonial history. During the process, Vietnamese citizens engaged in relatively open constitutional discussions on issues foundational to the socialist system, including the leading role of the Communist Party in the constitutional system,[14] human rights restriction according to the principle of proportionality,[15] land ownership,[16] the role of the state-owned enterprises in the national economy,[17] the role of the military, and other institutional questions.[18]

Participants in the Vietnamese constitutional dialogue included a wide range of national intellectuals. For example, 72 Vietnamese intellectuals in different fields (for example, law, journalism, economics, mathematics, music, and historical studies) signed a constitutional petition, which was later signed by more than 10,000 people. Famously known as Petition 72, it called for free elections, the separation of powers, and the protection of human rights by a constitutional court, among other things. Another notable initiative is the *Cùng Viết Hiến Pháp* (Let's Draw up the Constitution) group whose founders included, among others, Vietnamese mathematician Ngo Bao Chau and Vietnamese physician Dam Thanh Son, both at the Chicago University. The group created a

---

14 Bui Th, 'Constitutionalizing Single Party Leadership in Vietnam: Dilemmas of Reform' (2016) 11 Asian Journal of Comparative Law 219.

15 Vu GC and Tran K, 'Constitutional Debate and Development on Human Rights in Vietnam' (2016) 11 Asian Journal of Comparative Law 235.

16 Le T, 'Interpreting the Constitutional Debate over Land Ownership in the Socialist Republic of Vietnam (2012–2013)' (2016) 11 Asian Journal of Comparative Law 287

17 Pham DN, 'From Marx to Market: The Debates on the Economic System in Vietnam's Revised Constitution' (2016) 11 Asian Journal of Comparative Law 263.

18 Pham LP, 'The Procuracy as a Subject of Constitutional Debate: Controversial and Unresolved Issues' (2016) 11 Asian Journal of Comparative Law 309.

website to facilitate online constitutional discussion beyond the state-run fora, which drew the attention and engagement of many Vietnamese intellectuals and citizens.[19]

4.3.2 Prof. Hoàng's constitutional engagement

Prof. Hoàng Xuân Phú is a professor at the Institute of Mathematics in Hanoi, Vietnam. He holds a Habilitation (Doctor of Science) from the University of Leipzig, Germany.[20] Before joining Vietnamese constitutional debates in 2013, he had already engaged in public debates on other national issues, including legal issues, such as local authorities grabbing peasants' land,[21] citizens' rights to demonstrate,[22] and the parliamentary vote of confidence on government members.[23]

With that experience, when the state launched the initiative of constitutional amendments, it was not surprising that Prof. Hoàng vigorously engaged in constitutional debates. He is a member of the aforementioned 72 Petition group. In 2013, he wrote eight constitutional essays published on his personal website. Some of these essays were circulated on the website of the *Cùng Viết Hiến Pháp* group. Professor Hoàng's constitutional writings touched on some of the most controversial and sensitive constitutional questions. This explains why these writings were only published on his personal website or disseminated on other unofficial platforms, not in the official media due to censorship.

Professor Hoàng proposed eliminating from the Constitution the provisions on the leadership of the Communist Party of Vietnam and state ownership of

---

19 Https://Cungviethienphap.Wordpress.Com
20 See his CV at: Http://Hpsc.Iwr.Uni-Heidelberg.De/Hxphu/Index.Php?Page=Cv
21 Hoàng Xuân Phú, 'Một Số Khía Cạnh Hình Sự Của Vụ Án Tiên Lãng – Hải Phòng' ['Some Criminal Aspects Of The Tiên Lãng -Hải Phòng Case'], (Hoàng Xuân Phú, 16 February 2012), Http://Hpsc.Iwr.Uni-Heidelberg.De/Hxphu/Index.Php?Page=Readwriting&W=Motsokhiacanhhinhsucuavuantienlang-Haiphong-20120217c
22 Hoàng Xuân Phú, 'Quyền Biểu Tình Của Công Dân' ['Citizens' Right to Demonstration'], (Hoàng Xuân Phú, 09 August 2011), Http://Hpsc.Iwr.Uni-Heidelberg.De/Hxphu/Index.Php?Page=Readwriting&W=Quyenbieutinhcuacongdan-20130601
23 Hoàng Xuân Phú, 'Nhận Thức Mới: Lấy Là Bỏ, Bỏ Là Lấy' ['New Realization: Get Is Give up, Quit Is Get'], (Hoàng Xuân Phú, 18 October, 2012), Http://Hpsc.Iwr.Uni-Heidelberg.De/Hxphu/Index.Php?Page=Readwriting&W=Nhanthucmoi_Laylabo_Bolalay-20121018

lands.[24] He further called for popular sovereignty,[25] changing the nation's name (without the word "socialist"),[26] and constitutional protection of human rights,[27] including the right to demonstration.[28] These arguments challenged the ideological and institutional cores of the socialist constitutional system in Vietnam, while advocating for major ideas and institutions of liberal constitutionalism. Professor Hoàng's arguments are supported by references to comparative constitutional experiences in western liberal democracies such as Germany, the US, and the UK. To illustrate, he called for "opening the soul to learn from the American Constitution and the constitutions of other powerful countries to accumulate experiences for amending our country's constitution."[29]

After the amended constitution was adopted in late 2013, Professor Hoàng wrote four essays in 2014 to criticize this document. The first essay considers the new constitution a "misamendment," warning of the negative impact of new provisions restricting human rights, although it also recognizes some positive changes regarding the rights to counsel.[30] The second essay condemned the Constitution as an "unconstitutional constitution" as discussed below. The third essay took advantage of the official media news's misspelling *hien phap* (constitution) as *hiep phap* (rape law) to argue that new Constitution was imposed upon

---

24 Hoàng Xuân Phú, 'Hai Tử Huyệt Của Chế Độ' ['Two Death Points of the Regime'], (Hoàng Xuân Phú, 11 January 2013), Http://Hpsc.Iwr.Uni-Heidelberg.De/Hxphu/Index.Php?Page=Readwriting&W=Haituhuyetcuachedo-20130111; Hoàng Xuân Phú, 'Đảng Và Nhân Dân – Vị Thế Bị Tráo' ['Party and People – The Position Is Swapped'], (Hoàng Xuân Phú, 17 September, 2013), Http://Hpsc.Iwr.Uni-Heidelberg.De/Hxphu/Index.Php?Page=Readwriting&W=Dangvanhandan-Vithebitrao-20130917 ; Hoàng Xuân Phú, 'Uẩn Khúc Trong Điều 4 Hiến Pháp' ['Mystery in Article 4 of the Constitution'], 9Hoàng Xuân Phú, 29 August 2013), Http://Hpsc.Iwr.Uni-Heidelberg.De/Hxphu/Index.Php?Page=Readwriting&W=Uankhuattrongdieu4hienphap-20130829

25 Hoàng Xuân Phú, 'Chỗ Đứng Của Nhân Dân Trong Hiến Pháp' ['The People's Place in the Constitution'], (Hoàng Xuân Phú, 14 February 2013), Http://Hpsc.Iwr.Uni-Heidelberg.De/Hxphu/Index.Php?Page=Readwriting&W=Chodungcuanhandantronghienphap-20130214

26 Hoàng Xuân Phú, 'Quốc Hiệu Nào Hội Tụ Lòng Dân?' ['Which Nation's Name Converges People's Hearts?'], (Hoàng Xuân Phú, 17 May 2013), Http://Hpsc.Iwr.Uni-Heidelberg.De/Hxphu/Index.Php?Page=Readwriting&W=Quochieunaohoitulongdan-20130518

27 Hoàng Xuân Phú, 'Teo Dần Quyền Con Người Trong Hiến Pháp' ['Gradual Decline of Human Rights in the Constitution'], (Hoàng Xuân Phú, 15 January, 2013), Http://Hpsc.Iwr.Uni-Heidelberg.De/Hxphu/Index.Php?Page=Readwriting&W=Teodanquyenconnguoitronghienphap-20130115

28 Hoàng Xuân Phú, 'Là Thực Thi Quyền Hiến Định Ông Trọng Ạ!' ['It Is to Exercise the Constitutional Right, Mr. Trong Sir!'] (Hoàng Xuân Phú, 26 February 2013), Http://Hpsc.Iwr.Uni-Heidelberg.De/Hxphu/Index.Php?Page=Readwriting&W=Lathucthiquyenhiendinhongtronga-20130226

29 Hoàng Xuân Phú, The People's Place in the Constitution (note 25).

30 Hoàng Xuân Phú, 'Hiến Pháp 2013 – Sửa Nhầm Hay Đổi Thiệt?' ['Constitution 2013 – Misamendment or Correct Change?' (Hoàng Xuân Phú, 29 August, 2014), Http://Hpsc.Iwr.Uni-Heidelberg.De/Hxphu/Index.Php?Page=Readwriting&W=Hienphap2013-Suanhamhaydoithiet-20140829

the people and may be amended or replaced in the near future.³¹ The fourth essay (47 pages) critically evaluated the whole constitutional amendment process and the new substantive changes.³² In this essay, he concluded:

> Whether satisfied or disappointed with the results of the discussion on amendments to the Constitution, it is also an opportunity for many people to express their opinions. Whether or not you accept the other side's point of view, it is also an opportunity to understand each other's stance. The people have conditions to better understand the mind and reach of the ruling power and the National Assembly deputies. The authorities also better understand the people's frustrations, aspirations and capacities. This is perhaps the most remarkable achievement of the discussion on amending the 1992 Constitution.³³

Professor Hoàng recognized the procedural aspects of Vietnam's participatory constitutional amendments. The amendment process created a window of opportunity for a constitutional dialogue between the state and the people. He, however, retained strongly critical views about the substantive contents of the amendments. In his view, the amendments turn the constitution into an "unconstitutional constitution" as explored below.

4.4 Hoàng's account of unconstitutional constitution

4.4.1 What is an unconstitutional constitution?

Professor Hoàng believes that

> unconstitutional legislations are not rare. But the constitution that is also unconstitutional is so rare that it can be considered the "specialty" of the [Vietnam's] regime. Unfortunately, the 2013 Constitution – passed by the 13th National Assembly on November 28, 2013 – falls into that category.³⁴

He may not be aware of the comparative experience of unconstitutional constitutions and amendments elsewhere, but his explanation of the unconstitutional constitution in Vietnam resonates with the comparative insights.

---

31 Hoàng Xuân Phú, 'Bắt Mạch Hiến… Nháp' ['Pulsing The Draft Constitution'], (Hoàng Xuân Phú, 10 September, 2014), Http://Hpsc.Iwr.Uni-Heidelberg.De/Hxphu/Index.Php?Page=Readwriting&W=Batmachhiennhap-20140910
32 Hoàng Xuân Phú, 'Não Lòng Với Hiến Pháp' ['Affliction with The Constitution'], Hoàng Xuân Phú, 16 September, 2014), Http://Hpsc.Iwr.Uni-Heidelberg.De/Hxphu/Index.Php?Page=Readwriting&W=Naolongvoihienphap-20140916
33 ibid.
34 Hoàng Xuan Phu (n 4).

His theory of an unconstitutional constitution is based on logical inference rules, which understandably echoes mathematical reasoning due to his academic background. He formulates this logic:

> Since all provisions in a constitution are considered "norm", when two norms contradict each other, one can use one to negate the other and vice versa, and in the end, both become unconstitutional. However, we will not completely negate both, but "forgive" the term that takes precedence in the constitution and use it to evaluate other provisions. So, what is the basis for determining the priority position in the constitution? According to the framers' mindset, Chapter I must have the highest priority, and Chapter II has a higher (more important) priority than the following chapters. Within a chapter, what is put first is perhaps also considered more important than what is placed behind.[35]

Chapter I in Vietnam's Constitution established principles fundamental to the subsequent provisions on rights and state institutions. Within Professor Hoàng's logic, the subsequent provisions on rights and state institutions can be considered unconstitutional if they violate the constitutional principles established in Chapter I. He points out four such unconstitutional provisions which deal with human rights, citizens' military duty, military force, and land ownership. In addition, provisions on constitutional principles within Chapter I can be considered unconstitutional if the subsequent provisions violate the preceding provisions. On that basis, he points out three such unconstitutional provisions which established the leadership of the Communist Party of Vietnam, the role of the Vietnam Fatherland Front, and the role of the Vietnam Labor Union. He states:

> Three of the seven unconstitutional contents mentioned above have been commented and criticized a lot during the discussion of the Draft 1992 Amendment of the Constitution. However, the authorities still defied and tried to keep it … And as an instinct, every time it makes a mistake, the authorities' reasoning and propaganda machines often capture conflicting opinions as hostile or reactionary. Now, in this essay, all the arguments are purely based on the 2013 Constitution. So, if you still try to attribute the conclusions drawn here as reactionary, then it is no different than considering the Constitution of the contemporary regime as reactionary.[36]

Apart from the principles in the existing constitution, Professor Hoàng also refers to international law, particularly the United Nations Charter and the 1948 Universal Declaration of Human Rights, to prove that a certain provision of the 2013 Constitution is unconstitutional. However, he contends that this

35 ibid.
36 ibid.

international reference does not mean invoking external documents, but only to confirm that the provision under consideration violates Article 12 of the 2013 Constitution, which provides that the Socialist Republic of Vietnam complies with the United Nations Charter and international treaties to which it is a signatory.[37]

The next sections will focus on his arguments on three controversial issues which were prominent in the 2013 Vietnamese constitutional debates: human rights, land ownership, and popular sovereignty.

4.4.2 Human rights

The issue of human rights was one of the most contentious issues in the 2013 constitutional debates. The 1992 Constitution already included a provision on human rights and a lavish list of fundamental rights. In 2013, however, reformers advocated for a more universal understanding of human rights as opposed to the socialist conception of rights as given to citizens by the state. In another direction, reformers called for the inclusion of more rights in the new constitution in accordance with international human rights treaties that Vietnam ratified.[38]

Professor Hoàng's argument on the unconstitutionality of a human rights provision in the 2013 constitution echoed that broader human rights discourse in Vietnam. He argued that Article 14 on human rights in Chapter II contradicts the principle of human rights established in Article 3 of Chapter I. Article 3 newly added this provision: "The State ... acknowledges, respects, protects and guarantees human rights and citizens' rights."[39] Article 14 of the new Constitution basically retained a provision of the preceding 1992 Constitution, which states that human rights and citizens' rights "are recognized, respected, protected and guaranteed in concordance with the Constitution and the law."[40]

Professor Hoàng opines that:

> Citizens' rights can be unique to each country, but human rights are universal in the world, not something bestowed by the authorities of each country. Normally, the State must recognize all human rights, whether or not they are specifically mentioned in the Constitution and law or not. Human rights mentioned in Article 3 of the 2013 Constitution must carry such meaning. Therefore, the fact that Clause 1 Article 14 of the 2013 Constitution restricts human rights, only "recognizes ... according to the Constitution and the law", is a violation of Article 3 of the 2013 Constitution.[41]

---

37 ibid; Vietnam's 2013 Constitution, art 12.
38 Vu and Tran (n 15), 235
39 2013 Constitution, art 3.
40 2013 Constitution, art 14.
41 Hoàng Xuân Phú (n 4).

In other words, Article 14's statist position on human rights contradicts Article 3 on human rights which should be read as a universalist commitment (human rights beyond the state's positive creation by law). He said: "You can't specify or list everything in the constitution and the law, and if something isn't listed, it doesn't mean it's denied."[42] To justify this argument, he cited the Ninth Amendment to the US Constitution, which states that "The enumeration in the Constitution, of certain rights, shall not be construed to deny or disparage others retained by the people."[43] He then cited several provisions on the Universal Declaration of Human Rights to support his explanation of Article 3 as Vietnam's commitment to universal human rights.[44] On that basis, he moved on to argue that Article 14 also violates Article 12 of the Constitution, which states that Vietnam conforms to the Charter of the United Nations and international treaties in which it is a member.[45]

Why is there such an unconstitutional constitutional provision? Professor Hoàng explains:

> This unconstitutionality is not accidental, but a traditional product of "miraculous syndrome", which is the dominant way of thinking, that people can only do and enjoy only what the authorities allowed. It stems from the misconception that the rulers are "much higher than" all of the People and have "the right to kill" over the People's community. It is a serious disease, has bound our People and hindered the development of our people for decades, turning our People into a "thinking slave." The so-called "*doi moi*" (which has been carried out since the 80s of the 20th century) is just that the government is compelled to "untie", or more precisely speaking to "loosen", giving back to the People a portion of their inherently self-sustaining right to live and self-employment. Therefore, if you want to truly liberate the People, liberate the People from the chains, you must be determined to erase this "miraculous syndrome."[46]

The new 2013 Constitution presents a dissonant move. It signals a commitment to universal human rights, while retaining the hegemony of right statism. This constitutional disharmony creates space for the discourse on "unconstitutional constitution." This discourse is characterized by the contradiction between the pre-established statist provision and the newly introduced universalist provision on human rights as an example of an "unconstitutional constitution."

---

42 ibid.
43 US Constitution, IX Amendment.
44 Hoàng Xuân Phú (n 4).
45 ibid.
46 ibid.

4.4.3 Land ownership

Land ownership is another controversial issue in the 2013 Vietnamese constitutional discourse. The debates focused on the question of whether the Constitution should allow for private ownership of lands. The debates on this question were informed by several cases in which authorities confiscated peasants' lands for developmental projects, leading to violent protests. Reformers believed that the 1992 Constitution which provided for the state's exclusive ownership of lands was the source of land disputes and official corruption. Therefore, they called for the privatization of land ownership.[47]

As mentioned above, Professor Hoàng wrote several pieces on land issues before and during the constitutional amendment process. Understandably, this issue prominently returned in his account of the unconstitutional constitution. He argued that Article 53 of the 2013 Constitution, which continued to provide for state ownership of all lands, is unconstitutional. His argument was based on historical, contemporary, and international grounds.

First, he traced the unconstitutionality of the 2013 Constitution's continued nationalization of lands back to Vietnamese constitutional history. He demonstrated that the first constitution of the country enacted in 1946 protected "The ownership of property of Vietnamese citizens."[48] He infers that: "Obviously, land is a form of property, so the private ownership of land by citizens is also guaranteed by the 1946 Constitution. That is what has become evident and also the solemn commitment of this regime at its inception."[49] The next Constitution of 1959, Professor Hoàng indicates, continued to provide for the protection of private ownership of property generally and explicitly recognized the "ownership of land by peasants."[50] The third Constitution of 1980, however, nationalized all lands under the form of "people's ownership of lands"[51] which actually means the state's ownership of lands. This practice was continued in the 1992 Constitution. Professor Hoàng argued

> When the VI National Assembly (1976–1981) passed the 1980 Constitution on December 18, 1980, the 1959 Constitution was still in effect. Therefore, the vote of the 6th National Assembly to abolish private legal ownership of land and assert that all "land ... belongs to the entire people" (Article 19 of the 1980 Constitution) is a gross violence to the Constitution in effect.[52]

In other words, he believes the 1980 Constitution is unconstitutional because it violated the preexisting 1959 Constitution.

---

47 Le (n 16) 287
48 Vietnam's 1946 Constitution, art 12.
49 Hoàng Xuân Phú (n 4).
50 Vietnam's 1959 Constitution, arts 14 and 18.
51 Vietnam's 1980 Constitution, art 19.
52 Hoàng Xuân Phú (n 4).

Second, Professor Hoàng argued the 2013 Constitution is unconstitutional because it still retains the same provision nationalizing lands established by the 1980 and 1992 constitutions. Particularly, he contends that Article 53 of the 2013 constitution (which establishes the state ownership of lands and excludes the right to private ownership of lands) violates the constitutional right to private property established by Article 32 of the same constitution.[53]

Third, he castigated Article 53 of Vietnam's 2013 Constitution for violating Article 17 of the Universal Declaration of Human Rights, which guarantees the right to private property. That also means the violation of Vietnam's constitutional commitment to conforming with the international treaties it ratified.

Finally, Professor Hoàng proposed that to make the 2013 Constitution constitutional, it should abolish the provision nationalizing lands and allow for private land ownership.[54]

4.4.4 Popular sovereignty

The 2013 constitutional debates in Vietnam featured the two interrelated questions: people's sovereignty and the Party's leadership. Reformers questioned the constitutionalization of hegemonic power of the Communist Party on the grounds of people's power. Critics called for the elimination of Article 4 in the 1992 Constitution, establishing the leadership of the Communist Party, which may open the door for the practice of the people's power through free elections.[55]

As mentioned above, during the constitutional amendment process, Professor Hoàng wrote several articles criticizing the constitutionalization of the Communist Party. This question returned in his account of the new constitution as unconstitutional. He contends that Article 4 in the new Constitution, which continued to mandate the Party's leadership, is unconstitutional because it violates Article 2 of the same document which established the principle of popular sovereignty.[56]

Article 2 provides that "The Socialist Republic of Vietnam is a socialist rule of law State of the People, by the People and for the People," and that "the people are the masters of the Socialist Republic of Vietnam; all state powers belong to the people."[57] Article 4 confirms that "The Communist Party of Vietnam … is the force leading the State and society."[58] Professor Hoàng questioned the constitutionality of Article 4 on the ground of Article 2, reasoning that:

> If "all state power belongs to the People" then at least the right to choose and determine "the force leading the State and society" must also "belong to

---

53 ibid.
54 ibid.
55 Bui (n 14) 219.
56 Hoàng Xuân Phú (n 4).
57 Vietnam's 2013 Constitution, art 2.
58 Vietnam's 2013 Constitution, art 4.

the People". This is the most fundamental and core right among "state powers". Only when the people exercise that basic right can the State be considered "of the People, by the People", and that the State can be "owned by the People". But in reality, the People have never elected the Communist Party of Vietnam as "the force leading the state and society". Why then did the framers write in Article 4 of the 2013 Constitution that "The Communist Party of Vietnam ... is the force that governs the State and society?"[59]

Professor Hoàng has anticipated arguments that the people vest in the National Assembly (elected by the people) the constitution-making power to establish the leadership of the Communist Party. He, however, considers such an argument to be "sophism"[60] due to these reasons:

First, the National Assembly was elected among the candidates selected by the ruling force and therefore did not represent the will and aspiration of the entire people.[61]

Second, the Constitution does not have any provision empowering the National Assembly to select a vague force leading the state and the society. The Constitution only vests the five-year term of the National Assembly to select particular government offices corresponding to its specific terms. He underlined: "The National Assembly is only empowered for a five-year term and cannot be allowed to elect indefinite titles or powers as in Article 4 of the 2013 Constitution!"[62]

Third, the National Assembly is vested with the constitution-making power, but "constitution" must be understood in the "normal and sound sense."[63] He said:

> It is impossible to abuse the constitution-making power to arbitrarily write in the Constitution "abnormal" provisions. In normal constitutions of the world, it is not possible to constitutionalize a permanent leadership of a single political party towards the state and society. In the name of "special circumstances", the National Assembly may introduce some "unusual" contents to the Constitution, but that will only be considered "in accordance with the people's hearts" if it is approved by the majority of the people in a national referendum.[64]

Professor Hoàng Xuân Phú concludes:

> The people of this generation do not have the right to decide for the People of the generations to come ... In any case, the People of this generation and

---

59 Hoàng Xuân Phú (n 4).
60 ibid.
61 ibid.
62 ibid.
63 ibid.
64 ibid.

the incumbent National Assembly are not allowed to constitutionalize the eternal power to "lead of the State and society" of any "force".[65]

He suggests that to resolve the problem of unconstitutionality, either Article 2 or Article 4 of the Constitution must be amended or abolished:

> If Article 4 is kept, Article 2 must be amended to delete the contents "State of the People, by the People, for the People", "owned by the People", and "all state power belongs to the People" out of the Constitution. Since the deleted content is characteristic of the "Republic" regime, the country name must also be changed, for example replacing the word "Republic" with "Party Nation", similar to the model of "Kingdom". On the contrary, if Article 2 is kept intact with the institution of "Republic", then only way is to delete the content of Article 4.[66]

4.5 Comparative analysis

4.5.1 Unamendability vs unconstitutional constitution

Unamendability can be legal, judicial, or political. Legal unamendability is entrenched in the constitution; judicial unamendability stems from courts' constitutional interpretation; and political unamendability is created by politicians. The latter is connected to Richard Albert's conceptualization of *constructive unamendability*.[67] Apart from the procedural aspects, there are substantive aspects of the political construction of unamendability. Substantive aspects of the constitution are made unamendable not by the constitution itself or by judicial interpretation but by politicians in the amendment agenda.

Vietnamese political leaders are willing to amend the constitution, but their amendment agenda deliberately constructs basic socialist constitutional principles as unamendable to protect the existing socialist regime. This political construction of unamendability generates Professor Hoàng's discourse of unconstitutional constitution.

Vietnamese constitutional amenders established principles of constitutional amendments. Accordingly, amendments must continue to confirm the overall socialist political system, the leadership of the Communist Party of Vietnam, and the socialist-oriented market economy, and the inseparability between citizens' rights and their duties.[68] These principles of constitutional amendments actually establish political limits on the amendment power. Consequently, core

---

65 ibid.
66 ibid.
67 Richard Albert, *Constitutional Amendments: Making, Breaking, and Changing Constitutions* (OUP 2019) 158.
68 Báo cáo Thuyết minh về Dự thảo sửa đổi Hiến pháp năm 1992 ['Statement of Notes on the Draft Constitution Amendment in 1992'] (Nhan Dan, 06 January, 2013], https://nhandan.com.vn/chinhtri/bao-cao-thuyet-minh-ve-du-thao-sua-doi-hien-phap-nam-1992-384696/

commitments to the socialist political and economic system (such as party leadership, the statist form of land ownership, and statist rights) are politically unamendable despite the absence of formal constitutional barriers. Therefore, the 2013 Constitution continues these socialist constitutional identities established in the preceding 1992 Constitution, although there were vehement calls among the society for amending these aspects during the amendment process. The political limits of constitutional amendments in Vietnam aim to reject core norms of constitutionalism and to defend core norms of constitutional socialism. The new 2013 Constitution is conceived as unconstitutional not because of what it changes, but because of what it failed to change due to political unamendability.

4.5.2 Constitutionalism and unconstitutional constitution

In comparative scholarship, the doctrine of unconstitutional constitutional amendments and the doctrine of unconstitutional constitutions rest on the ideas of liberal constitutionalism. These doctrines attempt to ensure that existing holders of power cannot change fundamental norms defining their power to protect fundamental values of liberty.

Liberal constitutionalism influenced the Vietnamese constitutional discourse in 2013.[69] This is in part due to the diffusion of ideas of liberal constitutionalism in Vietnam via several channels, such as translations of works by liberal thinkers (such as Rousseau's *The Social Contract* and Montesquieu's *The Spirit of the Laws*), and writings by Vietnamese legal scholars educated overseas.[70] Professor Hoàng's theory of an unconstitutional constitution is also informed by ideas of liberal constitutionalism. Although he claims that he bases his theory exclusively on the 2013 Constitution, he in fact interprets its fundamental principles (such as popular sovereignty, protection of human rights, the right to private property) in line with liberal constitutionalism. He refers to the comparative experience of western constitutional governments to justify his argument. The fact that the 2013 Constitution includes vague principles creates the space for alternative interpretations, including this critical interpretation as an unconstitutional constitution.

Professor Hoàng uses the liberal construction of some fundamental principles of Vietnam's Constitution as the criteria to evaluate other provisions in the text. Consequently, his theory is actually that the 2013 Constitution is unconstitutional because some of its provisions contradict fundamental norms of liberal constitutionalism. In this regard, Professor Hoàng's theory of an unconstitutional constitution resonates with the arguments justifying unconstitutional constitutional amendment doctrines: namely, some core values of liberal constitutionalism (such

---

69 Bui Thiem, 'Liberal Constitutionalism and the Socialist State in an Era of Globalisation: An Inquiry into Vietnam's Constitutional Discourse and Power Structures' (2013) 5 (2) Global Studies Journal 43–54.
70 Bui Ngoc Son, *Constitutional Change in the Contemporary Socialist World* (OUP 2020) 17–80.

as fundamental rights and popular sovereignty) are so fundamental that they must be beyond the scope of constitutional amendments. It also echoes the Honduran Court's theory of an unconstitutional constitution: both emphasize that some parts of the constitution collide with other parts on fundamental rights.

4.5.3 International law and unconstitutional constitution

In comparative scholarship, the theory of unconstitutional constitutions conceives international law, particularly international human rights law, as "criteria for invalidating substantive constitutional provisions."[71] According to Landau, Dixon, and Roznai,

> the Honduran Court's explicit rationale focuses largely on a vision of Honduran constitutionalism that subordinates norms in the domestic constitution to certain precepts of international law, such as international human rights law. The Court suggests that it has the power to declare parts of the constitutional order to be incompatible with international principles and therefore to hold them "inapplicable". The Court thus suggests a hierarchy in which the domestic constitution is itself subordinate to some aspects of the international legal order.[72]

As indicated above, Professor Hoàng's theory of an unconstitutional constitution is also based on international law, particularly international human rights law. He uses international legal standards to evaluate some provisions in Vietnam's constitution regarding human rights and land ownership. However, he does not suggest a hierarchy: the domestic constitution is not subordinate to international law. Rather, his strategy is to construe some provisions in the constitution according to international legal standards and use this international interpretation as the framework to evaluate other constitutional provisions. He does not claim that some provisions are unconstitutional because they violate international law. His claim is that some provisions are unconstitutional because they violate the Vietnamese constitutional commitments to comply with international treaties the country signed. This claim still remains within the domain of domestic law.

4.6 Conclusion

This chapter presented Professor Hoàng's account of unconstitutional constitution as a political, critical, and normative discourse on Vietnam's Constitution. Professor Hoàng's criticisms of the constitutional entrenchment of statist human rights, state ownership of lands, and the dominant leadership of the Communist Party are informed by the Vietnamese public constitutional discourse during the

---

71 Landau, Dixon, and Roznai (n 9) 62.
72 ibid 60.

constitutional amendment process. In addition, his normative call for universal rights, the private ownership of lands, and democratic elections is also informed by several liberal and universalist arguments in the Vietnamese public constitutional discourse. He complicates the story by putting together the familiar critical and normative arguments in the public discourse to argue that Vietnam's new constitution is an unconstitutional constitution.

At the end of his paper, he concludes: "Regardless of how the National Assembly will explain it and deal with it itself, we have to wonder with the question: Is a document containing so many contradictory terms worthy of the Constitution?"[73] The internal contradictions of the constitution are framed in terms of unconstitutional constitution to render it not a real constitution. His account may not persuade the Vietnamese constitution-makers and intellectuals.[74] His account, however, complicates critical discourse on Vietnamese constitutional issues: to call the constitution as an unconstitutional constitution is another way to problematize it.

The comparative implication of this chapter is that the accounts of unconstitutional constitutions and unconstitutional amendments should not be limited to what is textually entrenched or/and judicially decided but should extend to what public intellectuals say about the unconstitutionality of the constitution in the public sphere.[75] Why does this matter? For one thing, this inquiry can shed light on the ideas circulating within public discourse on unconstitutional constitution and amendments. In addition, the inquiry into the public discourse on unconstitutional constitution and amendments can add to our understanding of the dynamic functions of a constitution. A constitution regardless of whether it is liberal-democratic or authoritarian is more than a legal document to be used in courts or a charter for governance structure. It can be a political document for social and public debates on national affairs ranging from land distribution to elections. Finally, and relatedly, the inquiry into public discourse on unconstitutional constitutions and amendments can enhance our understanding of socio-economic and political issues in a given country. One may not be convinced by Professor Hoàng's account of unconstitutional constitutions but may still gain a better understanding of contested issues pertaining to human rights, land ownership, and party leadership in Vietnam.

---

73 Hoàng Xuân Phú (n 4).
74 He may not also intend to convince them to accept his arguments.
75 For example, the public discourse on the unconstitutionality of informal constitutional amendments in Japan. See Koichi Nakano, Chapter 2 in this volume.

Part II
Denotive model

5 The law and politics of unconstitutional constitutional amendments in Malaysia

HP Lee and Yvonne Tew

5.1 Introduction

The judicial review of constitutional amendments is more than a matter of law, it is inescapably also a matter of constitutional politics. The question of whether a constitution possesses a foundational core immune from legislative alteration lies at the heart of how a particular polity conceives of its vision of constitutionalism.

The Malaysian experience with the notion of a constitutional basic structure over the last half century reveals a story about judicial power and constitutional politics. It is a story that cannot fully be told without understanding the courts' interaction with the political branches of government.[1]

Courts in Malaysia have long had – and continue – to navigate fraught political dynamics. For decades considered a dominant party regime, Malaysia had been governed by a single political coalition – Barisan Nasional – since its independence in 1957. In 2018, the Barisan Nasional government was voted out for the first time in the country's history. That unprecedented democratic regime change was followed by the Pakatan Harapan government's collapse in 2020, and a newly assembled Perikatan National coalition taking power, before itself succumbing to internal power struggles resulting in yet another change in leadership in 2021. Malaysia today is no longer, as it once was, characterized by a dominant political coalition that has never been ousted from power; it is, more than ever before, deeply fragile.

This chapter explores the rising trajectory of the unconstitutional constitutional amendments doctrine in Malaysia's constitutional landscape. The course of the doctrine's journey never did run smooth; it has been one of fits and starts. It traces the evolution of the Malaysian judiciary's engagement with the basic structure doctrine: from initial judicial resistance to the apex court's contemporary jurisprudence that established the judicial review of unconstitutional constitutional amendments in Malaysia's constitutional landscape. This chapter argues that although judicial approaches toward the basic structure doctrine still demonstrate some unevenness, the seeds of the doctrine of unconstitutional constitutional amendments have taken root, and begun to thrive, in Malaysia's constitutional soil.

---

1 See Yvonne Tew, *Constitutional Statecraft in Asian Courts* (OUP 2020) 57–65.

Section 5.2 begins with the birth and growth of the Malaysian nation from its independence in 1957 and outlines the key institutions of constitutional governance of the Malaysian state. It sets out the constitutional amendment procedures laid out in the Malaysian Federal Constitution and situates the ease of constitutional change within a broader context dominated by consolidated political power. Section 5.3 looks at early judicial dicta in the 1970s and 1980s expressing skepticism toward the idea of implied limitations on constitutional amendments. Of significance is the constitutional amendment passed in 1988 altering Article 121(1) of the Federal Constitution to remove the textual provision vesting judicial power in the courts, and the Malaysian judiciary's anemic response to that legislative intrusion on judicial power.[2]

Section 5.4 examines the judicial renaissance in developing a doctrine protecting unamendable constitutional features in Malaysia. It focuses on three principal cases that demonstrate the rise of the basic structure doctrine in Malaysian constitutional jurisprudence: *Semenyih Jaya*,[3] *Indira Gandhi*,[4] and *Alma Nudo*.[5] In this trilogy of cases, the Malaysian apex court affirmed and entrenched the basic structure doctrine to Malaysia's constitutional order. While there is still some judicial reluctance to recognize that the doctrine fully applies to the Malaysian context,[6] what seems undeniable is that the notion of judicial review of constitutional amendments now occupies a central part in judicial reasoning and constitutional practice in Malaysia. The final part of this chapter considers how the basic structure doctrine might apply to specific constitutional amendments excluding judicial review over an emergency proclamation and removing the requirement of royal assent to legislation. We conclude with reflections on the contemporary state of Malaysian constitutional adjudication and politics, and the judicial path forward.

5.2 The Malaysian constitutional system

5.2.1 The emergence of the Malaysian polity

Situated between the Indian Ocean and the South China Sea, the Malay Peninsula sits at the center of Southeast Asia, a location that made its port cities the nucleus of trade routes between the East and the West. Changing colonial hands from the Portuguese to the Dutch and then to the British, the Federation of Malaya eventually achieved independence in 1957, following negotiations between local representatives from Malaya and the British government.

An independent commission headed by Lord Reid was appointed to create the new federation's constitution; it was tasked with making recommendations "for a

---

2 *Public Prosecutor v Kok Wah Kuan* [2008] 1 Malayan LJ 1.
3 *Semenyih Jaya Sdn Bhd v Pentadbir Tanah Daerah Hulu Langat* [2017] 3 Malayan LJ 561.
4 *Indira Gandhi Mutho v Pengarah Jabatan Agama Islam Perak and Others* [2018] 1 Malayan LJ 545.
5 *Alma Nudo Atenza v Public Prosecutor* [2019] 4 Malayan LJ 1.
6 *Maria Chin Abdullah v Director-General of Immigration* [2021] 2 Current LJ 579.

federal form of constitution for the whole country as a single self-governing unit within the Commonwealth based on parliamentary democracy with a bicameral legislature."[7] The Reid Commission, constituted by five Commonwealth legal experts, gathered evidence from local groups and individuals before publishing a draft constitution, which was later modified after input by Malaya's Alliance coalition.

On August 31, 1957, the Federation of Malaya became a fully independent state, with the Independence Constitution coming into force. In 1963, the Federation of Malaysia was created when the polity expanded to include Singapore and the Borneo states of Sabah and Sarawak.

The Federal Constitution of Malaysia established a federal system of government, with a legislative, executive, and judicial branch, and a constitutional monarch.[8] Malaysia's constitutional framework is modelled after Westminster, with a bicameral Parliament and a Prime Minister and Cabinet as part of the executive. Significantly, Article 4(1) expressly declares that the Constitution is the supreme law of the land.[9] Courts are acknowledged to have the power to invalidate unconstitutional legislation and executive actions, and the Constitution also contains a chapter guaranteeing fundamental liberties.[10]

Malaysia's Constitution has often been said to embody a "social contract," reflecting the inter-communal compromise among the various racial and religious groups reached at the founding.[11] The elements of the constitutional framework include the establishment of a strong central government with the states and settlements enjoying a measure of autonomy, the safeguarding of the position and prestige of the Malay rulers, a constitutional head of state chosen from among the Malay rulers, a common nationality, and the safeguarding of the special position of the Malays and the legitimate interest of other communities.

5.2.2 The constitutional amendment process in Malaysia

Amendment rules are contained in Article 159 of Malaysia's Constitution. In general, amendments require an Act of Parliament that has been passed by a two-thirds majority of the total number of members of each House of Parliament.[12]

There are three categories of exceptions to this general requirement. First, the consent of the Conference of Rulers is additionally required for amending provisions dealing with citizenship, the Conference of Rulers, the Malay

---

7 Federation of Malay Constitutional Commission, Report of 1956–57 § Colonial No. 330.
8 Federal Constitution of Malaysia, ptVI, ch 1; pt IV, chs 3, 4; pt IX.
9 ibid art 4(1).
10 ibid arts 5–13.
11 See, for example, Tommy Thomas, 'The Social Contract: Malaysia's Constitutional Covenant' (2008) 1 Malayan LJ cxxxii.
12 Federal Constitution of Malaysia, art 159(3).

national language, the special position of the Malays, and the natives of Sabah and Sarawak.[13] A second category involves amendments affecting the constitutional position of Sabah and Sarawak, which requires the heads of these states to concur.[14] Third, for certain amendments – like those concerning supplementary citizenship provisions and the admission of a new state into the federation – a simple majority vote is all that is required.[15]

Formal amendment rules are one thing, amending the constitution in practice is another. The two-thirds legislative majority to amend most constitutional provisions has rarely posed a constraint for much of Malaysia's history. Since its enactment in 1957, the Malaysian Constitution has been amended extensively; estimates put the number at 51 amendment acts, or about 700 individual textual amendments.[16]

From the country's independence in 1957 to 2018, the Barisan Nasional ruling coalition typically controlled more than a two-thirds majority in parliamentary. As a result, constitutional amendments "had been apparently regarded by the government as a mechanism which could be exploited, as required, to enable the government and the ruling party to maintain and increase its grip on power."[17]

Things look somewhat different now. In the 2008 general elections, the Barisan Nasional lost its legislative supermajority for the first time in decades, and in 2018 was ousted from government. None of the governing coalitions that have come into power since 2018 have managed to control close to two-thirds of the parliamentary seats; indeed, the incumbent government appears to barely command a threadbare majority in Parliament. Still, it is relevant for our discussion on the basic structure that concerns about democratic legitimacy in Malaysia have historically not been focused on the difficulty of formal constitutional change, but on the ability of powerful political branches to amend the constitution at will.

---

13 ibid art 159(5). The Conference of Rulers is comprised of the Malay rulers and governors of individual states in Malaysia.
14 ibid art 161E(2).
15 HP Lee, 'The Process of Constitutional Change in Malaysia' in Tun Mohamed Suffian, HP Lee and FA Trindade (eds), *The Constitution of Malaysia – Its Development: 1957–1977* (OUP 1978), 369, 370–2.
16 Cindy Tham, 'Major Changes to the Constitution' (*The Sun*, 17 July 2007) https://perma.cc/5LU7-LRQ9, https://www.malaysianbar.org.my/article/news/legal-and-general-news/general-news/major-changes-to-the-constitution.
17 HP Lee, Richard Foo and Amber Tan, 'Constitutional Change in Malaysia' (2019) 14(1) Journal of Comparative Law 119, 138.

5.3 Judicial power, constitutional amendments, and constitutional politics

5.3.1 Early judicial resistance to implied limitations on the Constitution

An early glimmer of a notion of implied restrictions on the amendment power appeared in the 1963 case of *The Government of the State of Kelantan v The Government of Malaya and Tunku Abdul Rahman Putra Al-Haj*.[18] The case involved a challenge to the validity of the Malaysia Act 1963, which sought to amend the Federal Constitution to facilitate the enlargement of the Federation of Malaya by admitting three new states. Dismissing the challenge, Chief Justice Thomson wrote that the Federal Parliament had not done anything "so fundamentally revolutionary" as to require consultation with the state of Kelantan or any other state such that the amendment was unconstitutional.[19] That said, it seems highly likely that the Chief Justice's caveat was specifically tied to a narrow implied limitations notion confined to a requirement for consultation with the states in the event of a fundamental reconfiguration of the Malaysian federal scheme.[20]

In subsequent decisions in the 1970s and early 1980s, the Malaysian Federal Court gave short shrift to arguments that invoked the basic structure doctrine. In *Loh Kooi Choon v Government of Malaysia*,[21] Justice Raja Azlan Shah called the doctrine a "fallacy," observing that "it concedes to the courts a more potent power of constitutional amendment through judicial legislation than the organ formally and clearly chosen by the Constitution for the exercise of the amending power."[22]

A formalist approach was also taken in *Phang Chin Hock v Public Prosecutor*,[23] in which Lord President Tun Suffian stated that "Parliament may amend the Constitution in any way they think fit" as long it complied with the constitutionally prescribed amendment process.[24] But it's worth noting the Federal Court found that "none of the amendments" in the case actually "destroyed the basic structure of the Constitution," and so held it "unnecessary to express our view on

---

18 [1963] 1 Malayan LJ 355. See Johan Shamsuddin Sabaruddin, 'The Kelantan Challenge' in Andrew Harding and HP Lee (eds), *Constitutional Landmarks in Malaysia: The First 50 Years 1957–2007* (LexisNexis 2007) 47, 51.
19 [1963] Malayan LJ 355, 359. For criticisms of this implied restriction, see: S Jayakumar, 'Admission of New States' (1964) Malaya Law Review 181, 188; LA Sheridan and HE Groves, *The Constitution of Malaysia* (NY: Oceana Publications, 1967) 4.
20 The *Kelantan* case pre-dated the enunciation of the Indian basic structure doctrine in the 1973 case of *Kesavananda v. State of Kerala* AIR 1973 SC 1461 (India).
21 [1977] 2 Malayan LJ 187.
22 ibid 189. Justice Wan Suleiman FJ did not feel that the issue before the court would require him to determine whether there were "inherent or implied limitations to the power of amendment under Article 159." ibid 193.
23 [1980] 1 Malayan LJ 70.
24 ibid 73.

the question whether or not Parliament has power so to amend the Constitution as to destroy its basic structure."[25] Thus, in these early decisions, the Court left open the question as to whether the basic structure doctrine could be invoked in a future context.[26]

5.3.2 The 1988 constitutional amendment and judicial self-emasculation

Central to any discussion about the development of the basic structure doctrine in Malaysia is the constitutional amendment passed in 1988 to alter Article 121(1) of the Federal Constitution. In the decades following the founding of the Constitution, the Malaysian judiciary operated within a context of dominant political power; the courts tended to extensively defer to the political branches, adopting a strictly literal and legalistic approach to constitutional interpretation.[27] Article 121(1) as originally framed in the 1957 Independence Constitution expressly declared: "The judicial power of the Federation shall be vested in a Supreme Court and such inferior courts as may be provided by federal law."

A main impetus behind this constitutional amendment was the Supreme Court's decision in the 1987 case of *Public Prosecutor v Dato' Yap Peng*.[28] The Court invalidated a legislative provision that empowered the Public Prosecutor to order an inferior court to transfer a case pending before it to the High Court, declaring that the provision encroached on the judicial power of the federation, vested by Article 121(1) in the courts. The Supreme Court declared that the provision amounted to "both a legislative and executive intromission into the judicial power of the Federation,"[29] holding that the power to transfer cases from a subordinate court at any stage of the proceedings could not be conferred on any organ of government other than the judiciary.

Soon after, the Malaysian Parliament, under Prime Minister Mahathir Mohamad's administration, passed an amendment to Article 121(1). The amended Article 121(1) now provides that "the High Courts and inferior courts shall have such jurisdiction and powers as may be conferred by or under federal law." Conspicuously absent from the amended Article 121(1) were the words "The judicial power of the Federation shall be vested" from the text of the constitutional provision.[30]

---

25 ibid 74.
26 See Jaclyn Neo, 'A Contextual Approach to Unconstitutional Constitutional Amendments: Judicial Power and the Basic Structure Doctrine in Malaysia' (2020) 15 Asian Journal of Comparative Law 69, 84.
27 Tew (n 1) 46–53.
28 [1987] 2 Malayan LJ 311 (SC).
29 ibid 318 (SC).
30 Still, the phrase "Judicial power of the Federation" remains as a shoulder note to the current Article 121(1) provision.

The occasion for the judiciary to determine the meaning of the amended Article 121(1) provision arose in the 2007 case of *Public Prosecutor v. Kok Wah Kuan*.[31] At issue was a statutory provision for the detention of a juvenile offender convicted of murder at the pleasure of the King. The Federal Court ruled that the provision was constitutional and that it did not impinge on judicial power.

Taking a rigidly literalist view of Article 121(1), the majority in the Federal Court held that the amended provision meant that the courts' powers and jurisdictions must now depend on federal law.[32] Justice Abdul Hamid's majority opinion exhibits a stunningly narrow conception of judicial power:

> After the amendment, there is no longer a specific provision declaring that the judicial power of the Federation shall be vested in the two High Courts. What it means is that there is no longer a declaration that "judicial power of the Federation" as the term was understood prior to the amendment vests in the two High Courts. If we want to know the jurisdiction and powers of the two High Courts we will have to look at the federal law ... But, to what extent such "judicial powers" are vested in the two High Courts depend on what federal law provides, not on the interpretation the term "judicial power" [has] prior to the amendment. That is the difference and that is the effect of the amendment.[33]

The position taken by the *Kok Wah Kuan* majority was nothing short of judicial self-emasculation. As the entity tasked as the final arbiter of constitutional meaning, it bears mentioning that it was open to the Federal Court to interpret the amended article narrowly, in a manner that would have avoided undermining its own position in the constitutional system. Instead, the majority placed a construction on the amended Article 121(1) that in effect converted the courts into little more than entities with begging bowls into which Parliament might, as it pleased, pour jurisdictional crumbs.

Justice Richard Malanjum forcefully dissented in *Kok Wah Kuan*. Declaring that he was "unable to accede to the proposition that as a consequence of the amendment of Article 121(1) ... the courts in Malaysia can only function in accordance with what [has] been assigned to them by federal law,"[34] he wrote:

> The amendment which states that "the High Courts and inferior courts shall have such jurisdiction and powers as may be conferred by or under federal law" should by no means be read to mean that the doctrines of separation of powers and independence of the Judiciary are now no more the basic features

---

31 *Kok Wah Kuan* (n 2). See Richard SK Foo, 'Malaysia – Death of a Separate Constitutional Judicial Power' [2010] Singapore JL Studies 227.
32 *Kok Wah Kuan* (n 2) [11].
33 ibid.
34 ibid [37].

of our Federal Constitution. I do not think that as a result of the amendment our courts have now become servile agents of a federal Act of Parliament and that the courts are now only to perform mechanically any command or bidding of a federal law.[35]

Justice Malanjum's vision of the separation of powers and judicial independence as basic features stands in stark contrast to the majority's approach in *Kok Wah Kuan*, according to which the very existence of the separation of powers hinges on the mercy of the legislature.[36] For years to come, the majority's position of *de facto* parliamentary supremacy – of reflexive deference to the political branches – would pervade much of the Malaysian courts' approach to constitutional review.

5.4 A judicial renaissance? The evolution of the unconstitutional constitutional amendments doctrine in Malaysia

5.4.1 *The rise of the basic structure doctrine in Malaysia*

5.4.1.1 *Establishing the basic structure doctrine: Semenyih Jaya*

The Malaysian Federal Court's unanimous decision in the 2017 case *Semenyih Jaya Sdn Bhd v Pentadbir Tanah Daerah Hulu Langat* represented a landmark assertion of judicial power in Malaysia.[37] On the surface, *Semenyih Jaya* involved a dispute over the adequate amount of compensation for a compulsory land acquisition.[38] But, shorn of its minutiae, the case engaged a broader question about judicial power.

The Land Acquisition Act of 1960 provided for two lay assessors to assist the presiding judge to determine the compensation of acquired land. In 1997, the Act was amended to provide that "the amount of compensation shall be the amount decided upon by the two assessors,"[39] and that any such decision would be "final and there shall be no further appeal to a higher Court on the matter."[40] The question was whether the Land Acquisition Act provisions infringed the Article 121(1) judicial power provision because it allowed lay assessors to conclusively determine the amount of compensation. That set the context for the Federal Court to address the scope of Article 121(1) in light of the 1988 amendment that had removed the provision vesting "the judicial power of the Federation" in the courts.

In a unanimous decision, the Federal Court held that "the judicial power of the court resides in the Judiciary and no other" under Article 121(1) of the

---

35 ibid [38].
36 ibid [22].
37 *Semenyih Jaya* (n 3).
38 Fed. Const. (Malay.), art. 13 ("(a) No person shall be deprived of property save in accordance with law; (b) No law shall provide for the compulsory acquisition or use of property without adequate compensation").
39 Land Acquisition Act 1960 §40D(1).
40 ibid §40D(3).

Constitution.[41] The Court struck down the challenged Land Acquisition provision for imposing on the judge a duty to adopt the determination of the lay assessors regarding the compensation amount.[42] This undermined the judicial power of the court enshrined under Article 121(1),[43] wrote Justice Zainun Ali, as it "effectively usurps the power of the court in allowing persons other than the judge to decide on the reference before it."[44]

It was the first time in two decades that the Malaysian Federal Court had invalidated a federal law. The *Semenyih Jaya* decision is significant for at least three reasons. First, it established that judicial power is vested in the courts and can only be exercised by a judicial body. Second, it signaled a clear departure from the self-emasculating position taken by the majority in the *Kok Wah Kuan*.[45] Third, it gave judicial endorsement to the migration of the basic structure doctrine into the Malaysian constitutional arena.[46]

The *Semenyih Jaya* Court departed from the narrow view of Article 121(1) taken by the *Kok Wah Kuan* majority, instead affirming Justice Richard Malanjum's dissenting opinion. The Court endorsed the view that the courts are "a separate and independent pillar of the Federal Constitution and not mere agents of the federal legislature," and that Article 121(1) "is not, and cannot be, the whole and sole repository of the judicial role in this country."[47] Courts are required "to ensure that there is a 'check and balance' in the system, including the crucial duty to dispense justice according to law for those who come before them."

It is worth noting the Federal Court's invocation of judicial authorities from comparative contexts. In discussing the meaning of "the judicial power of the Federation shall be vested," the Court observed that the phrase had been taken by the framers of the Malaysian Constitution from the Australian Constitution.[48] Australia's Constitution has no express recognition of the separation of power; yet, the neat compartmentalization of the three different organs of government is understood to reflect the separation of powers, and judicial power is recognized as vested in the constitutionally created courts.[49]

The Federal Court in *Semenyih Jaya* affirmed that judicial power can be vested only in the courts, notwithstanding the amendment to Article 121(1):

---

41 *Semenyih Jaya* (n 3) [86].
42 ibid [50].
43 ibid [95].
44 ibid [52].
45 *Kok Wah Kuan* (n 2). See Foo (n 31) 227.
46 On the migration of the basic structure doctrine globally, see Yaniv Roznai, 'Unconstitutional Constitutional Amendments: The Migration and Success of a Constitutional Idea' (2013) 61 American Journal of Comparative Law 657.
47 *Semenyih Jaya* (n 3) [70].
48 ibid [64].
49 See *R v Kirby; Ex parte Boilermakers Society of Australia* (1956) 94 CLR 254, 276 (observing that "for upon the judicature rested the ultimate responsibility for the maintenance and enforcement of the boundaries within which governmental power might be exercised and upon that the whole system was constructed").

> [I]t is clear to us that the 1988 amendment had the effect of undermining the judicial power of the Judiciary and impinge on the following features of the Federal Constitution: (i) The doctrine of separation of powers; and (ii) The independence of the Judiciary.[50]

Denouncing the amendment for seeking to remove the judicial power from the judiciary, leaving the judicial institution "effectively suborned to Parliament, with the implication that Parliament became sovereign,"[51] the Court observed that "[t]his result was manifestly inconsistent with the supremacy of the Constitution enshrined in Article 4(1)."

In a ringing endorsement of the basic structure doctrine to the Malaysian Constitution, the Federal Court declared:

> It is worthwhile reiterating that Parliament does not have power to amend the Federal Constitution to the effect of undermining the features stated in (i) [the doctrine of separation of powers; and (ii) the independence of the judiciary].[52]

The Court bolstered its approach by referring to earlier decisions that had rejected parliamentary supremacy, citing the 2010 decision of *Siravasa Rasiah* for the proposition that "the fundamental rights guaranteed under Part II [of the Constitution] is part of the basic structure of the Constitution and that Parliament cannot enact laws (including Act amending the Constitution) that violate the basic structure."[53] It also invoked *Kesavananda*, the famous authority for the Indian basic structure doctrine, to emphasize that "it is not permissible for the legislature to encroach upon the judicial sphere."[54]

At the heart of the vision of constitutionalism articulated by the Federal Court in *Semenyih Jaya* is a conception of judicial power as foundational to the separation of powers:

> The Judiciary is thus entrusted with keeping every organ and institution of the State within its legal boundary. Concomitantly the concept of the independence of the Judiciary is the foundation of the principle of the separation of powers. This is essentially the basis upon which rests the edifice of judicial power. The important concepts of judicial power, judicial independence and the separation of powers are as critical as they are sacrosanct in our constitutional framework.[55]

---

50 *Semenyih Jaya* (n 3) [74].
51 ibid [75].
52 ibid [76].
53 ibid [79].
54 ibid [87].
55 ibid [88]–[90].

5.4.1.2 Entrenching the basic structure doctrine: Indira Gandhi

Barely a year after *Semenyih Jaya*, the Malaysian apex court further entrenched the constitutional basic structure doctrine in *Indira Gandhi Mutho v Pengarah Jabatan Agama Islam Perak and Others*.[56] In another constitutional landmark, the Federal Court declared the power of judicial review as essential to the role of the courts and inherent to the Malaysian Constitution's basic structure. By contrast with *Semenyih Jaya*, which appeared pragmatically concerned with land acquisition compensation, the dispute in *this* case concerned a highly fraught issue: religion, and the relationship of the civil courts vis-à-vis the religious courts.

Indira Gandhi and her husband were both non-Muslims when they were married. Unbeknown to Indira Gandhi, her husband later converted to Islam, and then obtained certificates of conversion to Islam for their three children, before securing custody orders for the children from the Sharia court. Unable to access the religious courts as a non-Muslim, Indira Gandhi sought an order from the civil court to quash the certificates of conversion and custody orders unilaterally obtained by her ex-husband. She faced the argument that conversion to Islam was a strictly religious matter that was solely within the jurisdiction of the Sharia courts, not the civil courts. Indira Gandhi's case worked its way through the High Court and Court of Appeal, eventually arriving at the Federal Court after almost a decade.

In a unanimous decision, the Federal Court voided all the certificates of conversion, ruling that the constitutional right to equality requires the consent of both parents for the conversion of minor children. It held that civil courts have jurisdiction over all constitutional matters even when matters of Islamic law are involved,[57] departing from a pattern over the last two decades of civil courts extensively deferring jurisdiction to the Sharia courts.[58]

Of particular significance, the Federal Court declared that the power of judicial review is inherent in the basic structure of the Constitution. The Court's unanimous opinion underscores the role of the Court: "Inherent in these foundational principles is the role of the Judiciary as the ultimate arbiter of the lawfulness of state action. The power of the courts is a natural and necessary corollary of the rule of law."[59]

Justice Zainun Ali, writing for the Court as she had in *Semenyih Jaya*, referred to that earlier decision as having "put beyond a shadow of doubt that judicial power is vested exclusively in the High Courts by virtue of art 121(1)."[60] "Judicial independence and the separation of powers are recognized as features in the basic structure of the Constitution," she wrote. "The inherent judicial power of the

---

56 *Indira Gandhi* (n 4).
57 ibid [104].
58 See Yvonne Tew, 'Stealth Theocracy' [2018] 58 Virginia Journal of International Law 31.
59 ibid [33].
60 ibid [42].

civil courts under art 121(1) is inextricably intertwined with their constitutional role as a check and balance mechanism."[61]

Referencing the Indian basic structure doctrine in *Kesavananda* and *Minerva Mills*,[62] the Malaysian court declared that "the power of judicial review is essential to the constitutional role of the courts, and inherent in the basic structure of the Constitution," and thus "cannot be abrogated or altered by Parliament by way of a constitutional amendment."[63]

It then turned to the Article 121(1A) provision, which provides that the civil courts "shall have no jurisdiction in respect of any matter within the jurisdiction of the Sharia courts." It's relevant to note that Article 121(1A) had been inserted when the Constitution was amended in 1988 to alter the Article 121(1) provision on judicial power. The *Indira Gandhi* Court made clear that the "vital role of the judicial review in the basic structure of the constitution" meant that "judicial power cannot be removed from the civil courts."[64]

Strikingly, the Federal Court, in effect, nullified Article 121(1A). It ruled that "the amendment inserting clause 1A into Article 121 does not oust the jurisdiction of the civil courts nor does it confer judicial power on the Sharia courts."[65] Civil courts are constitutionally created entities "invested with inherent judicial powers" whereas the Sharia courts are "creatures of state legislation."[66] "More importantly, Parliament does not have the power to make any constitutional amendment to give such an effect," wrote the Federal Court. "It would be invalid, if not downright repugnant, to the notion of judicial power inherent in the basic structure of the constitution."[67]

In a robust affirmation of judicial power, the Federal Court distilled the following principles in crystal-clear terms:

(a) under art 121(1) of the Federal Constitution, judicial power is vested exclusively in the civil High Courts. The jurisdiction and powers of the courts cannot be confined to federal law. The courts will continually and inevitably be engaged in the interpretation and enforcement of all laws that operate in this country and any other source of law recognised by our legal system;
(b) judicial power in particular the power of judicial review, is an essential feature of the basic structure of the Constitution;
(c) features in the basic structure of the Constitution cannot be abrogated by Parliament by way of constitutional amendment;
(d) judicial power may not be removed from the High Courts; and

---

61 ibid [42].
62 ibid [48], [49].
63 ibid [48].
64 ibid [51].
65 ibid [92].
66 Ibid [80].
67 ibid [92].

(e) judicial power may not be conferred upon bodies other than the High Courts, unless such bodies comply with the safeguards provided in ... the Constitution to ensure their independence.[68]

The apex court explicitly entrenched the basic structure doctrine in the Malaysian constitutional system:

> The powers of judicial review and of constitutional or statutory interpretation are pivotal constituents of the civil courts' judicial power under Article 121(1) .... As part of the basic structure of the constitution, it cannot be abrogated from the civil courts or conferred upon the Syariah Courts, whether by constitutional amendment, Act of Parliament or state legislation.[69]

Among the underlying principles on which the Malaysian Constitution is premised, the Court identified "the separation of powers, the rule of law and the protection of minorities."[70]

The Federal Court in *Indira Gandhi* affirmed the role of the civil courts as sole repositories of judicial power with the power of judicial review. *Indira Gandhi* not only reinforced the principles that were established in *Semenyih Jaya*, but also entrenched the doctrine of judicial review to protect the separation of powers and judicial power as part of the Constitution's basic structure.

5.4.1.3 Affirming the basic structure doctrine: Alma Nudo

In the 2019 case of *Alma Nudo Atenza v Public Prosecutor*, the Federal Court further affirmed the doctrine of a constitutional basic structure.[71] The Court struck down a statutory provision that allowed a double presumption against accused drug traffickers as disproportionate.

Delivering the judgment for a nine-member Court, Chief Justice Richard Malanjum observed that the "courts can prevent Parliament from destroying the 'basic structure' of the [Federal Constitution]."[72] Referring to the *Semenyih Jaya* and *Indira Gandhi*, the Chief Justice stated that:

> while the Federal Constitution does not specifically explicate the doctrine of basic structure, what the doctrine signifies is that a parliamentary enactment is open to scrutiny not only for clear-cut violation of the [Constitution] but also for violation of the doctrine or principles that constitute the constitutional foundations.[73]

---

68 ibid [58].
69 ibid [104].
70 ibid [90].
71 *Alma Nudo* (n 5).
72 ibid [73].
73 ibid.

In line with those earlier decisions, the Federal Court in *Alma Nudo* emphasized that the role of the judiciary is "intrinsic to the constitutional order."[74] "As the bulwark of the Federal Constitution and the rule of law," wrote the Chief Justice, "it is the duty of the Courts to protect the Federal Constitution from being undermined by the whittling away of the principles upon which it is based."[75]

5.4.2 An uneven judicial trajectory

5.4.2.1 Maria Chin Abdullah

In January 2021, in a sharply divided decision, the Federal Court revisited the relevance of the basic structure doctrine to Malaysia's constitutional system in *Maria Chin Abdullah v. Director-General of Immigration*.[76] The case involved a travel ban imposed by the immigration authorities on Maria Chin, a non-governmental organization leader, which prevented her from leaving Malaysia. A clause in the Immigration Act ousted judicial review of any decision made by the immigration authorities.[77] Maria Chin argued that the travel ban was beyond the power of the immigration authorities and, further, challenged the ouster clause as unconstitutional in light of the principles affirming judicial power and the separation of powers in *Semenyih Jaya* and *Indira Gandhi*.

The Federal Court ruled that the travel ban was unlawful on the grounds that the Immigration Director General does not have unfettered discretionary power to impose a travel ban on a citizen.[78] But the Court split 4–3 on the constitutionality of the Immigration Act clause preventing judicial review, an issue that brought to the fore the Article 121(1) provision on judicial power. Two opinions were delivered for the majority and two for the dissent.

Justice Abdul Rahman Sebli, writing one of the majority opinions, held that the ouster clause was consistent with Article 121(1), which provides that courts "shall have such jurisdictions and powers as may be conferred by federal law." Taking a "literal interpretation" of Article 121(1), Justice Abdul Rahman Sebli found the provision "irresistibly clear and unambiguous."[79] Since Parliament had determined through the Immigration Act that the courts' jurisdiction and powers are limited on immigration matters, the courts could not ignore the limitation imposed by the ouster clause.[80] The justice reasoned that the constitutional framers had not viewed that Article 121(1) set up conferral of the court's jurisdiction and powers by federal law as contrary to the separation of powers.[81]

---

74 ibid [74].
75 ibid [91]
76 *Maria Chin* (n 6).
77 Immigration Act 1959/63, §59A.
78 *Maria Chin* (n 6) [255] (Abdul Rahman Sebli FCJ).
79 ibid [85].
80 ibid [88]–[89].
81 ibid [98].

Constitutional amendments in Malaysia 101

This majority opinion contains an excursus on the basic structure doctrine that is openly skeptical about the doctrine's applicability to the Malaysian context: "Article 121(1) of the Federal Constitution cannot be suborned to any doctrine of law, including the Indian doctrine of basic structure and the common law doctrine of separation of powers."[82] "What poses a problem in the context of a written constitution is the application of the so-called 'doctrine' of basic structure,"[83] wrote Justice Abdul Rahman Sebli, "This leads to a situation where a law that is duly passed by Parliament is rendered void for offending the doctrine of separation of powers even where it is not inconsistent with the express terms of the Federal Constitution."[84] He dismissed the cases of *Semenyih Jaya*, *Indira Gandhi*, and *Alma Nudo* as inapplicable to the present case,[85] observing that the articulation of the basic structure doctrine in those cases was "at best *obiter dicta*."[86] In his view, "*Semenyih Jaya*, *Indira Gandhi*, and *Alma Nudo* cannot be read ... as deciding that Parliament has no power to amend the Federal Constitution."[87]

Justice Mary Lim wrote a concurring opinion, which was also joined by the other two of the majority justices.[88] In her view, it was unnecessary to determine the constitutionality of the ouster clause in light of *Semenyih Jaya* and *Indira Gandhi*; that question was unnecessary – in her words, "an overkill" – for determining the case.[89] Notably, though, Justice Mary Lim's opinion expressly acknowledges the basic structure doctrine in *Semenyih Jaya*:

> Where the jurisdiction and power of the court is interfered with in absolute terms as was the case in *Semenyih Jaya* ... the court has no hesitation in striking down such provision as offending the doctrine of basic structure as enshrined within art. 4.[90]

Two opinions were delivered for the three judges in dissent. In her dissent, Chief Justice Tengku Maimun defended the Federal Court's earlier decisions on judicial power as part of the basic structure:

> The principles set forth in *Semenyih Jaya* and *Indira Gandhi* are irrefutably clear ... no matter how art. 121(1) was or may have been amended, it being a basic feature of the [Federal Constitution], remains to be read as it was prior to the 1988 amendment.

---

82 ibid [122].
83 ibid [130].
84 ibid [131].
85 ibid [163]–[164].
86 ibid [165].
87 ibid [167].
88 ibid [257]–[377] (Mary Lim FCJ).
89 ibid [354]–[357].
90 ibid [282]. See also [272]–[273].

The 1988 amendment had "no effect whatsoever of diminishing or subordinating judicial power to Parliament or declaring Parliament supreme in any way."[91]

Where does this leave the current state of the basic structure doctrine in Malaysia's constitutional jurisprudence? For some commentators, the *Maria Chin* majority opinion heralded the demise of the basic structure doctrine in Malaysia.[92]

Rumors of the doctrine's death, we think, have been greatly exaggerated.[93] To be sure, there is much in Justice Abdul Rahman Sebli's opinion that stands at odds with the Federal Court's holdings in *Semenyih Jaya* and *Indira Gandhi* on the Article 121(1) judicial power provision and the constitutional basic structure. On careful inspection, though, the *Maria Chin* decision does not negate the basic structure doctrine established by the Malaysian Federal Court in *Semenyih Jaya, Indira Gandhi*, and *Alma Nudo*.

First, Justice Abdul Rahman Sebli's opinion was not the only majority judgment in *Maria Chin*, and his critique of the basic structure doctrine is not shared by most of the judges in the case. As noted earlier, Justice Mary Lim is clear that the Court would have "no hesitation in striking down" a provision that prohibits judicial scrutiny "as offending the doctrine of basic structure,"[94] and she specifically held that the question about the basic structure was not relevant for determining the *Maria Chin* decision. All four judges in the majority concurred with the opinion of Justice Mary Lim, in addition to that of Justice Abdul Rahman Sebli.[95] All of which is to say, the only common holding shared by the two majority judgments relates solely to the validity of the Immigration Act's ouster clause, not the basic structure doctrine. And, of course, all three dissenting justices repudiated Justice Abdul Rahman Sebli's criticisms of the basic structure doctrine. All told: "This leaves Abdul Rahman Sebli FCJ's judgment alone in its attack on *Semenyih Jaya* and the basic structure doctrine."[96]

Second, Justice Abdul Rahman Sebli acknowledges that the precedents of *Semenyih Jaya* and *Indira Gandhi* do not apply to *Maria Chin*; on his own account, then, his opinion's discussion of the basic structure doctrine is merely obiter. Justice Abdul Rahman Sebli observed that "not only are the facts in *Semenyih Jaya* and *Indira Gandhi* different" to the Immigration Act context in *Maria Chin*, "but the constitutional and/or legal issues raised were also different."[97]

---

91 ibid [453]–[454] (Tengku Maimun FCJ).
92 See, e.g., Iqbal Harith Liang, 'Maria Chin v Director General of Immigration: The Basic Structure Doctrine's Demise?' (*Malaysian Public Law*, 9 January 2021) https://malaysianpubliclaw.com/maria-chin-v-director-general-of-immigration-the-basic-structure-doctrines-demise/.
93 To paraphrase the quote popularly attributed to Mark Twain, https://www.oxfordreference.com/view/10.1093/acref/9780199990009.001.0001/acref-9780199990009-e-9198.
94 *Maria Chin* (n 6) [282] (Mary Lim FCJ).
95 ibid [377].
96 Tan Kian Leong and Shukri Shahizam, 'O Bitter Pill to Swallow: Separating Ratio from Dicta in Maria Chin Abdullah' [2021] 1 Malayan LJ ccccii.
97 *Maria Chin* (n 6) [70] (Abdul Rahman Sebli FCJ).

Since *Semenyih Jaya* and *Indira Gandhi* were both dismissed as inapplicable to the *Maria Chin* context, Justice Abdul Rahman Sebli's views on the constitution's basic structure appear to be no more than dicta.

More broadly, *Maria Chin* does not affect the central holdings in *Semenyih Jaya* and *Indira Gandhi* establishing that the judicial power of the courts is fundamental to the constitution's basic structure. The Federal Court held in *Semenyih Jaya* that the 1988 amendment to Article 121(1) could not remove the courts' judicial power, which constitutes a fundamental feature of the basic structure. According to Justice Abdul Rahman Sebli, "on the facts of the present case, [there is] no removal of judicial power or conferral of judicial power to a non-judicial branch;"[98] and so, "where no amendment is made to the Constitution, the doctrine has no application and is irrelevant."[99] His majority opinion itself acknowledges that *Maria Chin* does not directly involve any constitutional amendment nor the removal of judicial power from the courts. Indeed, Justice Abdul Rahman Sebli's opinion expressly accepts that "*Semenyih Jaya* is authority for the proposition that a non-judicial body cannot bind the superior courts," and "*Indira Gandhi* for the proposition that Syariah Courts are not of equal status to the superior civil courts."[100] It follows, then, that none of the opinions in *Maria Chin* undermine the central holdings concerning judicial power and the constitution's basic structure established in *Semenyih Jaya* and *Indira Gandhi*.

Viewed against the broader arc of the evolution of the basic structure doctrine in Malaysian constitutional law, *Maria Chin* might represent a speedbump, but it is hardly an impenetrable roadblock.

5.4.3 *The separation of powers, judicial power, and the basic structure doctrine*

With the trilogy of decisions in *Semenyih Jaya*, *Indira Gandhi*, and *Alma Nudo*, the Malaysian Federal Court carved out a role for the courts to protect a constitutional core of fundamental features as beyond the legislative intrusion. A striking aspect about the evolution of the basic structure doctrine in Malaysia is the judicial statecraft exhibited by the Malaysian Federal Court in developing the doctrine through bold, but also prudent, jurisprudence.[101]

The Federal Court developed its assertion of judicial power in careful stages, beginning with its 2017 decision in *Semenyih Jaya*, in which a unanimous Court established the foundation for the judicial review of constitutional amendments by identifying certain features as fundamental to the constitution and observing that these principles were beyond Parliament's amendment power.[102] Yet the

---

98 ibid [103].
99 ibid [141].
100 ibid [164]
101 Tew (n 1) 133–40.
102 *Semenyih Jaya* (n 3) [76].

Court did not expressly invalidate the constitutional amendment in *Semenyih Jaya*; instead, it read down the 1988 constitutional amendment, in effect nullifying the amendment by interpreting Article 121(1) to mean that judicial power continues to reside in the courts.[103] By refraining from striking down the amendment outright, the Court avoided provoking immediate political backlash while laying down the seeds for a doctrine of an immutable constitutional core.

Then, the following year, the Federal Court in *Indira Gandhi* powerfully entrenched and enforced the basic structure doctrine, declaring that "the power of judicial review is essential to the constitutional role of the courts and inherent in the basic structure of the Constitution," which "cannot be abrogated or altered by Parliament by way of a constitutional amendment."[104] In this unanimous judgment, the Court nullified the Article 121(1A) constitutional amendment and declared the principles foundational to the Constitution as "the separation of powers, the rule of law, and the protection of minorities."[105]

Later, in the 2019 case of *Alma Nudo*, a full bench of nine Federal Court justices reaffirmed the basic structure principles laid down in *Semenyih Jaya* and *Indira Gandhi*. The Court referred to both those decisions to reiterate that:

> This court has, on several occasions, recognised that the principle of separation of powers, and the power of the ordinary courts to review the legality of State action, are sacrosanct and form part of the basic structure of the [Federal Constitution].

More recently, some judgments reveal divisions on the Federal Court regarding the salience of the basic structure doctrine in the Malaysian constitutional order.[106] Like the *Maria Chin* majority decision by Justice Abdul Rahman Sebli, these cases show some backtracking about the doctrine's applicability

---

103 See Wilson Tay, 'Basic Structure Revisited: The Case of *Semenyih Jaya* and the Defence of Fundamental Constitutional Principles in Malaysia' (2019) 14 Asian Journal of Comparative Law 113.
104 *Indira Gandhi* (n 4) [48].
105 ibid [90].
106 See *Maria Chin* (n 6). See also *Rovin Joty A/L Kodeswaran v Lembaga Pencegahan Jenayah* [2021] 2 Malayan L J 822 (majority stating that the basic structure doctrine "should not be pressed into use in aid of interpretation" of the Federal Constitution, but acknowledging that the doctrine was not applicable for construing the constitutionality of the Prevention of Crimes Act in that case); *Zaidi bin Kanapiah v ASP Khairul Fairoz bin Rodzuan* [2021] 3 Malayan L J 759 (the majority upholding a provision of the Prevention of Crimes Act, relying on *Maria Chin* and *Rovin Joty* to state that the basic structure doctrine had no place in Malaysia, with the Chief Justice joined by another justice dissenting). However, *Rovin Joty* has been vacated on successful application for review by the Federal Court, to be heard de novo. The Chief Justice, writing for the Court, noted that the majority in *Rovin Joty* "did not allude to any suggestion by the respondents that basic structure doctrine is doctrinally wrong or most fundamentally, that it does not exist. *See Nivesh Nair v Abdul Razak Musa*, at [26] (Cr. Appl. No: 05(RJ)-2-03/2021(W)).

to Malaysia's Constitution. Even so, such judgments have far from definitively eroded the foundations of the basic structure doctrine established by the Federal Court's unanimous decisions in *Semenyih Jaya*, *Indira Gandhi*, and *Alma Nudo*. Those three unanimous decisions – joined by a total of 19 justices – laid down the groundwork for protecting foundational principles of separation of powers and judicial power, which Malaysian courts can build on to shape future constitutional adjudication.

5.5 The potential reach of the basic structure doctrine

5.5.1 Emergency powers and constitutional ouster clauses

What is the potential scope of the basic structure doctrine in Malaysia? This section speculates on the implications of the doctrine by examining constitutional amendment challenges that have already emerged on the horizon.

One challenge involves the constitutional amendment passed in 1981 to the Malaysian Constitution's Article 150 emergency powers provisions. In 1981, Article 150 was amended with the insertion of a clause that deprived the courts of jurisdiction to determine the validity of a proclamation of emergency and orders of preventive detention. Article 150(8) now provides that the King's satisfaction that a grave emergency exists "shall be final and conclusive and shall not be challenged or called in question in any court on any ground."[107] Moreover, "no court shall have jurisdiction to entertain or determine any application, question or proceeding, in whatever form, on any ground," regarding the validity of a proclamation of emergency or the continued operation of an emergency ordinance. As one of us has argued previously, the width of this constitutionally entrenched ouster clause amounts to an abrogation of the judicial power of the courts: "[T]he new clause (8) has undermined the basic structure of the Constitution as all questions concerning emergency powers are left to the absolute discretion of the Government of the day."[108]

In January 2021, the King issued a proclamation of emergency, pursuant to Cabinet advice, purportedly to combat the COVID-19 pandemic.[109] The state of emergency was slated to last till August 1, 2021. During this time, an emergency ordinance promulgated under the proclamation suspended the sitting of Parliament and the legislative assemblies of the States.

All of this occurred in the aftermath of the Perikatan Nasional coalition taking over governance in March 2020 after the breakdown of the Pakatan Harapan coalition. After taking power without an electoral mandate, Prime Minister

---

107 Article 150(8)(a).
108 HP Lee, 'Emergency Powers in Malaysia' in FA Trindade and HP Lee (eds), *The Constitution of Malaysia: Further Perspectives and Developments* (OUP 1986) 135, 151.
109 Muhyiddin Yassin, at the time the prime minister and head of the Perikatan Nasional government, had attempted to convince the King to proclaim a state of emergency in October 2020, but the King rejected the Prime Minister's plan.

Muhyiddin Yasin faced persistent calls to prove that he commanded the support of the majority in Parliament. Critics viewed the suspension of Parliament during this state of emergency as a move to prevent the Prime Minister's support from being tested on the floor of Parliament.

The emergency proclamation has led to two challenges before the High Court. In response to the first challenge, brought in March 2021 by three elected representatives, the High Court ruled that Article 150(8) precluded judicial review of the King's emergency proclamation and the enacted ordinances.[110] The second lawsuit brought by opposition leader Anwar Ibrahim challenged the constitutionality of the Prime Minister's advice to the King to suspend Parliament during the emergency.[111] In April 2021, the High Court rejected Anwar Ibrahim's application for judicial review, also on the grounds that Article 150(8) effectively precluded judicial review of matters relating to the proclamation of an emergency.[112] Should the Federal Court decide to hear these cases on appeal, the basic structure doctrine will likely be at the forefront of challenges to the validity of the Article 150(8) constitutionally entrenched ouster clauses.

5.5.2 Royal assent as a feature of the Constitution's basic structure?

That's not all. Another lawsuit brought by Anwar Ibrahim seeks to invalidate the National Security Council Act 2016 as well as the constitutional amendments involving the royal assent to legislation.[113] The National Security Council Act passed in 2016 empowers the Prime Minister, on advice of a national security council, to declare a security area, over which the Prime Minister has the power to deploy security forces. The Malaysian Bar Council has denounced the security law for enabling "the Prime Minister, either unilaterally or through the NSC, to exercise authoritarian executive powers," adding that "[t]hese powers are in

---

110 Bernama, 'Emergency proclamation cannot be challenged: High Court' (*The Malaysian Reserve*, 11 March 2021) <https://themalaysianreserve.com/2021/03/11/emergency-proclamation-cannot-be-challenged-high-court/> accessed 28 May 2021.
111 Ida Lim, 'Anwar sues PM over Parliament suspension in Emergency, seeks court order to declare Muhyiddin's advice to Agong illegal, unconstitutional' (*Malay Mail*, 26 January 2021) <https://www.malaymail.com/news/malaysia/2021/01/26/anwar-sues-pm-over-parliament-suspension-in-emergency-seeks-court-order-to/1944059 > accessed 28 May 2021.
112 'Court throws out Anwar's bid to challenge emergency proclamation' (*Free Malaysia Today*, 22 April 2021) https://www.freemalaysiatoday.com/category/nation/2021/04/22/court-throws-out-anwars-bid-to-challenge-emergency-proclamation/? accessed 28 May 2021.
113 *Datuk Seri Anwar Ibrahim v Government of Malaysia & Anor* [2020] 4 Malayan LJ 133. The basic structure issue was one of the questions posed to the Federal Court of Malaysia following a referral to the apex court by the High Court regarding questions raised in Anwar Ibrahim's application.

effect emergency powers, but without the need for a proclamation of an emergency under Article 150 of the Federal Constitution."[114]

One of the grounds on which the National Security Act was challenged is that it was passed without the assent of the King following what are argued to be unconstitutional constitutional amendments.[115] When the Barisan Nasional government tried to pass the National Security Council Bill in 2016, the King did not give his assent to the contentious security bill. Nonetheless, the national security law came into force because of the legislative procedure put in place by constitutional amendments that dispensed with the requirement for royal assent. As a result of these constitutional amendments, passed in 1983, 1984, and 1994, the Constitution now provides that after the Bill has been submitted to the King and 30 days have elapsed, the bill shall become law "in the like manner as if [the King] had assented thereto."[116]

Thus, the question was whether the National Security Council Act was unconstitutional because it had "become law pursuant to unconstitutional amendments," on the ground that those amendments violated the basic structure of the Constitution. In other words, the royal assent was argued to constitute a basic feature of the Constitution that cannot be removed by complying with the constitutional amendment process.

In a 5–2 decision delivered in February 2020, the Federal Court declined to answer the question on the constitutionality of the National Security Council Act and the constitutional amendments.[117] The majority ordered the case to be struck out, holding that the questions posed – on the constitutionality of the statute and the constitutional amendment – were abstract and purely academic. The dissenting justices were clear that they would have been prepared to find the statute unconstitutional for violating the Constitution's Article 149 anti-subversion provisions as well as being a disproportionate restriction on the constitutional right to freedom of movement. But on the basic structure point, Justice David Wong reasoned that the royal assent remains a part of the legislative process as a matter of construction, hence "the question as to the violation of the basic structure of the Constitution does not arise."[118]

---

114 Steven Thiru, 'Bar: Hallmarks of authoritarianism in government's NSC Act move' (*Malaysiakini*, 15 June 2016) <https://www.malaysiakini.com/news/345378> accessed 28 May 2021.
115 Shad Saleem Faruqi, 'A precedent but no blanket pass' (*The Star*, 23 June 2016) <http://www.thestar.com.my/opinion/columnists/reflecting-on-the-law/2016/06/23/a-precedent-but-no-blanket-pass-article-66-4a-permits-the-king-to-be-bypassed-but-cannot-apply-to-ot/> Steven Thiru, 'Bar: Hallmarks of authoritarianism in government's NSC Act move' (*Malaysiakini*, 15 June 2016) <https://www.malaysiakini.com/news/345378> accessed 28 May 2021.
116 Fed. Const. (Malay.), Section 66(4A).
117 *Anwar Ibrahim* (n 113).
118 ibid [146].

The majority and the dissenting justices in this 2020 decision avoided the question about the validity of the constitutional amendments, thus allowing the Federal Court to navigate out of having to determine whether the royal assent falls within the constitutional basic structure, a minimalist move that appeared prudent.[119] The invocation of the basic structure doctrine with regard to the royal assent is a double-edged sword when appreciated against the backdrop of Malaysian *realpolitik*. The constitutional amendments in 1993, 1984, and 1994 arose at a time when then-Prime Minister Mahathir Mohamad was engaged in a convulsive constitutional battle with the Malay rulers after the conduct of some of the Rulers had given rise to concerns that they were exceeding their role as *constitutional* monarchs;[120] these included reported instances of some Rulers withholding their assent to state legislation because they could not get their way with their state government. Writing in support of applying the basic structure doctrine to the Malaysian constitutional arena, Andrew Harding once remarked that "decisions must be guided by instinct."[121] Judicial instinct is needed to determine not just when to invoke the doctrine, but also when to avoid doing so.

More generally, although it remains to be seen how far the Malaysian apex court will extend the basic structure doctrine in cases to come, it seems apparent that the doctrine will increasingly play a role in future constitutional challenges.

5.6 Conclusion

Constitutional adjudication is bound up in constitutional politics. Courts in Malaysia, as in many other fragile democracies in Asia, face the sensitive task of navigating powerful political actors in seeking to enhance the judiciary's position as a constitutional stakeholder. That endeavor is ever more challenging – and ever more crucial – amidst a political landscape in flux.

For decades, Malaysia operated under a dominant ruling coalition, the Barisan Nasional alliance, which had held power since before the country's independence in 1957. That ended in 2018, when Barisan Nasional was voted out in an

---

119 Anwar Ibrahim subsequently filed an application to review the Federal Court's February 2020 decision. In January 2021, the Federal Court, after rehearing the case, reserved decision on the question regarding whether the National Security Act was unconstitutional because it did not receive the royal assent. At the time of going to print, it was reported that the Federal Court had delivered a decision in August 2021 in which it has rejected the challenge to the constitutionality of the National Security Council Act 2016, with the Court holding that the constitutional amendments to royal assent of legislation did not engage the basic structure doctrine. See *Datuk Seri Anwar Ibrahim v. Kerajaan Malaysia* (Civ. Appl. No. 06(RS)-1-03/2019(W)).
120 For an account of the constitutional battle over the royal assent, see HP Lee, *Constitutional Conflicts in Contemporary Malaysia* (2nd edn, OUP 2017) chapter 2. See also Raja Tun Azlan Shah, 'The Role of Constitutional Rulers in Malaysia' in FA Trindade and HP Lee (eds), *The Constitution of Malaysia: Further Perspectives and Developments* (OUP) chapter 5.
121 AJ Harding, 'The Death of a Doctrine? *Phang Chin Hock v Public Prosecutor*' [1979] 21 Malaya Law Review 365, 373.

unprecedented election outcome, resulting in the transfer of government power to the Pakatan Harapan coalition – the Alliance of Hope – in the country's first ever democratic transition.

And then came 2020. A domestic government crisis, and a global pandemic. In March 2020, the Pakatan Harapan government collapsed, following political defections and a leadership battle between political rivals. Prime Minister Muhyiddin Yassin was appointed premier by the King, at the helm of Perikatan Nasional, a hastily assembled coalition that returned many members of the Barisan Nasional government to power. Citing the coronavirus pandemic, in January 2021, a nationwide state of emergency was declared, followed by the government announcing the suspension of Parliament; by August 2021 however, internal power struggles within the Perikatan Nasional government saw Prime Minister Muhyiddin Yassin replaced by Ismail Sabri Yaakob, the country's third premier in three years.[122]

It is against this background of constitutional politics – of a long history of dominance by a single political alliance, and of deeply fragile political dynamics in transition – that the evolution of judicial power and the unconstitutional constitutional amendments doctrine in Malaysia must be understood. Faced with consolidated political power for much of the nation's post-independence history, the Malaysian judiciary's path toward becoming an effective constraint on the governing powers has been described as Sisyphean.[123]

Yet, in recent times, the Malaysian courts have shown signs of judicial willingness to reassert power, through the careful, but unmistakable, development of the basic structure doctrine. With strategic maneuvering, the Malaysian Federal Court set the groundwork for safeguarding foundational constitutional elements from being altered by the legislature in its 2017 decision in *Semenyih Jaya*.[124] A year later, in another display of judicial statecraft in *Indira Gandhi*, the apex court explicitly endorsed the constitutional basic structure doctrine, invoking the power to nullify a constitutional amendment that curtailed the civil courts' power of judicial review.[125] And in subsequent cases in 2019 and 2020, the Federal Court affirmed that the doctrine that "courts can prevent Parliament from destroying the basic structure of the Constitution" is now part of Malaysian constitutional jurisprudence.[126]

---

122 'Malaysia gets a new prime minister — the country's third in 3 years' (CNBC, 20 August 2021) <https://www.cnbc.com/2021/08/20/malaysia-king-appoints-ismail-sabri-yaakob-as-new-prime-minister.html> accessed 14 September 2021.
123 HP Lee and Richard Foo, 'The Malaysian Judiciary: A Sisyphean Quest for Redemption?' in HP Lee and Marilyn Pittard (eds), *Asia-Pacific Judiciaries: Independence, Impartiality and Integrity* (CUP 2018) chapter 11.
124 *Semenyih Jaya* (n 3).
125 *Indira Gandhi* (n 4).
126 *Alma Nudo* (n 5) [73]. See also *JRI Resources Sdn Bhd v. Kuwait Finance House* [2019] 3 Malayan LJ 561 [240] (Chief Justice Richard Malanjum observing that "the basic structure doctrine is very much part of this country's judicial landscape"); *Anwar Ibrahim* (n 113)

Judicial embrace of the basic structure doctrine in Malaysia has not been ubiquitous, however. Recent Federal Court judgments, like the Maria Chin judgment and other decisions delivered in 2021, underscore that some judges reject the basic structure doctrine's relevance in Malaysia's constitutional context.[127] That not all judicial quarters have embraced the notion that there can be implied limits on constitutional amendments is unsurprising, especially for judges navigating a fraught political context. But it does not decisively undermine the basic structure doctrine established by the apex court's contemporary jurisprudence.

Of course, the precise contours of the doctrine's operation in Malaysia remain to be worked out. What seems undeniable, though, is that the notion of an implied domain of unamendable features has begun to alter the landscape of Malaysia's constitutional order and that doctrine will increasingly be invoked in future constitutional litigation, as recent constitutional challenges only confirm.[128]

The trajectory of judicial power in a fragile democracy rarely moves in a straight line; it zigs and zags. With its unanimous decisions in *Semenyih Jaya*, *Indira Gandhi,* and *Alma Nudo* establishing judicial review over constitutional amendments, the Malaysian Federal Court put in place a firm foundation for a potent judicial mechanism that empowers courts to protect basic principles of separation of powers and judicial review as part of the constitution's foundational core. Even so, ultimately, the doctrine's effectiveness rests on judicial willingness to wield this powerful tool.

Dayung sudah di tangan, perahu sudah di air, as a Malay proverb goes, "The paddle is already in hand, the canoe is already in the water." While the exact shape of the Malaysian courts' path may yet be uncertain, the way forward has been clearly lit.

---

[110] (Justice David Wong observing "[w]hat remains clear at this juncture is that the assertion that there is no such thing as basic structure doctrine, may no longer be made").
127 *Maria Chin* (n 6) (majority opinion of Justice Abdul Rahman Sebli).
128 See, for example, *Datuk Seri Anwar Ibrahim v. Kerajaan Malaysia* (Civ. Appl. No. 06(RS)-1-03/2019(W); *Nivesh Nair v Abdul Razak Musa*, at [26] (Cr. Appl. No: 05(RJ)-2-03/2021(W)). See also recent cases revealing the Federal Court's divide on the basic structure doctrine (n 106).

6 Amending constitutional standards of parliamentary piety in Pakistan?
Political and judicial debates

Matthew J Nelson

6.1 Introduction

Notwithstanding extensive engagement with so-called "basic structure" jurisprudence, which the Supreme Court of India has used to strike down constitutional amendments seen as violating the essential features or implied basic structure of India's Constitution, the Supreme Court of Pakistan has never struck down any constitutional amendment duly promulgated by parliament. This chapter nevertheless considers an emerging debate regarding the possibility of unconstitutional constitutional amendments (UCA) in Pakistan. Focusing on what the Supreme Court of Pakistan has called the "salient" features of Pakistan's Constitution, with particular reference to underpinning *Islamic* features, this debate has divided politicians and judges alike.

Among politicians, one strain of this debate has focused on a constitutional clause known as Article 62(1)(f). Part of an omnibus constitutional amendment known as the Eighth Amendment – introduced in 1985 by a parliament convened under Pakistan's third military dictator, General Zia-ul-Haq – this clause outlines some of the standards qualifying individuals to stand for election and serve as parliamentarians. Inter alia, it requires such individuals to remain *ameen* or trustworthy in a religious (Qur'anic) sense.[1] A July 2017 Pakistan Supreme Court decision disqualifying Prime Minister Nawaz Sharif for failing to qualify as ameen, however, reignited a debate about the possibility of removing what some described as a link between "vague" Islamic norms and eligibility for parliamentary election.[2] Today, cross-party support for repealing Article 62(1)(f) is strong.

At the same time, turning to the judicial side of the debate, a number of questions have emerged regarding the *limits* of parliament's amending powers. These questions have intensified since an August 2015 Supreme Court judgment known as *District Bar Association Rawalpindi v Federation of Pakistan*.[3] This judgment did not strike down any constitutional amendments; it actually upheld Pakistan's

---

1 The term "ameen" refers to someone who is honest, reliable, or trustworthy – see for example Qur'an 28:26.
2 *Imran Ahmed Khan Niazi v Mian Muhammad Nawaz Sharif* (PLD 2017 SC 692).
3 *District Bar Association Rawalpindi v Federation of Pakistan* (PLD 2015 SC 401).

DOI: 10.4324/9781003097099-6

Eighteenth, Nineteenth, and Twenty-First Amendments. But, for the first time ever, a Supreme Court majority held that any duly promulgated constitutional amendment seen as violating the salient features or basic structure of Pakistan's Constitution could and should be annulled. (In previous judgments, this was a minority view. And, in *District Bar Association*, the majority found no specific violation.) Inter alia, building on several previous judgments, the Supreme Court cited Pakistan's "parliamentary form of government *blended with Islamic provisions*" as an unamendable salient feature of Pakistan's constitution. It may be that this reference linking a "parliamentary" form of government to "Islamic" provisions could limit the future amendability of Article 62(1)(f).

With respect to parliament's power of constitutional amendment, including amendments touching on Article 62(1)(f), the tussle between parliamentarians and judges has been particularly fraught since one portion of Pakistan's Eighteenth Amendment, known as Article 175A, sought to shift control over the *appointment* of superior-court judges – that is, both Supreme Court and provincial High Court judges – from the superior judiciary to parliament. Just six months after the Eighteenth Amendment was promulgated in April 2010, however, a preliminary Supreme Court short order known as *Nadeem Ahmed v Federation of Pakistan* responded to Article 175A, citing "judicial independence" with respect to judicial appointments as yet another unamendable salient feature of the constitution.[4] This in turn led the country's parliament to "reconsider" its approach to Article 175A with a further amendment – Pakistan's Nineteenth Amendment – restoring a leading role for the Supreme Court vis-à-vis all superior-court appointments. As such, there was no practical need for the Supreme Court to strike down parliament's initial approach to Article 175A when its full judgment (*District Bar Association Rawalpindi* 2015) was issued five years later.

In effect, the Supreme Court of Pakistan has used its articulation of (unamendable) constitutional "salient features" to craft an understanding in which (a) judges are empowered to assess the Qur'anic qualifications of individual parliamentarians (Eighth Amendment: Article 62(1)(f)) even as (b) parliamentarians are *not* empowered to assess the qualifications of individual judges (Eighteenth/Nineteenth Amendments: Article 175A). This understanding of the constitution's salient features – "judicial independence" on the one hand; a "parliamentary form of government blended with Islamic provisions" on the other – has, in many ways, clarified the *institutional* underpinnings of an ongoing debate regarding the religious parameters of parliamentary democracy in Pakistan.

If, responding to the disqualification of Prime Minister Nawaz Sharif and several other politicians described as insufficiently ameen, Pakistani politicians were to amend or repeal Article 62(1)(f), would Pakistan's Supreme Court intervene to annul that amendment as a salient-feature violation of Pakistan's "parliamentary form of government *blended with Islamic provisions*"? In what follows I combine the historical, political, and judicial elements of this question with a small set

---

4 *Nadeem Ahmed v Federation of Pakistan* (PLD 2010 SC 1165).

of interviews targeting senior political and judicial figures to illuminate the link between globally familiar forms of basic-structure jurisprudence and emerging debates regarding the parameters of Islamic constitutionalism in Pakistan.

6.2 Constitutional basic structure: From India to Islam

Even before India's Supreme Court clarified its notion of constitutional "basic structure" in 1973, debates regarding the *relative* power of parliament and the courts, vis-à-vis constitutional amendments, were travelling back and forth between India and Pakistan.

Within India's Constituent Assembly (1947–9), the dawn of these debates can be found in efforts to abandon British notions of unfettered parliamentary sovereignty in favour of a broadly American commitment to enumerated and enforceable rights. These efforts prompted numerous questions about the degree to which parliament's power of constitutional amendment, enshrined in Article 368 of India's Constitution, might extend to amending or abrogating basic rights – and, then, how India's Supreme Court might respond to any such manoeuvre. In fact, India's first constitutional amendment, seeking to protect government land reforms from any form of judicial review based on claims of inconsistency with a fundamental right to property, was reviewed – and subsequently upheld – in a Supreme Court case known as *Shankari Prasad v Union of India* (1951).[5]

A later case known as *I.C. Golak Nath v State of Punjab* (1967), however, offered a different view.[6] In this case, the Supreme Court cited a Pakistan Supreme Court case known as *Fazlul Quader Chowdhry v Muhammad Abdul Haque* (1963), which considered the "essential features" and "basic structure" of Pakistan's constitution.[7] Specifically, *I.C. Golak Nath* held that, henceforth, even duly promulgated constitutional amendments could not "take away" or "abridge" the essential features of India's constitution, including fundamental rights.

India's parliament, however, did not embrace the Court's decision in *I.C. Golak Nath*. In fact, India's parliament promulgated the Twenty-Fourth Amendment (1971) asserting that parliament's amending power was *not* limited by any articulation of fundamental rights. Yet, two years later, this back-and-forth prompted India's landmark basic-structure decision in *Kesavananda Bharati Sripadagalvaru v State of Kerala* (1973).[8] In this case, India's Supreme Court held that, although India's parliament was empowered to "amend" any provision of the constitution, the Supreme Court was empowered to strike down

---

5 *Shankari Prasad v Union of India* (AIR 1951 SC 450).
6 *I.C. Golak Nath v State of Punjab* (AIR 1967 SC 1643).
7 *Fazlul Quader Chowdhry v Muhammad Abdul Haque* (PLD 1963 SC 486) nullified an order issued by Pakistan's first dictator, General Ayub Khan, allowing cabinet members to serve as parliamentarians despite the "presidential" form of government Ayub introduced in Pakistan's second constitution (1962: Article 104).
8 *Kesavananda Bharati Sripadagalvaru v State of Kerala* (AIR 1973 SC 1461).

any amendment that might appear to "abrogate" whatever the Court chose to define as the (implied) basic structure of India's constitution, including (a) federalism, (b) a parliamentary form of government, (c) fundamental rights (including a "secular" approach to religion–state relations), and (d) judicial independence.

A similar debate emerged in Pakistan, but this time India's focus on *fundamental rights* was set aside in favour of a debate regarding the Supreme Court's power – possibly in conjunction with an associated "Mulla Board" – to review parliamentary actions for their compliance with *Islamic injunctions*.[9] In fact, one member of Pakistan's first Constituent Assembly (1947–54), Abdulla al-Mahmood, criticised the Indian Supreme Court decision in *Shankari Prasad* (1951) for its claim to provide parliament with unfettered powers of constitutional amendment. Al-Mahmood argued that, in Pakistan, the Federal Court (later, Supreme Court) must be empowered to review even duly promulgated constitutional provisions to ensure they were not "repugnant" to the injunctions of the Qur'an and *sunnah* (i.e. prophetic tradition).[10]

In Pakistan, this link between notions of constitutional basic structure and "Islam" is often associated with a feature of the constitution known as the Objectives Resolution. Approved by Pakistan's first Constituent Assembly in 1949, then preserved as a preamble in Pakistan's first (1956), second (1962),[11] and third (1973) constitutions, this Resolution was recast as a substantive article (Article 2A) via Pakistan's Eighth Amendment under General Zia-ul-Haq in 1985. The Resolution states that, while "sovereignty over the entire universe belongs to Almighty Allah" and the authority of Pakistan's people will be exercised within "the limits prescribed by Him" (as "a sacred trust"), the citizens of Pakistan will nevertheless exercise their authority via "chosen representatives" working alongside an "independent judiciary." Within this Resolution, the balance between Pakistan's "parliamentary form of government" and its commitment to "Islamic provisions" is clear.

Even apart from this Objectives Resolution, however, Pakistan's Constitution contains several references linking parliamentary authority to Islam. Its list of non-justiciable "Principles of Policy" notes that "steps shall be taken to enable … Muslims … to order their lives in accordance with the fundamental principles … of Islam" (1956 "Directive Principles": Article 25; 1962 "Principles of Policy": Article 8(1)(1); 1973: Article 31). A further portion entitled "Islamic Provisions" states that legislation considered "repugnant" to the injunctions of Islam will be barred – although, having said this, a strictly *advisory* Council of Islamic Ideology was established by the President to support the country's National and Provincial Assemblies with compliance (1956: Article 198; 1962: Article 204; 1973:

---

9 See Leonard Binder, *Religion and Politics in Pakistan* (California 1961), 104, 169, 236, 265, 279, 289–91, 324, 337–8, 342.
10 *Constituent Assembly Debates* (22 October 1953), 317.
11 The language of the preambular Objectives Resolution was diluted in Pakistan's second Constitution (1962) but restored to its original form in a First Amendment one year later.

Articles 227–30). Pakistan's president and prime minister are, in turn, constrained by a series of oaths ensuring that they must be "Muslims" (1956: Article 32; 1962: Article 19; 1973: Article 41) – indeed, after 1973, when Islam was finally specified as Pakistan's state religion (Article 2), that neither the president nor the prime minister would belong to a heterodox minority known as the Ahmadiyya.[12]

In 1985, the terms of Article 62 were also adjusted via Pakistan's Eighth Amendment to stipulate that Muslim parliamentarians must have "adequate knowledge of Islamic teachings" and "practice [the] obligatory duties prescribed by Islam" while "abstain[ing] from major sins" (Article 62(1)(e)) – indeed, that *any* parliamentarian facing a court judgment regarding dishonesty would stand disqualified for failing to meet the required standard of being "ameen" (Article 62(1)(f)).

The Eighth Amendment also moved beyond parliamentary to judicial power, supplementing the advisory work of Pakistan's Council of Islamic Ideology with *binding* powers for a new Federal Shariat Court and a "Shariat Appellate Bench" of the Supreme Court (Article 203D/E). Both courts were empowered to decide whether any law – apart from Muslim personal laws, various fiscal and financial laws, and, crucially, *the constitution itself* – might be deemed "repugnant" to Islam, rendering such laws ineffective until an alternative could be framed by Pakistan's elected representatives on the orders of the president or, in the case of provincial laws, the president's appointed governor.

Again, Abdulla al-Mahmood urged Pakistan's first Constituent Assembly to ensure that Pakistan's highest court was empowered to test for Islamic repugnancy up to and including the Constitution itself. But, when Pakistan's first constitution emerged in 1956, this view was set aside. Instead, recalling the views articulated by the Indian Supreme Court in *Shankari Prasad* (1951), Pakistan's first Constitution stipulated that any amendment duly promulgated by parliament would "not be questioned in any court" (Article 216).[13]

This clause regarding unfettered parliamentary powers of constitutional amendment was removed in Pakistan's second and third constitutions (1962: Articles 208–9; 1973: Articles 238–9). But, in 1985, Pakistan's Eighth Amendment imported two provisions directly from India's constitution to restore and strengthen it. Article 239(5) – in India, Article 368(4) – specified

---

12 The Ahmadiyya see themselves as Muslims; they recognise a late-nineteenth-century religious reformer named Ghulam Ahmad who claimed to receive revelations like a prophet, but in 1974 Pakistan's Second Amendment followed the constitution's Third Schedule in defining a "Muslim" as one who "does not believe in, or recognize as a prophet or religious reformer, any person who claimed or claims to be a prophet … after Muhammad" (Article 260).
13 Pakistan's second Constituent Assembly featured a sovereign parliament informed by an advisory Council of Islamic Ideology (Binder, 371). See also G.W. Choudhury, 'Constitution-Making Dilemmas in Pakistan', *Political Research Quarterly* 8:4 (1955), 589–600; I.H. Qureshi (then Education Minister) noted that "the legal Sovereign shall be the Muslim Law, but its definition shall be in the hands of a legislature representing the people," 591.

that "no amendment of the Constitution shall be called in[to] question by any court." Article 239(6) – in India, Article 368(5) – noted that, "for the removal of doubt ... there is no limitation whatever on the power of ... parliament to amend any of the provisions of the Constitution."[14] It is worth noting that India's Forty-Second Amendment (1976), which introduced these two provisions, was struck down by the Indian Supreme Court in a case known as *Minerva Mills Ltd v Union of India* (1980).[15] Specifically, *Minerva Mills* read these provisions as a violation of "judicial independence" (and, thus, a violation of India's constitutional "basic structure"). But, in Pakistan, both provisions remain in place.

In Pakistan, however, these two provisions prompted a number of questions regarding the degree to which parliament's "unlimited" powers of constitutional amendment might extend to Islamic provisions. These questions are particularly interesting insofar as (a) parliamentary considerations of Islamic repugnancy are *not* bound by the advice of Pakistan's Council of Islamic Ideology and (b) the binding power of Pakistan's Federal Shariat Court does *not* extend to an assessment of constitutional provisions. As such, parliament's power to shape and reshape ostensibly "Islamic" constitutional provisions would appear to remain quite unlimited, both with respect to the Council of Islamic Ideology and with respect to Pakistan's Federal Shariat Court. In fact, even *after* the 1962 removal of Article 216 (amendments will "not be questioned in any court"), but *before* the 1985 introduction of Article 239(6) (there is "no limitation" whatsoever on parliament's amending power) – Pakistan's Supreme Court continued to respect parliament's power to shape Pakistan's Constitution, including its Islamic provisions.[16]

In the Lahore High Court case of *Zia-ur-Rahman v The State* (1972), for instance, followed by a Supreme Court appeal known as *The State v Zia-ur-Rahman* (1973), the courts considered whether parliament was empowered to introduce changes in Pakistan's third Constitution (1973) that might be described as "repugnant to Islam."[17] In this context, Justice Afzal Zullah of the Lahore High Court focused on Pakistan's Objectives Resolution, describing it as a "supra-constitutional instrument" that was "so fundamental" it "[could] not ...

---

14 In the Constitution of India (1950), Article 368 stated that "parliament may, in exercise of its constituent power, amend ... any provision of this Constitution." India's Forty-Second Amendment added that "[n]o amendment of this Constitution ... shall be called in[to] question in any court on any ground" (Article 368-4) and, "[f]or the removal of doubts ... there shall be no limitation whatever on the constituent power of parliament to amend ... the provisions of this Constitution" (Article 368-5).
15 *Minerva Mills Ltd v Union of India* (1980 2 SC 591).
16 See the Second Amendment to Pakistan's third constitution, which removed state recognition for Ahmadis' fundamental right of religious self-identification as "Muslims" (1974), as well as the Fifth and Sixth Amendments, which altered patterns of judicial appointment (1975).
17 *Zia-ur-Rahman v The State* (PLD 1972 Lahore 382); *The State v Zia-ur-Rahman* (PLD 1973 SC 49).

be repealed or abrogated."[18] But, on appeal, the Supreme Court Chief Justice, Hamood-ur-Rahman, held that, while the Objectives Resolution could be said to provide some type of constitutional *grundnorm*, it was still just a constitutional preamble. As such, Rahman noted that this (non-justiciable) Resolution could *not* be used to strike down or test any other part of the constitution. In fact, departing from *I.C. Golak Nath* (1967) and the impending logic of *Kesavananda* (1973) in India, Chief Justice Rahman went out of his way to stress that, in Pakistan, the Supreme Court had "never claimed … the right to strike down any provision of the constitution."[19]

This deference to parliamentary power vis-à-vis constitutional amendments, including amendments pertaining to Islam, was further reiterated in cases like *Islamic Republic of Pakistan v Abdul Wali Khan* (1976) ("this court [remains] committed to the view that 'the judiciary cannot declare any [constitutional] provision … to be invalid or repugnant'") as well as *Fauji Foundation v Shamimur Rehman* (1983) (parliament's "amending power, unless it is restricted, can amend, vary, modify or repeal any provision of the Constitution").[20] It also appeared in cases like *Federation of Pakistan v United Sugar Mills* (1977), which reviewed Pakistan's Fourth Amendment (regarding, inter alia, reserved parliamentary seats for non-Muslims) before accepting it precisely insofar as it was duly promulgated by parliament.[21] In fact, until the Supreme Court's preliminary short order reviewing Pakistan's Eighteenth Amendment in *Nadeem Ahmed* (2010) and, then, its final decision in *District Bar Association Rawalpindi* (2015), the Supreme Court consistently deferred to parliament's amending power.

Even in *District Bar Association Rawalpindi* (2015), the Court's majority did not strike down any amendment duly promulgated by parliament. Instead, the majority simply indicated that, henceforth, such amendments could and should be struck down if, in the eyes of the Court, they were found to alter the constitution's essential features or abrogate its basic structure, including its "parliamentary form of government blended with Islamic provisions."

6.3 Constitutional amendments: From the Eighth (1985) to the Eighteenth (2010)

Within Pakistan, debates regarding unconstitutional constitutional amendments are not rooted in a history of judicial annulments. Instead, they grow out of enduring questions regarding the degree to which parliament's amending power might extend to "Islamic" provisions and, then, whether a parliamentary push to *amend* those provisions might lead Pakistan's Supreme Court to move away from

---

18 *Zia-ur-Rahman v The State* (1972).
19 *The State v Zia-ur-Rahman* (1973).
20 *Islamic Republic of Pakistan v Abdul Wali Khan* (PLD 1976 SC 57); *Fauji Foundation v Shamimur Rehman* (PLD 1983 SC 457).
21 *Federation of Pakistan v United Sugar Mills* (PLD 1977 SC 397).

its traditional deference to parliament's amending powers, effectively abandoning its "descriptive" account of the constitution's salient features in favour a more robust "proscriptive" approach in which amendments seen as *violating* those features are annulled.[22] So far this has not occurred. But, since 2015, politicians and judges have begun to consider whether it might.

Two closely related amendments have shaped the emerging debate. The first is Pakistan's Eighth Amendment (1985), which recast the Objectives Resolution as a substantive constitutional article (Article 2A) and indemnified several executive orders introduced by General Zia-ul-Haq after his military coup in 1977. This amendment also incorporated several provisions seeking to check the power of Pakistan's parliament – for example, Article 58(2)(b), which endowed Pakistan's president with discretionary powers to dissolve Pakistan's parliament as a whole,[23] as well as provisions affecting individual parliamentarians, including Article 62(1)(f).

In an effort to stem the anti-democratic effects of this Eighth Amendment, however, the second relevant amendment is the Eighteenth Amendment (2010), which removed Article 58(2)(b) but left several references to Islam, including Article 62(1)(f), intact. As such, the constitutional threat facing Pakistani parliamentarians has shifted: from the discretionary power of Pakistan's head of state or president under Article 58(2)(b) (1947–73, 1985–2010) to specific "Islamic" standards adjudicated by Pakistan's courts via Article 62(1)(f) (1985–present).

6.3.1 The Eighth Amendment, the Eighteenth Amendment, and Islam

To place these elements in context, it is important to note that Pakistan's third Constitution (1973) was suspended following a military coup led by General (later President) Zia-ul-Haq in 1977. Zia ruled by decree until 1985, when non-party elections ushered in a new parliament that, in exchange for ending martial law, restored Pakistan's third Constitution alongside an omnibus Eighth Amendment. Inter alia, this amendment recast Pakistan's preambular Objectives Resolution as Article 2A while restoring Article 58(2)(b) and adding Article 62(1)(f). In fact, to protect these alterations from any judicial review, the Eighth Amendment also imported Articles 239(5) and 239(6) from India. These articles clarified that, henceforth, no amendment should be "called in[to] question by any court" as there was "no limitation" whatsoever on the amending power of

---

22 See Waqqas Mir, 'Saying Not What the Constitution Is ... But What It Should Be: Comment on the Judgment on the 18th and 21st Amendments to the Constitution' (2015) 2 LUMS Law Journal 64, 69.

23 Article 58(2)(b) was derived from Article 19(2)(c) of the Government of India Act (1935), which allowed Britain's colonial Governor-General to dissolve India's Federal Assembly at his "discretion." After independence, this power was transferred to Pakistan's president in the country's first and second constitutions (1956: Article 50; 1962: Article 23). It was removed in 1973 but restored in 1985 (58(2)(b)).

parliament (at that time, a non-party parliament still dominated by General/President Zia).

During the late 1980s and 1990s, however, even *after* the death of General Zia, Pakistan's presidents routinely exercised the discretionary powers in Article 58(2)(b). Zia himself dissolved the government of Prime Minister Mohammad Khan Junejo in 1988. And, in 1990, Zia's successor President Ghulam Ishaq Khan dissolved the government of Pakistan People's Party (PPP) Prime Minister Benazir Bhutto. In 1993, President Khan went on to remove Pakistan Muslim League (PML-N) Prime Minister Nawaz Sharif. And, in 1996, Khan's successor Farooq Leghari removed Benazir Bhutto (again). When Nawaz Sharif returned to power in 1997 with a huge single-party majority, however, he used that majority to repeal Article 58(2)(b) via Pakistan's Thirteenth Amendment. Unfortunately, having repealed Article 58(2)(b), he was not removed by constitutional means but ousted in a military coup led by General Pervez Musharraf two years later. After cobbling together a new parliament in 2002, however, General (President) Musharraf pushed through a Seventeenth Amendment restoring Article 58(2)(b).

General (President) Musharraf later tried to sack Pakistan's Supreme Court Chief Justice, Iftikhar Muhammad Chaudhry, after Chaudhry entertained a case challenging Musharraf's bid to stand for re-election as president without first holding National and Provincial Assembly elections to create a fresh Electoral College for that purpose. Chaudhry successfully challenged Musharraf's attempt to remove him.[24] But, just a few months later, anticipating an adverse Supreme Court judgment regarding an element of the Seventeenth Amendment allowing Musharraf to serve, simultaneously, as president and Chief of the Army Staff (COAS), Musharraf declared a state of emergency (November 2007). Suspending the Constitution and postponing elections scheduled for January 2008, Musharraf removed Chief Justice Chaudhry and several other judges from their posts.

Protests led by district lawyers subsequently prompted Musharraf to resign as COAS. And, following the assassination of Benazir Bhutto (December 2007), elections were finally held in February 2008. Led by Benazir Bhutto's widower, Asif Ali Zardari, the PPP emerged from these elections as the leader of a ruling coalition alongside PML-N leader Nawaz Sharif, with both parties vowing to impeach Musharraf (still serving as president) and reinstate the judges he had sacked. Unfortunately, fearing that Chief Justice Chaudhry might revive a set of corruption cases targeting Zardari, the government proceeded with its impeachment campaign against Musharraf (prompting Musharraf to resign from the presidency in August 2008, after which Zardari was sworn in as president) *without* reinstating Chaudhry. This failure to reinstate Chief Justice Chaudhry, however,

---

24 *Chief Justice of Pakistan v President of Pakistan* (2007 PLD SC 578).

led the PML-N to abandon the PPP-led governing coalition and support a further round of protests until Chaudhury was finally reinstated in March 2009.[25]

In an enduring push to shore up the power of Pakistan's parliament after several years of military dictatorship, however, both the PPP and the PML-N came together in April 2010 to support Pakistan's Eighteenth Amendment, which, as noted above, removed Article 58(2)(b) even as it enhanced parliament's power vis à vis the appointment of judges (Article 175A). Steering clear of the Constitution's "Islamic" features, however, the Eighteenth Amendment did *not* remove or substantially alter Article 62(1)(f).[26] In fact, even as it sought to restore key features of Pakistan's 1973 Constitution, the final text appeared to accommodate an increasingly religious strand of public opinion. Specifically, PML-N leader Nawaz Sharif and Islamist parties like the Jama'at-e-Islami positioned themselves as defenders of religious values, resisting any alteration of Zia's ostensibly "Islamizing" amendments.[27] In short, the Eighteenth Amendment removed a threat posed by the discretionary powers of Pakistan's president (Article 58(2)(b)) even as it retained a broadly "Islamic" threat tied to the power of the judiciary (Article 62(1)(f)).

6.3.2 Political versus judicial power: "District Bar Association Rawalpindi"

Mindful of the role that Pakistan's Supreme Court had played in accepting earlier military coups,[28] as well as previous civilian efforts to massage the appointment of judges,[29] one key part of the Eighteenth Amendment sought to clarify parliament's role in the appointment of both High Court and Supreme Court judges.[30] Specifically, Article 175A created a Judicial Commission with a mix of judicial and non-judicial members to prepare a list of nominees for consideration by an eight-member Parliamentary Committee.[31] This Parliamentary Committee was

---

25 Iftikhar Muhammad Chaudhry continued to serve as Chief Justice until his retirement in December 2013.
26 In their 'Notes of Reiteration on the Constitutional Reform Package' (Annex D-II, 21 March 2010), Awami National Party leaders Haji Mohammad Adeel and Afrasiab Khattak argued that, within Article 62, "Sub Clauses (d), (e), (f), and (h) shall be omitted."
27 'Nawaz Himself Supported Article 62: Khursheed' (*Business Recorder*, 14 April 2018).
28 See *The State v Dosso* (1958 PLD SC 533); *Begum Nusrat Bhutto v Chief of the Army Staff and Federation of Pakistan* (1977 PLD SC 657); *Zafar Ali Shah v Pervez Musharraf* (PLD 2000 SC 869).
29 See n 17, above.
30 Article 175A responded to a case known as *Al-Jehad Trust* (PLD 1996 SC 324) wherein the Supreme Court tied the process of superior-court appointments to judicial independence as a "salient feature" of the constitutional "basic structure."
31 The Judicial Commission included the chief justice, two further Supreme Court justices, and a retired chief justice or Supreme Court justice plus the Federal Law Minister, the Attorney General, and a senior lawyer nominated by the bar. The Parliamentary Committee included four members from Pakistan's National Assembly and four from the Senate distributed evenly between the government and opposition benches.

empowered to *reject* the Judicial Commission's recommendations – citing reasons that were, nevertheless, justiciable.

Alongside a Twenty-First Amendment (2015) introducing time-limited military courts to try civilians accused of religious terrorism,[32] however, judicial concerns regarding this appointment process – and its implications for "judicial independence" – prompted the landmark basic-structure decision known as *District Bar Association Rawalpindi* (2015). As the Supreme Court pointed out, both the Eighteenth Amendment and the Twenty-First Amendment raised "a common ... question," namely, "whether there are any limitations on the powers of the Parliament to amend the Constitution" and, faced with a challenge to the independence of the judiciary (read as a constitutional "salient feature"), "whether the Courts possess jurisdiction to strike down a constitutional amendment" (Page 10, Para 5; Page 78, Paras 67, 69). Previously, the Supreme Court had responded to such questions with a definitive "no."[33] But, in *District Bar Association Rawalpindi*, the Court began to modify this view.

To understand the Court's change of focus, it is necessary to revisit the preliminary short order known as *Nadeem Ahmed* (2010), which urged parliament to "reconsider" its approach to Article 175A by expanding the Judicial Commission with two further Supreme Court justices (thus creating an absolute Supreme Court majority). Issued unanimously by a full bench of the Supreme Court on 30 September 2010, *Nadeem Ahmed* was led by Chief Justice Chaudhry, who, according to one senior lawyer, was "at the peak of his powers" having just been reinstated with support from a nationwide grassroots protest movement.[34]

In fact, two of the retired Supreme Court chief justices I interviewed explained that, for nearly three days before its *Nadeem Ahmed* order, the Court seriously considered striking down Article 175A; but, instead, it returned to its traditional focus on parliament's power of constitutional amendment and urged the parliament to avail its privileges under a special provision *within* the Eighteenth Amendment (Article 267A) allowing members to "reconsider" their work to remove any difficulties with a simple majority of both houses. In other words, the Court opted to avoid an annulment in favour of a staged approach – one that, according to both former chief justices, recognised (a) the importance of reinforcing parliamentary power after nearly ten years of dictatorship as well as (b) the broad parliamentary consensus underpinning the Eighteenth Amendment. If parliament had *refused* to heed the Court's recommendations, however, both

---

32 The Twenty-First Amendment's military courts were subject to renewal every two years (renewed in 2017; lapsed in 2019).
33 In *Pakistan Lawyers Forum* (2005 PLD SC 719), the Court stressed "almost three decades of settled law to the effect that even though there were certain Salient Features of the Constitution, no Constitutional Amendment could be struck down by the Superior Judiciary as being violative of those features." "The remedy ... lay in the political and not the judicial Process" (Para 57).
34 Interview, Feisal Naqvi, 29 September 2020.

chief justices suggested that Pakistan's first-ever basic structure annulment was very much in play.

It is impossible to know whether this historical, political, and judicial push in the direction of basic structure jurisprudence, underpinned by a popular chief justice with an activist judicial personality (i.e. Chief Justice Chaudhry), would have emerged without the momentum surrounding the 2007–9 Lawyers Movement. However, we do know that parliament's Nineteenth Amendment accommodated the unanimous recommendation in *Nadeem Ahmed*, thus removing any need to nullify Article 175A when the Eighteenth Amendment was fully reviewed in *District Bar Association Rawalpindi* five years later. As Khurshid Ahmad from the Jama'at-e-Islami – another member of the Parliamentary Committee on Constitutional Reforms in 2010 – told me, "the tone and temper of the judiciary during that period, particularly [that of Chief] Justice Chaudhry, was such that we didn't want a clash." As a result, he explained, parliament simply "conceded."[35]

It is, in many ways, difficult to read this pivotal moment as a simple clash of institutions: legislature vs. judiciary. Politically, the case of *Nadeem Ahmed* that prepared the ground for *District Bar Association Rawalpindi* was clearly underpinned by a powerful pro-democracy protest movement – a movement focused not only on the authority and independence of the judiciary, but also, on the restoration of a charismatic chief justice. The politics, as such, were not merely principled; they were also highly personalised.

6.4 Essential features: From 'District Bar Association Rawalpindi' to Islam

The decision in *District Bar Association Rawalpindi* ran to more than 900 pages. Four Supreme Court justices stressed the presence of Articles 239(5) and 239(6) and maintained that there was *no constraint whatsoever on parliament's power to amend Pakistan's constitution*: in short, neither the Eighteenth nor the Nineteenth Amendment (nor the Twenty-First) could be struck down.[36] In fact, responding to those who asked whether parliament could go so far as to amend "constitutional provisions regarding [an] Islamic way of life and Islam being the State religion," Justice Asif Saeed Khosa wrote that "Islam is not just ... a salient feature of the Constitution" but "a matter of faith transcending any constitutional dispensation," before immediately pivoting to a specific defence of parliament's unfettered amending powers: "if at some future stage the people of this country have a change of heart or mind" with respect to such provisions, he

---

35 Interview, Khurshid Ahmed, 31 October 2020. One of the Supreme Court judges I interviewed described this parliamentary "concession" as a moment of "political sagacity," recognising that, "in case we don't defer to the Supreme Court reference, it could be challenged [i.e. annulled]."
36 The four justices were Asif Saeed Khosa, Nasir-ul-Mulk, Mian Saqib Nisar, and Hameed-ur-Rehman.

noted, "the will of the people will have its way and the aspirations of yore ... may not be able to shackle it" (Para 6).

Still, others embraced a new approach. Justice Jawwad S. Khwaja, for instance, noted that while Articles 239(5) and 239(6) might oust the "courts" from any review of duly promulgated amendments, they did not prevent the country's *highest* court, that is, the Supreme Court, from defending the constitution's "basic structure" (Para 18). In fact, *rejecting* the Court's history of deference to parliament's power of constitutional amendment, Justices Ejaz Afzal Khan, Ijaz Ahmed Chaudhry, and Dost Muhammad Khan built on Khwaja's view to support an annulment of the Eighteenth Amendment, the Twenty-First Amendment, or both. Justices Ejaz Afzal Khan and Ijaz Ahmed Chaudhry were particularly keen to stress the "Islamic" underpinnings of Pakistan's constitutional basic structure.[37]

In the end, however, eight justices speaking for the Court's majority sought to carve out a certain middle ground. While recognising the Court's power to annul amendments that appeared to conflict with the constitution's salient features, they chose to uphold the Eighteenth/Nineteenth and Twenty-First Amendments as duly promulgated changes that were *consistent* with the constitution's salient features: "Parliament, in view of Articles 238 and 239, is vested with the power to amend the Constitution as long as the Salient Features of the Constitution are not repealed, abrogated, or substantively altered," they noted.[38] But, having said this, they stressed that the Court was still empowered "to examine ... any Constitutional Amendment so as to determine whether any of the Salient Features ... ha[d] been repealed, abrogated or substantively altered." And, then, turning to the case at hand, they argued that, "in view of the provisions of the 19th Constitutional Amendment," Article 175A "d[id] not offend against the Salient Features."[39]

Before *District Bar Association Rawalpindi* (2015), a majority within the Court had never favoured striking down a duly promulgated constitutional amendment. But in 2015 this changed, prompting numerous questions regarding future constitutional amendments – including those touching on Islamic provisions. If, in keeping with the constituent powers and procedures outlined in Article 239(5) and 239(6), Pakistan's parliament were to move beyond the realm of "judicial independence" (Article 175A) to consider an amendment touching on "Islamic provisions" (Article 62(1)(f)), would Pakistan's post-2015 Supreme Court consider nullifying that amendment as an essential-features violation of the constitution's parliamentary form of government "*blended with Islamic provisions*"?

---

37 See also the *District Bar Association Rawalpindi* opinion by Justice Sarmad Jalal Osmany.
38 The eight justices were Shaikh Azmat Saeed, Umar Ata Bandial, Sarmad Jalal Osmany, Gulzar Ahmed, Mushir Alam, Maqbool Baqar, Anwar Zaheer Jamali, and Amir Hani Muslim.
39 See the *District Bar Association Rawalpindi* opinion by Justice Jawwad S. Khwaja (Para 96).

6.5 "Islamic" constraints on parliament's amending power?

Decades before, in the case of *Zia-ur-Rahman* (1973), Pakistan Supreme Court Chief Justice Hamood-ur-Rahman noted that preambular references to Islam in Pakistan's Objectives Resolution could *not* be used to test other parts of the constitution. But, then, as a result of this judgment, Pakistan's Eighth Amendment (1985) elevated the Objectives Resolution to the status of a substantive article within the constitution itself (Article 2A), leading Justice Tanzil-ur-Rahman of the Sindh High Court to hold, in *Bank of Oman Ltd v East Trading Co. Ltd.* (1987 Karachi), that "[a]ny provision of the constitution ... found repugnant to [Article 2A]" could be "declared ... as void."[40] In fact, Rahman went even further in the case of *Irshad H. Khan v Parveen Ijaz* (1987), noting that Article 2A's reference to "the sovereignty of Almighty Allah" should be seen as controlling the rest of the constitution.[41]

Still, this high court push for a "proscriptive" basic structure reading of Article 2A rooted in references to the "sovereignty" of Allah and the "limits" prescribed by Him invariably failed in the Supreme Court. In *Hakim Khan v Government of Pakistan* (1992), for instance, the Supreme Court considered Pakistan's Qisas and Diyat Ordinance (1990), which provided for an "Islamic" approach to retribution in cases of physical injury as well as monetary compensation for murder.[42] In Islamic law, those who suffer injury, in addition to the heirs of murder victims, are empowered to pardon offenders. But in Pakistan, some argued that Article 45 of the Constitution, which gave the president unlimited powers of pardon, cut against Article 2A's references to injunctions "set out in the Holy Qur'an and Sunnah." In fact, pointing to a possible clash between Article 45 and Article 2A, some argued that Article 45 should be annulled. But, in *Hakim Khan*, the Supreme Court disagreed, noting that Article 2A was merely equal to every other constitutional provision. Specifically, Justice Nasim Hasan Shah noted that, where two articles appeared to clash, the only remedy lay in a duly promulgated constitutional amendment reconciling or correcting that clash.

Indeed, the same view resurfaced with reference to Article 58(2)(b). As allegations emerged that military elites and opposition parties had conspired with various presidents to bring down elected governments rather than waiting for fresh elections in 1988, 1990, 1993, and 1996, the dissolution of Prime Minister Bhutto's second government by President Farooq Leghari in 1996 was challenged in a basic structure case known as *Mahmood Khan Achakzai v Federation of Pakistan* (1997).[43] This case looked beyond the president's discretionary actions under Article 58(2)(b) to consider the constitutionality of the Eighth Amendment as a whole. Specifically, it examined the degree to which a focus on

---

40 *Bank of Oman Ltd v East Trading Co. Ltd.* (PLD 1987 Karachi 404, 445).
41 *Irshad H. Khan v Parveen Ijaz* (PLD 1987 Karachi 466).
42 *Hakim Khan v Government of Pakistan* (PLD 1992 SC 595).
43 *Mahmood Khan Achakzai v Federation of Pakistan* (PLD 1997 SC 426).

"presidential" powers in Article 58(2)(b) might be seen as a distortion of Article 2A's description of the Constitution's "parliamentary" basic structure.

Still, Supreme Court Chief Justice Sajjad Ali Shah returned to the reasoning articulated by Justice Nasim Hasan Shah in *Hakim Khan*. Dismissing the case, the Chief Justice noted that, although Article 2A "when read with other provisions" could be said to reflect "salient features" of the constitution – including (for the first time) "[a] parliamentary form of government blended with Islamic provisions" – Article 58(2)(b) also gave certain powers to the president as a matter of "checks and balances" (ostensibly, "to forestall a situation in which martial law could be imposed").[44] In fact, Shah read *both* Article 2A *and* Article 58(2)(b) as amendments duly promulgated by parliament that could not be struck down precisely insofar as their mix of parliamentary, presidential, and religious checks and balances did not irredeemably alter "a parliamentary form of government blended with Islamic provisions" (Para 27). As Justice Saleem Akhtar went on to declare in his concurring opinion, "the theory of basic structure" had been "completely ... rejected" in Pakistan (Para 34): Article 58(2)(b) could be altered or removed, but only by a further amendment.

In short, there was no indication during the late 1980s, 1990s, or 2000s that Pakistan's Supreme Court might nullify a duly promulgated constitutional amendment as an essential-features or basic-structure violation rooted in the Islamic features of Article 2A (or, for that matter, any other Islamic provision). Departing from the Court's traditional deference to parliament's amending power, that step emerged in conjunction with a series of cases tied to the "Islamic" features of Article 62(1)(f).

6.5.1 Debating Article 62(1)(f): Judges versus parliamentarians

Embracing a broad interpretation of Article 62(1)(f), some judges sought to frame a rather expansive sense of the requirement that parliamentarians must be "ameen." But, while agreeing that such religious terms were obscure, vague, or subjective (*Ishaq Khan Khakwani v Mian Nawaz Sharif* PLD 2015 SC 275),[45] the Supreme Court generally saw fit to disqualify parliamentarians found guilty by a court of dishonesty.[46] In fact, politicians from all major parties were disqualified

---

44 See *Achakzai* short order (Para 3).
45 Khosa described Article 62(1)(f) as "a feast of legal obscurities" (Para 3(f)) based on the ideal qualities of a Prophet rather than a practical standard for a government of "sinful mortals."
46 See *Mudassar Qayyum Nahra v Ch. Bilal Ijaz* (2011 SCMR 80); *Malik Iqbal Ahmad Langrial v Jamshed Alam* (PLD 2013 SC 179); *Abdul Ghafoor Lehri v Returning Officer PB-29* (2013 SCMR 1271); *Muhammad Khan Junejo v Federation of Pakistan* (2013 SCMR 1328); *Allah Dino Khan Bhayo v Election Commission of Pakistan* (2013 SCMR 1655). The Court refused to disqualify individuals where clear evidence was not established: *Waqas Akram v Dr. Tahir-ul-Qadri* (PLJ 2003 SC 9); *Rana Aftab Ahmad Khan v Muhammad Ajmal* (PLD 2010 SC 1066).

for bogus academic credentials, false declarations regarding their dual citizenship, and so on.

The most important case, by far, was *Imran Ahmed Khan Niazi v Mian Muhammad Nawaz Sharif* (2017), which removed Prime Minister Nawaz Sharif for withholding information in an application to stand for re-election – information regarding unaccrued payments (read as an "asset") for his service as the chairman of a Dubai-based company owned by his son. Already, a related judgment regarding unclear funding for four flats with a rather complex ownership structure in London had cited an expanding body of caselaw treating legal evidence of dishonesty as a breach of Article 62(1)(f).[47] But, even then, the precise meaning of "ameen" remained unspecified. In fact, a frustrated Supreme Court Justice Khosa noted in the case of *Imran Ahmed Khan Niazi* that, in the absence of any clarifying amendment, the Court itself was obliged to intervene and suggest a meaning for such terms. In particular, and despite his own earlier comments regarding the "obscurity" of terms like ameen, Khosa explained that, although Article 62(1)(f) applied to Muslims and non-Muslims alike,[48] its meaning should be clarified with reference to Qur'anic sources (Para 115).[49]

Justice Azmat Saeed responded that the Court should not "arrogation [sic.] unto itself the power to vet candidates on moral grounds" (Para 37) – a view he reiterated in a related judgment known as *Sami Ullah Baloch v Abdul Karim Nowsherwani* (2018),[50] wherein he argued that the constitutionally unspecified *duration* of any Article 62(1)(f) disqualification should be clarified, not by the Court, but by parliamentarians. Overall, however, the Court's majority in *Sami Ullah Baloch* disagreed. The majority returned to Khosa's claim that, in the absence of any amendment clarifying the duration of Article 62(1)(f) disqualifications, the judiciary was compelled to intervene. In particular, returning to Islamic standards rooted in the Qur'an and sunnah (Paras 3, 14–19), the Court built on several prior cases to declare that a ban for "illegal" dishonesty was permanent so long as the judgment finding that dishonesty remained in place (Para 23). "If at all the period of embargo … is to be relaxed," noted Justice Umar Ata Bandial, writing for the majority, this would follow "only from a Constitutional amendment by the Parliament" (Para 3).

In short, parliament was empowered to amend the Constitution, *including Article 62(1)(f)*. But, until it exercised that power, the Court was obliged to define the constitutional meaning of terms like ameen and, then, to define the duration of any disqualification for those judged "not ameen" within the

---

47 See *Constitution Petitions 29* and *30* (2016) as well as *Constitution Petition 03* (2017).
48 Previously, in *Raja Muhammad Afzal v Muhammad Altaf Hussain* (1986 SCMR 1736), the Court noted that, because Article 62(1)(f) applied to non-Muslims, its "spiritual" and "religious" content had to be "ignored" (Para 14).
49 Khosa endorsed (Para 121) the Qur'anic verses highlighted by Justice Qazi Faez Isa while Isa was serving as Chief Justice in Balochistan (*Molvi Muhammad Sarwar v Returning Officer PB-15* 2013 CLC 1583).
50 *Sami Ullah Baloch v Abdul Karim Nowsherwani* (PLD 2018 SC 405).

(Qur'anic) parameters set by the Court. Historically, in India, basic structure jurisprudence has been used to remove elected legislators for a failure to reflect the terms of "secularism" (as defined by India's Supreme Court).[51] In *Imran Ahmed Khan Niazi* and *Sami Ullah Baloch*, Pakistan simply embraced a similar approach, disqualifying parliamentarians seen as insufficiently ameen in an "Islamic" sense (as defined, again, by the Supreme Court).

"There is no cavil with the fact that Article 62(1)(f)—introduced by a dictator—should be repealed/amended," noted Saad Rasool (2018), "because it holds the possibility of becoming a tool for moral witch-hunts." Still, Rasool felt that any repeal should be treated as "a choice [for the] … legislature."[52] And, yet, with Article 62(1)(f) increasingly tied to the Islamic elements of a constitutional basic structure that was, itself, tied to "a parliamentary form of government blended with Islamic provisions," one might reasonably ask: was a repeal of Article 62(1)(f) really an option for the legislature?

6.5.2 Debating Article 62(1)(f): Parliamentarians versus parliamentarians

By 2018, the cases of *District Bar Association Rawalpindi*, *Imran Ahmed Khan Niazi*, and *Sami Ullah Baloch* had revitalised an important debate regarding the degree to which Pakistani parliamentarians were empowered to promulgate amendments touching on Islamic provisions – specifically, provisions concerning the Qur'anic qualifications of individual parliamentarians as a marker of Pakistan's parliamentary form of government "blended with Islamic provisions."

With headlines like "[PML-N] Government Reveals Plans to Amend Articles 62, 63" (2017) and "[PML-N] PM Abbasi Hints at Scrapping 62(1)(f) with Help of Political Parties" (2017), it is clear that, although initial efforts to repeal Article 62(1)(f) were rebuffed by the PML-N during parliamentary debates surrounding the Eighteenth Amendment, such a step was still under discussion even within the PML-N.[53]

During an October 2020 interview with PPP Senator Raza Rabbani, the Chairman of the Committee on Constitutional Reforms that formulated Pakistan's Eighteenth Amendment (2010), I was told that, with respect to Article 62(1)(f), the Committee initially faced "resistance from the PML-N and … Islamist parties."[54] But "now … most if not all of the political parties," especially opposition parties hounded by periodic campaigns for "accountability," perceive "a

---

51 See *S.R. Bommai v Union of India* (3 SCC 1 1994).
52 Saad Rasool, 'The Promise of Democracy' (Common Many Initiative, 2018) http://commonman.org/wp-content/uploads/2018/10/The-Promise-of-Democracy.pdf
53 APP, 'PM Abbasi Hints at Scrapping 62(1)(f) with Help of Political Parties', *DAWN*, 9 August 2017, <https://www.dawn.com/news/1350368>; Iftikhar A Khan, 'Government Reveals Plans to Amend Articles 62, 63' *DAWN* (Karachi, 23 August 2017) <www.dawn.com/news/1353269>.
54 Interview, Raza Rabbani, 28 October 2020.

misuse ... [of] this provision." In fact, referring to "the overall tone and tenor" of ongoing efforts to promote greater accountability for individual parliamentarians in Pakistan, Rabbani felt that current trends would produce "[an] amendment in that [provision]."

Former Jama'at-e-Islami Senator Khurshid Ahmed, however, disagreed. Ahmed did not see any interest in repealing Article 62(1)(f) at all. "[I]t was introduced in the Eighth Amendment ... and with great debate it was retained in the Eighteenth Amendment," he noted, "and now it has the support of all the parties." Even the secular Pashtun-nationalist Awami National Party, which initially "opposed it," he added,[55] "they [have] also accepted it, so now it is a unanimous part of the constitution"." "It is," he stressed, "an integral part of the Islamic rules of the constitution."

Indeed, former Council of Islamic Ideology Chairman and ad hoc Shariat Appellate Bench member Khalid Masud agreed that Pakistan's religious parties would "not ally with other political parties to amend this ... provision."[56] "Opening this box," he explained, could "mean repealing the whole Islamization process" associated with General Zia. And, politically, he argued, "I do not believe this article would be amended," even if, broadly speaking, the Supreme Court "would not and should not annul a constitutional ... amendment." In short, Masud argued, the barriers to repeal were neither constitutional nor judicial, but political.

Everyone I interviewed expected the level of support for repealing Article 62(1)(f) to falter among religious activists. In fact, returning to the views of Senator Ahmed, all felt that, if a constitutional amendment were introduced to remove the word ameen, street protests led by religious activists would follow. Some religious parties "just want ... an excuse to come out in protest," noted one retired Supreme Court Chief Justice, adding that an amendment targeting Article 62(1)(f) would almost certainly amount to "a very good excuse." In fact, Ahmed himself confirmed this, noting that, if parliament took steps to repeal Article 62(1)(f), he would expect "an uproar." "[The] Qur'an says it in clear terms: give your authority ... to people who are honest," he noted. "Politicians cannot say anything ... against [the Holy] Qur'an."

Still, only Ahmed felt that religious protests would (or should) deter specific constitutional reform efforts initiated by parliamentarians. Protests can be "awkward, even for semi-secular parties [like the PPP]," noted Senator Rabbani. But, in the end, he felt, such protests would not be "fatal" for any legislative majority.

---

55 See n 27.
56 "If you remove ameen," noted Senator Rabbani, "that would be difficult for [religious party constituencies] to live with." But, then, adopting a more cynical tone, he added, "the actual question as to whether the Islamic parties would kick up a storm" will hinge on "how they come into the net of accountability" (that is, the degree to which their own members might be disqualified). Khurshid Ahmad from the Jama'at-e-Islami dismissed such concerns: Jama'at candidates, he insisted, were "spotless."

6.5.3 Debating Article 62(1)(f): Principles versus personalities

If a repeal of Article 62(1)(f) were supported by most parliamentarians while remaining broadly unobjectionable to most voters, however, there is still a chance that such a repeal might fail at the hands of Supreme Court justices concerned about their relative authority vis-à-vis individual parliamentarians. Indeed, this institutional tussle might be cast as an "essential-features" problem focused on the *judiciary's* power to defend the Constitution's "parliamentary form of government blended with Islamic provisions."

Recalling views articulated by Syed Abul ala Maududi and Muhammad Asad targeting Pakistan's first Constituent Assembly,[57] this position was clearly expressed by Senator Ahmed: "If anything has been done which violates the constitution, then [the] judiciary has a right to rule on [it]," he noted. "[P]arliament has powers," he clarified, but "even the parliament cannot legislate against the Qur'an and sunnah." Pakistan has "[a] democratic constitution," he argued, but "not absolutely as in the other secular democratic constitutions." Indeed, returning to Pakistan's first Constituent Assembly, he echoed the views of Abdulla al-Mahmood, who favoured a "religious" check on parliament's power vis-à-vis the Constitution.

Returning to a plain reading of Articles 239(5) and 239(6), however, Senator Rabbani disagreed. "I have a lot of questions [about] the essential features doctrine," he said. "I believe ... parliament is sovereign," and "parliament can amend the constitution in whatever manner ... it wants." "I'm sure ... there may be ordinary citizens or other vested interests who would put in an appeal challenging [an amendment repealing Article 62(1)(f)]," so the Supreme Court "may examine [that] on the touchstone of the constitution and the general atmosphere [favouring] accountability [for individual parliamentarians]." But, in the end, Rabbani did not believe there would be "much of a fuss ... from the Court." "[M]ore than the Supreme Court," he felt, resistance to any repeal of Article 62(1)(f) "may come from the ... [military] establishment." After all, he noted, Article 62(1)(f) was introduced by a parliament acting at the behest of General Zia to be "as ambiguous as possible," so as to "serve as ... a tool for allowing or disallowing the candidature of any one whom [the establishment might see as] working against ... their ideology."

Faced with a constitutional amendment repealing Article 62(1)(f), however, none of those I interviewed felt that the work of Pakistan's Supreme Court would be shaped by core constitutional *principles* referring to broad institutional priorities, including parliamentary sovereignty (Articles 239-5 and 239-6). In particular, they argued, earlier patterns of judicial deference to parliamentary authority vis-à-vis constitutional amendments could no longer be taken for granted; instead, all focused on the case of former Chief Justice Muhammad Iftikhar Chaudhry and stressed that any future reference to basic-structure jurisprudence would depend

---

57 See n 9.

on the *personality* of the chief justice: "I think the personality [of the Chief Justice will] matter," noted one of the former Supreme Court chief justices I interviewed. Whereas basic-structure jurisprudence elsewhere in the world might be tied to stable constitutional principles or broad institutional priorities, in other words, my respondents felt that relevant patterns in Pakistan were now more closely tied to historically specific personalities and the politically contingent patterns of judicial activism (or reticence) attached to them.

"Judicial activism is very much there," noted Senator Rabbani. "But ... it has had its ups and downs." In particular, he added, "it ... depends upon the temperament of the chief justice." "Obviously, nobody would like to see a waning of their [institutional] power," Rabbani added. But "the degree varies [with each chief justice]." Or, as Senator Ahmed noted, "the whole trend is towards judicial activism ... [and Chief Justice] Saqib Nisar ... and Iftikhar Chaudhry, they were sometimes overstepping." But even so, he stressed, it always depends on the views of individual jurists. "Every judge is independent," noted one former chief justice. So "it depends on ... who are the judges at that particular time." Specifically, noted another former chief justice, "the judiciary ... has become [more] assertive" since "Chaudhry." So "I think ... there may be a [broader] change." "The past pattern" of judicial deference "may not continue," he added, not only with respect to military regimes, but also with respect to civilian regimes and even "hybrid" civilian-military regimes like that of Prime Minister Imran Khan. Still, he concluded, echoing the views of both Rabbani and Ahmed, "a lot depends on the composition of the bench." "When it comes to religious issues [in particular]," he argued, it "depends on individual judges."

Focusing on the intersection of basic-structure jurisprudence and religious issues, these comments reiterate the special link between two key salient features, namely "judicial independence" as this relates to judicial appointments and, then, Pakistan's "parliamentary form of government blended with Islamic provisions." The institutional politics, however, are often highly personal. *Who* controls who sits on the courts? *Which* judges determine which parliamentarians are "ameen"?

6.6 Conclusion

Descriptions of judicial activism are often associated with broad notions of public interest: judges encroach on the policy-making domain to protect – of their own accord (e.g. via *suo motu* powers) – the interests of ordinary citizens. With reference to constitutional "basic structure," however, judicial activism is also associated with broad *institutional* interests: judges encroach on parliament's constituent power to protect the interests of the judiciary. In Pakistan, however, patterns of judicial activism rooted in basic-structure jurisprudence are often more idiosyncratic than institutional.

According to one retired Supreme Court chief justice, the future of basic-structure jurisprudence in Pakistan should be framed as a choice between (a) broad constitutional *principles* tied to an institutional balance-of-power and (b) specific judicial *personalities*. He saw little evidence supporting an entrenched commitment to principles; after all, he noted, 8 of the 13 justices who asserted that Pakistan's Supreme Court was empowered to strike down duly promulgated constitutional amendments in *District Bar Association Rawalpindi* did *not* agree on a list of constitutional salient features. In fact, he saw occasional references to constitutional "salient features" as little more than passing *obiter dicta*. Specifically, turning to the historical contingencies surrounding basic-structure jurisprudence in Pakistan, he noted that, with reference to "religious issues" like Article 62(1)(f), the role of "individual judges" was crucial.

Given this focus on historical and political contingencies alongside the idiosyncratic work of individual judges, one might ask whether assertive forms of basic-structure jurisprudence will persist in Pakistan *without* an unusually assertive chief justice backed by a popular protest movement. This is a hypothetical question. But, after the short order in *Nadeem Ahmed* was handed down under Chief Justice Chaudhry in 2010, the fact that 13 out of 17 justices in *District Bar Association Rawalpindi* (2015) endorsed a "proscriptive" understanding of basic-structure jurisprudence two years *after* Chaudhry retired in 2013 is telling. The vastly different personnel associated with *District Bar Association Rawalpindi* (2015) might suggest that, while individual judges are important, the Court as a whole still matters.

Precisely insofar as individual judges *underpin* the pursuit of institutional interests, however, it is difficult to overlook the importance (indeed, the judicial politics) surrounding judicial appointments – arguably the most common and contentious area within the realm of basic structure jurisprudence worldwide. Indeed, what might be described as the "curation" of Supreme Courts – in Pakistan, a Court empowered to frame the legal parameters of Islam within which the careers of individual parliamentarians are defined – is crucial. As I have noted elsewhere, the link between basic structure jurisprudence and religion often unfolds *via* debates regarding the appointment of individual judges.[58]

Few in Pakistan believe the state should avoid articulations of religious standards for public life. The question is merely which branch of the state, and which individuals within that branch, might have the *final* word when articulating these standards? Historically, parliamentarians have been too divided to meet the threshold for amendments touching on Islamic provisions (not only with respect to constitutional amendments but also ordinary legislation).[59] Cross-party coalitions face special hurdles. But, even when single-party governments have succeeded in securing the majorities needed for constitutional amendments – for example, after 1997 – those governments have come to power on a platform

---

58 Nelson, 'Indian Basic Structure Jurisprudence in the Islamic Republic of Pakistan: Reconfiguring the Constitutional Politics of Religion' (2018) 13 (2) Asian Journal of Comparative Law 333–57.
59 Matthew J Nelson, 'Inheritance Unbound: The Politics of Personal Law Reform in Pakistan and India' in *Comparative Constitutionalism in South Asia*, S Khilnani, V Raghavan, and A Thiravengadam, eds. (OUP 2012) 219–46.

stressing "Islamic" credentials, making them even *less* likely to amend (let alone repeal) the constitution's Islamic provisions.

Indeed, notwithstanding widespread political interest in repealing "obscure" terms like ameen, Justice Khosa noted that Pakistan's parliament was "most unlikely" to "amend the Constitution for achieving something which may offend against any express Divine [i.e. Qur'anic] command." In Pakistan, he noted, doing so could "negate the raison d'être of the country's conception, creation, and existence." But, he added, returning to his own focus on parliament's constituent power, if Pakistan's parliament *were* to proceed in this direction, the Supreme Court would not be in a position to "shackle it."

In Pakistan, familiar controversies regarding the possibility of "unconstitutional constitutional amendments" are closely tied to debates regarding the meaning of Islamic constitutionalism. Justice Khosa's view, regarding the unfettered power of parliament, is broadly in keeping with the position of Pakistan's Supreme Court before 2010. But, since 2015, Justice Khosa's view is no longer the majority view.

7 Limiting constituent power?
Unconstitutional constitutional amendments and time-bound constitution making in Nepal

Mara Malagodi

7.1 Introduction

Judicial interventions in questions of constitutional unamendability are usually contentious, but become even more controversial when they encroach upon the activity of constitution making. Adjudication over unconstitutional constitutional amendments already interrogates the appropriate limits to judicial involvement in the constitutional sphere. However, when this kind of adjudication is coupled with direct judicial interference in the exercise of constituent power, the notion of constitutional supremacy clashes even more directly with that of popular sovereignty, and the realm of law and the realm of politics explosively collide. I argue that such a clash between the legal and the political is exasperated when judges intervene in a constitution-making process that is carried out through a Constituent Assembly. This is because a Constituent Assembly embodies the highest modality of constitution making and represents an instance of extraordinary constitutional politics. As Andrew Arato explains, Constituent Assemblies are the archetype of revolutionary constituent power: they are conceptualised as sovereign institutions with unlimited powers; they embody the unified will of the people and promise a total rupture from the old regime through a foundational moment.[1] However, this contribution aims to show that in practice Constituent Assemblies – even highly representative and diverse bodies like the one in Nepal – are often sidelined in constitution-making processes and the task of actually writing the constitution is carried out by a much smaller group of political actors belonging to the dominant elites resulting in the effective exclusion of already marginalised groups.[2] So under what circumstances is judicial encroachment on the life and work of a Constituent Assembly warranted, and what is its long-term impact?

This chapter explores the relationship between adjudication on constitutional amendments and constitution making through an in-depth analysis of a single case study, that of Nepal's first Constituent Assembly ("CA1"), which operated

---

1 Andrew Arato, *Post Sovereign Constitution Making* (Oxford University Press 2016) 91, 108.
2 For a critique of constituent power see Hèctor López Bofill, *Law, Violence and Constituent Power* (Routledge 2021).

DOI: 10.4324/9781003097099-7

between 2008 and 2012 in a post-conflict context. Nepal represents an extreme instance of the politics of constitutional unamendability. The chapter focuses on the interventions by the Supreme Court of Nepal in the disputes over the extension of the CA1 time limit through constitutional amendment, and the political context of this protracted litigation. The initial two-year term of CA1 (May 2008–May 2010) was extended four times by way of constitutional amendment of the initial Assembly's term under Article 64: first, by a year (May 2010–May 2011) under the 8th Amendment of the 2007 Interim Constitution; second, by three months (May–August 2011) under the 9th Amendment; third, by other three months (August–November 2011) under the 10th Amendment; and finally by six months (November 2011–May 2012) under the 11th Amendment. A fifth attempt to extend the Assembly by other three months (May–August 2012) was made by tabling the 13th Amendment Bill, but was ultimately unsuccessful.

Judicial activism in this area grew exponentially after the third extension of CA1 with the 10th Amendment of the Interim Constitution in August 2011. Until that point the Supreme Court had been rather deferential to the elected branches by deploying the doctrine of necessity. However, as new petitions kept coming in to challenge the constitutionality of the amendments, on 25 November 2011, the Supreme Court took a firmer stance and held that any further extensions of the Assembly's term would be a violation of the 2007 Interim Constitution and that the amendment would be held unconstitutional.[3] However, when CA1 failed to complete the drafting of the new constitution within the extended timeframe, on 22 May 2012 the government tabled another bill to amend the constitution and extend the CA1 term further. Immediately, yet another petition was filed in the Supreme Court seeking a stay order on the proposed amendment. On 24 May, the court issued the order demanded by the petitioners and effectively disallowed any further extensions. It therefore effectively placed constitutional limitations to the existence of CA1 beyond its term.[4]

Last-minute political negotiations over finalising the new constitution became frantic in the shadow of the judicial ban and the looming definitive deadline. Ultimately, any last-minute attempts to salvage the constitution-making process were unsuccessful and CA1 was dissolved on 27 May 2012 by the President on the recommendation of the Prime Minister. New elections for a second Constituent Assembly ("CA2") were called for immediately, but did not take place until November 2013. As a result, Nepal remained without a functioning legislature and constitution-making body for over a year and half in a crucial phase of the peace process. Moreover, Supreme Court Chief Justice Khil Raj Regmi, who had

---

3 *Adv. Bharat Mani Jangam and Adv. Bal Krishna Neupane v. Prime Minister and Cabinet Office et al.* Writ N. 068-WS-0014. The petition was filed on 21 September 2011 and the decision was handed down on 25 November 2011.
4 *Adv. Rajkumar Rana, Adv. Kanchan Krishna Neupane and Adv. Bharat Mani Jangam v Prime Minister and Cabinet Office et al.* Writ N. 068-WS-1085, 1086, 1087. The decision was handed down on 24 May 2012.

adjudicated the majority of the controversial cases on the CA1 dissolution, was appointed as the Head of the Interim Cabinet to lead the country through the transition. This represented a clear violation of the doctrine of separation of powers and proved to be a disastrous move for the Court's reputation. As a result, the country's constitutional moment was irremediably lost. The failure of CA1 set the trajectory of Nepal's constitution making under CA2 onto an entirely different political course, which did not prioritise inclusion in its agenda and sought to rein in the judiciary, in particular the Supreme Court. As a result, the new constitutional settlement reached under the 2015 Constitution alienated many segments of Nepali society and engendered long-term political instability.

The focus on Nepal as a case study teases out the importance of the political context in adjudicating the constitutionality of a constitutional amendment. It is not sufficient to conduct a purely doctrinal analysis of the judicial reasoning in the key decisions and an analysis of the constitutional framework to examine the question of unamendability. It is also critical to include a broader political view of the events and context of the litigation, and consider the balance of power between different political actors. To do so, the chapter examines, first, the constitutional context of Nepal to explain from a historical perspective the powers of the Supreme Court and the configuration of constitutional amendments. Second, it explores the context and outcomes of the litigation over the dissolution of CA1 with a specific focus on the unconstitutionality of constitutional amendments. Third, it analyses the impact of the Supreme Court decisions concerning the constitutionality of the CA1 extension on both the constitutional position of the judiciary and the long-term political and institutional developments in Nepal.

This chapter draws four sets of conclusions from the Nepal case study that fit neatly with the classification of the Nepali experience as an instance of the "denotive model" by the volume editors.[5] First, the language of the basic structure doctrine has seeped into Nepal's constitutional discourse, partly through the inclusion of eternity clauses under the previous 1990 Constitution and through constitutional borrowing from other South Asian jurisdictions – India *in primis*. This was the case even if the 2007 Interim Constitution did not contain any eternity clauses, pointing to a consolidation of the Supreme Court's powers, activism, and constitutional role. Second, the contested nature of constitutional unamendability coupled with the explosive issue of adjudication on the life of the Constituent Assembly raised questions not just about the appropriate constitutional bounds of the judiciary, but about the partisan nature of judicial decision-making under these circumstances. Third, Nepal's post-conflict constitution-making process fits what Silvia Suteu has characterised as the "fraught context" of divided, conflict-affected societies.[6] As such, this contentious process was both the backdrop of *and* the substantive core issue in the protracted litigation over the validity of the constitutional amendments seeking to extend the

---

5 Rehan Abeyratne and Ngoc Son Bui, Chapter 1 in this volume.
6 Silvia Suteu, Chapter 14 in this volume.

136 *Mara Malagodi*

term of CA1. Finally, the voluble way in which the Supreme Court and its justices conducted themselves during Nepal's most embattled litigation bore a profound influence on the outcome of the constitution-making process itself, especially with respect to the structure and powers of the higher judiciary.

7.2 The constitutional context of Nepal

To understand the controversies over the Supreme Court's adjudication on constitutional amendments and the dissolution of CA1, it is crucial to appreciate Nepal's constitutional developments since 1990 and the newly acquired role of the Supreme Court.

7.2.1 *The development of the principle of constitutional supremacy in Nepal*

One of the few Asian countries that was never colonised, Nepal historically played an important strategic function at the margins of the British Empire. Featuring a long history of authoritarian governance, the country's first experiment with constitutional democracy in the 1950s was short-lived and saw a return to autocracy in 1960.[7] After 30 years of monarchical absolutism under the Panchayat regime (1960–90), in 1990, a pro-democracy movement launched by the underground political parties succeeded in forcing the king to dismantle the Panchayat regime and to initiate a process of re-democratisation centred on drafting a new constitution.[8]

The 1990 document – Nepal's fifth constitution – established a constitutional monarchy with a parliamentary system. The drafters looked at the British Constitution for political mechanisms to keep the monarchy within constitutional bounds. However, they ultimately opted for legally enforceable mechanisms of executive accountability and explicitly borrowed India's model of constitutional supremacy. The 1990 Constitution gave the Supreme Court the power to review the constitutionality of legislation and entertain public interest litigation (PIL). It also included an extensive list of justiciable fundamental rights opening the courthouse doors to extensive constitutional litigation.

The 1990s also saw another political development that would alter the course of Nepali history. In 1996, the Communist Party of Nepal (Maoist) launched from the countryside a ten-year insurgency against the government that they called the "People's War" (1996–2006). Treated by the government as a

---

7 Bhuwan Joshi and Leo Rose, *Democratic Innovations in Nepal* (University of California Press 1966) 396; Mara Malagodi, 'Constitution Drafting as Cold War *Realpolitik*: Sir Ivor Jennings and Nepal's 1959 Constitution' in Harshan Kumarasingham (ed), *Constitution-Making in Asia* (Routledge 2016) 154–72.
8 Mara Malagodi, *Constitutional Nationalism and Legal Exclusion in Nepal* (Oxford University Press 2013).

slow-burning local problem at first, the conflict eventually intensified and became a country-wide emergency. Politically, it progressively led to the marginalisation of the parliamentary political parties and a standoff between the Maoist insurgents and King Gyanendra Shah, who was supported by the Army.[9] Resolution of the conflict became inextricably intertwined with constitutional change in 2001, when the Maoist demands for the abrogation of the 1990 constitution and the election of a Constituent Assembly became non-negotiable. From the outset, the insurgents' demands had included radical constitutional change to abolish the 250-year-old Shah monarchy, declare Nepal a secular state, and achieve greater social inclusion through a sweeping programme of state restructuring. As such, constitutional reform became the main goal and battleground of identity politics in the country. In fact, the re-democratisation of 1990 had merely exacerbated economic and political inequality among the many socio-cultural groups in the country.[10]

The changes to the judiciary under the 1990 Constitution encouraged a great deal of constitutional litigation. In terms of access to justice, the relaxation of the rule of *locus standi* also opened the courtroom's doors to a growing number of litigants. The Supreme Court sought to streamline PIL petitions,[11] but the number of PIL petitions continued to increase. Since 1990, the Supreme Court has also heard a number of high-profile constitutional cases on salient political issues. These cases have provoked questions about whether the courts are the most appropriate venue to resolve political controversies, as well as allegations of increasing politicisation of the judiciary. This trajectory began with a 1991 judgment in which the Supreme Court decided the first and only case concerning the actions of the king.[12] Soon after, Nepal's apex Court was called upon

---

9 On the People's War see Sara Shneiderman, Luke Wagner, Jacob Rinck, Amy Johnson, and Austin Lord, 'Nepal's Ongoing Political Transformation: A Review of Post-2006 Literature on Conflict, the State, Identities, and Environments' (2016) 50 *Modern Asian Studies* 2041.
10 Nepal features a highly diverse social fabric. According to the 2011 census, of the country's 125 caste and ethnic groups, only the largest 6 account for more than 5 percent of the total population. Moreover, the various groups are intermingled rather than territorially concentrated, and none of them constitutes an absolute majority in any particular region. The two biggest groups are the Chetri (lit. Kshatriyas, a warrior class of local Khas origins), who make up 16.6 percent of the population, and the Bahun (lit. Pahari or "hill" Brahmins – priestly class) who make up another 12.2 percent. Together, these two high-caste Hindu groups constitute the dominant Khas-Arya group (28.8 percent of the population) to which Nepal's royal family and most of the elites belong. In terms of historically marginalised groups, dalits (lit. "former untouchables") form about 14 percent of Nepal's population. The 63 groups classified under the umbrella term Adivasi Janajati (lit. "indigenous people"), who can be described as ethno-linguistic groups that do not use Nepali as their mother tongue, account for 36 percent of the total population. Madhesi groups (lit. non-Pahari "Terai plain dwellers," often erroneously described as "of Indian origins") constitute slightly less than 20 percent of the population. Government of Nepal, 'Population Monograph of Nepal' (*Central Bureau of Statistics* 2014).
11 *Radheshyam Adhikari v. Council of Ministers* NKP 2048 (1991) Vol. 33, N. 12, 810.
12 *Adv. Radheshyam Adhikari v. Council of Ministers*, NKP, 2048/1992, Vol. 33, N. 12, 810.

with increasing frequency to intervene in quintessentially political disputes. In the mid-1990s the Supreme Court became embroiled in four cases pertaining to the dissolution of Parliament's lower chamber, the House of Representatives.[13] The Supreme Court struggled to articulate a consistent "political question" doctrine and appeared to decide cases in a partisan fashion according to the political party at the helm of government. In the last of these cases, the Supreme Court upheld in 2002 the validity of the dissolution by the Prime Minister over the House's inability to secure an extension of the state of emergency at the height of the civil war.[14] In this instance, the dissolution of the House and its judicial validation reopened the door to monarchical autocracy with a takeover by King Gyanendra.[15]

It was only in 2005 that the Maoists and the mainstream political parties eventually agreed to repeal the 1990 Constitution and adopt a new constitution to be drafted by a directly elected Constituent Assembly. In April 2006, they launched a joint movement against the autocratic monarchy and succeeded in restoring parliamentary democracy. The Interim Constitution was adopted on 15 January 2007 to pave the way for the election of the Assembly. It was under this document that the litigation over the extension of the CA1 term was conducted. Significantly, much debate over the structure and power of the judiciary took place within the Drafting Committee – with strong pushes from the Maoists and other left-wing parties to limit the powers of the judiciary.[16] In the end, the Interim Constitution remained silent on the issue of the monarchy, declared Nepal a secular state, retained ample similarities with the 1990 Constitution, created a unicameral Interim Legislature, and preserved the wide powers of the Nepali judiciary.[17]

7.2.2 Post-conflict constitution making in Nepal

Nepal's peace process essentially entailed two steps: the integration of Maoist combatants into the Nepal Army, which was completed by April 2012, and the drafting of a new Constitution – Nepal's seventh – by a directly elected body

---

13 *Hari Prasad Nepal v. Prime Minister*, NKP, 2052/1994, Vol. 37, N. 1, 88; *Ravi Raj Bhandari v. Prime Minister*, Supreme Court Bulletin, 2052/1995, 4, Bhadra 16-31; *House Dissolution (N. 3) Case*, 6 Sarvocca Adalat Bulletin, 2054/1996, 1, Magh 16-30; *Adv. Bharat Mani Jangam and Adv. Bal Krishna Neupane v Prime Minister and Cabinet Office et al.* Writ N. 068-WS-0014.
14 'Nepal court upholds Parliament's dissolution' *The Hindu* (Chennai, 7 August 2002). See: https://www.voanews.com/archive/nepal-supreme-court-upholds-decision-dissolve-parliament-2002-08-06
15 Mara Malagodi, 'Nepal' in D Law, H Lau, and A Schwartz (eds) *Oxford Handbook of Constitutional Law in Asia* (Oxford University Press 2022, forthcoming).
16 See: http://www.martinchautari.org.np/files/The_Media_Coverage_of_the_Drafting_of_Nepals_2007_Interim_Constitution_by_Mara_Malagodi.pdf
17 Mara Malagodi, 'Godot Has Arrived! Nepal's Federal Debates' in G Anderson and S Choudhry (eds), *Territorial Cleavages and Constitutional Transitions* (Oxford University Press 2019) 161–80.

deputed to secure the inclusion of the country's many marginalised groups by institutional means. Radical constitutional change became the primary intended vehicle for state-restructuring and the peace process' mantra of "*nayā Nepāl banāune*" (building new Nepal). This agenda was controversial and many of the political forces involved in constitution making did not subscribe to it – indeed, they fiercely opposed it in any way possible.

The election of CA1 eventually took place in April 2008 and delivered a relative Maoist majority to the surprise of many observers. At its first meeting, CA1 abolished the Shah monarchy and declared Nepal a republic. The sense of anticipation was enormous as the new constitution was expected to deliver on the promises of the People's War. However, the life of CA1 was marred by political instability from its inception. Functioning as both the constitution-making body and the legislature, the Assembly became embroiled in the controversies and tussles of both ordinary and extraordinary politics. Moreover, as the Assembly was divided along both party and identitarian lines, the place of identity and demands for recognition proved to be the most contested aspects in the drafting the new constitution. By May 2010, all of the Thematic Committees' reports had been discussed in plenary sessions, but no consensus could be reached on the most contentious issues: federal restructuring along identity lines, presidential versus parliamentary government, and the judiciary. As a result, the new constitution could not be finalised even if agreements had been reached at the Committee stage with a few members dissenting.[18]

CA1 then bought itself more time by amending the Interim Constitution to extend its own term by one year in May 2010 through an amendment of Article 64 of the Interim Constitution (8th Amendment). At this point, the task of resolving these issues was removed from the open public debates of the body directly representative of the Nepali people and put into the hands of the old guard leaders of the main parties. These men negotiated crucial decisions about Nepal's new constitutional settlement, mostly through the High Level Political Committee (HLPC), which had been set up in January 2010. As a result, no inclusive and transparent deliberations within CA1 were allowed to iron out the differences between the various political forces. Ultimately, backdoor secret negotiations, opaque deals outside the Assembly, and the overall lack of transparency undermined the legitimacy of the constitution-making process itself. At the same time, the political leaders failed to forge a compromise solution, notwithstanding three further extensions of the CA1 term, while effectively side-lining the Constituent Assembly itself. "Postponing," or rather "delaying," the entire constitution-making process was the strategy adopted by the political parties in opposition, since no consensus could be found on key issues. The opaque *modus operandi* of the party leaders effectively legitimised to a certain degree this set of increasingly forceful judicial interventions.

---

18 Mara Malagodi 'The Rejection of Constitutional Incrementalism in Nepal's Federalisation' (2018) 46 (4) Federal Law Review 521–40.

7.2.3 *The constitutional treatment of amendments in Nepal*

Nepal's recent permanent constitutions have adopted eternity clauses, unlike the 2007 Interim Constitution. Nepal first adopted an Indian-inspired basic structure doctrine under the 1990 Constitution through an eternity clause that forbade amendments contrary to the spirit of the Preamble under Article 116. The rationale for this choice was to preserve constitutional monarchy and multiparty democracy, which represented the basis of the political compromise behind the 1990 document: on the one hand, the king endeavoured to prevent a republican turn, while on the other hand, the political parties sought to preclude a return to monarchical absolutism.[19] Meanwhile, left-wing parties were dissatisfied with the arrangement as they feared that it would lead to judicial activism and prevent the political branches from carrying out essential reforms.

The 2007 Interim Constitution lacked such an eternity clause because it was expected merely to provide the legal basis for the Constituent Assembly to adopt a permanent constitution. However, it was under the 2007 Interim Constitution that the Supreme Court restricted the Constituent Assembly's ability to adopt amendments that would extend the Assembly's own term.

The inclusion of an eternity clause in the 2015 constitution can be viewed as implicitly recognising the role of the courts in striking down unconstitutional constitutional amendments. Nepal's 2015 constitution is difficult to amend and Article 274 requires a qualified majority of two-thirds of the members of both Houses of the Federal Parliament and the assent of the President. The eternity clause further specifies that no amendment may violate the constitution's basic structure by contravening Nepal's independence, self-rule, territorial integrity, or the principle of popular sovereignty.[20]

7.3 The litigation over the dissolution of the first Constituent Assembly

The failure of CA1 to finish drafting the constitution and its eventual dissolution resulted from a number of factors. First, the behaviour of top political leaders marginalised the Assembly as the forum of deliberation relating to key constitutional issues. By undercutting the only truly representative body entrusted with the task of constitution drafting, the entire constitutional process was delegitimised. Second, inter- and intra-party squabbles over offices and seats took precedence over meaningful and long-awaited institutional reforms. Third, both the Executive and the Supreme Court became progressively more involved in matters relating to the proceedings of CA1, leading to an unhealthy tension between the various branches of the Nepali state. As a result, public frustrations with CA1 also resulted from the Assembly's inability to complete its task notwithstanding the

---

19 Mara Malagodi, (n 8) 126, 172.
20 Constitution of Nepal 2015, Art. 274(1).

Limiting constituent power? 141

total of four extensions of its term by way of constitutional amendment. From the original timeframe of two years, the term of CA1 was doubled through four separate constitutional amendments.

CA1 extended its original term of two years by another year (May 2010–May 2011) through the 8th Amendment, which altered Article 64 of the Interim Constitution. Shortly after the amendment was passed, a number of lawyers filed a series of PIL petitions in the Supreme Court challenging the validity of the amendment itself. In the first petition, the Court decided the case on 4 November 2010.[21] A special bench of three judges upheld the constitutional validity of the 8th Amendment and ruled that the term of the Constituent Assembly could be extended until the new constitution was finalised. The respondents invoked the doctrine of necessity to legitimise the government's action. Constitutional lawyer and former advisor to the President of Nepal, Surya Dhungel, excoriated the Supreme Court for this judgment. He argued that the court's reasoning based on hypothetical scenarios failed to provide a cogent and sound interpretation of the Interim Constitution, and, most importantly, that its role had become politicised:

> The court has entered into the regime of "constitutional politics" in order to help stretch and safeguard the longevity of the Constituent Assembly. It is therefore bound to be controversial as it has failed to respond to the genuine question of a fresh poll of CA in case the present CA is unable to even draft a "skeletal framework" before May 28 [2011] to justify its possible extension through another amendment of Article 64, which is solely a jurisdiction of CA. Despite the Supreme Court's numerous hypothetical discourses of political nature, the question is still alive as to what would happen if the CA fails to produce a new Constitution and the Legislative wing of CA is unable to pass an amendment bill. Let this hypothetical question not be a reality.[22]

The confusion engendered by the lack of guidance provided by the Supreme Court in this first decision was further exacerbated by a second decision of the Court a few months later. This case arose from a separate petition that also challenged the constitutional validity of the 8th Amendment. On 25 May 2011, a full bench of five judges including Chief Justice Khil Raj Regmi came to the opposite conclusion on the constitutionality of the 8th Amendment.[23] The Court held that the 8th Amendment was unconstitutional, but refused to issue an order invalidating it because its decision was handed down just three days before the expiry of

---

21 *Adv Vijaya Raj Sakya v President of Nepal; Adv. Kamlesh Dwivedi v President of Nepal*, NKP 2067, Vol. 52, Part 9 Decision N. 8457. Writ Petition N.066-WS-0050 decided on 4 November 2010 (BS 2067/07/18).
22 See: https://www.spotlightnepal.com/2011/03/14/the-disturbing-verdict/ (14 March 2011).
23 *Adv. Bal Krishna Neupane v President of Nepal; Bharatmani Jangam v President of Nepal* NKP 2068, Vol. 53, Part 4, Decision N. 8588. Writ Petition N.066-WS-0056 decided on 25 May 2011 (BS 2068/02/11).

the extended term: 28 May 2011. This second judgment directly contradicted the earlier one; while it was not a re-examination of the first judgment as they arose from two separate petitions, it effectively overruled it.

Constitutional expert Bipin Adhikari offers an insightful analysis of the second judgment in the CA1 extension litigation, especially given that this decision was handed down after the government had tabled the 9th Amendment Bill to extend CA1 term further by three months:

> Commenting on the earlier ruling, Chief Justice Khilraj Regmi, Justices Damodar Prasad Sharma, Ram Kumar Prasad Shah, Kalyan Shrestha and Tahir Ali Ansari said the term cannot be extended an infinite number of times. Without mentioning anything about the Interim Constitution (Ninth Amendment) Bill 2011, awaiting the order of the Chairperson Subash Nemwang to introduce it in the house at that time, the SC specifically stated that extension of the house on any basis for more than six months is not contemplated by the constitution. In other words, the Interim Constitution (Eighth Amendment) Bill 2010, by which Article 64 of the constitution was amended, meant a one-year house term extension did not meet the constitutional requirement. The court pointed out that while it accepts the unconstitutionality of the eighth amendment, it does not want to overrule it for the simple reason that there have already been many developments in the constitution building process. Based on the (unconstitutionally) extended period, annulment of these developments is not in the interest of the public. However, it is clear that if the eighth amendment extending the mandate of CA in normal times for one year was unconstitutional, then the ninth amendment proposing the same for another additional year cannot be constitutional ipso facto.[24]

Adhikari concluded his analysis by saying that this kind of litigation was there to stay. In fact, the two lawyers behind the second petition had already filed another PIL in the Supreme Court to challenge the validity of the 9th Amendment extending the CA1 term by three months (May–August 2011) as soon as it was passed.

In this third case, on 28 August 2011, Nepal's Supreme Court quashed the petition and upheld the constitutional validity of the 9th Amendment on the basis of the doctrine of necessity.[25] In this convoluted judgement, the Supreme Court, on the one hand, upheld its earlier decision of 25 May 2011 in the second petition concerning the 8th Amendment, but, on the other hand, refused to strike down the 9th Amendment noting the brevity of the three-month extension. Moreover, the Supreme Court again had to decide a case on the constitu-

---

24 See: https://bipinadhikari.com.np/opinions/final-hearing/ (24 June 2011).
25 *Adv. Bal Krishna Neupane v President of Nepal; Bharatmani Jangam v President of Nepal* Writ Petition N.067-WS-0071 decided on 28 August 2011 (BS 2068/05/11).

tional validity of an amendment extending the CA1 term when the extended term had already ended. The timing of the decision had serious policy implications, including that declaring these amendments unconstitutional would invalidate the previous work of CA1, which was also Nepal's legislature.

Bipin Adhikari criticised the Supreme Court for straying from a literal interpretation of the Interim Constitution and becoming involved in essentially political matters outside of its purview and competence:

> Article 64 of the Interim Constitution is very clear. It clearly states that unless otherwise dissolved earlier by the Constituent Assembly (CA) itself, the term of the house shall be two years. There is only one exception to this rule. The term of the house may be extended for up to six months in the event that the task of drafting the constitution is not complete due to the proclamation of a state of emergency in the country. The court could have delivered its decision based on this clear-cut provision … the Supreme Court tried this time to read the political situation in the country which was not necessary. It ignored the fact that the Constituent Assembly was a fixed term house, and there was no emergency in the country in May 2011 to allow it extension on exceptional ground. When the constitutionality of the eighth amendment bill was challenged last year, the court agreed that there could be no extension beyond six months, whether there is an emergency or any other dire necessity. But it declined to declare the unconstitutional extension null and void at that time because it thought that would negatively affect the achievements of the CA made during this extended period. But the judgment of the court left little space for the CA to work on another extension after the completion of this unconstitutionally acquired one year additional term. It is therefore natural that the issue was taken up once again by public interest litigants, when the house passed Interim Constitution (Ninth Amendment) Bill extending the term of the house for another three months. But the Supreme Court annulled the writ petition on the ground that despite the efforts of political parties, the twin tasks of peace building and constitution drafting processes remain incomplete and the extension of CA's tenure was necessary to complete these tasks. Apparently, it ignored the emergency clause, and in the absence of the enabling provision in the constitution, it relied on the doctrine of necessity to validate the extension. This interpretation is not sound. The court has become unnecessarily generous. It has misread the political economy of the peace process and constitution building. There is a fear that the House may not complete the tasks for several reasons even though the court is prepared to give unlimited extension to the house.[26]

---

26 See: http://constituent-assembly.blogspot.com/2011/09/doctrine-of-necessity-is-vulnerable-on.html (August 2011).

Adhikari presciently concluded that this line of judicial reasoning centred on political expediency and deference to the executive would also invite further litigation along these lines as CA1 was already extending its own term for a third time. In fact, on 31 August 2011, CA1 passed the 10th Amendment to extend its term by another three months (August–November 2011). As predicted, on 21 September 2011, Advocates Bharat Jangam and Balkrishna Neupane filed yet another PIL petition in the Supreme Court arguing that it was a violation of Article 64 of the Interim Constitution to extend again the Assembly's term under the 10th Amendment.

On 25 November 2011, a special bench of the Supreme Court comprising then Chief Justice Khil Raj Regmi, Justices Damodar Prasad Sharma, Rajkumar Prasad Shah, Kalyan Shrestha, and Prem Sharma ruled on this writ petition. The bench ordered CA1 to complete the drafting of the new constitution before the expiry of the six-month extension (before May 2012). In this respect, the Court issued an order stating that "if the Constituent Assembly was to fail to promulgate the new constitution within the next six months, its term would automatically expire after those six months."[27] This order effectively served as constructive notice forbidding further extensions of the Assembly's term by way of constitutional amendment to the Interim Constitution. The reasoning deployed the language of the basic structure doctrine to interpret Article 64 concerning the term of the Constituent Assembly, which was defined as "unamendable and mandatory" also in the previous two decisions on the extension of the CA1 term. It further infers that the framers of the Interim Constitution did not intend for frequent amendments to the document. In its reasoning, the Supreme Court also focused on the Preamble of the Interim Constitution and extensively referenced democracy as the guiding principle of its interpretation. As such, the Court reclaimed its role of guardian of the constitution and enforcer of the rule of law, claiming that the Constituent Assembly ought to answer to the people and respond to their aspirations by finalising the new constitution. The Court went on to state that the CA1 work schedule included in the written replies of the respondents lacked credibility and the progress on the constitution-making front was negligible.

The Supreme Court, however, stopped short of invalidating the 10th Amendment and stated that if the Constituent Assembly were to be unable to complete the task of constitution drafting within the extended period, it would be *ipso facto* terminated. Of course, at the time of the decision the 11th Amendment Bill was being tabled in CA1 to extend the terms of the Assembly for a fourth time by six months (November 2011–May 2012).

Nonetheless, the decision caused outrage. The Supreme Court was accused by many politicians (especially Maoists) of overreaching and overstepping its

---

27 *Adv. Bharat Mani Jangam and Adv. Bal Krishna Neupane v. Prime Minister and Cabinet Office et al.* Writ N. 068-WS-0014. For the English translation of the judgment on the Supreme Court website, see: http://www.supremecourt.gov.np/web/assets/downloads/judgements/Constitution_Assembly_Case.pdf

Limiting constituent power? 145

constitutional role as the question of constitution making was essentially political and outside of the Court's jurisdiction. Former Chief Justice Kalyan Shrestha, in an interview that I conducted with him later on, reflected on the case and stood by the decision the Supreme Court had reached in November 2011. He said that the Supreme Court at that time was greatly concerned about interfering with constitutional amendments, but that the Constituent Assembly was not making any progress with the drafting. Justice Shrestha argued that constitution making is not an exercise that can continue indefinitely without a fresh electoral mandate, and that the Court had to resort to the doctrine of necessity under those circumstances.[28]

The Constituent Assembly, however, was unable to complete the new dispensation even within the extended timeframe under the 11th Amendment. Thus, on 22 May 2012, the Government tabled the Constitution (13th Amendment) Bill supported by the main four political parties to extend the term of the Constituent Assembly by a further three months until August 2012. Immediately, two petitions were filed in the Supreme Court.

In the first case, Advocates Rajkumar Rana, Kanchan Krishna Neupane, and Bharat Mani Jangam sought a stay order on the 13th Amendment Bill tabled in the Assembly. The single bench of Chief Justice Khil Raj Regmi found for the petitioners and issued a stay order on the Amendment Bill, effectively disallowing any further extensions of the Assembly's term. The Chief Justice found the government to be in violation of the Supreme Court Order issued in November 2011 and to be in breach of their duty to complete drafting the new Constitution by May 2012.[29]

In the second case, on 24 May 2012, a single bench composed by Justice Kalyan Shrestha entertained a contempt of court petition filed by Advocate Kamal Prasad Itani against Maoist Prime Minister Baburam Bhattari and Nepali Congress Minister for Law and Justice Krishna Prasad Sitaula claiming that the government decision to seek the Constituent Assembly's term extension went against the Constitution and violated the Supreme Court's November 2011 decision. Justice Shrestha responded to the petition by issuing an order demanding that the defendants furnish written replies before the Supreme Court.[30] He went so far to tell two very senior politicians and party leaders that they could not send their representatives in such a case, and that they would have to attend the hearing in person.[31] The backlash against this bold decision was immediate. Kalyan Shrestha recounted in an interview with me that a few days after his decision in the contempt case, his father rang him on the telephone to tell him that he had heard on

---

28 Author's personal communication with Kalyan Shrestha, Kathmandu, 7 August 2018.
29 *Adv. Rajkumar Rana, Adv. Kanchan Krishna Neupane and Adv. Bharat Mani Jangam v Prime Minister and Cabinet Office et al.* Writ N. 068-WS-1085, 1086, 1087.
30 See: http://kathmandupost.ekantipur.com/printedition/news/2012-05-24/sc-summons-pm-sitaula.html
31 See: https://www.himalini.com/supreme-court-summons-pm,-dpm-sitaula.html

the radio that the Maoists were preparing an impeachment motion against him and the Chief Justice; eventually they dropped the plan.[32]

In response to the two adverse judicial decisions, last-minute negotiations took place amongst the main political party leaders outside the Assembly, but to no avail. When the leaders failed to reach a compromise on federalism on 27 May 2012, Prime Minister Bhattarai advised the President to dissolve CA1 and immediately called for new elections. The dissolution of the Assembly left Nepal with neither a legislature nor a constitution-drafting body in place for over a year and a half. It also led to a major constitutional crisis in which the Supreme Court became directly embroiled.

7.4 The aftermath of the dissolution

The impact of the Supreme Court cases on the extension of the CA1 term and the unconstitutionality of constitutional amendments had several effects on the reputation and constitutional position of the Court. In the short term, the Court appeared to take a partisan position. Indeed, the Court was openly accused of that, especially after the Chief Justice became the Head of the Interim Cabinet, which created an unprecedented constitutional crisis. In the long term, these judgments gave sufficient justification to constitution-makers to rein in the Supreme Court and to attempt a significant curtailment of its role and function. The result was a compromise, but it is clear that the 2015 Constitution has effectively sought to curb the judicial activism of the Supreme Court.

First, in February 2013 negotiations to form a government began amongst the main political parties, and Chief Justice Khil Raj Regmi was put forward as a candidate for Prime Minister. Ironically, the prospective government was named "Nepal Interim Election Council" to obscure the fact that Nepal's key executive institution was to be led by the Head of Nepal's judiciary – a blatant violation of the doctrine of separation of powers. Regmi was also the adjudicator on the key constitutional cases that had led to the dissolution of CA1. The International Commission of Jurists, amongst other organisations, called for Regmi to step down from his judicial appointment as he was only on temporary leave from his post. In fact, the agreement amongst the four main political parties provided that Regmi would refrain from participating in his duties as Chief Justice of the Supreme Court while exercising the powers of the Prime Minister, but that after the elections had taken place, he would resume his position and regular duties as Chief Justice.[33]

On 26 February 2013, Advocates Chandra Kanta Gyawali and Om Prakash Aryal filed a writ petition in the Supreme Court demanding that the appointment of Khil Raj Regmi as Prime Minister, which had been made by Nepal's President

---

32 Author's personal communication with Kalyan Shrestha, Kathmandu, 7 August 2018.
33 See: https://www.icj.org/icj-calls-on-nepali-chief-justice-to-step-down-as-judge-after-app ointment-as-prime-minister/

Ram Baran Yadav, be withdrawn. The Supreme Court, however, kept the petition pending and refused to entertain it. In an effort to close ranks and present a united front, the deafening silence of the Supreme Court dented its image even further. On 14 March 2013, a new consensus government was constituted. It was composed of ministers appointed by the political parties and headed by Chief Justice Regmi. This caused an unprecedented constitutional crisis, even if the CA2 elections were eventually held in November 2013 after two postponements.

On 22 January 2014, CA2 held its first meeting. As a result, in February 2014, Chief Justice Regmi stepped down from his executive post, and was replaced by the Nepali Congress President Sushil Koirala. Finally, on 28 March 2016 the Supreme Court entertained the petition filed in 2013 by Advocates Gyawali and Aryal on the appointment of Khil Raj Regmi as Prime Minister – over two years after Regmi had stepped down. The Constitutional Bench comprising Chief Justice Kalyan Shrestha, and Justices Sushila Karki, Baidyanath Upadhyaya, Gopal Parajuli, and Om Prakash Mishra, quashed the writ petition on the basis that it had become irrelevant as that Council of Ministers was no longer in place. Kalyan Shrestha and Sushila Karki, however, registered a differing view in the majority's decision and maintained that the move of appointing Regmi as Prime Minister was against the Interim Constitution, the doctrine of separation of power, and the principles of checks and balances.[34] But it was too little too late. Sushila Karki, in a BBC interview on 1 July 2016, reiterated that the Nepali judiciary was still paying the price for Regmi's appointment as Prime Minister while serving as Chief Justice.[35]

Second, the controversial constitutional litigation that led to the demise of CA1 and the saga of Chief Justice Regmi gave ammunition to the politicians openly advocating for a diminished role of the Supreme Court. These arguments had already emerged during the drafting of the Interim Constitution and were even more forcefully proposed by left-wing parties in CA1. In December 2011 – a month after the controversial Supreme Court decision barring further extension of the Assembly – a report by the International Crisis Group summarised the debates over judicial reform within CA1:

> The issue of the judicial system ... remains controversial in legal circles. A constitutional court has been proposed, as well as appointment of judges by an independent body that includes representatives from parliament. This is a considerable change from the original concept, primarily put forward by the Maoists, which would have limited the authority of the Supreme Court; provided that constitutional disputes would be settled by a parliamentary body; and would have made all judges political appointees. The legal community

---

34 See: https://thehimalayantimes.com/kathmandu/sc-endorses-regmis-appointment-in-executive/
35 See: http://archive.nepalitimes.com/article/from-nepali-press/I-will-not-spare-the-corrupt,3156

is a significant constituency for politicians to alienate, given the increasing appeals to the Supreme Court on the peace process and politically important issues such as extension of the CA and pardons for crimes committed by party members.[36]

After years of lobbying by the legal profession, eventually a compromise was reached in CA2: the proposal for a separate Constitutional Court was scrapped, and instead a Constitutional Bench within the Supreme Court was created. It remains an unsatisfying compromise for many judges and lawyers, who identify this as part of a wider, concerted assault on the Nepali judiciary.

The 2015 Constitution weakens the position of the Supreme Court in three respects:

(i) Under the 2015 Constitution, the ability to review legislation is confined to the newly established Constitutional Bench, which is now the only judicial organ allowed to adjudicate on the validity of legislation on the basis of constitutionality, resolve disputes between the various tiers of government, and determine electoral controversies. The reliance on the smaller Constitutional Bench is causing the Court's already sizeable constitutional backlog to increase considerably and thus undermines the viability of the combination of judicial review and PIL.

(ii) The 2015 Constitution has relaxed the requirements for impeachment, threatening to undermine the independence of the judiciary.[37] Indeed, the easing of the impeachment requirements under Article 101 has already facilitated two failed impeachment attempts at the Supreme Court level in September 2016 against Justice Ananda Mohan Bhattarai,[38] and another in April 2017 against Chief Justice Sushila Karki.[39]

(iii) The 2015 Constitution retains the procedure for judicial appointments introduced by the 2007 Interim Constitution. It requires all nominations to Chief Justice and all Supreme Court Justices, members of Judicial Council, Head or official of Constitutional bodies, and ambassadors be reviewed by the Parliamentary Hearings Committee (PHC). Article 293 clearly states that "constitutional bodies must be accountable and responsible to the Federal Parliament" embedding the principle of parliamentary scrutiny and oversight. This procedure is redundant as the constitutional bodies, in which the executive is in a majority, already perform the function of vetting candidates

---

36 See: https://d2071andvip0wj.cloudfront.net/b131-nepal-s-peace-process-the-endgame-nears.pdf [Accessed 6 January 2019].
37 Article 101.
38 The impeachment complaint failed to secure the necessary one-fourth support and was quashed by Parliament's Impeachment Recommendation Committee as spurious.
39 The Supreme Court issued an interim order staying the impeachment motion and reinstating the Chief Justice. Ultimately, the three main political parties simply agreed to withdraw the impeachment motion as part of a political deal to reshuffle the Cabinet.

and finding an agreement among the various institutional actors. The Parliamentary Hearings Committee is borrowed from the American model, which aims to ensure parliamentary oversight of presidential nominations. In Nepal, the PHC procedure has been considered a formality until very recently, but in August 2018 the PHC rejected the nomination of Acting Chief Justice Deepak Raj Joshi in what appeared to be a politically motivated decision by lawmakers from the government's party. Moreover, the effectiveness of the constitutional bodies in dealing with issues pertaining to the judiciary – including misconduct – had already been tested in March 2018, when the Constitutional Council removed Chief Justice Parajuli from his post on the basis of the mandatory age requirement for retirement.

7.5 Conclusions

Four sets of conclusions on unconstitutional constitutional amendments in the context of constitution making can be drawn from the Nepal case study. First, the language of the basic structure doctrine has seeped into Nepal's constitutional discourse. Significantly, Nepal's saga over unconstitutional constitutional amendments took place under the 2007 Interim Constitution, which unlike its 1990 predecessor and 2015 successor did not contain any eternity clauses. In this respect, I argue that the increase in the stature and activism of the Supreme Court of Nepal since the 1990s emboldened the court to extend its power of judicial review to constitutional amendments extending the term of CA1 and to deploy the language of the basic structure doctrine to justify its intervention.

Second, the contested nature of constitutional unamendability coupled with the explosive issue of adjudication on the life itself of the Constituent Assembly raised questions not just about the appropriate constitutional bounds of the judiciary, but about the partisan nature of judicial decision-making under these circumstances. Both the constitutional context and the political milieu of post-conflict Nepal are crucial factors in explaining the high degree of judicial intervention by the Supreme Court as well as the consequences of that degree of involvement. In the short term, the court appeared to take a partisan position and was openly accused of doing just that.

Third, Nepal's post-conflict constitution-making process fits what Silvia Suteu has characterised as the "fraught context" of divided, conflict-affected societies.[40] As such this contentious process was both the backdrop of *and* the substantive core issue in the protracted litigation over the validity of the constitutional amendments seeking to extend the CA1 term. The problematic nature of the Nepal Supreme Court's interventions in the life of CA1 resulted from a combination of judicial activism and partisan politics. On the one hand, the constitution-making process could not continue indefinitely especially since the party leaders had already highjacked the drafting process from the Constituent

---

40 Silvia Suteu, Chapter 14 in this volume.

Assembly. Moreover, the Supreme Court only put a stop to further extensions by way of constitutional amendment after the fourth time in May 2012, only when a fifth extension was attempted. On the other hand, the involvement of Chief Justice Regmi in executive politics after the dissolution of CA1 retrospectively casted a nefarious light on the intentions of the bench in adjudicating those cases. Moreover, the fact that the 2015 Constitution proved to be such an embattled settlement makes it easy for the groups unhappy with it to place the blame with the Supreme Court.

Finally, the way in which the Supreme Court and its Justices conducted themselves during Nepal's most embattled litigation bore a profound influence on the outcome of the constitution-making process itself, especially with respect to the structure and powers of the higher judiciary. In the long term, the move by the court gave enough justification to constitution-makers to rein in the highest court and to attempt a significant curtailment of its role and function. The result was a compromise, but it is clear that the 2015 Constitution has effectively sought to curb the judicial activism – and the power – of the Supreme Court.

Part III
Decisive model

8 Beyond unconstitutionality

The public oversight of constitutional revision in Taiwan

Jiunn-rong Yeh

8.1 Introduction

Taiwan's Constitutional Court (the Court) issued Judicial Yuan Interpretation (J.Y. Interpretation) No. 499 declaring unconstitutional the constitutional amendments passed by the National Assembly on the ground that these amendments infringed the constitutionally embedded basic structure on substantive and procedural grounds. With this ruling, the Court was hailed as a brave and active court that dared to challenge public sovereignty in constitutional revisions.[1]

Judicial review has become a popular mechanism in modern constitutional democracies, but judicial checks on the constitutionality of constitutional amendments have been rare and exceptional in practice. Upon ruling constitutional amendments unconstitutional, the courts, even individual justices, might be hailed as heroic and the constitutional doctrines used to support the decision, such as basic structure doctrine, eternal clauses, or inherent limitations to sovereign constitutional revision powers, could well be over-dramatized without sufficient contextual rationalization.[2] By looking into ad hoc judicial cases in this way, this leading case approach often fails to account for the spectrum and dynamics of constitutional amendment mechanisms and processes on the one hand and public perceptions of constitutional amendments on the other. Worse, single case doctrinal analysis often fails to recognize public ambivalence towards constitutional change and the spectrum of constitutional amendment mechanisms.

This chapter looks into Taiwan's J.Y. Interpretation No. 499 with contextual underpinnings, including atypical transitional arrangements of elections, presidential electoral imperatives, party politics, and negotiated constitutional engineering. Other earlier judicial settlements that set the foundation of procedural rationality in exercising sovereign power of constitutional amendment are also reviewed to

---

1 See Jiunn-rong Yeh and Wen-Chen Chang, 'An Evolving Court with Changing Functions: The Constitutional Court and Judicial Review in Taiwan' in Albert HY Chen and Andrew Harding (eds), *Constitutional Courts in Asia: A Comparative Perspective* (CUP 2018).
2 David KC Huang and Nigel NT Li, 'Unconstitutional Constitutional Amendment in Taiwan: A Retrospective Analysis of Judicial Yuan Interpretation No. 499 (2000)' (2020) 15 University of Pennsylvania Asian Law Review 424.

DOI: 10.4324/9781003097099-8

154 *Jiunn-rong Yeh*

better present a holistic picture of judicial review, against the backdrop of public oversight, on constitutional amendment. This chapter argues that the alleged global diffusion of the idea of unconstitutional constitutional amendment is in fact a continuous struggle of public oversight on constitutional amendment, in which not only the judiciary but the general public plays an integral role too.

8.2 Judicial reasoning and contextual imperatives

The 1946 ROC Constitution (the Constitution) set forth the National Assembly as the monopolistic institution to revise the constitution.[3] Since the launch of democratic reform, the National Assembly has completed seven rounds of constitutional amendments in 1991, 1992, 1994, 1997, 1999, 2000, and 2005.[4] In the 1999 amendment, the fifth one, the National Assembly concluded three main schemes: (1) parliamentary reform on the structure of the National Assembly and Legislative Yuan; (2) elimination of temporary clauses on provincial election; (3) incorporation of basic national policies.[5] Among these revisions, proportional-appointment and term-extension clauses were highly controversial, considered as a political and constitutional surprise to the new democracy.[6] Unlike previous rounds of constitutional revisions, this revision provoked public outcry amidst the upcoming presidential election. Not surprisingly, agents of major political parties appealed to the Court, arguing that these revisions were unconstitutional.

It was absolutely within the Court's discretion to avoid the tight rope by resorting to the political question doctrine while confronting the justiciability of constitutional amendments.[7] The Court, nevertheless, took a hard look at the

---

3 Article 174 of the ROC Constitution provides two methods of constitutional revision. (1) Upon the proposal of one-fifth of the total number of the delegates to the National Assembly and by a resolution of three-fourths of the delegates present at a meeting having a quorum of two-thirds of the entire Assembly, the Constitution may be amended. (2) Upon the proposal of one-fourth of the members of the Legislative Yuan and by a resolution of three-fourths of the members present at a meeting having a quorum of three-fourths of the members of the Yuan, an amendment may be drawn up and submitted to the National Assembly by way of referendum. Such a proposed amendment to the Constitution shall be publicly published half a year before the National Assembly convenes. In practice, however, the second procedure has never been used.
4 For a general review of these seven rounds of constitutional amendments and future prospects, see Jiunn-rong Yeh, 'Taiwan's Constitution: Incremental Reform and Prospects for Future Revisions' in Ryan Dunch and Ashley Esarey (eds), *Taiwan in Dynamic Transition: Nation Building and Democratization* (University of Washington Press 2020).
5 For the full content of the 1999 constitutional revision: Office of the President, Republic of China (Taiwan) < https://www.president.gov.tw/Page/326> accessed 22 May 2021.
6 Huang and Li (n 2) 424.
7 For judicial application of the political question doctrines in Taiwan and other east Asian democracies, see Jiunn-rong Yeh, 'Judicial Strategies and Political Question Doctrine: An Investigation into the Judicial Adjudications of the East Asian Courts' in Chang-fa Lo, Nigel NT Li and Tsai-yu Lin (eds), *Thoughts between the East and the West in the Multilevel Legal Order* (Springer 2016).

dynamics of constitutional revision without acknowledging that this revision was in fact undertaken as a part of the ongoing incremental constitutional engineering for better democratic representation within a transforming Taiwan.

8.2.1 Judicial reasoning on unconstitutionality

The court reviewed the case from procedural and substantive angles, both leading to the conclusion of unconstitutionality. On reviewing the procedural flaws in the reading sessions, the Court made it clear that the amendment process contradicted certain basic principles of the Constitution, which rendered the entire revision void. In addition, using the theory of constitutional unamendability, the Court went on to strike down both proportional-appointment and term-extension clauses, based on the violation of principles concerning popular sovereignty and democratic republic that are the integral part of the constitutional order.

8.2.1.1 Procedural grounds

In its reasoning, the Court declared that the 1999 constitutional revision was inconsistent with certain fundamental principles that sustain the validity of constitutional amendments. In the Court's view, an amendment process requires openness and transparency as the fundamental principles to facilitate democratic deliberation and rational communication. Moreover, a constitutional amendment should be deemed void if there is a "manifest and gross flaw" in the amendment process.[8]

Yet, as the Court observed, the procedural requirements were not fulfilled by the National Assembly during the reading sessions. Among the various procedural flaws, the use of secret ballots was considered as manifest and gross, and had already undermined the legitimacy and validity of the amendment. In the second and third reading sessions, Su Nan-Cheng, the Speaker of National Assembly, denied the request for an open ballot pursuant to Article 38 of the Rules of Procedure and the application of a secret ballot was then approved by the majority.[9] The Court condemned the application of the secret ballot in the amendment process as a clear contravention of the principle of openness and transparency.[10] Based on these procedural grounds, the Court struck down the disputed revision in its entirety, even though Articles 9 and 10 of the Additional Articles were not challenged at all.

---

8 J.Y. Interpretation No. 499 (2000).
9 See Li Bingnan, *2000 Taiwan Xiangai* (Taiwan's Constitutional Change in 2000) (Straits Academic Press 2004) 21–2; Xie zhengdao, *Zhonghua Minguo Xiuxian Shi* (The History of Constitutional Change in Taiwan) (Hurng-Chih Book Co., Ltd. 2007) 386.
10 J.Y. Interpretation No. 499 (2000).

8.2.1.2 Substantive grounds

The Court further examined substantive matters within the disputed constitutional revisions, holding that some contradicted constitutional provisions that are "integral to the essential nature of the Constitution."[11] For the Court, these essential provisions cannot be undermined even through constitutional amendment as they would otherwise destroy the constitutional order in its entirety. Despite the fact that the Constitution does not explicitly include any provision within its essential nature, the Court still made its own list of unamendable provisions, including Article 1 (the principle of democratic republic), Article 2 (the principle of popular sovereignty), Chapter II (the protection of constitutional rights), and those providing for the separation of powers and the principle of checks and balances.[12] The rationale behind the concept of unamendability is arguably inspired by constitutional theory from Germany that distinguishes between the essential and non-essential part of the Constitution.[13]

By applying the theory, the Court struck down both proportional-appointment and term-extension clauses based on their contradictions with the essential provisions of the Constitution. The National Assembly was granted tremendous constitutional powers including the power to amend the constitution, which by nature should be vested with the elected representatives. In this sense, the Court required that the members of National Assembly must be directly elected by the people, but representatives elected pursuant to the proportional-appointment clause were merely "appointed by individual political parties, rather than representatives of the people."[14] Therefore, the Grand Justice found this clause incompatible with the principle of democratic republic under Article 1 of the Constitution.

Similarly, the Court did not struggle too much to reach the conclusion that the term-extension clause was also unconstitutional. Based on its previous decisions in J.Y. Interpretation Nos. 31 and 261, the Court held that regular elections must take place to reflect the will of the people unless an extraordinary circumstance exists to justify preclusion. The Court took the position that it is not constitutionally allowed to change the term limit of the National Assembly alone while leaving its structural and functional reform for future political resolution. By denying the necessity of extending the fixed term of the National Assembly, the Court considered such an extension as a betrayal of the people, which should be deemed inconsistent with the principle of popular sovereignty.

---

11 J.Y. Interpretation No. 499 (2000).
12 J.Y. Interpretation No. 499 (2000).
13 It was so argued by the authors of one of the three applications. See Huang and Li (n 2) 443–4.
14 J.Y. Interpretation No. 499 (2000).

8.2.2 Contextual imperatives for judicial activism

The holding and reasoning in the ruling were ironclad and harsh, but there could well be contextual imperatives for the Court to do so. By looking into the context, judicial decisions can be conceived as reflecting the political tide, moving the Court towards politicization. Three contextual imperatives provided the impetus for the determinate ruling. They are: (1) incremental constitutional reform, (2) the status of the National Assembly, and (3) the presidential election.

8.2.2.1 Incremental constitutional reform since the 1990s

During the time of democratic transition, Taiwan underwent seven rounds of constitutional revision from 1991 to 2005.[15] This incrementalist model of constitutional reform was actually a compromise through the negotiations of political powers, rather than a composition of mere incidental events. Fierce debates occurred on the choice between "incrementally amending the constitution" and "making a new constitution" in reflecting the changing landscape of constitutional order. However, in order to preserve the symbolic "*Fatung*" of the ROC Constitution, the latter proposal was strongly opposed by the then-ruling Kuomintang (KMT) government.[16] The main scheme of Taiwan's incremental constitutional reforms lay in the reconstruction of popular representation to strengthen the connection between the central government and the people themselves. This constitutional project was eventually completed with the abolishment of the National Assembly and the desirable installation of a public referendum in the seventh constitutional revision of 2005.[17]

Similar to the past four rounds of constitutional revision, the fifth in 1999 was still the product of partisan negotiations for incremental constitutional engineering. After the fourth constitutional revision passed in 1997, the National Assembly became the next target of reform. Proposals for reorganizing the National Assembly varied from its entire abolishment to structural reform by transforming it into a bicameral parliament.[18] Consensus was finally achieved in the fifth constitutional revision to approve the proposal of unicameralism, which included both proportional-appointment and term-extension clauses aiming not only to reflect the outcome of political negotiations but to reduce the cost of holding national elections.[19]

---

15 Yeh (n 4) 80–92.
16 Jiunn-rong Yeh, 'The Cult of Fatung: Representational Manipulation and Reconstruction in Taiwan' in Graham Hassall and Cheryl Saunders (eds), *The People's Representatives: Electoral Systems in the Asia-Pacific Region* (St Leonards, N.S.W.: Allen & Unwin 1997).
17 Jiunn-rong Yeh, *The Constitution in Taiwan: A Contextual Analysis* (Hart 2016) 38–9.
18 Jiunn-rong Yeh, 'Cong XinGuohui Guandian Lun Guohui Gaige' (*Parliamentary Reform from the Perspective of a "New Parliament"*) (1999) 6 Xinshiji Zhiku Luntan (The Think Tank Forum) 28, 30–2.
19 Li (n 9) 2.

8.2.2.2 National Assembly as a sunset agency

Looking back to Taiwan's constitutional history, the National Assembly was established, under Sun Yat-Sen's blueprint, as a significant body to represent the will of the people and reflect popular sovereignty. Article 27 of the Constitution granted the National Assembly the power to elect and recall the president and the vice president, as well as to amend the Constitution. Yet, during the time of democratization, the National Assembly was considered the "sunset agency." For one thing, the constitutional image of the National Assembly was based on the illusion of Mainland China as the ruling territory. Moreover, under the authoritarian regime governed by the Temporary Provisions, representatives of the National Assembly had not been reelected for over 40 years. It is therefore questionable whether the structure and function of the National Assembly could still satisfy the people's demand for democratic transformations.

As the monopolistic institution to approve constitutional amendments, the National Assembly abused its power for "rent-seeking" tradeoffs for its own political interests.[20] According to the Constitution, constitutional amendments could be proposed by the National Assembly or Legislative Yuan, but the Assembly was the only branch to hold the power of approving those proposed amendments. Yet in practice, almost every constitutional revision, including those to the Temporary Provisions, was proposed and approved by the National Assembly alone.[21] After the second and third constitutional revision, the Assembly not only made the structural reform a permanent institution that would be involved in more political affairs, but also expanded its own powers, *inter alia*, to confirm the appointments of the Judicial, Examination, and Control Yuan.[22]

In addition, the creation of the National Assembly and Legislative Yuan generated conflicts over the nature and scope of power sharing between the two political branches. To elaborate, unlike the bicameral system in some countries, it is argued that such division tears apart the power that has been conventionally perceived to be in the hands of the legislature. Even worse, competition for representing the supreme legislative body took place between the National Assembly and Legislative Yuan, especially when they were both recognized as "parliaments" by the Court in a previous decision, J.Y. Interpretation No. 76.[23]

---

20 Jiunn-rong Yeh, *Zhenxi Xianfa Shike* (Constitutional Moment) (Angle Publishing Co., Ltd. 2000) 47–50.
21 See Jiunn-rong Yeh, 'Jiuqi Xiangai yu Taiwan Xianfa Bianqian de Moshi' (Constitutional Revision of 1997 and the Model of Taiwan's Constitutional Change), *Minzhu Zhuanxing Yu Xianfa Bianqian* (Democratic Transition and Constitutional Change) (Angle Publishing Co., Ltd 2003) 11, 121, and 131; see also Xu Zhengrong, 'Woguo Xiuxian Jiguan Wenti zhi Yanjiu' (A Research on Taiwan's Constitutional Amendment Body) in Wu Zhongli and Wu Yushan (eds), *Xianzheng Gaige: Beijing, Yunzuo Yu Yingxiang* (Constitutional Reform: Its Context, Process and the Impact) (Wu-Nan Book Inc 2006) 108.
22 Article 11 of the Additional Articles (1992); Article 1 of the Additional Articles (1994).
23 "The National Assembly, the Legislative Yuan and the Control Yuan ... are composed of representatives or members that are directly or indirectly elected by the people. Their functions

In this context, demands for parliamentary reform became increasingly urgent to clarify the relationship between the National Assembly and the Legislative Yuan.

8.2.2.3 Presidential election and constitutional politics

Before the fifth constitutional revision in 1999, four rounds of constitutional reforms had been completed. One of the main schemes of these reforms focused on the institutional design of presidential powers and presidential elections. The first direct presidential election was held in 1996, making Taiwan a success story, marching towards a more democratic state. Moreover, the next presidential election in 2000 gave birth to the first regime change where the KMT lost its ruling power over the island for the first time in 50 years. With the Democratic Progressive Party (DPP) mounting a strong challenge, this election was critical for the KMT government as to whether it could still hold power for the next four years. The conference for the fifth revision was adjourned after the negotiations between the KMT and DPP, waiting for the decision from James Soong, another political superstar, on whether he would split from the KMT and run on an independent ticket for his presidential candidacy.[24]

Notably, the president in Taiwan has played a significant role throughout the course of Taiwan's constitutional reforms. In response to people's outcry for democratization, President Lee Teng-hui convened a National Conference in 1990, which settled the issues for multi-stage constitutional reforms and reached a consensus on repealing the Temporary Provisions.[25] As the leader of the KMT government, President Lee delivered his announcement to complete the engineering of constitutional reform with his term of presidency after attending a national meeting in 1998. On April 1999, the National Assembly soon requested President Lee to convene a conference for amending the constitution.[26]

In addition, the timing of the court's ruling was politically sensitive, being so close to the upcoming presidential election, which was only a week later. As the KMT's presidential candidate, Lien Chan had criticized the fifth revision as totally irresponsible.[27] On the other hand, President Lee cautiously remained silent on the revision.[28] In such a context, the issuance of J.Y. Interpretation No. 499 was conceived as the "x" factor of the presidential election. If the Court had struck down the fifth constitutional revision before the election day, it was a clear message from the Grand Justice that the fifth constitutional revision was unac-

---

and powers are similar to those important powers exercised by the parliaments of democratic nations. All of them from the perspective of the nature of their statuses and functions in the Constitution, should be considered as equivalent to the parliaments of democratic nations."
J.Y. Interpretation No. 76 (1957).
24 Xie (n 9) 383.
25 See Yeh (n 17) 38.
26 Li (n 9) 10–11.
27 See Yeh (n 17) 45.
28 Li (n 9) 28.

160 *Jiunn-rong Yeh*

ceptable. In this sense, the Grand Justice seemed to avoid criticisms for being involved in such political turbulence.

8.3 The Constitutional Court as the instrument for people's veto power over constitutional revision

Conventional understanding of judicial review is to confine the function of political powers in the orbit of constitutional space, and that is done so that the court rules independently. Investigating the contextual underpinnings of judicial rulings, one may find people engaged collectively in the making of judicial activism. The Court in J.Y. Interpretation No. 499 functioned exactly like that, serving as the instrument for the people to exercise their veto power against the discredited National Assembly that enjoyed monopolistic power over constitutional revision.

8.3.1 The notorious National Assembly and incremental constitutional reform

The issuance of J.Y. Interpretation No. 499 served not only as a denial of the constitutional amendments but also an institutional check on the notorious National Assembly. Indeed, the National Assembly had long been condemned as illegitimate and politically unaccountable. Representatives of the National Assembly had been denounced as "old thieves" (老賊) since their seats had not been up for election for some 40 years.[29] In addition, the Assembly's monopolistic amendment power became troublesome as a "Leviathan" that could hardly be controlled by any constitutional mechanism of checks and balances.[30] By the time of the fifth constitutional amendment, the National Assembly was therefore targeted for both functional change and institutional reorganization. Yet, the obstacles underlying such reforms lay in the National Assembly itself. A paradox of constitutional reform could be clearly observed: whether the self-interested National Assembly would be willing to lessen its own political powers by exercising its monopolistic constitutional revision power.

The general public had been disappointed with the Assembly's rent-seeking manipulations in each round of constitutional revisions, resulting in increasingly louder calls for its reorganization or total abolishment. The well-known term "Legends in the Mountain" had been used as the metaphor to literally describe the unexpected result of political games in the amendment conferences, which had been held in the scenic Yangming Mountain adjacent to the national capital Taipei.[31] During the Wild Lily Movement in 1990, student groups and activists had launched an appeal to dissolve the National Assembly, with the slogan "we

---

29 See Yeh (n 17) 39–40.
30 Yeh (n 20) 137–8.
31 Li Hongxi, 'Fei Guomin Dahui, Ci Qi Shi Ye' (It Is the Right Moment to Abolish the National Assembly) (2000) 10 Xinshiji Zhiku Luntan (The Think Tank Forum) 32, 36.

don't want hundreds of emperors."[32] After the fifth constitutional revision was passed by the National Assembly, there were sweeping criticisms condemning the National Assembly as "shameless" for its self-imposed term-extension as well as against the whole revision.[33] Even the ruling KMT, the political party that enjoyed a super majority in the Assembly, was divided on whether Speaker Su Nan-cheng should be responsible for the failure of the revision. Conflicts inside the KMT eventually led to Su's departure from the KMT.[34] Not surprisingly, a party cadre moved to appeal to the Court, arguing for the profound unconstitutionality of the revision.

Public distrust of the uncontrollable National Assembly in exercising constitutional revision powers was taken seriously by the Court years before the controversial fifth round of revision. Responding to the charge that the National Assembly sought to push through constitutional revision without prior notice, the Court was keen to impose a judicial check on the process of constitutional amendment to prevent possible procedural manipulation by the National Assembly. In J.Y. Interpretation No. 314, the Court made it clear that constitutional amendments cannot be passed through a temporary meeting; otherwise, the National Assembly would bypass higher procedural requirements for amending constitutional provisions. Notably, as the Court emphasized, the process of constitutional amendment should be conducted in such a way that people can have the opportunity to know its purpose and be able to express their opinions.[35]

In J.Y. Interpretation No. 342, the Court was asked whether the process of legislation in the Legislative Yuan was subject to judicial review. Based on the rules of the Legislative Yuan and the Constitution, the Court ruled the legislative process shall not be subject to scrutiny by the authority responsible for interpretation of the Constitution unless it clearly contravenes the Constitution. The Court viewed the legislative process an internal matter which falls within the scope set by the Legislative Yuan by virtue of the principle of parliamentary autonomy.[36]

J.Y. Interpretation No. 342 and J.Y. Interpretation No. 499 were all about the due process of legislation, even though one concerned a legislative bill and the other concerned a constitutional revision proposal. Yet, the Court treated the two cases differently. In J.Y. Interpretation No. 342, the Court respected the autonomy of the Legislative Yuan. But in J.Y. Interpretation No. 499, the Court

32 Fan Yun, 'Yebaihe Xueyun de Si Da Suqiu yu Si ge Yuanze' (Four Appeals and Principles in the Wild Lily Movement) (*Radio Taiwan International*) <https://www.rti.org.tw/radio/programMessagePlayer/programId/1580/id/102514> accessed 22 May 2021.
33 Li Suzhen, 'Guomin Dahui Ying Liji Tingzhi Kaihui, Quanli Jinxing Guodai Gaixuan' (The National Assembly Should Adjourn the Conference and Immediately Commence the Reelection) *China Times* (Taipei, 8 April 2000).
34 Fan Jiajie, 'Paohong Yanren An, Chaoye Liwei Tongpi Su Nancheng' (Legislators Condemned Su Nan-cheng for the Term-Extension Clause) *China Times* (Taipei, 30 October 1999).
35 J.Y. Interpretation No. 314 (1993).
36 J.Y. Interpretation No. 342 (1994).

took a hard stand. The Court thought there were manifest and gross flaws in the process of the fifth constitutional revision and held it unconstitutional. The contextual imperatives set forth above could be the drivers of the judicial about-turn.

8.3.2 Public sentiment towards frequent constitutional amendments

Incremental constitutional revisions require the National Assembly to convene and pass constitutional amendments frequently. Although constitutional revision was directed to resolving political crisis for democratization, public dissatisfaction with constitutional revisions arose as a clear reflection of public distrust in the politics of constitutional amendment. As observed, constitutional reforms in Taiwan have been criticized as "elite settlements," with political parties exerting control in the monopolistic National Assembly and leaving little room for public participation.[37] This elite model of amendment would hardly win the heartfelt support of civil society but instead increasingly generate public alienation over constitutional reforms. Even worse, the elite settlement of constitutional revision in Taiwan centers around the discredited National Assembly that seeks to expand powers and collect political gains in every round of constitutional revisions.

In addition, frequent constitutional amendments would have a negative impact that undermines the stability of the constitutional order. Five rounds of constitutional revisions by the same institution in only nine years inevitably lead to calls for reforming the National Assembly itself.

8.3.3 Constitutional re-revision and political retaliation against the Court

The Court ruling on the unconstitutionality of the constitutional amendment was not surprising to the public at all. Many celebrated the decision as a successful resistance to the expansion of the National Assembly and a safeguard for constitutionalism. Yet, the Court choose to downplay, if not completely ignore, the fact that this revision should be in fact taken as a part of the incremental constitutional engineering for Taiwan's improved democratic representation. Indeed, the constitutional revision institution and process as specified by the Constitution is itself the source of the problem. Taking the constitutional revision to the Court and having it ruled unconstitutional was a short cut to this rather deep-rooted institutional problem.

Having issued a popular decision, the court nevertheless paid the price later on. After the ruling was made, Speaker Su was upset about judicial intervention,

---

37 See Jiunn-rong Yeh 'Xiangai de Quanshi: Xianfa Bianqian de Dianfan Zhuanyi' (An Interpretation on Taiwan's Constitutional Revision in 2005: A Paradigm Shift of Constitutional Change) in Jhou Zhihong, Xu Zhixiong, and Cai Maoyin (eds), *Xiandai Xianfa De Lilun Yu Xianshi* (Theory and Practice of Modern Constitutional Law) (Angle Publishing Co., Ltd 2007) 145, 153.

criticizing the Court's ruling as inappropriate and ridiculous and stating that it would cause further constitutional crisis.[38] Moreover, Lin Yi-hsiung, then Chairman of the DPP, concurred with Speaker Su in arguing that the Court's power unconstitutionally overrode the amendment power.[39] Consensus was reached among the KMT, the DPP, and the New Party to convene the conference for the next revision. For the KMT, the reelection of the National Assembly was not the priority after losing the presidential election in March. On the other hand, it was another opportunity for the DPP to abolish the National Assembly.[40] In 2000, the same National Assembly gathered and passed a constitutional amendment that removed the pension of the grand justices who were not transferred from the judiciary.[41] This political retaliation was considered as punishment to the grand justices with scholarly backgrounds, to the lament of the judiciary.[42] One grand justice responded with concern over the possible impact on judicial independence.[43]

8.4 Politicization of the Constitutional Court and public scrutiny of constitutional revision

Similar to other Asian courts, the Court has been observed to be politicized, engaging itself more frequently in dynamic interactions among political branches and with the civil society.[44]

8.4.1 The shaping of a political court

It is not surprising that the Court was willing to take a hard look at the fifth constitutional revision with the people and political forces behind it. The Court went with the political tide to strike down constitutional amendments as a whole, leaving no room for the National Assembly to deliberate further. As Martin Shapiro

---

38 Wang Zhengning, 'Dangji Bei Kaichu, Su Nancheng Yao Gao Lianzhan, ye Pi Dafaguan, Ren Yanren An Weixian Jieshi Huangqiangzouban, Jiang Zhi Xianzheng Weiji' (Su Nancheng Would Sue Lien Chan after the Removal of His KMT Membership, and Also Criticized the Judicial Interpretation as Ridiculous That Would Lead to Constitutional Crisis) *United Evening News* (Taipei, 25 March 2000).
39 Peng Weijing, 'Lin Yixiong: Sifa Lingjia yu Renmin Yizhi zhi Shang' (Lin Yi-hsiung Considered that Judiciary Has Unconstitutionally Prevailed over People Themselves) *United Daily News* (Taipei, 25 March 2000).
40 Li (n 9) 77.
41 Article 5 of the Additional Articles (2000).
42 Guo Zihong and Huang Jinlan, 'Guoda Paichu Dafaguan Youyu, Weng Yuesheng Yihan' (Weng Yueh-sheng Felt Disappointed with the Removal of Grand Justices' Pension by the National Assembly) *China Times* (Taipei, 26 April 2000).
43 Zhang Tesheng, 'Dafaguan Youyu Quebao Chaoran Duli' (The Pension for Grand Justices Is the Guarantee of Judicial Independence) *United Daily News* (Taipei, 23 April 2000).
44 See Jiunn-rong Yeh, 'Politicization of Constitutional Courts in Asia: Institutional Features, Contexts and Legitimacy' in Henning Glaser (ed), *Constitutional Jurisprudence: Function, Impact and Challenges* (Nomos Verlagsgesellschaft 2016).

puts it, however, courts are indeed part of the political process, relying on support from the political system.[45] From this perspective, judicial reasoning in J.Y. Interpretation No. 499 can be regarded as the reflection of the underlying political and social tide in which the Court was situated. Grand justices may be well aware that they were confirmed then by the National Assembly. However, they still wiped out the entire constitutional revision in the midst of the heated presidential election with strong and clear public opinion behind them. What they did not anticipate then was the retaliation from the National Assembly in their next constitutional revision.

Though it was not the first time for the Court to deal with such politically charged issues, judicial intervention in constitutional amendment disputes marked a turning point in the trajectory of constitutional reform and democratic transition in Taiwan. Moreover, engaged civic groups and vibrant civil society, which have flourished since the 1980s, made a significant contribution to Taiwan's constitutional reform even when their sovereign power over constitutional change was taken away by the National Assembly. Reading beyond the determinate normative construction in the decision, the Court is indeed a "people's court" that plays an integral role by engaging itself in the stream of constitutional reform with public support deeply felt.

8.4.2 *Judicial strategies and risk management*

The issue behind J.Y. Interpretation No. 499 was a politically charged one. Grand justices did not choose the case before them, but they could exercise judicial strategies to minimize political backlash. The Court strategically went with the mainstream opinion as chanted by major political parties in the presidential election to avoid contradicting the will of the majority. The National Assembly, on the other hand, was treated as the "underdog" facing vigorous condemnation from the public. Indeed, the constitutional petition against the Assembly was then formed by a cross-party coalition in the Legislative Yuan representing major political parties and launched attacks on this notorious constitutional revision. However, this "majoritarian" judicial strategy did not exempt the Court from political retaliation as seen above.

8.4.3 *The integral role of popular sovereignty and public scrutiny in reviewing constitutional amendments*

In the contextual analysis of J.Y. Interpretation No. 499, one can find public scrutiny played an integral role in judicial review of constitutional amendments. The problem behind the fifth constitutional revision lies primarily in public dissatisfaction with the National Assembly itself. In this sense, the Court functions

---

45 Martin Shapiro, *Courts: A Comparative and Political Analysis* (University of Chicago Press 1981) 63.

not only as an institutional check on the constitutionality of the revision but as an instrument of the people's veto power against constitutional amendments to make the National Assembly politically accountable.

8.4.3.1 Popular sovereignty and the Court

From the perspective of judicial politics, there is a profound relationship between popular sovereignty and the judiciary. On the one hand, popular sovereignty provides legitimacy to all governmental powers including the one vested with the judicial branch. Judicial power has been commonly criticized on democratic grounds as the long-standing "counter-majoritarian difficulty" is primarily based on the premise that judges are not selected by the people.[46] In this sense, popular sovereignty not only serves as a checking mechanism on the exercise of judicial power but also plays a critical role in reinforcing the Court's constitutional legitimacy. On the other hand, courts may adopt the strategy to decide cases in accordance with the will of the people in order to obtain public support. As the "least dangerous branch," the judiciary is powerless to directly implement its preferred policies. By rendering "majoritarian" decisions, courts can build up their institutional capacity as well as reputation to compete with other political branches.[47]

Indeed, to theorize the role of popular sovereignty in interacting with the judiciary is not new. Larry Kramer's popular constitutionalism asserts a significant role for public interpretation of the constitution, against judicial supremacy in which the opinions of judges are placed as final and absolute in the shaping of constitutional order and rights recognition.[48] Similarly, the idea of civic constitutionalism as observed in the maturing democracy of Taiwan also highlights the constitutional function of civil society as it remains watchful and engaged not only in constitutional politics but also with respect to judicial review on rights protection and government integrity. Civil groups in Taiwan, often with the support of one-third of the Legislature, could bring issues to the courts for resolution, engaging in constitutional discourse, and pushing forward the consolidation of constitutional rights and principles. On the other hand, while weaving the fabric of the constitution, the Court keeps abreast of public views on matters concerning constitutional adjudication.[49] These insights remind us that courts do

---

46 See Alexander M. Bickel, *The Least Dangerous Branch: The Supreme Court at The Bar of Politics* (2 edn, Yale University Press 1986) 16–23.
47 To view Taiwan's Constitutional Court as an example of majoritarian judicial review, see Chien-Chih Lin, 'Majoritarian Judicial Review: The Case of Taiwan' (2014) 9 NTU Law Review 103.
48 See Larry D Kramer, *The People Themselves: Popular Constitutionalism and Judicial Review* (Y Oxford University Press 2004).
49 See Jiunn-rong Yeh, 'Marching towards Civic Constitutionalism with Sunflowers' (2015) 45 Hong Kong Law Journal 315, 319–21.

not make decisions independently by leaving the people's will aside, which echoes Martin Shapiro's observation of courts as part of the political process.

8.4.3.2 *Popular sovereignty as a catalyst in J.Y. Interpretation No. 499*

The Court ruled in J.Y. Interpretation No. 499 in accordance with the people's will. By looking into historical context, one can therefore understand the role of popular sovereignty behind, beneath, and beyond this case. Since Taiwan's democratization in the late 1980s, civil society has remained vibrant, leading to significant political change by engaging constitutional revisions, major legislation, and the judicial process, including appeals to the Constitutional Court.[50]

In previous constitutional interpretations, the Grand Justices had paved the way for popular sovereignty to play a critical role in constitutional revision, notwithstanding the fact that the Constitution vests the National Assembly with monopolistic power to revise the constitution. The Court issued J.Y. Interpretation No. 261, nearly a decade before No. 499, holding that the postponed reelection of representatives must be held in light of social and political changes.[51] During the Court's deliberation, students chanting for constitutional reform, including abolishing the National Assembly, before the Chang Kai-shek Memorial, culminated in the renowned Wild Lily Movement that contributed to consecutive rounds of constitutional reform for democratic change.[52]

It is due to the continuous public dissatisfaction with the National Assembly that the Court took a strong step in J.Y. Interpretation No. 499 to repeal the whole constitutional revision. As mentioned above, the notorious National Assembly monopolized constitutional amendment power for its political interests. To be more specific, the term-extension clause in the fifth constitutional revision was considered to have probably recalled the resurrection of the authoritarian tradition of life-long tenure of the national representatives.[53] Indeed, citizens in Taiwan did not pay attention to constitutional theories such as unconstitutional constitutional amendment or the principles of popular sovereignty. Rather, what people really opposed was the nightmare that might have been imposed by the National Assembly. Public antagonism to the fifth constitutional revision was expressively written in all the three separate applications to the Court, which sent a clear message to the Court that the people were highly dissatisfied with both constitutional revision as well as the National Assembly itself.

---

50 See Wen-Chen Chang, 'Public Interest Litigation in Taiwan: Strategy for Law and Policy Changes in the Course of Democratization' in Po Jen Yap and Holning Lau (eds), *Public Interest Litigation in Asia* (Routledge 2010) 136.
51 J.Y. Interpretation No. 261 (1990).
52 See Yeh (n 20) 38.
53 See Huang and Li (n 2) 423.

8.4.3.3 Beyond unconstitutionality: the triumph of public scrutiny of Taiwan's constitutional revision

In the contextual analysis of J.Y. Interpretation No. 499, one can find public scrutiny playing an integral role in the judicial review of constitutional amendments. The problem behind the fifth constitutional revision lay primarily in public dissatisfaction with the National Assembly itself. In this sense, the Court functioned not only as an institutional check on the constitutionality of the revision but an instrument of the people's veto power to constitutional amendment to make the National Assembly itself politically accountable. The paradox of constitutional reform in Taiwan was therefore resolved to some extent since the will of the people would be taken into serious account and the Assembly's exercise of monopolistic amendment power could be checked by the Court. The final abolition of the National Assembly and the inception of a public referendum in the 2005 constitutional revision by a mission-oriented National Assembly, formed from party lists proportional to aggregate votes from congressional election, represent the final triumph of public oversight of constitutional revision.

Even though the National Assembly, by design, functioned as the representative of the people to exercise its constitutional power, the people themselves and the idea of popular sovereignty were not absent in the dynamics of Taiwan's constitutional reforms. The Court repeatedly highlighted the role of the people in the amendment process through series of judicial interpretations. Procedurally, people should have the opportunity to express opinions and to engage in rational deliberation during the process. Moreover, constitutional amendments would be unconstitutional if the principle of popular sovereignty was undermined. Indeed, civil society remained watchful and engaged during the time of constitutional reform as a guardian of the constitutional revision power enjoyed solely by the National Assembly.[54]

It is very unlikely that the Court would vote down a constitutional amendment in the current system where a constitutional amendment is done through public referendum. But the case would have been different had the National Assembly not exercised monopolistic control over the constitutional revision process. This is not mere speculation. Nearly 15 years after J.Y. Interpretation No. 499, the Court once again reviewed constitutional amendments passed in 2005. Not surprisingly, the same Court upheld the legitimacy and constitutionality of the amendments in J.Y. Interpretation No. 721, holding that the electoral reform does not violate the principle of popular sovereignty in the constitutional revision. Observe the contextual differences between these two judicial rulings. While J.Y. Interpretation No. 499 dealt with amendments passed by the National Assembly, J.Y. Interpretation No. 721 dealt with the constitutional revision proposed for the first time by the Legislative Yuan, rather than the National Assembly, and passed through a more democratic process.

---

54 See Yeh (n 20) 244–6.

8.5 Conclusion

Taiwan's constitutional reform for democratic transformation has taken a path of incremental revisions. From 1991 to 2005, there were seven rounds of constitutional revision with the fifth round in 1999 declared unconstitutional by the Court. Reading into the holding and reasoning of the judicial ruling, one may be impressed with the Court's strong determination and iron-clad position to uphold constitutional basic structure and principles. As we looked into the political and social context, we found the Court took the easy way out. The fifth constitutional revisions by the National Assembly should be taken as a continuous part of the incremental constitutional engineering for improved democratic representation in Taiwan. With growing general distrust of the National Assembly and an unresolved constitutional crisis of representation, including the National Assembly, the Court in J.Y. Interpretation 499 served as the guardian of the constitutional revision process with the support of the general public. The Court functioned, therefore, not only as an institutional check on the constitutionality of the revision but as an instrument of the people's veto power against constitutional amendments to make the National Assembly itself politically accountable. The ruling reflects a continuous struggle of public oversight over constitutional amendment, in which the general public has struggled to regain their sovereign power over constitutional revision.

9 Thailand's unamendability
Politics of two democracies

Khemthong Tonsakulrungruang

9.1 Introduction

Constitutional law scholars often eye constitutional changes with the suspicion that they could pave the way for authoritarian usurpation. This hesitation is fair, as there are growing concerns that the modern-day autocratic leaders are rising not through military coups but through constitutional, yet illiberal, means.[1] They win elections through controversial populist campaigns and, once in office, entrench their repressive regimes. Abusive constitutionalism, as Landau calls it, results in constitutional amendment, or replacement, that silences the government's critics, extends their terms, or dismantles the check-and-balance mechanisms.[2] Abusive constitutionalism slowly erodes a healthy and vibrant democracy into an illiberal authoritarian regime. The principle of unamendability is meant to safeguard a constitution from such an act of sabotage.[3] An amendment must not destroy the original sprit of the constitution and the courts shall enforce that limitation on would-be usurpers.

From 2011 to 2014, the government of Yingluck Shinawatra in Thailand sought to introduce changes to the 2007 Constitution (2007–14) via constitutional amendments. Thrice it tried and thrice the court rejected the proposals before all descended into the chaos of street politics that ended in the 2014 coup. Superficially, these decisions fit within the idea of abusive constitutionalism as the Constitutional Court condemned a populist authoritarian for abusing an electoral victory to destroy democracy. Therefore, the Court invoked the concept of unamendability, citing the theory of constituent power as well as several implicit unamendable features, to protect the rule of law and the 2007 Constitution.

However, a deeper investigation into the series of 2011–14 amendments raises doubts about the above narrative. Conventionally, a suspicion toward constitutional change assumes that the original charter is already democratic while a change may or may not be of lower democratic quality. Hence, the notion

---

1 Kim Lane Scheppele, 'Autocratic Legalism' (2018) 85 University of Chicago LR 545.
2 David Landau, 'Abusive Constitutionalism' (2013) 47 UC Davis LR 189, 195–6.
3 Yaniv Roznai, *Unconstitutional Constitutional Amendments: The Limit of Amendment Powers* (OUP 2017) 5–8.

DOI: 10.4324/9781003097099-9

of unamendability seeks to maintain that liberal democratic arrangement. That assumption, this chapter argues, is not applicable to the case of Thailand. Rather, Thailand complicates this narrative. The 2007 Constitution represented an already ailing democracy, which was hampered by the 2006 coup d'état. As a response, the people, not yet ready to draft another constitution, endeavoured to amend the existing constitution in order to rescue the sinking democracy. But can the people invoke the secondary constituent power to supersede the primary constituent power to build a more democratic constitution? The Constitutional Court's response was adamantly negative.

This chapter argues that the Thai judiciary abused the concept of unamendability to entrench an undemocratic constitutional structure. It discusses the four amendment cases in the context of the recent political crisis where two political ideologies clashed and the Constitutional Court failed to be a reliable umpire. In these decisions, the Constitutional Court, at length, expressed its understanding of democracy, which was markedly different from liberal democracy and more aligned with what is termed Thai-style democracy adopted by the conservative faction. Thai-style democracy, however, is sometimes regarded as a euphemism for authoritarianism. In this circumstance, the roles are reversed. The amendments represented the people's will to challenge the authoritarian legacy in the 2007 Constitution, but the Constitutional Court's invocation of unamendability thwarted that will, ultimately, to the detriment of democracy and the rule of law.

9.2 The constitutional politics of two democracies

This section provides the political background leading up to the amendment attempts. The period of 2011–13 was a rare moment in Thai politics. These years were relatively calm, wrapped between two large street protests, the 2010 pro-Thaksin protest and the 2014 anti-Thaksin protests, and the two coups of 2006 and 2014.[4] This hiatus allowed civilian politicians to endeavour to bring about constitutional change via a formal channel.

Why would Thais then wish to amend the 2007 Constitution, which had been enacted only a few years earlier and approved by a national referendum? It turned out that the 2007 Constitution was deeply unpopular for several reasons, not least because it represented an ideology that was averse to the beloved previous charter. Thus, the latter half of this section discusses a battle between Thai-style and liberal democracies that has haunted Thailand for decades.

9.2.1 *The unpopular constitution*

The 2007 Constitution was the conservatives' reaction to politics in the final years of the 1997 Constitution (1997–2006). The 1997 Constitution was

---

4 Pavin Chachavalpongpun, 'Introduction: A Timeless Thailand' in Pavin Chachavalpongpun (ed) *Routledge Handbook of Contemporary Thailand* (Routledge 2020) 9–11.

part of a post-authoritarian reform that enjoyed a decisive mandate to consolidate Thailand's fragile democracy which had often been interrupted by the military. The consensus was clear: to rid Thailand of military coups, the country needed a strong and capable civilian government with even stronger checks and balances.[5] The 1997 Constitution adopted an electoral system that favoured large-sized parties that would result in a less fractious government. It also broadened public participation, most notably replacing senatorial appointments with popular elections. Many new courts and watchdog agencies were also introduced. Although the 1997 Constitution eventually led to the rise of Thaksin Shinawatra, a controversial strongman prime minister (2001–6), it left a deeply positive impression on the public. The 2006 coup, and the subsequent 2007 Constitution, aimed to dismantle the legacy of the 1997 Constitution, against strong public disapproval.

To appease the public, the 2006 junta copied the 1997 drafting procedure. The 1997 Constitution was unique in that it was born not of a coup but a popular uprising. The constitution drafting council comprised not only constitutional experts but also provincial representatives, such as academics, businessmen, and NGOs.[6] Thousands of local forums were held to gather opinions. The 2006 junta set up a similar council of 100 members and ordered opinion forums.[7] Moreover, it compensated for its undemocratic origins with a national referendum, the first of its kind for Thailand.[8] The 2006 junta boasted it was making the most democratic constitution ever.

The major goal of the 2007 Constitution was to prevent Thaksin, who was in self-exile, from returning to politics. While the drafters feigned the participatory drafting procedure of the 1997 Constitution, they dismantled the spirit. The government was significantly weakened through a new electoral system that favoured small to mid-sized parties.[9] The people also lost their right to vote for senators as the new senate would be half-appointed, half-elected.[10] A political party could be dissolved if a single member violated an election law.[11] Executive

---

5 Andrew Harding and Peter Leyland, *The Constitutional System of Thailand* (Hart 2010) 22–3; Duncan McCargo, 'Introduction: Understanding Political Reform in Thailand' in Duncan McCargo (ed) *Reforming Thai Politics* (Nordic Institute of Asian Studies 2002) 9–21.
6 Prawase Wasi, 'An Overview of Political Reform' in McCargo, *Reforming Thai Politics* 24–6.
7 2006 Interim Charter, sec 19, 22.
8 2006 Interim Charter, sec 29.
9 Michael Nelson, 'Delaying Constitutionalism to Protect Establishment Hegemony in Thailand: Designing the Election System and the Senate in the Constitution of 2007' in Marco Buente and Bjoern Dressel, *Politics and Constitutions in Southeast Asia* (Routledge 2017) 52–3.
10 See Michael Nelson, 'Constitutional Contestation over Thailand's Senate, 1997 to 2014' (2014) 36 Contemporary Southeast Asia 51; Paul Chambers, 'Superfluous, Mischievous or Emancipating? Thailand's Evolving Senate Today' (2009) 28 Journal of Current Southeast Asia Affairs 3.
11 2007 Constitution, sec 237.

prerogative was subject to an unelected judiciary and watchdog agencies.[12] In sum, the 2007 Constitution displayed a disdain for electoral politics. Yet, as Tom Ginsburg has shown, the drafters decided to retain some features of the 1997 Constitution in the 2007 one as a form of afterlife in order to boost its legitimacy.[13]

Calls to reject the 2007 Constitution began as early as the drafting council convened – a fact that the drafters must have known. The 2007 Constitution was unpopular because of its design as well as its origin. For the democratic camp, to reject the draft was symbolically to reject the 2006 coup. But several junta sympathizers pleaded with the public to vote for the constitution, to get the country going, to have a general election, and to rid the military of power. Thereafter, they promised, there should be another round of drafting for the real "popular" constitution.[14] Ultimately, the 2007 Constitution was approved by a thin margin.[15]

Despite the high likelihood of amendment, the amendment rule was surprisingly simple.[16] There was no requirement for a special council or another referendum. Procedurally, it required 50,000 voters to petition the Parliament, where both the House of Representatives and Senate must consider the motion together. If the motion was filed by the people, public opinion had to be sought. It required an absolute majority from the Parliament. As for substance, all was allowed except changes to the form of the state. An amendment must not overthrow the democratic regime with the king as the head of the state. In other words, Thailand must always be a democratic kingdom.

Most importantly, the 2007 Constitution assigned no body to review amendments. Amendments were not ordinary legislation so they were not subject to the Constitutional Court's judicial review.[17] Was this simplicity in the amendment

---

12 Borwornsak Uwanno, 'Economic Crisis and Political Crisis in Thailand: Past and Present' (2009) 4 National Taiwan University Law Review 141, 161–5.
13 See Tom Ginsburg, 'Constitutional Afterlife: The Continuing Impact of Thailand's Postpolitical Constitution' (2009) 7 International Journal of Constitutional Law 83.
14 จรัญระบุ รธน ไม่สมบูรณ์แต่วอนรับก่อน-แก้ทีหลัง/นิธิชี้ตั้งโจทย์แคบ [Jaran Admitted the Constitution Draft Imperfect but Plead for Acceptance-Later Amendment/Nidhi Complained the Objective too Narrow] InfoQuest News (3 August 2007) <https://www.ryt9.com/s/iq02/317185> (accessed by 12 January 2021); ปชป แสดงจุดยืน รับร่างรัฐธรรมนูญ 2550 เพื่อฟื้นฟูประชาธิปไตย [Democrat Party Vowed to Vote for the 2007 Constitution Draft to Restore Democracy] InfoQuest News (8 July 2007) <https://www.ryt9.com/tag/%E0%B8%A3%E0%B8%B1%E0%B8%90%E0%B8%98%E0%B8%A3%E0%B8%A3%E0%B8%A1%E0%B8%99%E0%B8%B9%E0%B8%8D+2550/20070708T191021> (accessed 12 January 2021).
15 Election Commission of Thailand, ข้อมูลการออกเสียงประชามติ พ.ศ. 2550 [Information and Statistics of the 2007 Referendum] (ECT Office, 2007) at <https://www.ect.go.th/ect_th/ewt_dl_link.php?nid=234>.
16 See Khemthong Tonsakulrungruang, 'Constitutional Amendment in Thailand: Amending in the Spectre of Parliamentary Dictatorship' (2019) 14 Journal of Comparative Law 173, 175–6.
17 Khemthong Tonsakulrungruang, 'The Constitutional Court of Thailand: From Activism to Arbitrariness' in Andrew Harding and Albert HY Chen (eds), Constitutional Courts in Asia: A Comparative Perspective (Cambridge University Press 2018) 197–8.

procedure a mistake when the drafters were aware of the likely prospect of amendment?

9.2.2 Politics of two democracies

The 2007 Constitution must be understood in a broader context of fierce contestation over election and political legitimacy.[18] The democratic revolution in 1932 ended absolute monarchy and introduced constitutional democracy. Unfortunately, infighting as well as resistance from the royalists prevented successful consolidation.[19] The royalist camp could not reintroduce absolute monarchy but they began instead to offer an alternative to liberal democracy by adopting a relativistic approach. They proposed Thai-style democracy, a version of democracy that fit the Thai context. The descriptor Thai-style signifies that the Thai democratic ideal does not conform with the universal standard.

Thai-style democracy first appeared in the administration of Field Marshall Sarit Thanarat (1959–63). Sarit was a staunch royalist military man who staged a coup in 1957 against Pibun, the last member of the 1932 Revolution Party. In contrary to the republican Pibun, Sarit hailed the monarchy supreme. He rejected the Western notion of democracy while creating his own version that justified his repressive despotic regime.[20]

Central to Thai-style democracy is the king as the core of the political arrangement. Based on the traditional belief in a hierarchical socio-political pyramid,[21] people are not equal. The basis of one's power is not popular consent but personal virtues. The king reigns at the top of the pyramid because of his exalted charisma and wisdom.[22] Thai-style democracy directly attacked the 1932 revolution by claiming that the revolution was premature. Most ordinary Thais were illiterate and therefore were not ready for self-governance. Meanwhile, King Prajadhipok was said to be already contemplating introducing democracy to the nation via a Meiji-style constitution but his goodwill was overlooked by the 1932 revolutionaries.[23] Regardless of truth, this narrative of Thai-style democracy identified prematurity and unpreparedness as the cause of democratic failure. The

---

18 See Kevin Hewison, 'Thailand: Contestation over Elections, Sovereignty, and Representation' (2015) 51 Representation 51; Bjoern Dressel, 'When Notions of Legitimacy Conflict: The Case of Thailand' (2010) 38 Politics and Policy 445.
19 Harding and Leyland (n 5) 11–17; Kevin Hewison, 'Thailand: Contestation over Elections, Sovereignty and Representation' (2015) 51 Journal of Representative Democracy 51, 53–4.
20 Kevin Hewison and Kengkij Kitirianglarp, 'Thai-Style Democracy: The Royalist Struggle for Thailand's Politics' in S. Ivarsson and L. Isager (eds) *Saying the Unsayable: Monarchy and Democracy in Thailand* (NIAS 2010) 186–7.
21 ibid 181–9.
22 ibid 189; Michael K Connors, 'Article of Faiths: The Failure of Royal Liberalism in Thailand' (2008) 38 Journal of Contemporary Asia 143, 145; Prince Dhani Niwat, 'The Old Siamese Concept of the Monarchy' (1946) 36 Journal of Siam Society 91.
23 Thongchai Winichakul, 'Toppling Democracy' (2008) 38 Journal of Contemporary Asia 11, 22–3.

majority voted for the wrong or selfish MPs who failed to represent the people's interest. Ultimately, an elected government was ousted by the military.

To uplift Thai-style democracy, electoral democracy is framed as an adversary. Thai-style democracy portrayed the military government in a much more positive light than elected politicians. The military presented itself as the guardian of the crown.[24] Sarit, in particular, claimed that he, with his father-figure characteristics, was a better representative of the people.[25] Politicians are guided by their voters' short-term interests, he argued, not the nation's long-term genuine benefit. More importantly, he was dedicated and, more importantly, loyal to Thainess and the king. Under the authoritarian regime, emphasis was given not to rights and liberties, which were a foreign and too individualistic concept, but to order and unity.[26] This narrative upended the definition of democracy. It normalized coup d'états as part of democracy. It was able to amalgamate royalism, authoritarianism, and liberalism into one ostensibly coherent system.[27]

By the 1980s, Thai-style democracy was successfully in operation. Constitutionalism was foreign and not fully compatible.[28] Collective prosperity was preferred over personal freedom. Thai politics oscillated between elections and coups. Elections were regular, so were coups. Whenever parliamentary disputes or corruption scandals loomed, the army staged a coup – the safety valve to release tension. Following some of the worst clashes, the king personally intervened.[29] Therefore, while the minimum element of democracy was maintained, it was not the only game in town. The king and the army served as a *deus ex machina*. Civilian politicians learned to coexist with conservative elites in the palace, military, and business world, as well as the bureaucracy.

But the spirit of liberal democracy, instilled since 1932, had not gone away either. It manifested intermittently through mass uprisings in the 1970s.[30] Eventually, in the 1990s, political and economic liberalization in East Asia rendered military dictatorship obsolete. The middle class, who received a westernized education, began to demand full democracy. Thus, when the army staged the 1991 coup, and in 1992, appointed the junta leader as prime minister, thousands rose up against the army in the bloody uprising known as the Black May.[31] The king, sensing the change, intervened in the bloodshed by urging the junta

---

24 See Paul Chambers and Napisa Waitoolkiat, 'The Resilience of Monarchised Military in Thailand' (2016) 46 Journal of Contemporary Asia 425.
25 Hewison and Kengkij (n 20)187.
26 ibid 190–1.
27 See Connors (n 22)
28 Ginsburg (n 13) 88–9.
29 See Thongchai (n 23) 20–1.
30 See the struggle through Kasian Tejapira, 'The Irony of Democratization and the Decline of Royal Hegemony in Thailand' (2016) 5 Southeast Asian Studies 219.
31 Thongchai Winichakul, *Thailand's Hyper-Royalism: Its Past Success and Present Predicament* (ISEAS-Yusok Ishak Institute 2016) 5.

leader, General Suchinda Kraprayoon, to resign. The aftermath was a constitutional convention to draft the 1997 Constitution.

Thus, the 1997 Constitution was not born from a popular revolution that defeated the authoritarian past. It was a social experiment sanctioned by the more progressive wing of the conservatives. With its emphasis on rights and liberties, strong leadership, and rigorous checks and balances, the 1997 Constitution introduced a different model of democracy. It was more liberal, with a long list of rights, and newly founded administrative and constitutional courts to enforce these rights.[32] It strengthened the leadership of the government by adopting a new electoral system that favoured mainly a few large parties. It instilled the sense of constitutionalism with a participatory drafting procedure and new designs of many state apparatuses to replace the king and the army as arbiters of political disputes.[33] Nonetheless, Thai-style democracy did not simply vanish. It was recognized in the clause pertaining to the democratic regime with the king as the head of the state which the Constitutional Court invoked often.[34]

The 1997 Constitution was hugely successful. But its success, unfortunately, led to its demise. Thaksin utilized the aforementioned electoral rule to strengthen his position so much that he monopolized Thai politics.[35] When Thaksin dared to challenge the old powerful conservative network, they reacted with the 2006 coup to revive Thai-style democracy.[36] The year 2006 was a watershed year in Thai political history as the tide turned against liberalization.[37] The conservatives were convinced, once again, that liberal democracy was not compatible with Thainess. But notably this time, the judiciary, not the military, would lead the attack as discussed below.

In this sense, Ginsburg's constitutional afterlife is simply a compromise between the two democracies. The series of constitutional amendment cases is only a small part of a larger ideological and physical battle that raged from 2006 to 2014. While Yingluck, with a popular mandate vested in her, tried to amend the 2007 Constitution to regain control over politics, the Constitutional Court, spurred by distrust in the majority's wisdom, struck down all her government's attempts. Meanwhile it accepted the 2014 coup as a normal component of Thai-style democracy. This inconsistency showed how Thai-style democracy worked. On the ideological front, Thai-style democracy condemns the idea of majority rule. During normal politics, it enlists the Constitutional Court,

---

32 Harding and Leyland, *The Constitutional System of Thailand* 23.
33 Duncan McCargo, 'Alternative Meanings of Political Reform in Contemporary Thailand' (1998) 14 Copenhagen Journal of Asian Studies 5, 15–17.
34 2017 Constitution, sec. 5 para 2.
35 See Kasian Tejapira, 'Toppling Thaksin' (2006) 39 New Left Review 5, 28–9.
36 Kevin Hewison, 'Thaksin Shinawatra and the Reshaping of Thai Politics' (2010) 16 Contemporary Politics 119, 127–9.
37 See Hewison, *Contestation over Elections*; Bjoern Dressel, When Notions of Legitimacy Conflict: The Case of Thailand' (2010) 38 Politics and Policy 445.

among other apparatus, to contain the government. At its most extreme, it permits a coup.

9.3 Yingluck's amendment series

Thaksin's clique returned as soon as elections resumed. His proxies, Samak Sundaravej, and subsequently Somchai Wongsawat, led a fragile government in 2008. They faced massive street protests, hostile senators, and contentious court cases.[38] The Constitutional Court quickly ousted them through frivolous lawsuits.[39] Late in 2008, the army brokered a deal to promote Abhisit Vejajiva, the opposition leader and the leader of the royalist Democrat Party, as the new prime minister. Abhisit enjoyed the army's backing, which helped him disperse the 2009 and 2010 anti-government protests, but he lost the 2011 election. Yingluck Shinawatra, the youngest sister of Thaksin, led the Phue Thai Party (PT) to victory. One of PT's promises was to amend the 2007 Constitution which Yingluck began in earnest.

Prior to Yingluck, Samak Sundaravej initiated an amendment campaign, targeting the disproportionately harsh party dissolution and the amnesty for the 2006 junta.[40] But his government collapsed before his efforts materialized. In contrast, Abhisit amended the electoral system but his effort was minimal.[41] Yingluck ambitiously vowed to replace the whole charter. It was part of her election campaign, and her government added it to the policy priority list.[42]

This section will discuss four cases concerning constitutional unamendability in the Constitutional Court. In each case, there are issues of jurisdiction and procedural irregularities, but this section is interested primarily in the topic of unamendability, which was the focus of these judgments.[43]

9.3.1 A new constitutional drafting council (2012)

In February 2012, the Yingluck cabinet proposed a motion to amend the 2007 Constitution to replace the existing amendment provision with the aim of establishing a constitution drafting council. The new council would consist of 99 members, 77 elected from the provinces and 22 recruited by the parliament. Again, this copied the 1997 drafting council model. Yingluck faced strong resistance from Thaksin's opponents: the former 2006 junta members, the Democratic

---

38 See Marc Askew, 'Confrontation and Crisis in Thailand, 2008–2010' in Mac Askew (ed) *Legitimacy Crisis in Thailand* (Silkworms 2010).
39 See Bjoern Dressel, 'Judicialization of Politics or Politiciazation of the Judiciary? Considerations from Recent Events in Thailand' (2010) 23 Pacific Review 671, 682–3.
40 Askew (n 38) 33–4.
41 See Tonsakulrungruang (n 16) 180.
42 See point 1.16 of the Yingluck Cabinet's Policy Statement at <https://www.nesdc.go.th/ewt_dl_link.php?nid=5057> accessed 12 January 2021.
43 Details at Tonsakulrungruang (n 16).

MPs, and other right-wing figures. Believing that she was rebuilding Thaksin's political empire, they coordinated to file five petitions to the Constitutional Court asking for the dissolution of PT.

Because an amendment draft was not explicitly under the court's jurisdiction, the Constitutional Court controversially accepted the case under Section 68.[44] However, Yingluck's opponents directly filed a petition without the Attorney General's approval. The Constitutional Court accepted that circumvention by describing the case as urgent.[45]

The government defended its proposal that an amendment was not an act to overthrow the democratic government with the king as the head of the state. The government prepared to install a list of procedural safeguards. The procedure adhered to the participatory democratic principle as it would seek approval both from the people's representatives in the council and directly from the national referendum. The council would act independently of the legislature. Finally, there was a substantive guarantee that the Speaker of the House must review the new draft to determine if it would endanger the democratic form of government with the king as the head of the state. The Constitutional Court was not convinced.

The Court referred to the primary constituent power of the 2007 Constitution, which was voted by the people in the 2007 national referendum.[46] Therefore, the Parliament could not amend the Constitution through the normal legislative process. The Constitutional Court opined that, were the government to draft a new constitution, it should hold another referendum to acquire popular approval of the plan. Otherwise, the Parliament may invoke the current amendment process to amend the 2007 Constitution by section.[47] The Constitutional Court did not discuss this issue at length; its discussion consisted of only two short paragraphs in a terse and ambiguous style. But it seemed to recognize, though not explicitly, the difference between constitutional amendment and replacement and demanded a different track for each. Its reasoning resonated with the idea that an amendment that is closer to a replacement shall require a procedure that resembles the primary constituent power.

The Constitutional Court's innovation, recommending a referendum, was unusual for the judiciary, often known for a conservative, textualist approach to interpretation. However, the Constitutional Court did not find PT had overthrown the democratic government yet. That fear was speculative. The Constitutional Court refused to entertain a request to dissolve PT.

During the trial, it should be noted that four judges tried to withdraw themselves as they were former drafters or had previously expressed their opinion

---

44 2007 Constitution, Section 68 (providing that a person who witnesses the overthrow of a democratic government with the king as the head of the state shall file a complaint to the Attorney General who, after investigation, may ask the Constitutional Court to issue an order to halt such act and, if applicable, dissolve the political party which commits that act).
45 Constitutional Court Decision 18-22/2555 (2012), 21–2.
46 ibid 23.
47 ibid.

regarding the possible constitutional amendment. Jaran Pakdithanakul, the intellectual and moral powerhouse of this conservative bench and one of the 2007 drafters, once remarked publicly that the draft was not really democratic while promising that the people could amend it later. He was allowed to withdraw.[48] Two judges, Nurak Mapraneet and Suphot Kaimook, who were also 2007 drafters, were told to stay on the bench.

Yingluck and her followers were upset by this setback. They even contemplated impeaching these judges but eventually they decided to pursue a less ambitious path by amending the 2007 Constitution in a piecemeal manner. They would focus on some particular pain points.

9.3.2 A senatorial election (2013)

In March 2013, the government MPs and some friendly senators submitted three proposals to amend the 2007 Constitution to the Parliament. These proposals would (1) reintroduce a fully elected senate, (2) revise the treaty-making power, and (3) amend the party dissolution clause. In essence, the three amendment proposals aimed to rebuild the government's leadership by reducing vague or unnecessary oversight from the legislature and the judiciary. Both senator selection and party dissolution had long been identified as problems. Problems with the treaty-making power were discovered only after the 2008 border dispute with Cambodia.[49] Again, the same coalition of former junta members, senators, Democrat MPs, and right-wing figures bypassed the Attorney General to file a complaint directly to the Constitutional Court. The Court accepted these three cases notwithstanding a clear breach of procedure.

Since 1997, the Senate has approved candidates to watchdog agencies. Under the 1997 Constitution, when the Senate was elected, it served as an important link between the people and the watchdog agencies, supplying them with democratic legitimacy. Unfortunately, Thaksin had covertly co-opted senators, so there was a good reason to reconsider whether the senate should be elected.[50] But appointments, too, were vulnerable to secret lobbying.[51] Only people with connections would be chosen. Appointed senators were elitist by nature and inclined to express a negative attitude toward civil politicians. They were coup sympathizers, and their mission was to uphold the undemocratic arrangement.

The Constitutional Court struck down the reintroduction of a fully elected senate for two reasons. On procedural grounds, the House Speaker had deliberately allocated too little time for the amendment debate, in effect coercing the

---

48 Duncan McCargo, *Fighting for Virtue: Justice and Politics in Thailand* (Cornell University Press 2020) 192–3.
49 See Pavin Chachavalpongpun, 'Temple of Doom: Hysteria about the Preah Vihear Temple in the Thai Nationalist Discourse' in Askew, *Legitimacy Crisis in Thailand*.
50 Chambers (n 10) 13–19.
51 ibid 24–5.

opposition into silence. Some MPs were filmed voting on behalf of their absent friends.[52]

More interesting is the substantive review of a fully elected senate. First, the Constitutional Court made a reference to the preamble of the 2017 Constitution as the intention of this charter; that every political institution serves with righteousness, fairness, independence, and honesty for the benefit of all Thais; that the charter does not wish any political institution to usurp any part of the law to enrich itself.[53]

Then, the Constitutional Court sought to explain what democracy was. The Constitutional Court warned that, despite the principle of majority rule, democracy forbade the majority from abusing its superior status to harass the minority, which would result in the tyranny of the majority.[54] To prevent such tyranny, separation of powers was installed. The Court continued that each political branch was not independent or immune from the others but subject to checks and balances. Otherwise, unchecked power would lead to damage, and the country would suffer because of the blindness and greed of those in power.[55] In addition to written laws, all state apparatuses must adhere to the rule of law. The Constitution introduced the rule of law as a "pure and selfless" principle to restrain the exercise of power to prevent a conflict of interest which would result in "decadence of the nation" or serious division.[56] Most importantly, the Constitutional Court was assigned to enforce the rule of law upon politicians.[57]

Was a fully elected senate intended to overthrow democracy? According to the Constitutional Court, the 2007 Constitution had revised senatorial selection to ensure its independence from the House, as the senate served as a check-and-balance mechanism within the legislature.[58] The Court foresaw that a senatorial election would collapse this mechanism and the principle of bicameralism. It would result in two crony houses full of friends and family members, learing to the loss of public trust.[59] It would, in other words, promote dynastic politics. Therefore, the Court held that the amendment was unconstitutional: it constituted an act to overthrow a democratic regime with the king as the head of state, which was part of the Constitution's unamendable core.

9.3.3 The treaty-making procedure (2014)

By late 2013, Bangkok was experiencing another mass protest when Yingluck Shinawatra pushed for an amnesty law that would allow Thaksin's return to

---

52 Constitutional Court Decision 15-18/2556 (2013) 26–8.
53 ibid, 19.
54 ibid 20.
55 ibid.
56 ibid 20–1.
57 ibid 29.
58 ibid 30.
59 ibid 30.

Thailand. The anti-amnesty bill protest escalated into calls for a coup. In response to the protest, Yingluck dissolved the House and called for an election but the protesters demanded that she resign, suspend the constitution partially, and appoint an interim national government. She refused.[60] As Thailand descended into chaos, the Constitutional Court delivered another decision in the series that further weakened the Yingluck administration and emboldened anarchic protesters. This one concerned the treaty-making power.

The 2007 Constitution subjected treaty-making, once principally within the executive's power, to more stringent legislative oversight.[61] A treaty that had an adverse social or economic impact needed to obtain legislative approval prior to and after the negotiation. The Constitutional Court was empowered rule if a particular treaty had such an impact. However, "adverse social or economic impact" was an ambiguous and subjective standard. In 2008, when the Thai government was about to sign the Thai-Cambodia Joint Communique on the Preah Vihear Temple along the border, anti-Thaksin elements launched a senseless nationalist campaign which triggered massive unrest and jeopardized this foreign relationship. The Constitutional Court, with benefit of hindsight, cited that incident as the reason to blame the government and invalidate the signing of the Joint Communique, which led to a criminal case against the foreign minister.[62] Yingluck proposed an amendment which would require legislative approval only for a treaty with an obvious social or economic impact. This was the cabinet's attempt to retake control over foreign affairs from the legislature and the Constitutional Court.

In January 2014, the Constitutional Court asserted itself as the guardian against the usurpation of the 2007 Constitution and the rule of law. Here, the Constitutional Court once again reiterated that democracy was not simply the rule of the majority and that Thailand was still under the rule of law.[63] Thus, it was capable of reviewing the amendment despite a clear written constitutional mandate.

Similar to the 2013 decision, the Constitutional Court referred to the preamble to claim that power must be exercised with righteousness, independence, and honesty, for the collective benefit of all Thais, without conflict of interest, abuse of power, or total monopoly of politics.[64] Also, the Constitution did not allow a political body to abuse any law to support its unlawful gains.[65] Were the government to ignore the rule of law, it would corrupt democracy into majoritarian dictatorship.[66] Thus, separation of powers and checks and balances were necessary

---

60 See Duncan McCargo, *Thailand in 2014: The Trouble with Magic Swords* (Institute of Southeast Asian Studies 2014).
61 2007 Constitution, sec 190.
62 Decision 6-7/2551 (2008).
63 Constitutional Courtt Decision 1/2557 (2014) 13–14.
64 ibid 11–12.
65 ibid 12.
66 ibid.

to prevent such abuse that would lead to ignorance and greed by those in power who would ruin the country. Again, the Constitutional Court described the rule of law as a pure and unprejudiced morality superior to the written text.[67]

The Constitutional Court ruled that the substance of the amendment was unconstitutional. Treaty-making power was of utmost importance so it had to be exercised with transparency and prudence.[68] The Constitutional Court posited that the Constitution, therefore, designed the treaty-making procedure to achieve a balance among the executive, legislative, and members of civil society who may participate in public hearings on particular treaties.[69] The amendment that limited the public's access to the treaty-making procedure, the Court held, was unconstitutional as it was considered an act to overthrow a democratic regime with the king as the head of state.

9.3.4 Party dissolution (2014)

In March, the Constitutional Court delivered the final decision in the series. The fourth amendment bill aimed to amend, first, Section 68 itself, and second, Section 237, the party dissolution provision. This bill was clearly aimed to retaliate against the judiciary. Section 68 allowed the judiciary to interfere with the amendment plan while the problematic Section 237 was repeatedly used to dissolve PT's predecessor and allies. The same group of anti-government senators and activists filed a complaint to the Court under Section 68.

By May 2014, the political protest reached a dead end. The February election was blocked by anti-democratic protesters and later invalidated by the Constitution. But Yingluck remained at the head of an interim government, neither resigning nor leaving the country as protesters demanded. In any event, the demonstrations were losing steam. The shutdown of the government complex and the business district caused much inconvenience to commuters. Finally, General Prayuth Chan-ocha staged a coup and abolished the 2007 Constitution. The case was then rendered moot, so the Constitutional Court dismissed it. But it is highly likely that, were the case not moot, the Constitutional Court would have also ruled that these two sections were unamendable as well.

In summary, the 2007 Constitution set a low bar for amendment but, through a series of decisions, the Constitutional Court significantly raised that bar. Despite the absence of an obvious mandate, the Constitutional Court expanded its jurisdiction to review amendment proposals. In the first case, where the government intended to allow a special assembly to rewrite the whole charter, the Constitutional Court differentiated between replacement and amendment and concluded that, for the first category of constitutional change, a normal amendment procedure was inadequate. Here, it invoked the idea of constituent power

---

67 ibid 13.
68 ibid 15–16.
69 ibid 20–5.

and controversially suggested gathering public input. In this sense, it resembled the national referendum that approved the 2007 Constitution despite the absence of a written requirement. In the cases that followed, the Constitutional Court arbitrarily expanded implicit unamendability under the claim that these changes would contradict the original purpose of the constitution, which emphasized strong checks and balances. The amendment procedure became extremely rigid.

9.4 Reverse abusive constitutionalism and illiberal judicial activism

In the end, despite the Constitutional Court's rigorous defence, Thai democracy succumbed, not to unscrupulous and opportunistic politicians as the Constitutional Court had feared, but to a military coup d'état just as before. Once the conservatives were convinced that the 2007 Constitution was inadequate to resist Thaksin, the 2014 National Council of Peace and Order (NCPO), a group of armed force commanders, staged a coup that ended the 2007 Constitution and suspended democracy for five long years. Military dictatorship is clearly opposed to liberal democracy. There is no check-and-balance mechanism. Nor is there independence or the rule of law. Politics return to rampant and blatant cronyism.[70] However, contrary to its previous aggressive scrutiny, the Constitutional Court raised no objection to the junta. It lay dormant. The few decisions it issued were to endorse the junta's legality.[71]

This juxtaposition – the fact that the Constitutional Court was so concerned about abusive constitutionalism but failed to resist an outright coup – suggests that unamendability may actually be invoked to safeguard regimes that are distinct from the liberal democratic model. Indeed, the Court's decisions reflected fear of the majority's wisdom, which is the root of Thai-style democracy. This section tries to unravel the judiciary's link to Thai-style democracy and its role in the politics of unamendability.

It was not fear or intimidation that co-opted the judiciary. Thai judges have never been cowed into rubberstamping the coup; rather, they were persuaded to willingly entrench the illiberal regime.[72] The court has long been a faithful accomplice of Thai-style democracy. The judiciary and the army are two modern institutions founded by King Chulalongkorn over a century ago during the modernization of the Siamese Kingdom. Both have remained unchanged ever since. Through royal visits, countless audiences, and other symbolic ceremonies, Thai kings, especially King Bhumibol, inculcated close and personal connections

---

70 See Prajak Kongkirati and Veerayooth Kanchoochat, 'The Prayuth Regime: Embedded Military and Hierarchical Capitalism in Thailand' (2018) 6 TRaNS 279.
71 See Khemthong Tonsakulrungruang, 'Thailand' in Richard Albert et al. (eds) *The I·CONnect-Clough Center 2016 Global Review of Constitutional Law* (IConnect 2017) 214–15.
72 David Landau and Rosalind Dixon, 'Abusive Judicial Review: Court against Democracy' (2020) 52 UC Davis Law Review 1315, 1338–43, 1345–50.

with high-ranking men in cloaks and uniforms.[73] Army commanders may stage a coup and appoint themselves prime ministers but former supreme court judges too were appointed prime ministers in times of political crisis.[74] Several presidents of the supreme court and army generals became privy council members, personal advisors to the king, after retirement.[75] The two institutions therefore are the bastions of conservative royalists. They were part of a vast network of the king's allies.[76] Citing the success of a coup as evidence of the junta as the rightful de facto sovereign, no judges ever challenged the legality of a coup regime.[77] Quietly, then, the judiciary is a supporting pillar of the coup regime.

The 1997 Constitution assigned the judiciary as the guardian of the constitutional order. However, before the 2006 crisis, when Thaksin won a landslide victory and dominated Thai politics, King Bhumibol granted an audience to newly appointed judges where he gave a speech encouraging the judiciary to rescue the nation from political deadlock.[78] That speech arguably galvanized the judiciary and mobilized it to be more politically active.[79] The Constitutional Court, and later the Supreme Administrative Court, responded by invalidating the 2006 election, paving the way for the coup.[80] The decision marked the beginning of judicial activism which has lasted until today. The 2007 Constitution equipped the judiciary with more tools to control politicians, such as the power to dissolve political parties. Courts were granted more independence. Judges would be appointed to watchdog agencies. The judiciary and independent watchdog agencies had their jurisdiction expanded. Most importantly, they felt compelled to take the lead in politics. Should politicians try to disrupt this arrangement, as Yingluck did, they would be axed. The Constitutional Court transformed from an umpire into serving the needs of Thai democracy.[81]

When the Constitutional Court is to deliver a decision that is of huge public attention, it is read aloud before the parties and televised countrywide. The performance served two purposes. First, it publicly reprimanded the government of

---

73 See Duncan McCargo, *Fighting for Virtue: Justice and Politics in Thailand* (Cornell University Press 2019) chapter 4; Chambers and Napisa, *Monarchised Military*.
74 Sanya Thammasak (1973–5) and Thanin Kraivixien (1976–7).
75 Both Sanya and Thanin were appointed after their political posts.
76 See Duncan McCargo, 'Network Monarchy and Legitimacy Crises in Thailand' (2005) 18 Pacific Review 499.
77 McCargo (n 73) 89–94. See Piyabutr Saengkanokkul, ศาลรัฐประหาร: ตุลาการ ระบอบเผด็จการ และนิติรัฐประหาร [Court of Coup: Judiciary, Dictatorship, and the Judicial Coup] (Same Sky Book, 2017).
78 Dressel (n 39) 680.
79 See Luis Roberto Barroso, 'Countermajoritarian, Representative, and Enlightened: The Roles of Constitutional Courts in Democracies' (2019) 67 The American Journal of Comparative Law 109, 112–17.
80 Khemthong Tonsakulrungruang, 'An Abuse of Judicial Review' in Po Jen Yap (ed), *Judicial Review of Elections in Asia* (Routledge 2016) 179.
81 Eugenie Meriaeu, 'Thailand's Deep State, Royal Power and the Constitutional Court (1997–2015)' (2016) 46 Journal of Contemporary Asia 445.

Yingluck for its stubbornness. Second, and more important, it set the narrative for what democracy officially is.

In the 2013 and 2014 decisions, the Constitutional Court repeatedly warned about a possible abuse of democracy to undermine the democratic regime. The Constitutional Court did not regard an election as a sufficient criterion for a genuine democratic regime, which, according to the Court, must be for the benefit of all people. An elected government, meanwhile, only enjoyed temporary endorsement of some but not the whole polity, and acted only for the benefit of those voters. Thus, what is democracy? In addition to the majority rule, the Constitutional Court posited that the rule of law must be maintained. The rule of law meant, at least, the separation of powers and respect for rights and liberties. A truly democratic regime had to shield the minority's interest from abuse by the majority.

While the Constitutional Court was right that the concept of democracy extends beyond mere elections, it adopted a very negative view of politicians who may, in the Court's own words, be ignorant and drunk on power. Power might be used to lead to corruption and conflicts of interest. The Court criticized politicians for abuse, ignorance, greed, conflicts of interest, and unduly enriching one's family, while it promoted values such as selflessness, the benefit of the whole nation, honesty, righteousness, and independence. In summary, these sermon-like decisions showed the Constitutional Court's fear that the shrewd politicians would claim the majority's mandate to dismantle democracy, to grab power, and to enrich themselves. It repeated the mantra of the rule of law so as to take the moral high ground while undermining elected politicians.

But when it came to unamendability, the Constitutional Court remained vague about the fundamental structure of the democratic regime with the king as the head of state. There were no tiers of importance or well-demarcated provisions where politicians could not venture. The Constitution appeared very fragile as every topic, every change the 2007 Constitution had introduced, was not to be amended. This vagueness confirms that unamendability served as a pretext for this regressive judicial activism.

The effect of the Constitutional Court's judicial review of amendment was illiberal. The Constitutional Court may have condemned politicians and criticized the majority. It may have claimed that it was safeguarding constitutional democracy from abuses. However, these claims are inaccurate. What Thailand was experiencing under the 2007 Constitution was not abusive constitutionalism, where politicians employed constitutional means to dismantle democracy. The roles are reversed in the Thai case. The 2007 Constitution could hardly claim to be democratic. With benefit of hindsight, the 2007 Constitution operated in a transitional phase between the vibrant liberal democracy of 1997 and the 2017 hybrid Thai-style democracy. The 2007 Constitution did not succeed from its popular predecessor, the 1997 Constitution. That succession was interrupted by the coup. It did not represent the will of the people. The 2006 coup was controversial and Thailand was divided. It was drafted against the will of many, if not the majority. Drafters were picked from the junta's friends. There was little participation as the country was then under the military-backed nonpartisan government. The Constitutional Court's emphasis on a referendum as the source of democratic justification, while ignoring the nature of the whole process, was therefore misleading.

Even the referendum was questionable. Proponents of the 2007 Constitution enticed voters by acknowledging all the flaws but promising that they could amend the constitution later. They encouraged people to be strategic. By accepting the 2007 Constitution, they explained, the junta would cease to function and a general election would be called. The referendum was passed by a very thin margin. The Constitutional Court ignored such irregularities.

As a result, Thailand's amendment cases present a more complicated situation. An amendment could not be said to be an undemocratic sabotage of a properly democratic constitution. To the contrary, Yingluck's amendments could be seen as practical attempts to correct the wrongs of the 2007 Constitution. She was fully aware that a new constitution was unrealistic as the network of conservatives who had just staged the 2006 coup would never allow her to abolish its legacy, so amendment was the only solution. Yet, these amendment proposals contradicted the primary constituent power, which derived from the coup makers and was arguably less democratic than the amendments themselves.

In this circumstance, the principle of unamendability was invoked to hinder, not to protect, constitutional democracy. The senatorial appointment power, and the treaty-making power, as well as the party dissolution power, all of which were described by the Constitutional Court as part of the identity of the 2007 Constitution, were introduced into law without approval of the majority in order to constrain their representatives. They deviated from the people's will in 1997 and the amendments aimed to reset such provisions. In theory, the people were left only with the choice of abolishing the 2007 Constitution and drafting another charter. But constitutional replacement, of course, could not take place. The army then staged another coup against the very constitution it had sponsored once it realized that the 2007 Constitution had failed to stop Thaksin.

9.5 Unamendability of the future past

The 2007 Constitution has gone but the precedent on unamendability might have a far-reaching impact on the current politics. Following the first general election in 2019, the calls for amendment grew. In 2020, the country witnessed several large protests where tens of thousands marched to make several demands to end the ongoing Thai-style democratic regime. One major demand was a new constitution.[82] Despite initial resistance, the government was forced to consider the demand.

---

82 'Protesters Reiterate 3 Key Demands' *Bangkok Post* (9 October 2020) <https://www.bangkokpost.com/thailand/politics/1998947/protesters-reiterate-3-key-demands> (accessed 12 January 2021).

The current 2017 Constitution is the product of the 2014 coup. Unlike its unsuccessful predecessor, the National Council of Peace and Order (NCPO) learned from the 2006 coup's mistake. It did not hasten to promulgate a constitution. Nor did they copy the 1997 spirit. Over three years, the NCPO carefully selected drafters and instructed them to follow its command. The NCPO officially demanded a constitution with democracy that matched the Thai context, another reference to the idea of Thai-style democracy.[83] The result was a draft constitution that, instead of restoring electoral democracy, facilitated the junta's transformation into a civilian government.[84] The junta would appoint members to the Constitutional Court and watchdog agencies, as well as the senate.

The 2016 referendum was no less problematic than the 2007 one. The questions were prepared in ambiguous language: most people later admitted they had no knowledge of what they voted for.[85] Such ambiguity cloaked the real intention of the draft which was to allow Prayuth a channel to become a civilian prime minister. The NCPO heavily suppressed critics, with lawsuits, intimidation, and even torture. Many opponents fled abroad. Meanwhile, it bombarded the public with misinformation about the new constitution.[86] The Constitutional Court upheld the referendum law that was used to crush criticism of the charter draft.[87] In sum, only praise was allowed. Moreover, the junta employed the tactic of fear and uncertainty. Should Thais vote down the draft, the junta would stay on and draft another constitution, this time without public consent.[88] Through coercion and deceit, the public voted for the 2016 draft.

The 2016 draft constitution faced more hurdles after the referendum. Mainly, King Bhumibol died in October 2016. King Vajiralongkorn refused to sign the law unless the government amended it upon his request, which granted him the power to intervene in politics.[89] He did not sign the Constitution into effect until April 2017. Then, the NCPO kept postponing a general election until March 2019 when its proxy was ready.[90] These factors – that Vajiralongkorn was able to

---

83 2014 Interim Charter, sec 35 (2).
84 Duncan McCargo, 'Ordering Peace: Thailand's 2016 Constitutional Referendum' (2017) 39 *Contemporary Southeast Asia* 65, 68–71; Eugenie Merieau, 'Thailand in 2018: Military Dictatorship under Royal Command' (2019) *Southeast Asian Affair* 326, 3309–11.
85 McCargo (n 84) 75.
86 ibid 71; ANFREL, *Thailand Constitutional Referendum: A Brief Assessment Report* (ANFREL 2016) 11 [ANFREL Referendum Report]; Hataikarn Treesuwan, *Cultural Politics of Thailand's Constitutional Referendum in 2016* (MA Thesis, Thammsat University 2017) 119–24.
87 Constitutional Court Decision 4/2559 (2016); Khemthong, *2016 Global Review of Constitutional Law* 214–15.
88 Hataikarn, *Cultural Politics of Thailand's Constitutional Referendum* 22–9.
89 Eugenie Merieau, 'Thailand's New King Is Making a Power Grab' *The Diplomat* (4 February 2017) at <https://thediplomat.com/2017/02/thailands-new-king-is-making-a-power-grab/>.
90 Asian Network for Free Election (ANFREL), *The 2019 Thai General Election: A Missed Opportunity for Democracy* (ANFREL Election Observation Mission Report, 2019) 69.

change the constitution post-referendum, and that the NCPO was able to ignore constitutional mandates easily – raised serious questions about the primary constituent power of this law. Whose will does this constitution represent?

Prayuth's electoral victory owed much to the malicious 2017 Constitution that designed a poor electoral system and biased election commission.[91] At best, the 2017 Constitution facilitated farcical democracy, which places the majority and electoral politics under the guidance and manipulation of courts and watchdog agencies, populated by a network of conservative elites. Again, the pro-democratic camp had been contemplating constitutional amendments before its promulgation. Nonetheless, unlike the 2007 Constitution, the new procedure imposes almost impossible requirements for an amendment.[92] An amendment must acquire consensus from the government, the opposition, as well as the senate. An amendment to certain provisions requires a national referendum. It is also subject to the Constitutional Court's review prior to going into effect. Again, an amendment must not change the basic form of the democratic kingdom.

All of a sudden, in 2020, Thailand was plunged back to the years 2011–14. The sheer number of protesters in the streets indicated that a significant portion of Thais wished for constitutional change, which they wanted to achieve through formal amendment.[93] There was a cacophony of voices, demanding various sections of the constitution be abolished or amended, including senatorial appointment. Protesters also asked for another constitutional council and the restoration of the 1997 Constitution. Arguably, this call is more democratic and genuine than the referendum outcome. One amendment bill even gained signatures from more than 100,000 voters.[94] The government skilfully rejected most of the proposals, including the popularly initiated one, but was pressured to accept amendment bills that would create another constitution drafting assembly in the 1997-style council. Eventually, the government figured out how to resist the people's demands by referring the case to the Constitutional Court.

Following its 2012 decision, the Constitutional Court identified the amendment bill as a replacement, which therefore needed more procedural safeguards. Citing the people as the holder of the primary constituent power, the Constitutional Court ruled that the government must hold an extra referendum to determine whether the public desired a new constitution. If the public

---

91 See ANFREL *The 2019 Thai General Election*; Duncan McCargo and Saowanee T. Alexander, 'Thailand's 2019 Election: A State of Democratic Dictatorship?' (2019) 26 Asia Policy 89; Jacob I. Ricks, 'Thailand's 2019 Vote: The General's Election' (2019) 92 Pacific Affairs 443.
92 2017 Constitution, Section 291. See Khemthong, *Constitutional Amendment in Thailand* 186.
93 'Inside Thailand's Youth Revolution' *Financial Times* (5 November 2020) <https://www.ft.com/content/c2a530ba-a343-4007-a324-c2d276b95883> (accessed 12 January 2021).
94 'iLaw Submits Bill Backed by 100,000' *Bangkok Post* (22 September 2020) <https://www.bangkokpost.com/thailand/politics/1989851/ilaw-submits-bill-backed-by-100-000> (14 September 2020).

approved, the draft constitution must be approved by another referendum.[95] The pending amendment bill soon collapsed, much to the public's fury. The government offered a less ambitious choice of amendment, not replacement. It remains to be seen if these attempts will hit a roadblock in the form of explicit unamendability, as in 2013 and 2014.

9.6 Toward constitutional revolution?

The Constitutional Court's politicization of unamendability is a dangerous bet. So far, it successfully helped to prevent disruption to Thai-style democracy. But at what cost? The public is increasingly upset and has increasingly realized that the judiciary is not a trustworthy umpire. A constitution that cannot be amended by peaceful means can be abolished by force. The Constitutional Court's loathing of democracy can be contrasted with its deferral to dictatorship. All this generates a sense of public hopelessness and anger. If the people could not invoke the secondary power to amend the constitution, can they, as the Constitutional Court confirmed twice in 2012 and 2021, re-establish the unlimited primary constituent power and write a new constitution?

The new primary power means destruction of the existing constituent power, a decisive break from Thai-style democracy. In practice, that could entail violence, disruption, and drastic changes. The next constitution-making attempt may propel the country into a whirlwind.

---

95 Constitutional Court 4/2564 (2021).

10 Constitutional politics over (un)constitutional amendments

The Indian experience

Surya Deva *

10.1 Introduction

This chapter provides critical insights on politics in India over unconstitutional constitutional amendments (UCA). The Indian Constitution is not only one of the longest constitutional documents but is also one that has been amended quite frequently: 104 times in 71 years (January 1950 to December 2020).[1] Article 368 of the Constitution empowers the parliament of India to amend the Constitution *formally*.[2] In terms of their amendability, provisions of the Constitution can be divided into four categories. First, the amendment of certain provisions[3] is not treated as an amendment for the purpose of Article 368: such provisions can be amended by a "simple majority" and without following the procedure of Article 368. Second, a majority of constitutional provisions require a "special majority" – a majority of the total membership of each House of parliament and a majority of not less than two-thirds of the members of that House present and voting – for amendment. Third, some provisions (including Article 368) require a "special majority and ratification" by resolution passed by not less than one-half of the state legislatures.[4] Fourth, although not expressly provided for or originally envisaged, certain provisions of the Indian Constitution

---

* I would like to thank Binit Agrawal and Tse Long Hei Ronnie for providing research assistance for this chapter, and acknowledge the grant provided by a private foundation to City University of Hong Kong for research about the "Relevance of the Basic Structure Doctrine to the Basic Law" of the HKSAR.
1 See http://legislative.gov.in/constitution-of-india (accessed 1 May 2021).
2 The original heading of Article 368 had provided a "Procedure for amendment of the Constitution." This was revised by the 24th Constitution Amendment to read "Power of parliament to amend the Constitution and procedure thereof." Even without this amendment, it is arguable that Article 368 provides for both power and procedure of amendment, as procedure implies the presence of power, which was not conferred on the parliament by any other constitutional provision.
3 Creation of new states or reconstitution of existing states (Art 4), creation or abolition of Upper Chambers in states (Art 169(3)), and constitution of centrally administered areas (Art 239-A).
4 Proviso to Article 368(2). Provisions falling into this category relate to the centre-state relation and the higher judiciary. An amendment of the Tenth Schedule of the Constitution was

DOI: 10.4324/9781003097099-10

are "unamendable" because of the basic structure doctrine developed by the Supreme Court. The last category is the subject matter of this chapter.

However, the Indian Constitution has also been amended *informally*, for example, through judicial interpretation and ordinary legislation. As articulated in this chapter, constitutional law scholars should pay greater attention to such informal ways of amendment, because governments are using innovative tools to bypass limits on their power to amend the Constitution. Similar to what I have argued in the context of Hong Kong,[5] any legislative, executive, or judicial action which has the "effect" of amending a constitution should be treated an amendment and be subjected to express as well as implied limitations on the power of amendment. Such an effect, for example, will arise if an action contradicts or modifies an express provision, or overrides permissive constitutional silence on certain issues.[6]

Article 368 (or any other constitutional provision) does not impose any explicit limits on the power of Indian parliament to amend the Constitution. Nevertheless, the Supreme Court of India found certain implied limits. While these limits were initially found in the unamendable nature of fundamental rights, the basic structure doctrine became the subsequent basis of unamendability.[7] In fact, the evolution and application of the basic structure doctrine since the early 1970s provides the axis around which the debate about UCA has unfolded in India both inside and outside courts. This chapter will analyse critically this debate as a two-strand political dispute over values embodied in the Indian Constitution. The first strand has been of the *politics of supremacy* between the executive-legislature and the judiciary as to who has the final say on what the Constitution means. This started as a battle over the right to property versus agrarian reforms aimed at achieving a social revolution, but extended to cover a wide terrain over the years, including the power to appoint judges. The second strand is the *politics of legitimacy* between the executive-legislature and "We, the people of India," those members of the public who feel that the government – despite having a parliamentary majority – has no power to trample the spirit of the Indian Constitution. This strand has also involved the legitimacy of judicial interpretations or decisions.

This chapter will advance three main arguments. First, that greater attention should be paid to analysing informal amendments (e.g., judicial interpretations,

---

declared unconstitutional for not complying with the ratification requirement. *Kihoto Hollohan v Zachillhu* AIR 1993 SC 412.

5 Surya Deva, 'Threats to Hong Kong's Autonomy from the NPC's Standing Committee: The Role of Courts and the Basic Structure Doctrine' (2020) 50 Hong Kong Law Journal 901.

6 One can find several examples of permissive silence in the Indian Constitution. For example, the protection against discrimination under Articles 15(2) and 16(2) is not expressly limited to being available only against the state. Similarly, Article 58(1)(a) requires that the President is a citizen of India, but does not require the President to be a "natural born citizen."

7 See Mahendra P Singh, *VN Shukla's Constitution of India* (12th edn., Eastern Book Company, 2008) 1074–87.

ordinal legislation, and constitutional conventions) of constitutions to ensure that governments are not able to do indirectly what they cannot do directly. Second, the basic structure doctrine is perhaps more relevant today in view of growing democratic deficits, the rise of populism and nationalism, and traits of power concentration shown by political leaders all over the world. Third, the doctrine should be seen as part of a wider constitutional mechanism of checks and balances, rather than as a judicial *brahmastra* (a weapon with no defences) against the legislature and/or the executive. Seen in this context and considering how judicial interpretations too could amend a constitution, the doctrine should also bind courts.

I will use two case studies to examine the politics around UCA. First, the 2015 Supreme Court decision in the *Supreme Court Advocates on Record Association v Union of India*[8] (the *Fourth Judges* case) which declared unconstitutional the Constitution (Ninety-ninth Amendment) Act and the National Judicial Appointments Commission Act 2014 (NJAC Act). This constitutional amendment sought to replace the collegium system of judges' appointment with a National Judicial Appointment Commission (NJAC) and thus reverse judicial supremacy in this arena. Second, the twin August 2019 President's Orders – the Constitution (Application to Jammu and Kashmir) Order 2019,[9] and the Declaration under Article 370(3) of the Constitution[10] – coupled with the Jammu and Kashmir Reorganisation Act 2019 (JKR Act), which take away the special constitutional status and autonomy of Jammu and Kashmir conferred by Article 370 of the Constitution but without amending this provision. The second case study involves amending the Indian Constitution without an actual amendment. It is therefore contended that we should consider the term UCA in a broad sense to capture not only formal amendments but also laws or policies which have the effect of amending the Constitution.

I begin in Section 10.2 by unpacking various strands of constitutional politics in India and situate the evolution and application of the basic structure doctrine in this context. This section also analyses theoretical underpinnings of the basic structure doctrine and proposes that the doctrine should be considered part of a system of checks and balances. Section 10.3 then examines constitutional politics around two case studies – the second of which is a work in progress as the constitutional validity of government actions taking away the autonomy of Jammu and Kashmir is still pending before the Supreme Court. Since the second case study is an example of informal amendment, I also discuss what ought to be the scope of basic structure doctrine. Section 10.4 draws some common conclusions.

---

8 (2016) 4 SCC 1.
9 See http://egazette.nic.in/WriteReadData/2019/210049.pdf (accessed 1 May 2021).
10 See http://egazette.nic.in/WriteReadData/2019/210243.pdf (accessed 1 May 2021). This order was pursuant to a resolution adopted by Rajya Sabha, the Upper House of the parliament: https://pib.gov.in/newsite/PrintRelease.aspx?relid=192487 (accessed 1 May 2021).

10.2 Constitutional politics and the basic structure doctrine

10.2.1 Politics over vision and objectives of the Constitution

The drafters of Indian Constitution tried to create a founding document which balances competing interests of diverse groups of people, preserves diversity as well as the spirit of inclusiveness, and provides a pathway for "social revolution" by bringing transformative changes to economic, political, social, cultural, and religious practices.[11] The Preamble of the Constitution outlines some of these goals. It acknowledges that the people of India "resolved to constitute India into a SOVEREIGN SOCIALIST SECULAR DEMOCRATIC REPUBLIC." The Preamble also expresses the resolve of people

> to secure to all its citizens: JUSTICE, social, economic and political; LIBERTY of thought, expression, belief, faith and worship; EQUALITY of status and opportunity; and to promote among them all FRATERNITY assuring the dignity of the individual and the unity and integrity of the Nation.[12]

As readers will note below, many sites of constitutional politics in India have revolved around some of these objectives outlined in the Preamble.[13] For example, one can analyse affirmative action provisions for Scheduled Castes, Scheduled Tribes, and other backward classes of citizens in terms of social "justice" and substantive "equality."[14] At the same time, we can examine affirmative action laws and policies in terms of the politics of *supremacy* (whether legislative/executive is the best judge of these transformative measures or courts should put certain limits on the substantive equality agenda) as well as the politics of *legitimacy* (whether the government measures are merely a "vote bank tactic" or meant to bring about real change in the situation of historically disadvantaged groups). Another example of constitutional politics is provided by agrarian reforms aimed at the redistribution of land which were underpinned by the quest for economic justice and equality of status and opportunity. A challenge to the constitutional validity of these government measures triggered the politics of *supremacy*: whether the

---

11 Granville Austin, *The Indian Constitution: Cornerstone of a Nation* (Clarendon Press 1966) 27, 50–2, 124–6, 144–56, 308–9, and generally.
12 Bhatia suggests the trinity of liberty, equality, and fraternity in the Preamble is reflective of the Indian Constitution being a transformative constitution. Gautam Bhatia, *The Transformative Constitution: A Radical Biography in Nine Acts* (HarperCollins Publishers India 2019) xxvii–xxxi.
13 See, e.g., Sujit Choudhry, 'How to Do Constitutional Law and Politics in South Asia' (2014), https://www.law.berkeley.edu/files/csls/Choudhry1Dec2014.pdf (accessed 1 May 2021).
14 Mahenendra P Singh, 'Are Articles 15(4) and 16(4) Fundamental Right?' (1994) 3 SCC (Jour) 33.

government or the judiciary should be the final arbiter of the appropriateness of the tools employed to bring social revolution.[15]

One can find several other similar sites of constitutional politics in India which can be analysed from the supremacy or legitimacy angle (or from other angles for that matter).[16] For instance, the rise of judicial activism around public interest litigation, especially in the post-emergency era, could be seen in terms of the Supreme Court not only trying to regain its public *legitimacy*, but also asserting its *supremacy* in public governance and upholding constitutionalism.[17] In fact, by adopting this approach, the judiciary can claim itself to be "an arm of social revolution."[18] Similarly, the contours of religious freedoms, the meaning of secularism, and the enactment of the Uniform Civil Code have been a prominent site of politics of *legitimacy*, as critics have questioned whether certain laws and policies were really driven by *Sarva Dharma Samabhāva* (equal treatment of all religions) or driven by a desire to appease religious minorities for political gains.[19] In more recent years, India under Prime Minister Modi is embarking on the politics of Hindu nationalism in the name of national unity and integrity,[20] which raises questions about the *legitimacy* of some of the measures taken by his government even if supported by the parliament and acquiesced by the Supreme Court.

The two case studies selected in this chapter can also be analysed in terms of the politics of supremacy and/or legitimacy. For example, the battle of *supremacy* has been at play in the power of the President to appoint judges of the Supreme Court and High Courts (Articles 124 and 217) and to transfer judges of High Courts (Article 222) as well as the four cases related to the exercise of this power.[21] As discussed in detail in Section 10.3, the Supreme Court wrested the power of judicial appointments from the executive in *S C Advocates on Record*

---

15 "In India, Parliament and the judiciary have been and are likely to remain competitors when it comes to interpreting the Constitution." Pratap Bhanu Mehta, 'India's Unlikely Democracy: The Rise of Judicial Sovereignty' (2007) 18(2) Journal of Democracy 70, 75.
16 See Granville Austin, *Working a Democratic Constitution: The Indian Experience* (Oxford University Press 1999); AG Noorani, *Constitutional Questions and Citizens' Rights: An Omnibus Comprising Constitutional Questions in India: The President, Parliament and the States and Citizens' Rights, Judges and State Accountability* (Oxford University Press 2006).
17 See Ashok H Desai and S Muralidhar, 'Public Interest Litigation: Potential and Problems' in BN Kirpal et al. (eds.), *Supreme but not Infallible – Essays in Honour of the Supreme Court of India* (Oxford University Press 2000) 159; Upendra Baxi, 'The Avatars of Indian Judicial *Activism*: Explorations in the Geographies of [In]justice' in SK Verma and Kusum (eds.), *Fifty Years of the Supreme Court of India – Its Grasp and Reach* (Oxford University Press 2000) 156; SP Sathe, *Judicial Activism in India – Transgressing Borders and Enforcing Limits* (Oxford University Press, 2002); Surya Deva, 'Public Interest Litigation in India: A Critical Review' (2009) 28 Civil Justice Quarterly 19.
18 Austin, *Cornerstone of a Nation* (n 11) 164.
19 See Gerald James Larson (ed), *Religion and Personal Law in Secular India: A Call to Judgment* (Indiana University Press 2001).
20 See Ramachandra Guha, 'Politics and Current Affairs', http://ramachandraguha.in/archives/category/politics-and-current-affairs (accessed 1 May 2021).
21 See Austin, *Working a Democratic Constitution* (n 16) 123–38, 328–47, 435–41, and 516–33.

194 *Surya Deva*

Association v Union of India[22] (the *Second Judges* case) through a judicial interpretation. Although doubts remain about the opaque process adopted by the judiciary in recommending judges for appointment as well as the quality of recommended judges, the Court in the *Fourth Judges* case rebuffed an attempt made by the government to introduce a system of sharing of such power among various organs. One can also see the politics of *legitimacy* at play in the Supreme Court not trusting the executive to exercise its judicial appointment power in a way that wouldn't undermine judicial independence. Meanwhile, the government considered the NJAC to be a more legitimate body to make recommendations because judicial primacy is not constitutionally legitimate.

The second case study (taking away the special status of Jammu and Kashmir under Article 370) again demonstrates the *supremacy* of the central government over states under the federal system established by the Indian Constitution. The Supreme Court's slow reaction to dealing with the constitutionality of this government action as well as the detention of many political leaders indicates the judiciary's willingness to concede supremacy – at least for now – on this matter to the executive. On the other hand, in the absence of any consultation with people, political leaders, or institutions of Jammu and Kashmir, the central government tried to derive *legitimacy* for its action in narratives of economic development and national integration.[23] Serious questions arise about the legitimacy of the government actions as well as the underpinning legitimacy narratives.

10.2.2 The basic structure doctrine

The origin, evolution, and application of the basic structure doctrine in India could also be seen in terms of the politics of supremacy and legitimacy.[24] The Supreme Court relied on the doctrine to gain supremacy over the executive-parliament and strike down certain constitutional amendments which "sought to overturn judicial decisions which the regime in power claimed obstructed social

---

22 AIR 1994 SC 268.
23 See, e.g., Ministry of Home Affairs, 'Economic Development of Jammu and Kashmir after the Abrogation of Article 370' (4 February 2020), https://pib.gov.in/PressReleaseIframePage.aspx?PRID=1601843 (accessed 1 May 2021); '"Removal of Article 370 Brought Socio-Economic Development in J-K, Ladakh": MHA' (15 September 2020), https://www.hindustantimes.com/india-news/removal-of-article-370-has-brought-socio-economic-development-in-j-k-ladakh-mha/story-0ioxNZ6veZsgL5Xlby9ViM.html (accessed 1 May 2021); 'Revocation of Article 370 Has Paved Way for National Integration: Anurag Thakur' (6 August 2019), https://www.indiatoday.in/india/story/revocation-of-article-370-has-paved-way-for-national-integration-anurag-thakur-1577528-2019-08-06 (accessed 1 May 2021).
24 See Rajeev Dhavan, *The Supreme Court of India and Parliamentary Sovereignty* (Sterling Publishers 1976); Upendra Baxi, *The Indian Supreme Court and Politics* (Eastern Book Company 1980); TR Andhyarujina, *Kesavananda Bharati Case: The Untold Story of Struggle for Supremacy by Supreme Court and Parliament* (Universal Law Publishing Co. 2011).

justice and the nation's progress."[25] One can also see the politics of legitimacy at play: the legitimacy of the parliament's exercise of its amendment power (different from its legislative power) as well as the legitimacy of the Supreme Court's power to invalidate a constitutional amendment when no express limitations are imposed by the Constitution.

In 1973, the Supreme Court in *Kesavananda Bharati v State of Kerala*[26] held that the parliament does not have the power to amend the basic structure of the Constitution.[27] By doing so, "the Court assured for itself, a new and impregnable role in the constitutional politics of India"[28] and created what Albert and Oder describe as "informal unamendability."[29] This decision "results in a co-sharing with Parliament of constituent power by the Apex Justices."[30] The roots of such implied limits on the parliament's amendment power in the form of a basic structure (or certain basic features) could be traced to Justice Mudholkar's dissenting judgment in *Sajjan Singh v State of Rajasthan*:

> [The Constituent Assembly] formulated a solemn and dignified preamble which appears to be an epitome of the basic features of the Constitution. Can it not be said that these are indicia of the intention of the Constituent Assembly to give a permanency to the basic features of the Constitution?[31]

Then came the majority judgment in *Golak Nath v State of Punjab*,[32] which held that the parliament could amend any provision of the Constitution but not fundamental rights, because a constitutional amendment is "law" for purpose of Article 13 of the Constitution.[33] In other words, unlike earlier cases, the majority

---

25 Raju Ramachandran, 'The Supreme Court and the Basic Structure Doctrine' in Kirpal et al. (eds.), (n 17) 107.
26 (1973) 4 SCC 225.
27 Judges used a range of terms such as "essential elements," "basic features," "basic structure," "basic foundation and structure," "fundamental features," "essential features," "basic elements of the Constitutional structure," and "essential elements of the basic structure." PK Tripathi, 'Kesavananda Bharati v. The State of Kerala Who Wins?' (1974) 1 SCC (Jour) 3, http://www.ebc-india.com/lawyer/articles/74v1a2.htm (accessed 1 May 2021).
28 Ramachandran (n 25) 108.
29 Richard Albert and Bertil Emrah Oder, 'The Forms of Unamendability' in Richard Albert and Bertil Emrah Oder (eds.), *An Unamendable Constitution? Unamendability in Constitutional Democracies* (Springer 2018) 1, 9–11.
30 Upendra Baxi, 'Law, Politics, and Constitutional Hegemony: The Supreme Court, Jurisprudence, and Demosprudence' in Sujit Choudhary, Madhav Khosla, and Pratap Bhanu Mehta (eds.), *The Oxford Handbook of the Indian Constitution* (Oxford University Press 2016) 94, 101.
31 (1965) 1 SCR 933, 966.
32 (1967) 2 SCR 762.
33 Article 13(2) provides: "The State shall not make any law which takes away or abridges the rights conferred by this Part and any law made in contravention of this clause shall, to the extent of the contravention, be void."

in *Golak Nath* saw no distinction between the parliament's legislative power and constituent power.[34]

Both *Golak Nath* and *Kesavananda Bharati* imposed limits on the parliament's amendment power. However, the limits under the former were narrow and specific (only fundamental rights provisions were unamendable), while flexible and open-ended under the latter. Moreover, the basic structure doctrine was invoked to justify implied or inherent limitations on the amendment power only in the latter case (*Kesavananda Bharati*). Unlike the *Golak Nath*'s majority, the majority in *Kesavananda Bharati* accepted a distinction between a constitutional amendment and ordinary legislation. Yet, it imposed implied substantive limits even on the parliament's constituent power, as the power to amend the Constitution could not be used to abrogate or destroy it altogether.

It is worth noting that the Court did not place limits on the parliament's amendment power in initial years. For example, in *Sankari Prasad v Union of India*,[35] the Supreme Court ruled that there are no limits on the parliament's constituent power and consequently, the parliament can amend any provision of the Constitution. This view was affirmed by the majority in *Sajjan Singh v State of Rajasthan*,[36] just two years prior to the *Golak Nath* decision. What explains this major shift in the Court's attitude? The end of Nehru's era in May 1964 might have provided the Supreme Court an opening to assert its supremacy, because the Court appears to be more deferential to powerful prime ministers. The other reason may be that the judiciary got a sense of executive authoritarianism in the making[37] and thus started preparing for what was to unfold later.[38] The doctrine has become an integral part of Indian jurisprudence since its application by the Court in *Indira Nehru Gandhi v Raj Narain*,[39] a case decided during the emergency, and subsequent cases decided in normal times.[40]

How can we justify the basic structure doctrine in a functional democracy? Is it anti-democratic or could it be defended as a counter-majoritarian bulwark to preserve the essence of democracy? Scholars and lawyers have debated these questions. Commenting on the application of the basic structure doctrine to ward off abuses of power during emergency in India, Ramachandran highlights the paradoxical nature of the doctrine: "An anti-democratic doctrine had to be used to

---

34 For a critique of ignoring this distinction, see PK Tripathi, *Some Insights into Fundamental Rights* (University of Bombay 1972).
35 (1952) SCR 89.
36 (1965) 1 SCR 933.
37 See Ramachandran (n 25) 112–13.
38 Baxi argues that the doctrine emerged from a fear that "if you do not apply brakes, the engine of amending power would soon overrun the Constitution." Upendra Baxi, *Courage, Craft, and Contention: The Indian Supreme Court in the Eighties* (NM Tripathi 1985) 68.
39 (1975) Supp SCC 1.
40 *Minerva Mills v Union of India* (1980) 3 SCC 625; *Waman Rao v Union of India* (1981) 2 SCC 362; *Ismail Faruqui v Union of India* (1994) 6 SCC 360; *L Chandra Kumar v Union of India* (1997) 3 SCC 261.

prevent the murder of democracy by a grotesque mutilation of the Constitution."[41] Writing in 2000, he argues that the doctrine "proceeds upon a distrust of the democratic process," but in effect it "stifles democracy" and therefore "must now be buried."[42] Nariman notes that the doctrine "upset the balance-of-powers in the Constitution" and that by "propounding 'the basic structure theory', the guardians *of* the Constitution (it was said) had at once become guardians *over* the Constitution."[43] Writing much earlier in 1974, Tripathi had observed in relation to the ruling in *Kesavananda Bharati*:

> It will be some irony if a Court so severely concerned with saving the "essential elements" or the "basic structure and framework" of the Constitution should end up with destroying the most essential and basic principle of constitutional law, namely, that the restrictions, if any, on the power of the amendment of a sovereign constitution can be imposed only by the Constituent Assembly or its nominee, the amending authority, both of whom operate upon the Constitution, and not by a Court which must operate under the Constitution and subject to it.[44]

On the other hand, Austin justified the doctrine as some constitutional amendments tried to destroy the seamless web of protecting national unity and integrity, establishing the institutions and spirit of democracy, and fostering a social revolution.[45] Krishnaswamy goes further and defends the basic structure doctrine as an independent implied power of judicial review which covers all types of state action (not merely a constitutional amendment).[46] Roznai has also countered many theoretical, practical, and textual objections raised against the unamendability of certain constitutional provisions,[47] something which the basic structure doctrine embodies.

I will argue that the doctrine of basic structure should be treated as part of a wider system of checks and balances in times with serious democratic deficits in all institutions of governance. Nariman, a leading Indian lawyer, in his autography wrote: "One of the lessons of the Internal Emergency (of June 1975) was not to rely on constitutional functionaries. These functionaries failed us – ministers of government, members of Parliament, judges of the Supreme Court, even

---

41 Ramachandran (n 25) 117.
42 Ibid, 130.
43 Fali S Nariman, *The State of the Nation: In the Context of India's Constitution* (Hay House India 2013) 195 (emphasis in original).
44 Tripathi, 'Who Wins?' (n 27).
45 Austin, *Working a Democratic Constitution* (n 16) 258.
46 Sudhir Krishnaswamy, *Democracy and Constitutionalism in India: A Study of the Basic Structure Doctrine* (Oxford University Press 2009) 44.
47 Yaniv Roznai, 'Necrocracy or Democracy? Assessing Objections to Constitutional Unamendability' in Albert and Oder (eds.) (n 29) 29. See also Yaniv Roznai, *Unconstitutional Constitutional Amendments: The Limits of Amendment Powers* (Oxford: Oxford University Press 2017).

the president of India."[48] Nariman's assessment is relevant in non-emergency times too. For example, although Prime Minister Modi has not declared any internal emergency, his governance traits are not dissimilar to those shown by Indira Gandhi before or during the infamous Emergency. Modi has practiced a highly centralised and opaque model of decision making with almost no effective checks on his powers from any source (internal or external to the executive).[49] The autonomy of independent institutions has been undermined, opposition parties have been systematically dismantled both inside and outside the parliament, most media outlets have shown appetite for self-censorship or buying uncritically the government narrative, and even the judiciary has not shown the courage to question many controversial government decisions.[50] In such a scenario, the doctrine of basic structure should be relevant in controlling the propensity of the government to destroy the core constitutional values embodied in the Indian Constitution.

Critiquing the reasoning behind the basic structure doctrine in *Kesavananda Bharati*, Tripathi contended that "the argument that Parliament does not represent the people is a dangerous argument, because it questions a fundamental assumption not only of our Constitution but of the democratic or representative form of government."[51] There is some merit in this argument: if the parliament – comprising representatives of people elected in a democratic election – enacts a law (such as the JKR Act or the CA Act discussed below) or passes a constitutional amendment for that matter, this should be regarded as legitimate expression of the people's will. Such an argument, however, ignores the realities of parliamentary democracy in which the executive (being the leader of a political party with a majority in both houses) controls the parliament with little scope for any critical scrutiny, debate, or dissent.[52] If the Supreme Court interprets and applies the basic structure doctrine not in a self-serving manner but as the guardian of core values embodied in the Constitution, the doctrine may in fact be defended as an exercise of power on behalf of "We, the people of India" as the source of the ultimate constituent power.

---

48 Fali S Nariman, *Before Memory Fades ... An Autography* (Hay House India 2010) 171.
49 Surya Deva, 'With Coronavirus Crisis, China Sees a Chance to Export Its Model of Governance', *South China Morning Post* (29 March 2020), https://www.scmp.com/comment/opinion/article/3077320/coronavirus-crisis-china-sees-chance-export-its-model-governance (accessed 1 May 2021).
50 See Tarunabh Khaitan, 'Killing a Constitution with a Thousand Cuts: Executive Aggrandizement and Party-State Fusion in India' (2020) 14 Law and Ethics of Human Rights 49.
51 Tripathi, 'Who Wins?' (n 27).
52 The executive may also make laws by bypassing the parliament. Shubhankar Dam, *Presidential Legislation in India: The Law and Practice of Ordinances* (Cambridge University Press 2014).

10.3 Formal and informal amendments: Two case studies

The first case study analysed in this section concerns a formal constitutional amendment (the 99th Constitutional Amendment coupled with the NJAC Act), whereas the second involves no formal constitutional amendment but merely executive orders and ordinary legislation (the JKR Act) which have the effect of amending the Constitution. It is argued that the doctrine of basic structure should have a role to play in both these situations.

10.3.1 Formal constitutional amendment: Continuing battle over judicial appointments

Judicial independence has been a key issue in the *Fourth Judges* case as well as in several other previous cases relating to the appointment and/or transfer of judges.[53] It is clear from the detailed debate as well as constitutional provisions regarding the appointment, tenure, salaries, retirement age, and removal of the judges that the framers of the Indian Constitution considered judicial independence an important aspect of Indian constitutionalism.[54] Special attention was paid to the procedure of appointment as "an independent judiciary begins with who appoints what calibre of judges."[55]

However, the appointment and transfer of judges have always been under controversy, inviting protracted litigation, from the very beginning.[56] In the *First Judges* case, the Court held that the independence of the judiciary is a basic feature of the Constitution and that there must be "full and effective" consultation between all the constitutional functionaries on the question of appointment. The majority rejected the suggestion that the Chief Justice of India has any primacy in recommending a person for appointment to the High Court or the Supreme Court. As the government misused its primacy in appointing judges, the issue again came before the Supreme Court in the *Second Judges* case in which it overruled its decision in the *First Judges* case on the point of primacy. The Court held that the procedure for the appointment of the judges was an "integrated participatory consultative process" in which "all the constitutional functionaries must perform this duty collectively with a view primarily to reach an agreed decision ... so that the occasion of primacy does not arise."[57] However, in case of a difference of opinion between different constitutional functionaries, the opinion of the Chief Justice of India has primacy. The proposal for the appointment of

---

53 *Union of India v Sankalchand Sheth* AIR 1977 SC 2328.
54 Austin, *Cornerstone of a Nation* (n 11) 176–83.
55 Austin, *Working a Democratic Constitution* (n 16) 124.
56 Ibid 125–38, 278–89, 344–6, and 516–33; Mahendra P Singh, 'Securing the Independence of the Judiciary: The Indian Experience' (2000) 10 Indiana International and Comparative Law Review 245, 265–6.
57 AIR 1994 SC 268, 442.

judges must be initiated by the Chief Justices of the respective courts, but only after consulting the two senior-most judges of the concerned Court.

This judgment received a mixed response[58] and in view of the difficulties in applying the collegium system, the President referred the issue to the Supreme Court to clarify certain doubts.[59] The Court clarified those doubts in the *Third Judges* case: it held that an opinion of the Chief Justice of India not formed according to the majority judgment in the *Second Judges* case was not binding on the government. The Court also raised the strength of the collegium from three to five judges. The collegium is expected to make its decision by consensus but no appointment to the Supreme Court could be made unless the appointment is in conformity with the opinion of the Chief Justice of India. However, the appointment must not be made if it is favoured by the Chief Justice but not by the majority of the collegium. In other words, the Court tried to refine the collegium system, including to avoid the exercise of power solely by the Chief Justice of India.

It is clear that the Supreme Court in the *Second* and *Third Judges* cases "in effect" amended Article 124 and other provisions of the Constitution by superimposing a position which was rejected during the drafting of the Constitution.[60] The apparent justification for this position was to exclude the possibility of the executive making political appointments and transferring or superseding inconvenient judges.[61] However, such instances of the executive's misuse of power were not new: they existed even prior to the *First Judges* case. So, what explains this shift? I will suggest that this turnaround in the Court's position was reflective of waiting for the "right opening" to win the long see-saw battle of supremacy in constitutional adjudication: the era of coalition governments from the early 1990s coupled with the incremental consolidation of roles in political governance through public interest litigation provided the Court an ideal opportunity to snatch power from the executive in a way which appeared legitimate.

However, controversies around the appointment and transfer of judges continued along with growing incidents of misconduct and corruption among the judges with no effective mechanism of accountability. Against this background, suggestions for the establishment of a National Judicial Commission to deal with the issues of appointment and misconduct of judges were made, including by the National Commission to Review the Working of the Constitution.[62] In 2003, a Bill to amend the Constitution and establish a National Judicial Commission (comprising the Chief Justice of India as chair, the two senior-most judges of the

---

58 Lord Cooke of Thorndon, 'Where Angels Fear to Tread' in BN Kirpal et al (eds.) (n 17) 97–106.
59 See Singh, 'The Indian Experience' (n 56) 274.
60 There are many instances of the Court doing this: introduction of substantive due process in *Maneka Gandhi v Union of India* 1978 AIR 597 is a case in point.
61 See Austin, *Working a Democratic Constitution* (n 16) 278–89, 344–7.
62 Report of the National Commission to Review the Working of the Constitution (2002), vol. I, paras 7.3.7 and 7.3.8.

Constitutional politics in India 201

Supreme Court, the Union Law Minister, and a nominee of the President to be appointed on the recommendation of the Prime Minister) was moved.[63] In view of differences about the composition of the Commission and doubts about its effectiveness, the attempt did not materialise.

Then came the 99th Constitutional Amendment of 2015, which (along with the NJAC Act) sought to replace the collegium system of judicial appointment with a NJAC and thus reverse judicial supremacy in this arena. The NJAC was envisaged to comprise the following six people: the Chief Justice of India, the two most senior judges of the Supreme Court, the federal Law Minister, and two "eminent persons" to be nominated for three-year terms by a committee consisting of the Chief Justice, the Prime Minister, and the Leader of the Opposition in the Lower House of Parliament. While the 2003 Amendment Bill sought to preserve judges' majority in the Commission (3 out of 5), the 99th Constitutional Amendment brought down the judges' presence to 50 per cent (3 out of 6). This difference could again be explained in view of Vajpayee leading a coalition of political parties in 2003, while Modi had a clear majority in 2014.

The Supreme Court in the *Fourth Judges* case, by a 4:1 majority, held the entire 99th Constitutional Amendment unconstitutional. To put it simply, the Court's reasoning was that the independence of the judiciary is part of the basic structure, judicial primacy in appointments – which is not only mandated by the Constitution but is also part of the basic structure – is required to preserve judicial independence, and judicial primacy is undermined by the NJAC having three out of six non-judicial members or the possibility of them vetoing a nominee proposed by three judges.[64] Even if it is accepted "that the 'manner of selection and appointment' of Judges to the higher judiciary, is an integral component of 'independence of the judiciary',"[65] and thus part of the basic structure, it does not follow that judicial primacy is the *only* "manner" to achieve independence of the judiciary.[66] The Supreme Court in the *Fourth Judges* case insisted on "micro-managing" what appointment process will (or will not) preserve judicial independence.[67] It seems, from the majority's reasoning, that any other process

---

63 The Constitution (98th Amendment) Bill 2003.
64 For a critical analysis, see Rehan Abeyratne, 'Upholding Judicial Supremacy in India: The NJAC Judgment in Comparative Perspective' (2017) 49 George Washington International Law Review 569.
65 *Fourth Judges* case (n 8), Justice Khehar opinion, para 93.
66 Justice Chelameswar in his dissenting opinion observed: "Primacy of the opinion of judiciary in the matter of judicial appointments is not the *only* means for the establishment of an independent and efficient judiciary." *Fourth Judges* case (n 8), Justice Chelameswar opinion, para 98 (emphasis in original).
67 "In earlier cases, the Supreme Court had prescribed a set of meta-principles that formed part of the basic structure of the Constitution. The Court's role was to ensure that these meta-principles were preserved. The Fourth Judges Case took a step further, by not only prescribing what those meta-principles are, but also how they ought to be achieved." Chintan Chandrachud, 'Constitutional Falsehoods: The Fourth Judges Case and the Basic Structure Doctrine in India' in Albert and Oder (eds.) (n 29) 149, 162–3 (footnotes omitted).

which does not confer primacy on the judiciary in appointing judges will not be acceptable to the Supreme Court.

Chandrachud argues that the Court's decision in the *Fourth Judges* case exacerbates the "disjunctures between constitutional text and constitutional practice."[68] I think a more problematic falsehood is that judicial primacy in the appointment of judges is sine qua non for judicial independence. By replacing executive primacy with judicial primacy, the Supreme Court in the *Second Judges* case replaced (and entrenched in the *Third Judges* case and the *Fourth Judges* case) one evil by another: the executive misuse of the appointment power was replaced with judicial arbitrariness in appointing judges.[69] Although the power to appoint judges is related to judicial independence, judiciaries do not necessarily lose their independence when judges are appointed by the executive.[70] Conversely, conferring the appointment power solely to the judiciary may not automatically ensure judicial independence. Abeyratne has convincingly argued that the *Fourth Judges* case majority "judgment does not explain why judicial primacy promotes or secures judicial independence."[71] For example, the Chief Justice of India may in practice assert her primacy within the collegium,[72] or self-appointed judges may lack "internal" independence.[73] An opaque process may also result in the appointment of less-deserving candidates[74] or judges with suspect integrity.[75] There are also concerns about the "reciprocity" culture "amongst the members of the collegium particularly, and amongst judges generally."[76]

To address some of these concerns, the Court in the *Third Judges* case expanded the collegium from the three senior-most judges to the five senior-most judges and brought in the majority rule in making recommendations. However, this tweaking did not address the inherent problems with a non-transparent self-appointing system. Although hardly anyone will disagree with the importance of judicial independence, this concept has been utilised by both the judiciary and

---

68 Ibid, 150.
69 Justice Chelameswar in his dissenting opinion in the *Fourth Judges* case provides examples of successive Chief Justices not following even the collegium system. *Fourth Judges* case (n 8) Justice Chelameswar opinion, paras 57–63.
70 However, Gautam argues that judicial primacy in appointment is needed to save the system from nepotism and political patronage. Khagesh Gautam, 'Political Patronage and Judicial Appointments in India: A Comment on the Fourth Judges Appointments (NJAC) Case' (2017) 4 Indonesia Journal of International and Comparative Law 653. While this concern is legitimate, it ignores the problems with judicial patronage.
71 Abeyratne (n 64) 570 and generally 598–9.
72 Nariman, *Before Memory Fades* (n 48) 397–8.
73 On internal judicial independence, see Article 1.4 of the Bangalore Principles of Judicial Conduct (2007), and Article 9 of the Mount Scopus International Standards of Judicial Independence (2008).
74 See Nariman, *Before Memory Fades* (n 48) 398–401; Mehta (n 15) 74.
75 See Prannv Dhawan, '"Reform That You May Preserve": Rethinking the Judicial Appointments Conundrum' (2020) 9 Indian Journal of Constitutional Law 186, 188–9.
76 Dushyant Dave, 'Give and Take: The Supreme Court's Way of Business' (16 May 2019), https://thewire.in/law/supreme-court-judiciary-collegium-njac (accessed 1 May 2021).

the executive for a secondary institutional purpose, that is, to gain *supremacy* in picking judges with a final say in interpreting the Constitution and judging the constitutionality of government decisions. Both sides also tend to resort to the politics of *legitimacy*. The Supreme Court finds support for judicial primacy in the appointment of judges, among others, in the executive's track record of exercising the judicial appointment power for political reasons. The executive similarly contends that judicial primacy is not constitutionally legitimate. Nor is the collegium system legitimate, including because of the lack of transparency in the appointment process.

In the current situation, two broad reform options are feasible to ensure both judicial independence and transparency in the appointment process. The first is to reintroduce the idea of an NJAC with a composition (as well as the decision-making process) which may be acceptable to the judiciary.[77] It is, however, unlikely that the Modi government would like to create a system that essentially keeps the judicial appointment power with the judiciary. The second, and perhaps more plausible system, will be for the Supreme Court to "reform the practice" of the current collegium system.[78] Instead of operating opaquely within a small club of five senior-most judges, the collegium should institutionalise the practice of formally consulting a range of stakeholders (e.g., other Supreme Court judges, Chief Justices of High Courts, bar associations, senior lawyers, the Attorney General of India, the Solicitor General of India, and academics) before making recommendations to the President for appointment.[79]

10.3.2 Informal constitutional amendment: Unilateral withdrawal of Jammu and Kashmir's autonomy

Should the basic structure doctrine have a role in relation to informal constitutional amendments? This raises two inter-related questions about the scope of this doctrine. First, should the doctrine only constrain a constitutional amendment or also apply to ordinary legislation and other informal amendment pathways? Second, should the doctrine also apply to actions of the executive and the judiciary?

Regarding the first question, it seems that the doctrine was originally meant to apply only to constitutional amendments – it had the effect of elevating the status

---

77 See, e.g., Chintan Chandrachud, 'Collaboration, Not Confrontation: The Indian Supreme Court on Judicial Appointments' (17 October 2015), http://www.iconnectblog.com/2015/10/collaboration-not-confrontation-the-indian-supreme-court-on-judicial-appointments/ (accessed 1 May 2021).
78 The Court in the *Fourth Judges* case in fact agreed to consider introducing "appropriate measures, if any, for an improved working of the 'collegium system'." Fourth Judges case (n 8), Order of the Court, para 5.
79 The "most important consideration for appointment of any person as judge of the Supreme Court is to make all possible inquiries (from all possible sources) and then, and only then, recommend his/her name." Nariman, *Before Memory Fades* (n 48) 404.

of certain provisions or principles to a "super constitution" in that even a constitutional amendment could not tamper with them. It is also arguable that the doctrine is perhaps not required for ordinary legislation because it cannot infringe any constitutional provision.[80] This issue will not matter much if an aspect of the basic structure is also a provision of the Constitution. However, it will be consequential if the basic structure involves an abstract constitutional principle. Despite expressing a contrary view in cases such as *Kuldip Nayar v Union of India*,[81] the Supreme Court has invoked the doctrine to test the constitutionality of ordinary legislation as well as executive action.[82] If the objective of the doctrine is to preserve certain core values, the form of amendment should not matter. I will argue that the basic structure doctrine should operate as a check against all these pathways of change, because governments are using creative ways to amend constitutions, that is, without introducing any formal amendments as shown by the second case study of this chapter. In other words, we should look at both the *form* and the *effect* of an instrument of change.[83]

Regarding the second question, although the doctrine was primarily intended to control the unlimited power of legislatures to amend constitutions, it should also constrain powers of the executive and the judiciary.[84] If the basic structure of a constitution signifies certain core values which even peoples' representatives cannot amend while acting collectively, the executive or the judiciary may have less democratic legitimacy to amend it. As argued above, the doctrine as part of a broader scheme of checks and balances should bind all three government organs. Bringing the judiciary within the purview of the doctrine will also ensure that courts do not end up becoming a supra-constitutional institution, especially if a constitution does not specify unamendable provisions. Taking such a position would in practice mean that lawyers should be able to argue before the Indian Supreme Court that deciding a given case in a particular way may infringe the supremacy of the constitution, separation of powers, secularism, or federalism.

Krishnaswamy draws a distinction between two types of constitutional change (constitutional amendment and constitutional interpretation),[85] and argues that the basic structure doctrine judicial review should apply to all types of state action to ensure that such action does not destroy "basic features of the constitution."[86] Beshara similarly sees value in utilising the doctrine as a theory of judicial review

---

80 See Ramachandran (n 27) 123–4.
81 (2006) 7 SCC 1.
82 *L Chandra Kumar v Union of India* (1997) 3 SCC 261; *IR Coelho v State of Tamil Nadu* (2007) 2 SCC 1; *SR Bommai v Union of India* AIR 1994 SC 1918. For discussion, see Krishnaswamy (n 46) 43–69. See also Christopher J Beshara, 'Basic Structure Doctrines and the Problem of Democratic Subversion: Notes from India' (2015) 48(2) Verfassung und Recht in Übersee [Law and Politics in Africa, Asia and Latin America] 99.
83 Deva, 'Threats to Hong Kong's Autonomy' (n 5).
84 Singh, *Shukla's Constitution of India* (n 7) 1088–9.
85 Krishnaswamy (n 46) 183–9.
86 Ibid, xxix.

in dominant-party democracies like India.[87] My position regarding the scope of the doctrine articulated above is both narrower and broader than taken by Krishnaswamy and Beshara: it is narrower because the doctrine should apply only to an action which amends the text or practice of the Constitution; and it is broader because it should bind even the judiciary. The narrower scope is desirable; otherwise an open-ended doctrine could result in significant uncertainty if all types of state action are challenged before courts on the ground of infringing the basic structure. Such a view is also in line with the real purpose of the doctrine: to safeguard core values of a constitution from amendment. At the same time, the broader scope is vital because even non-formal pathways (including judicial interpretations) could destroy the core values of a constitution. This position also ensures that the judiciary too is subject to the rules that it develops for the other two branches of government, thus building an internal system of checks and balances in the basic structure doctrine. This, in turn, should alleviate Mehta's concerns about "judicial supremacy."[88]

With this analysis about the scope of the basic structure doctrine, let us now turn to the second case study illustrative of an informal constitutional amendment. Article 370 of the Constitution appears in Part XXI entitled "Temporary, Transitional and Special Provisions." This part contains provisions conferring special status on several states. However, Article 370 – with the headnote "Temporary provisions with respect to the State of Jammu and Kashmir" – is unique, because the "State of Jammu and Kashmir is the *only* State in the Union of India which *negotiated* the terms of its membership with the Union."[89] In other words, Article 370 embodies an accession agreement, which neither "side can amend or abrogate ... unilaterally."[90] Although the headnote of Article 370 uses the phrase "temporary provisions," Mustafa has argued that this provision conferring a special status on Jammu and Kashmir, as well as governing the centre's relationship with Jammu and Kashmir, was meant to be permanent: "Article 370 is nothing but a constitutional recognition of the conditions mentioned in the Instrument of Accession that the ruler of Kashmir signed with the Government of India in 1948."[91]

Article 370 cannot be amended by the parliament in exercise of its generic constituent power under Article 368 of the Constitution. Rather, the power to amend (or even abrogate) Article 370 lies with the executive: Article 370(3)

---

87 Beshara (n 82).
88 "In India, unelected judges have effectively replaced the notion of the separation of powers among three governmental branches with a 'unitarian' claim of formal judicial supremacy." Mehta (n 15) 72.
89 AG Noorani, *Article 370: A Constitutional History of Jammu and Kashmir* (Oxford University Press, 2011) 1 (emphasis in original).
90 Ibid, 1.
91 Faizan Mustafa, 'Article 370, Federalism and the Basic Structure of the Constitution' (27 September 2019), https://www.theindiaforum.in/article/article-370-federalism-and-basic-structure-constitution (accessed 1 May 2021).

empowers the President of India to amend it by issuing a notification but *only after* "the recommendation of the Constituent Assembly of the State" of Jammu and Kashmir. In addition to Article 370, prior to the August 2019 changes, "three documents were governing the State of Jammu & Kashmir and its relationship with India – the IoA [Instrument of Accession], the Basic Order, and the Constitution of Jammu & Kashmir."[92]

Article 370 limits the parliament's legislative power over Jammu and Kashmir "to three subjects – defence, foreign affairs, and communications."[93] The President of India could extend, in consultation with the government of Jammu and Kashmir, other provisions of the Indian Constitution to Jammu and Kashmir provided they relate "to the matters specified in the Instrument of Accession." However, the "concurrence" of the said government is required to extend other provisions of the Indian Constitution. This scheme again shows the centrality of consent of Jammu and Kashmir's government before changing the status quo. There is, however, a catch which, as noted below, the Indian government exploited.

It is worth noting that the autonomy of Jammu and Kashmir has been undermined "incrementally" by a series of President's Orders over the years.[94] Therefore, what separates the August 2019 President's Orders and the JKR Act from previous actions of the central government is the "complete" abrogation of the special constitutional status and autonomy of Jammu and Kashmir. As Bhatia explains, the central government used a clever pathway to achieve this goal and overcome technical obstacles built into Article 370 to prevent its amendment easily: the amendment of an Article requires the recommendation of the Constituent Assembly of the State of Jammu and Kashmir, but no such Assembly exists any more.[95] To overcome this difficulty, the government amended the interpretive provision of Article 367 to provide that the expression "Constituent Assembly of the State" referred in proviso to Article 370(3) shall mean "Legislative Assembly of the State." As Jammu and Kashmir's Legislative Assembly was under suspension, a resolution by Rajya Sabha (the Upper House of the Indian parliament) – which was given the power to act as the State's Assembly during suspension – in effect became "the recommendation of the Constituent Assembly of the State" to repeal the existing text of Article 370. Moreover, the amendment of Article 367 also provides that references to the "Government of the said State" shall be construed as references to "the Governor of Jammu and Kashmir acting on the advice of his Council of Ministers." In other words, the central government

---

92 Zaid Deva, 'Basic Without Structure?: The Presidential Order of 1954 and the Indo-Jammu and Kashmir Constitutional Relationship' (2020) 4(2) Indian Law Review 163, 166.
93 Noorani, *Article 370* (n 89) 5.
94 Ibid, 8–28.
95 Gautam Bhatia, 'The Article 370 Amendments: Key Legal Issues' (5 August 2019), https://indconlawphil.wordpress.com/2019/08/05/the-article-370-amendments-key-legal-issues/ (accessed 1 May 2021).

repealed Article 370 by replacing *strong* limitations built in this provision with some *symbolic* limitations.

The constitutional validity of the twin President's Orders and the JKR Act is pending before the Supreme Court. One of the arguments raised by the petitioner is that they violate three elements of the basic structure: federalism, democracy, and the rule of law.[96] For example, "substituting the concurrence of the state with concurrence by the governor under President's rule, is a violation of democracy."[97] The fact that Article 370(3) required the recommendation of the Constituent Assembly to amend or abrogate Article 370 implies a critical role of the "constituent power," which is enjoyed by people of Jammu and Kashmir or their delegates specifically entrusted with such power. It was a constitutional fraud to use legal manoeuvres to deny any say to the people in a process that effectively amended the Constitution. In fact, the central government did not consciously allow any possibility of *even informal consultation* with people because of complete clampdown, communication blackout, and preventive detention of all major political leaders. Moreover, if the status of a state like Jammu and Kashmir could be demoted with such ease, the autonomy of other states would be totally at the mercy of the central government with little constitutional cushion (as opposed to political cushion). It is worth noting that unlike the infamous emergency of 1975, the Modi government achieved such domination during normal political times.

The August 2019 actions of the Indian government vis-à-vis the special status of Jammu and Kashmir under Article 370 could again be analysed from the perspective of the politics of supremacy and legitimacy. Who is supreme under a unique model of federalism,[98] which tends to become unitary in times of emergency, established by the Indian Constitution? Could the central government erode at will the constitutionally guaranteed autonomy of states like Jammu and Kashmir without following the letter and spirit of the Constitution, or are there any effective legal checks on this power? Moreover, will the judiciary defer to the executive and let it enjoy supremacy over what Article 370 entails because of the so-called national unity and integrity at stake? The legitimacy of the President's Orders is also suspect because these Orders were issued after a "symbolic" consultation with the governor, who lacks any autonomy or democratic legitimacy at the state level, or on the recommendation of an Upper House of parliament controlled by the government. As the abolition of Article 370 was part of the political manifesto of Bharatiya Janata Party,[99] it is arguable that people gave it the political mandate to do so at the 2019 general elections. However, does this

---

96 See V Venkatesan, 'Eight Cases That Will Test Whether "Basic Structure Doctrine" Can Safeguard India's Democracy' (20 October 2020), https://thewire.in/law/eight-cases-that-will-test-whether-basic-structure-doctrine-can-safeguard-indias-democracy (accessed 1 May 2021).
97 Ibid.
98 Singh, *Shukla's Constitution of India* (n 7) A-32-36.
99 See https://www.bjp.org/en/manifesto2019 (accessed 1 May 2021).

confer legitimacy on the government's decision or should the will of the majority (even if true) triumph over constitutional limitations in the absence of strong political opposition?

Analysing the constitutional politics around the basic structure doctrine, Choudhry noted that it

> arose in the context of the domination of the Indian Parliament by the Congress Party, which alone, and with its allies, controlled the process of constitutional amendment. The course of the doctrine holds lessons for how one Supreme Court managed to check the power of a dominant political party through constitutional adjudication.[100]

Times have changed and now the Bharatiya Janata Party (coupled with Prime Minister Modi) is perhaps more powerful in the parliament than Congress used to be under Nehru or Indira Gandhi. Will the Supreme Court stand up to address the assault on the rule of law as well as the federal character of the Constitution? In the past, the Indian Supreme Court stepped up in the *Bommai* case to prevent the central government from misusing Article 356 to take over governance in states, especially if they were ruled by an opposition political party. The August 2019 executive actions pose a single but equally significant assault on the federal and democratic character of the Indian Constitution. It is yet to be seen whether the Court will again rise to the occasion or, alternatively, find a convenient reasoning to normalise the emasculation of Article 370.

10.4 Conclusion

Nariman, a noted Indian lawyer, is right in observing that "our present leaders have failed to live up to the ideals of the founding fathers."[101] Successive governments in India failed to read correctly and implement consistently the constitutional vision of bringing a socio-economic transformation in Indian society and developing a limited democracy. How could the Supreme Court use the basic structure doctrine for occasional course corrections? I have argued in this chapter that although the doctrine should not be seen as a device to address all types of misuse of power by the executive and the legislature, it should be employed to check against all formal and informal pathways of constitutional amendments. Moreover, the doctrine should also bind the judiciary to address fears of judicial arbitrariness and achieve a "constitutional equilibrium" rather than an absolute supremacy of either the judiciary or the legislature/executive. After all, "there is no reason to assume that judges any more than politicians will always protect our liberties."[102]

---

100 Choudhry (n 13) 9–10.
101 Nariman, *The State of the Nation* (n 43) 15.
102 Mehta (n 15) 80.

The real value of the basic doctrine will be in those situations when the judiciary invokes it to preserve core values of a constitution from assault from a dominant government and not merely for a self-serving purpose[103] or against weaker governments. There is no doubt that the Indian Supreme Court has been "a centre of *political* power" from the very beginning of an independent India.[104] However, if it continues to use this power in a selective, incohesive, or self-serving manner, the Court will erode further its legitimacy and in turn its supreme status under the Indian Constitution.

---

103 Kumar laments the fact that "the executive and the judiciary find themselves on the same page when it comes to trampling all over the Constitution." Alok Prasanna Kumar, 'Judiciary vs Executive: Is the Country's Constitution Becoming a Victim in This Pursuit for Supremacy?' (28 October 2017), https://www.firstpost.com/india/judiciary-vs-executive-is-the-countrys-constitution-becoming-a-victim-in-this-pursuit-for-supremacy-4180783.html (accessed 1 May 2021).
104 Baxi, *The Indian Supreme Court and Politics* (n 24) 10 (emphasis in original).

11 The politics of unconstitutional amendments in Bangladesh

Ridwanul Hoque *

11.1 Introduction

That a constitutional amendment can be unconstitutional despite its procedural compliance with the amendment rule is not a new concept in public law. The idea of "unconstitutional constitutional amendment" (UCA) is rather a well-developed, living concept. The idea is premised on the theorising that a constitution comprises certain essential cores and, therefore, an amendment that dismantles one or more of those essentials is unconstitutional. The idea of unconstitutional constitutional amendment is famously known as "the doctrine of basic structure" in South Asia.[1] The Supreme Court of Bangladesh subscribed to the idea in its 1989 decision in *Anwar Hossain Chowdhury v Bangladesh* (the 8th Amendment Case).[2]

In *Chowdhury*, the Appellate Division had struck down part of the 8th Amendment[3] that diffused the Supreme Court's High Court Division (HCD)[4] into several regional permanent branches.[5] Its reasoning was that the 8th

---

* I would like to dedicate this chapter to the loving memory of my mentor Prof M Shah Alam, who passed away on 31 August 2020. Prof Alam's seminal work on the legality of state religion amendment in Bangladesh is cited in this chapter.
1 See R Hoque, 'Implicit Unamendability in South Asia: The Core of the Case for the Basic Structure Doctrine' (2018) 3 Indian J of Const and Administrative L 23; A Choudhuri and K Shivani, 'Determining the Constitutionality of Constitutional Amendments in India, Pakistan and Bangladesh: A Comparative Analysis' (2017) 10 National U of Juridical Sc L Rev 3.
2 (1989) BLD (Special) 1, Justice Afzal dissenting.
3 The other part made Islam the "state religion." On the legality of the state religion part of the 8th Amendment, see S Alam, 'The State-Religion Amendment to the Constitution of Bangladesh: A Critique' (1991) 24(2) Verfassung und Recht in Übersee 209.
4 The Supreme Court comprises the Appellate Division (hereafter "SCAD") and the High Court Division (hereafter "HCD"). The HCD exercises the original jurisdiction of constitutional judicial review. The SCAD hears appeals from any decision, order, and judgment of the HCD. The Constitution of Bangladesh (16 December 1972) structured the HCD as an integral lower division of the Supreme Court. See arts 94, 102, and 103 of the Constitution of Bangladesh.
5 The literature on the Bangladeshi perspective includes the following: MJU Talukder and JA Chowdhury 'Determining the Province of Judicial Review: A Re-Evaluation of "Basic Struc-

DOI: 10.4324/9781003097099-11

Amendment violated an important basic feature of the Constitution: the unitary character of the state. Later, in 2010 and 2011, the Appellate Division of the Supreme Court (SCAD) declared unconstitutional with finality three more amendments – the 5th, 7th, and 13th Amendments. Further, in 2017, the Appellate Division by a unanimous decision struck down the 16th Amendment, but the decision has yet not become final because of a petition for review.[6] The Constitution of Bangladesh has so far gone through 17 amendments; the first one was in 1973 while the latest was in 2019. In regard to other constitutional amendments that confronted judicial scrutiny, the court either endorsed their constitutionality[7] or lent to them some legitimacy but not without questioning their legality.[8]

Apart from the judiciary, multiple political factors contributed to those annulment decisions while the political branches too had their own share in the doctrine's usage. As we will see below, the lawyers' movement against executive encroachments into judicial independence in the 1980s coupled with a public mobilisation against autocracy paved the way for the idea of UCA in Bangladesh. On the other hand, the elected branches had overly self-interested political gains in mind when enacting most, if not all, constitutional amendments. In most constitutional systems, party-interest and constitutional amendment objectives often converge. In Bangladesh's case, however, the ruling party in successive regimes has used constitutional amendments to exclude the opposition, realise incumbency advantage, and deepen the political divide that exists in the confrontational, polarised politics of the two major parties. It is indeed the design of excluding the opposition that has made the "self-interest" of the ruling party in constitutional amendments so problematic. At one point, for example, the current ruling party – the Bangladesh Awami League – resorted to the 15th Amendment in

---

ture" of the Constitution of Bangladesh' (2008) 2(2) Metropolitan U Journal 161; S Khan, 'Leviathan and the Supreme Court: An Essay on the "Basic Structure" Doctrine' (2011) 2 Stamford J of L 89; R Hoque, *Judicial Activism in Bangladesh: A Golden Mean Approach* (Cambridge Scholars Publishing 2011) 112–19; Hoque (n 1); R Chowdhury, 'The Doctrine of Basic Structure in Bangladesh: From "Calf-path" to *Matryoshka* Dolls' (2017) 14 Bangladesh J of L 43.

6 *Bangladesh v Asaduzzaman Siddiqui* (2017) CLR (AD) (Spl) 1, endorsing the HCD's opinion in *Asaduzzaman Siddiqui v Bangladesh* (Writ Petition (WP) No. 9989 of 2014; judgment 5 May 2016). See further R Hoque, 'Can the Court Invalidate an Original Provision of the Constitution?' (2016) 2(1) Univ of Asia Pacific J of L and Policy 13 (critiquing the HCD's decision).

7 In some cases, the SCAD declined to invalidate amendments that increased the number of reserved women's seats in parliament. See *Fazle Rabbi v Election Commission* (1992) 44 DLR (HCD) 14; *Dr. Ahmed Hossain v Bangladesh* (1992) 44 DLR (AD) 109; *Farida Akhter v Bangladesh* (2007) 15 BLT (AD) 206.

8 In a 1981 curious decision, the HCD found the 2nd and 4th Amendments to the Constitution to be violative of "essential features of the Constitution" but refused to invalidate them. See *Hamidul Huq Chowdhury v Bangladesh* (1981) 33 DLR (HCD) 381. On appeal, the SCAD eschewed the question altogether. See *Hamidul Huq Chowdhury v Bangladesh* (1982) 34 DLR (AD) 190.

212 *Ridwanul Hoque*

2011 to abolish the system of election-time "non-party caretaker government" (NPCTG), which was brought to the Constitution in 1996 in fulfilment of a demand of that party itself when it was in the opposition.

Arguably, behind every amendment, which can be considered unconstitutional, was the narrow party politics that was invariably exclusionary. Yet, the available literature has largely failed to capture the political dimension of unconstitutional constitutional amendments in Bangladesh. This chapter seeks to close this gap by examining the politics of two "unconstitutional" constitutional amendments – the 8th and the 15th Amendments. It will investigate how different political forums – the legislature, judiciary, political parties, and the constituent people – have influenced, and become informed of, the growth of the idea of UCA. The central argument of this chapter is that the politics of unconstitutional amendment in Bangladesh is deeply tied to diverse parameters of local (constitutional) politics whereas the concerned actors operate both cooperatively and incongruously, depending on their self-interest.

A note on the scope of this chapter should be made at the outset. The present chapter examines only two constitutional amendments – the 8th and the 15th. The 8th Amendment had two parts: one introduced six regional permanent branches of the High Court Division contrary to the original scheme of the Constitution, and the other part made Islam the state religion. The judicial restructuring part of the 8th Amendment was declared unconstitutional by the SCAD, but the state religion part has never been invalidated. Nevertheless, this paper considers the state religion amendment as unconstitutional for being incompatible with one of the founding cores and analyses the background politics thereof. The other amendment examined is the 15th Amendment which has not been challenged in court. The 15th Amendment has many parts, which form a curious mix of constitutional and unconstitutional amendments. This chapter examines two such 15th Amendment changes as unconstitutional amendments – the abolition of the NPCTG system and the insertion of an extraordinarily broad eternal clause.[9]

11.2 The politics of (un)constitutional amendment

The idea that a constitutional amendment can be unconstitutional first figured in the political discourse not too long after the nation's founding Constitution was adopted on 4 November 1972. The 2nd Amendment of 1973 was enacted to legalise executive detention without trial on state security grounds and to protect any constitutional amendment from the allegation of unconstitutionality for being incompatible with fundamental rights.[10] Because of democratic decline and increasing party dominance at the time, criticisms and debates over the 2nd Amendment's unconstitutionality were quite limited.

---

9 Now see art. 7B of the Constitution of Bangladesh.
10 The Constitution (Second Amendment) Act 1973.

The genesis of the idea of UCA, however, can be traced to pre-1971 (un)constitutional politics. In *the 8th Amendment Case* of 1989, the lead counsel emphasised that the idea of unamendability of basic constitutional features was not an alien concept but rather was an old one, first mooted in the 1963 Dacca High Court case of *Muhammad Abdul Haque v Fazlul Quader Chowdhury*.[11] In *Abdul Haque*, Mr Haque, who was a member of the National Assembly of Pakistan, challenged Mr Chowdhury and other respondents' eligibility to continue as members on the grounds that they lost their membership to the Assembly upon their appointment as ministers per article 104 of Pakistan's undemocratic Constitution of 1962.[12] Acting under article 224(3), the President in the meantime promulgated an "Order" making it lawful for a minister to continue as a member of parliament. More importantly, article 6 of the President's Order deprived the Court of the power to review the validity of the Order. There is little doubt, therefore, that the Order was sort of an executive constitutional amendment in disguise.

The Attorney-General sternly opposed the Court's jurisdiction to test the legality of Presidential Orders "removing" any difficulty in the operation of the Constitution. Justice Murshed, with whom Justices Siddiky and Chowdhury agreed, dismissed the government's case, and found the Order to be unconstitutional. Murshed, J observed as follows:

> Art. 104(1) and the allied articles relating to the same subject constitute one of the *main pillars of the Constitution* which envisages a sort of [p]residential form of [g]overnment where the Ministers are not responsible to the Legislative Assembly, but to the President himself ... This concept of a separation of the executive body from the [l]egislature ... is *the very basis* of [sic] present Constitution. *Mr. Brohi has aptly described it as the corner-stone which supports the arch of the Constitution.* (Emphasis added)[13]

As Murshed, J further held, the impugned Order was a *de facto* constitutional amendment and it "wiped out" a "vital provision" of the Constitution without resorting to the special machinery of constitutional amendment. On appeal, Pakistan's Supreme Court unanimously rejected the appeal. Chief Justice Cornelius observed that judicial review is a fundamental provision that could not be taken away from the Constitution and that "franchise" and the "form of Government" were fundamental features that were not subject to alteration by

---

11 (1963) 15 DLR (Dacca) 355. On this, Justice Ahmed in the *8th Amendment Case* (n 2) 131 said as follows: "Dr. Kamal Hossain has emphasised that the doctrine of basic structure as applied by the Indian Supreme Court had originated from a decision of the then Dhaka High Court which was upheld in appeal by the Pakistan Supreme Court."
12 Article 104(1) of the 1962 Constitution of Pakistan provided that a member of parliament would cease to be a member upon becoming a minister.
13 (1963) 15 DLR (Dacca) 355, 382 (para 76).

a Presidential Order under that Constitution.[14] Both courts annulled article 6 of the Order and, thus, unanimously placed higher normative value on the principle of judicial review.[15]

This case clearly shows how the executive resorted to unconstitutional politics to amend the constitution with an ulterior motive. At the time, the executive branch was authoritarian, and the regime was extra-constitutional itself. As *Abdul Haque* further depicts, political figures nevertheless relied on constitutional arguments to challenge what they considered an unconstitutional constitutional amendment. On the other hand, the Court intervened into politics for a right cause during a politically challenging time of a dictatorial regime.

The 1962 Constitution of Pakistan was written and promulgated by the military ruler Ayub Khan on 1 March 1962, who assumed power in October 1958 after suspending the first Constitution of 1956. Ayub Khan had an utter distrust of political parties and parliamentary democracy. From the early 1960s, political dissatisfaction and public mobilisation against Ayub's regime began to grow. In the meantime, disturbances broke out in East Pakistan where leaders threatened to fight against the undemocratic Constitution, and members of parliament demanded the withdrawal of the ban on party politics, and "Pakistani students and residents in London" organised a public meeting on 18 February 1962 "protesting against the continuation of military dictatorship."[16]

The temporal aspect of the judicial role in *Abdul Haque* vis-à-vis unconstitutional constitutional amendment probably signifies that the Court garnered legitimacy for its decision from the people's aspiration for constitutional democracy at the time. The political climate and the facts and politics surrounding *Abdul Haque* bear a striking similarity with Bangladesh's first basic-structure case,[17] analysed below.

11.3 The entrenchment of the idea of unconstitutional constitutional amendment: The 8th Amendment

Before dealing with the 8th Amendment of 1988, which was enacted during the second military regime since Bangladesh's independence, a short summary of national politics from 1971 to 1991 would be useful. Following its independence

---

14 *Fazlul Quader Chowdhury v. Muhammad Abdul Haque* (1963) PLD (SC) 486. Two years later, in his dissenting opinion in *Sajjan Singh's Case* (AIR 1965 SC 867) Justice Mudholkar of the Indian Supreme Court approvingly cited Cornelius J's above reasoning in support of his view that parliament's amendment power was not unbridled. Arguably, Justice Mudholkar's dissent had a critical impact on the majority view in *Kesavananda Bharati v State of Kerala* AIR 1973 SC 1461 that first authoritatively established the basic-structure doctrine in India.
15 See further R Braibanti, 'Pakistan: Constitutional Issues in 1964' (1965) 5(2) Asian Survey 79.
16 DP Singhal, 'The New Constitution of Pakistan' (1962) 2(6) Asian Survey 15, 17.
17 See *Chowdhury* (n 25).

in 1971 from Pakistan, Bangladesh adopted a parliamentary form of democracy that faced a tragic demise in 1974,[18] when the 4th Amendment installed an authoritarian, one-party government.[19] The 4th Amendment, enacted by Bangladesh's first parliament, was indeed a constitutional replacement or what many consider a "mini constitution." In August 1975, the founding leader of the country, Bangabandhu Sheikh Mujibur Rahman, was brutally assassinated along with almost all of his family. Soon thereafter, the military intervened, and a lingering period of autocratic rule began. From August 1975 to December 1990, there was no democratic government at all despite intermittent national elections. The second military ruler, General H.M. Ersahd, stepped down in December 1990, yielding to a public upsurge for democracy. In 1991, a general election was held under a consensus-driven mechanism under the stewardship of the then-Chief Justice. Multiparty democracy returned and the country reembraced a parliamentary government system through the 12th Amendment to the Constitution.[20]

11.3.1 *Judicial restructuring*

During the autocratic regime of General Ershad (1982–90), a pliable parliament enacted the 7th to 10th Amendments to the Constitution. Upon assumption of power in 1982, the general suspended the Constitution, which was "restored" in 1986. While the Constitution was suspended, Ershad issued decrees to amend the martial law "proclamation" (his "mini constitution") with a view to enacting rules of a constitutional nature. In May 1982, one such decree gave power to the President to set up "permanent Benches" of the Supreme Court's High Court Division. The President then diffused the HCD into seven permanent benches (each composed of three judges), with six located outside of Dhaka. The judges could be transferred from one High Court to another.[21] When the suspended Constitution was revived, the then-Chief Justice issued some notifications declaring those "permanent" or "circuit" Benches of the High Court Division as "sessions" within the meaning of article 100 of the Constitution but allowed those Benches to function as "permanent" courts.[22]

---

18 See JSA Choudhury, *Bangladesh: Failure of a Parliamentary Government 1973–1975* (Jamshed Foundation 2005); ZR Khan, 'Bangladesh's Experiments with Parliamentary Democracy' (1997) 37(6) Asian Survey 575.
19 The Constitution (Fourth Amendment) Act of 1975 (effective 25 January 1975). This Amendment destroyed many of the founding values of the nation (e.g., the independence of the judiciary), abrogated civil rights including freedom of the press, and stripped the Supreme Court of its judicial review power.
20 See the Constitution (Twelfth Amendment) Act 1991.
21 Justice M Kamal, *Bangladesh Constitution: Trends and Issues* (University of Dhaka 1994).
22 Article 100, before amendment in 1988, provided as follows: "The permanent seat of the Supreme Court shall be in the capital, but sessions of the High Court Division may be held at such other place or places as the Chief Justice may, with the approval of the President, from time to time appoint."

Presidential decrees and the Chief Justice's notifications raised a serious question of their constitutional validity. Against this backdrop, lawyers initiated and "continued a sustained and powerful agitation and movement since 1986 against the dismantling of the High Court Division."[23] As Kamal wrote, perhaps "to put at rest the unrest this created,"[24] the Constitution (Eighth Amendment) Act 1988 was enacted to legitimate these changes to the judicial structure, by replacing article 100 of the Constitution.

In *Anwar Hossain Chowdhury*,[25] the Appellate Division entrenched the idea of UCA, known as the "basic-structure doctrine" (BSD) in South Asia, by invalidating the part of the 8th Amendment that amended article 100. Mr. Anwar Hossain Chowdhury was Chairman-elect of a local government body (Union Council) in Sunamganj. He could not assume office as his opponents filed a lawsuit in the HCD, which issued an injunction on releasing the election results. Mr. Chowdhury wanted to have that injunction vacated, for which he needed to file a counter-affidavit. The Commissioner of Affidavits refused to allow him to affirm the counter-affidavit in Dhaka because the concerned case stood transferred to the Sylhet Bench of the High Court Division pursuant to the rules framed by the Chief Justice under art. 100(6) as amended by the 8th Amendment. Mr. Chowdhury then filed a writ petition (No. 1252 of 1988) challenging the vires of the 8th Amendment and said Rules arguing that the Amendment materially altered the basic structure of the Constitution and hence was beyond the Parliament's amendment power. The High Court Division, Dhaka Bench, summarily rejected his petition on 15 August 1988, against which Mr. Chowdhury appealed to the Appellate Division (SCAD).[26]

In a 3:1 majority, the SCAD held that Parliament's amendment power under art. 142 of the Constitution was "limited," as it was a "derivative" power, not an "original" constituent power. As such, a limited amendment power could not be exercised to alter "basic structures" of the Constitution, the Court reasoned.[27] The Court accepted the petitioner's following arguments: (i) the diffusion of the High Court Division breached the unitary character of the Supreme Court that was an unamendable basic feature, and (ii) a parliament with unlimited amendment power would be incompatible with the notion of constitutional supremacy, another basic pillar of the Constitution.[28] The lead counsel Dr Kamal Hossain

---

23 Kamal (n 21) 94.
24 ibid.
25 *Anwar Hossain Chowdhury v Bangladesh* (1989) BLD (AD) (Special) 1.
26 This was Civil Appeal No. 42 of 1988. There were two other proceedings seeking similar remedies – *Jalaluddin v Bangladesh* (SCAD, C.A. No. 43 of 1988) and *Ibrahim Sheik v Bangladesh* (SCAD, C.P.S.L.A. No. 3 of 1989) – that were heard jointly with *Chowdhury*.
27 Per Ahmed J in *Chowdhury* (n 25) 143.
28 Even the lone dissenting judge, Justice Afzal, agreed that the parliament cannot "destroy" the character of the Constitution in the name of amendment. *Chowdhury* (n 25) 212–13. For Afzal J, a destruction by an amendment would occur if any of the three organs of the state ("structural pillars") is destroyed or emasculated "in such a manner as would make the Constitution unworkable."

successfully argued that the independence of the judiciary as a basic feature was dismantled too.[29]

It is interesting to note that the bar deployed tremendous resources in arguing for an unconstitutional constitutional amendment in this case. First, the arguments were based both on substantive and procedural grounds.[30] Second, attempts were made to ensure that the Chief Justice could not hear the appeal because he had a conflict of interest. Powers to be exercised by the Chief Justice under the amended article 100 and notices he issued were challenged. Third, the lawyers arguing the case were not simply individual lawyers hired by the clients. They indeed were representing the profession, as the Supreme Court Bar had adopted several resolutions condemning the then-President's encroachments into the judiciary and the autonomy of the legal profession. Moreover, the lawyers for the petitioners were the most influential members of the bar. Dr Kamal Hossain was engaged as the lead counsel of Mr Chowdhury's appeal. For the other two appeals that were conjoined, Mr Syed Ishtiaq Ahmed and Mr Amir-Ul Islam argued the case. Dr Hossain was the Chairman of the Constitution Drafting Committee, while Mr Ahmed and Mr Islam both were esteemed constitutional lawyers of the country with experience from the pre-1971 years. Dr Hossain in particular had the experience of arguing the case of *Abdul Haque*, noted above, which is considered the first South Asian case to have flagged the idea of UCA. Fourth, all the lawyers who argued the case were arrested by the Ershad government during the lawyers' movement against the diffusion of the High Court Division.

These factors arguably had some impact on the outcome. As reflected in the judgment, the Court took notice of the protracted lawyers' movement and the growing anti-autocracy protests by the general public and civil society. Such public reactions may have led the Court to acknowledge the "undemocratic nature" of the amendment "in the absence of consultation with any stakeholders, lawmakers and the public."[31]

A not-so-discussed aspect of the 8th Amendment is the motive of the executive government that had spearheaded the change. This Amendment enacted two major changes: judicial restructuring and the introduction of Islam as the state religion. Ershad proffered the justification of bringing the Supreme Court within

---

29 As Dr Hossain further explained, "[i]ntroduction of transferability of Judges underlines the inconsistency of the amendment with the concept of the integrated Supreme Court and violates the provision of Art. 147(2) which provides that terms and conditions of service of Judges of the Supreme Court cannot be altered to their disadvantage during their tenure of office." See *Chowdhury* (n 25) 26.
30 On the procedural front, for example, it was argued that the 8th Amendment did not comply with the amendment rule of the Constitution as the long title of the amendment Bill did not set out the specific articles that were to be amended. It was argued that this requirement was a vital condition for the exercise of amendment power in the first place, and, as such, there was *fraud on the Constitution*. ibid.
31 C Farid, 'New Paths to Justice: A Tale of Social Justice Lawyering in Bangladesh' (2014) 31(3) Wisconsin Int'l LJ 421, 444.

the reach of the people by decentralising the higher judiciary. In reality, however, the military regime wanted to emasculate the judiciary by placing judges under the constant fear of being transferred out of Dhaka. Similarly, with regard to the state religion part, the reasoning advanced was that in a Muslim-majority country Islam should be given constitutional recognition. Behind the projected justification, the military ruler wanted to achieve fresh support from the general public and the right-wing parties in the wake of increasing opposition to his regime.

The judiciary had its own stake too. Constitutional judges, in the aftermath of the intervention of the military into politics in 1975, were not allowed to enforce the Constitution at all until late 1986 and their freedom was often restricted by the regime. Judges generally were also not happy with the way the Chief Justice, who had close ties with the regime, exercised his administrative powers. Moreover, the fact that some judges disliked their postings in divisional cities figured within the context of the discourse over the idea of inalterability of basic constitutional features. These judges' personal feelings vis-à-vis their terms and conditions probably played a role in the outcome of *Anwar Hossain Chowdhury*.[32]

11.3.2 Islam as state religion

As regards the other part of the 8th Amendment which constitutionalised Islam as state religion (article 2A), there were several challenges before the Supreme Court that remained undecided. The challenges were based on the grounds that the state religion clause breached the principles of equality and secularism. Interestingly, at the time the state religion part of the 8th Amendment was challenged, the Constitution did not have the fundamental principle of secularism as a founding value. The first military ruler since independence, General Ziaur Rahman, amended the Constitution by issuing decrees and initiated a process of Islamisation of the Constitution. Specifically, he amended the preamble and article 8 to replace the fundamental principle of secularism with the principle of "absolute trust and faith in Almighty Allah." When a parliament was formed, these changes were legitimated by the 5th Amendment, enacted by a pliable parliament. The second military ruler, General Ershad, completed the Islamisation project by making Islam the state's religion via the 8th Amendment.

In 2010, the Court invalidated the 5th Amendment that removed the principle of secularism from the Constitution. A far-reaching limitation of this SCAD-decision was that the Court could not, nor was it asked to, declare unlawful the state religion clause inserted by the 8th Amendment. The decision nevertheless added a twist in the trajectory of Islam's constitutional status. In the wake of the 5th Amendment decision, the state religion challengers renewed their petition on

---

32 Some even accused that the 8th Amendment decision reflected the Court's elitist mindset and resulted from an "invisible" compromise between the judiciary and the Dhaka-based elite lawyers. See M Rahman, *Unveiling Democracy: State and Law* (Parama Publications 1999) 61.

11 June 2011.[33] In September 2011, the Awami League government that led the drafting process of the founding Constitution with secularism as a fundamental principle enacted the 15th Amendment, discussed further below, to re-instate "secularism." Intriguingly, alongside the principle of secularism, the state religion clause was kept intact albeit with a new wording.[34] This would probably have pleased the right-wing parties and the Bangladesh Nationalist Party (BNP), the founder of which, General Zia, first omitted the principle of secularism.

However, since the 15th Amendment did not restore "secularism" in its original form, but rather conjoined it with the state religion clause, human rights activists and some progressive-minded intellectuals made a supplemental challenge to the state religion part of the 8th Amendment based on the argument of the restoration of "secularism." Initially, the Court agreed to hear the challenge. In a dramatic turn of events, however, the challenges to the state religion clause were summarily dismissed in March 2016, some 23 years after their lodgement.[35] When the challenges were due to be heard, some religious groups commenced demonstrations against the state religion challenge and the petitioners. They condemned the case as an act of atheists and warned that it would trigger disturbances. Another Islamist group "requested" that the Court reject the petition. They met with the Chief Justice in the morning of the day the case was scheduled for hearing. In an unprecedented move, the Court dismissed the challenges citing the lack of *locus standi* of the petitioners. It is not difficult to see that there were underlying politics as well as lobbying by religious groups that led to the rejection of the challenge to the state religion clause.

11.4 The 15th Amendment: Where party and judicial politics converge

11.4.1 Abolition of the caretaker government

As noted above, Bangladesh transitioned to democracy from military rule in 1991, and the 12th Amendment to the Constitution reintroduced parliamentary democracy.[36] It was the BNP that assumed power through a credible general election in 1991. At the end of its first post-transition term, the ruling party, however, began to corrupt the electoral system. In 1996, following a lingering political crisis, an election-time NPCTG system to conduct general elections

---

33 See R Hoque, 'Constitutional Challenge to the State Religion Status of Islam in Bangladesh: Back to Square One?', Int'l J of Const. L. Blog, 27 May 2016 <http://www.iconnectblog.com/2016/05/islam-in-bangladesh> accessed 11 May 2021.
34 See Hoque (n 62) 207.
35 *Sirajul Islam Chowdhury v Bangladesh*, WP No. 1834 of 1988 (Order of 28 March 2016). For a commentary on this decision see Hoque (n 33). On the illegality of the official religion clause, see generally Alam (n 3). See also ER Huq, 'The Legality of a State Religion in a Secular Nation' (2018) 17 Washington U Global Stud L Rev 245.
36 See MA Hakim, *The Changing Forms of Government in Bangladesh: The Transition to Parliamentary System in 1991, in Perspective* (Bangladesh Institute of Parliamentary Studies 2000).

was installed by the 13th Amendment.[37] From 2006, NPCTG system became intensely controversial mainly because the then-ruling party, the BNP, attempted to corrupt it through the 14th Amendment which raised the retirement age of Supreme Court judges from 65 to 67 with a particular Chief Justice in mind who, after retirement, would likely head the caretaker government.[38]

Not too long after the 13th Amendment introduced the NPCTG, some practising lawyers challenged the Amendment as unconstitutional and undemocratic. In *M Saleem Ullah v Bangladesh*,[39] the HCD in August 2004 held that the NPCTG was not unconstitutional. An appeal against this decision remained pending in the SCAD from 2004. In a dramatic development, the Appellate Division by a preliminary ruling ("short order") on 10 May 2011 declared the NPCTG system undemocratic and unlawful.[40] Interestingly, however, it observed that the next two general elections could be held under an NPCTG. The Court also advised for the reform of the NPCTG, saying that parliament was "at liberty to bring necessary amendments excluding the provisions of making the former Chief Justices of Bangladesh or the Judges of the Appellate Division as the head of the [NPCTG]." Thereafter, the Awami League government, which had an absolute majority in parliament, got the 15th Amendment enacted to abolish in haste the NPCTG system without the participation of the main opposition parties and with an ulterior political motive of taking incumbency advantage.[41] Seen in light of the SCAD's short order nullifying the NPCTG, the Awami League's choice not to follow the Court's advice to allow the NPCTG system for another two general elections does not seem wrong. As the background politics involved, however, shows, the thing is not that simple. A political process to reform, and not to abolish, the NPCTG system began long before the SCAD handed down its "short order" on the 13th Amendment. Given this political process, the Court ought not to have delivered the short order in the first place.

---

37 The Constitution (Thirteenth Amendment) Act 1996. NPCTG is an apolitical 11-member government of a 3-month duration that used to take charge following the dissolution of parliament, with the principal duty of conducting "fair and free" national elections. See, for details, H Zafarullah and MY Akhter, 'Non-Political Caretaker Administrations and Democratic Elections in Bangladesh: An Assessment' (2000) 35(3) Government and Opposition 345; N Ahmed, *Non-Party Caretaker Government in Bangladesh: Experience and Prospect* (University Press Limited 2004); SZ Khan, *The Politics and Law of Democratic Transition: Caretaker Government in Bangladesh* (Routledge 2017).
38 The Constitution (Fourteenth Amendment) Act 2004 (16 May 2004).
39 (2005) 57 DLR (HCD) 171. The challenge was first made in 1999 (HCD, WP No. 4212 of 1999).
40 *Abdul Mannan Khan v Bangladesh* (2012) 64 DLR (AD) 1 (*13th Amendment Case*). This was a four-to-three decision, and the Chief Justice allegedly expedited the disposal of the case before his retirement. He wrote the full judgment only after his retirement. For details, see R Hoque, 'Judicialization of Politics in Bangladesh: Pragmatism, Legitimacy, and Consequences' in M Tushnet and M Khosla (eds), *Unstable Constitutionalism: Law and Politics in South Asia* (CUP 2015).
41 See R Hoque, 'Deconstructing Public Participation and Deliberation in Constitutional Amendment in Bangladesh' (2021) 21 (2) Australian J of Asian L 7.

The abolition of the NPCTG system, thus, occurred within two months of the Court's short order and in disregard of strong objections from the opposition parties and civil society members. In 1996, the adoption of NPCTG system was a constitutional necessity based on the need for a context-specific constitutional mechanism to ensure free and fair elections.[42] It was in fact the Awami League, then in the opposition, that spearheaded a strong movement for the installation of a neutral government system. The then-ruling party BNP amended the Constitution to establish the NPCTG system. The abolition by the current ruling party Awami League of the system by the 15th Amendment, despite the opposition of major political parties, therefore, begs the question of legitimacy if not constitutionality. Moreover, the full 13th Amendment judgment was issued many months after the 15th Amendment abolishing the NPCTG. As noted below, shying away from its own promise, the ruling party did not wait for the full judgment before enacting the amendment. Justice Ali in the 13th Amendment Case commented in dissent that in the political context of the 1996 constitutional crisis, the people chose the NPCTG as a solution, and, therefore, any solution to that crisis must have come from the representatives of the people.[43] It seems that the ruling party made an abusive use of its constitutional amendment power, by excluding the opposition parties from a major structural constitutional decision-making.

The 15th Amendment is a consequential amendment. The next general elections of January 2014 were non-participatory and boycotted by all major opposition parties because the ruling party shunned the NPCTG system. Bangladesh has since embraced virtually one-party rule without formally amending the Constitution. And the December 2018 elections were in fact sham elections, with the ruling party winning 293 seats out of 300 general seats. The abolition of the NPCTG has since proved that, in the context of confrontational Bangladeshi politics, elections under a political government are not fair, but rather engineered or sham.

The 15th Amendment, which is said to be necessitated by the SCAD's annulment of the 5th Amendment to the Constitution,[44] sought to restore certain founding constitutional values such as secularism. Ironically, however, the 15th Amendment ultimately contained certain changes that arguably have elements of unconstitutionality. One such change was the abolition of the NPCTG system, the legitimacy of which is seriously doubtful. The second change of both doubtful legitimacy and legality brought forth by the 15th Amendment was the incorporation of an unwieldy eternity clause, which I will analyse later in this part.

---

42 As Justice M Imman Ali in dissent observed in *the 13th Amendment Case* (n 40) 472, "the Thirteenth Amendment was neither illegal nor ultra vires the Constitution and does not destroy any [of its] basic structures."
43 ibid 457.
44 See *Khondker Delwar Hossain v Bangladesh Italian Marble Works Ltd.* (2010) 62 DLR (AD) 298. See also *Siddique Ahmed v Government of Bangladesh* (2013) 65 DLR (AD) 8, invalidating the 7th Amendment that legitimated the second military regime.

First, the legitimacy question of the abolition of NPCTG system can be taken up. On 21 July 2010, the ruling party constituted a 15-member Special Committee to consider a proposal for the Fifteenth Amendment Bill, but the question of NPCTG was not specifically on its agenda. The Committee consisted of politicians mostly from the ruling party, excluding the opposition BNP and its allies.[45] The Committee, however, invited the BNP to its "hearing," but the party refused to attend citing that the whole process was a "farce."[46] As the history of the Committee proceedings shows, the political motivation behind the proposed constitutional change was to give the ruling party a strong incumbency advantage.

Although the Special Committee was established a year before the enactment of the 15th Amendment, the committee in fact took a very short time to deliberate on the issue of NPCTG.[47] It took up the NPCTG issue only in late March 2011. Notably, however, the Committee had had some quick consultations with politicians, civil society actors, and constitutional experts including former Chief Justices. The Committee was advised by almost all consultees not to discard the NPCTG system. In its 14th meeting on 29 March 2011, it unanimously decided to retain the system.[48] Mr Suranjit Sengupta, the co-chairperson, stated that they agreed that "in spite of all the limitations of the present system of the [NPCTG], the conclusion is that it should remain."[49]

On 27 April 2011, Prime Minister Sheikh Hasina appeared before the Special Committee and said that the people do not want unelected and undemocratic caretaker government anymore. In the end, she recommended the reform of NPCTG and not its abolition.[50] Two weeks later, on 10 May 2011, the SCAD handed down the short order in the 13th Amendment Case declaring the system unconstitutional, as noted above. Shortly thereafter, the Committee in its 24th meeting of 16 May 2011 decided "to reopen the issue" after "receiving the final judgment of the Appellate Division of the Supreme Court."[51] Without waiting for the final judgment of the Court, however, the Committee on 29 May made

---

45 There were three non-AL members, but they all belonged to parties in the government's coalition.
46 AA Khan, 'The Politics of Constitutional Amendments in Bangladesh: The Case of the Non-Political Caretaker Government' (2015) 9 Int'l Rev of L 1, 12.
47 The committee had the mandate of considering changes in view mainly of the SCAD's decision invalidating the 5th Amendment. The decision invalidating the 7th Amendment came on 15 May 2011 by which time the Committee almost completed its process.
48 The agenda of this meeting was "solely [to] assess the policy of the caretaker government regime." See Khan (n 46) 3, 15.
49 ibid 13.
50 BA Majumder, 'Legitimacy and Legality of 15th Amendment', 31 October 2013, The Daily Star, Dhaka <https://www.thedailystar.net/news/legitimacy-and-legality-of-15th-amendment> accessed 11 May 2021.
51 ibid.

some recommendations for the reform, and not abolition, of the NPCTG system.[52] According to reports, the Committee arbitrarily changed its mind after it met with the Prime Minister the next day, on 30 May 2011, just a few days before they submitted the final report on 5 June 2011. The Committee added to its final report a long list of 51 recommendations for reform, but did not say anything about the NPCTG system.[53] This dramatic tampering with the Committee's decision suggests "an inappropriate degree of influence by the executive."[54]

The 15th Amendment, therefore, abolished the NPCTG system rather undemocratically. The above-described process was arguably a sham deliberative exercise as reflected in the Committee's drastic change of mind from a decision to suggest reforms of the system to a complete abolition thereof.[55] That the 15th Amendment abolishing the NPCTG was exclusionary and suffered a problem of legitimacy is evident in the fact that the Bill passed the House amidst an opposition boycott by a 291–1 vote and quite easily.[56] The lone dissent was by the one and only independent member. The Bill was introduced in parliament on 25 June 2011 and passed the House the same day, and it was signed into law on 3 July 2011. The time spent for passing the Bill and its voting-pattern, thus, indicate the absence of internal deliberations in abolishing the NPCTG that was installed through a cross-party consensus.

The judicial decision that was relied upon as a justification by the ruling party for the abolition of the NPCTG system was not released in its full version before the enactment of the 15th Amendment. The issue of the legality of NPCTG was a pending matter before the SCAD from 2004, but it was only after Justice Haque took office as Chief Justice on 30 September 2010 that the appeal was heard. Such an important case of a structural issue was heard only for ten days beginning on 1 March 2011, a time that followed the formation of the Special Committee on the 15th Amendment in July 2010. The Court's "short order" of 10 May 2011, written by Chief Justice Haque, was delivered only eight days before his retirement on 18 May 2011 and in disregard of the opinions of all but two of the eight *amici curiae*. All the three judges who concurred with Chief Justice in the *13th Amendment Case* eventually became Chief Justices of Bangladesh,[57]

---

52 It recommended two minor changes to the system: first, the imposition of a time-limit of 90 days for the NPCTG and, second, the introduction of a restriction on signing foreign or international treaties. ibid.
53 Khan (n 46) 11–13; Majumder (n 50).
54 Khan (n 46) 11–13.
55 See further Hoque (n 41).
56 A Riaz, 'Bangladesh in Turmoil: A Nation on the Brink? (Testimony before the Subcommittee on Asia and the Pacific of the Committee on Foreign Affairs, United States House of Representatives, 20 November 2013) 7 <https://docs.house.gov/meetings/FA/FA05/20131120/101512/HHRG-113-FA05-WstateRiazA-20131120.pdf> accessed 11 May 2021. See Khan (n 46) 9.
57 They are Justices Md. Mozammel Hossain, SK Sinha, and Syed Mahmud Hossain (the latter is the incumbent Chief Justice).

while one of the dissenting judges, Mr Mia,[58] was superseded by the current Chief Justice who was in the majority. Notably, after his retirement, Chief Justice Haque assumed the role of the Chairman of Bangladesh Law Commission. These events probably show that the ruling party had a plan to unilaterally do away with the NPCTG system much earlier than the (deliberative) political process for the 15th Amendment actually began. These facts also probably show that there was some communication between the then-Chief Justice and the incumbent government in regard to the government's desire.

The abolition of the NPCTG led to a protracted constitutional crisis over the question of multi-party, competitive, and free and fair general elections that now seem to be completely ousted from the scene of Bangladeshi constitutionalism since the tenth general election in 2014.[59] As the above analysis shows, in stripping the Constitution of the NPCTG system, party and judicial politics coincided quite ingeniously. Quite clearly, the ruling party abusively used the SCAD's above judgment annulling the NPCTG system as well as the constitutional institution of the Special Committee to enact the 15th Amendment in furtherance of their narrow political gains.[60] The 15th Amendment's deletion of the NPCTG was indeed against the will or participation of the people. Let it be explained a little further. Although the Awami League was elected to power in a fair general election in 2008, the abolition of the NPCTG was not on its electoral manifesto. Second, the internalisation of the NPCTG system via the 13th Amendment, despite its limitations, was a response to a deepening political crisis over the matter of free and fair elections which is a founding objective.[61] Third, the 13th Amendment was a consensus-driven amendment in that all parties agreed to a neutral election-time government, irrespective of whether they actually voted for this change in parliament. Fourth, at the time the ruling party switched its agenda of reforming the system to abolishing it, there was a massive protest by the major opposition parties against the abolition of the NPCTG system. Verily, the amendment abolishing the NPCTG was procedurally legal, but it arguably lacked the popular support needed for the legitimacy of any constitutional change.

---

58 The other two dissenting judges were Justice Nazmun Ara Sultana (retired) and Justice M Imman Ali (currently the senior most judge after the Chief Justice).

59 R Hoque, 'The Making and Founding of Bangladesh's Constitution' in KYL Tan and R Hoque (eds), *Constitutional Foundings in South Asia* (Hart Publishing 2021) 117–19.

60 Similarly, Khan (n 46) 3 argues that these institutions and the SCAD's judgment "have been manipulated in an attempt to lend credibility to a controversial amendment [15th Amendment])."

61 See Hoque (n 41).

11.4.2 Making the constitution unamendable[62]

The second 15th Amendment change of questionable legitimacy and legality that this chapter analyses is the incorporation of an extraordinarily wide eternity clause, article 7B. The eternity clause does not specify any fundamental cores that would be impervious to amendment rules. Instead, it catalogues a lengthy list of "provisions" as unalterable. Article 7B makes unamendable the following: the preamble (that contains four "high ideals" of the state), all fundamental principles of state policy, all fundamental rights provisions, and "the provisions of articles relating to the basic structures."[63]

Eternity clauses are pretty common in constitutions across the world. An eternity clause prohibiting the amendment of certain constitutional features can indeed be seen as a legislative version of the basic structure doctrine. Bangladesh's eternity clause, however, is not a legitimate form of legislative entrenchment of constitutional unamendability in that it has bound tightly the hands of future generations vis-à-vis the amendment of a long list of provisions. In a 1998 decision, the SCAD held that the legislature cannot bind its successor.[64] Instead of entrenching certain basic principles, something like the German Constitution of 1949, the Bangladeshi eternity clause has indeed retarded democracy itself by prohibiting, for example, even an improvement of fundamental rights. Article 7B says, *inter alia*, that "all articles of Part III" (of fundamental rights) "shall not be amendable *by way of insertion, modification, substitution, repeal or by any other means*" (emphasis added). An ideal eternity clause would rather have protected the fundamental rights from a wholesale deletion or suspension as was the case during the military regimes in Bangladesh. For being unwieldly broad and for incapacitating the future parliament in amending a large part of the Constitution, I have elsewhere argued that this eternity clause is unconstitutional.[65] Here, I focus on the politics that prompted the insertion of the eternity clause, that is, the fact that it was a selfish political motive of the ruling party that influenced the design of article 7B.

While the 15th Amendment generally sets a classic example of abusive constitutional amendment for party interests, article 7B in particular is probably a result of micro-politics that quite often keeps the two major parties – the BNP and the Awami League – engaged in conflict and political mudslinging over certain fundamental constitutional principles and facts. As regards the question of who declared Bangladesh's independence in 1971, for example, there is a longstanding

---

62 In this section, I have relied on a 2017 work of mine. See R Hoque, 'Eternal Provisions in the Constitution of Bangladesh: A Constitution Once and For All?' in R Albert and BE Oder (eds), *An Unconstitutional Constitution?: Unamendability in Constitutional Democracies* (Springer 2017).
63 See art. 7B of the Constitution of Bangladesh.
64 *Shahriar Rashid Khan v Bangladesh* (1998) BLD (AD) 155, para 54. See further M Islam, *Constitutional Law of Bangladesh* (3rd edition, Mullick Brothers 2012) 31.
65 See Hoque (n 62).

rivalry and denials between the two parties. The 15th Amendment amended article 150 to insert 5th, 6th, and 7th Schedules to the Constitution, incorporating therein certain constituent instruments and historical speeches including the Declaration of Independence by Bangabandhu Sheikh Mujibur Rahman, the founding leader of the country. The BNP does not recognise the founding leader as the declarant of Bangladesh Independence,[66] but rather claims that its founder, General Ziaur Rahman, was the declarant of Bangladesh Independence. The author-party of the 15th Amendment, the Awami League, was probably wary of probable deletion of the recognition of Bangabandhu's declaration of independence. Similarly, the founder of BNP had taken "secularism" out of the Constitution and inserted into it the principle of "absolute faith in the Almighty Allah." The BNP also replaced "Bengali nationalism" by "Bangladeshi nationalism" as a fundamental constitutional principle. The 15th Amendment restored "secularism" and "Bengali nationalism," although it made them co-exist with, respectively, the state religion of Islam and Bangladeshi nationalism. Article 7B sought to ensure that these restored principles cannot be amended in the future at all. This is not an unusual political move, and this type of constitutional tinkering is part of politics. However, the very design of the eternity clause, which, as already noted, is extraordinarily broad, is incompatible with the basic structural feature of popular sovereignty. Its constitutionality is therefore open to a serious question. Bangladesh's eternity clause has strong potential of leading to dead-hand constitutionalism regarding the reform of a large number of provisions. Moreover, the way this unusual eternity clause was enacted was undemocratic and politically exclusionary. There was not participation of major opposition parties, nor was there any public deliberation at all on this matter.

11.5 Factors and actors in unconstitutional constitutional amendments discourse

The idea of UCA has provided a vehicle for judicial engagement with constitutional amendment in several ways. Applying the doctrine or based on it, the court can declare a constitutional amendment unconstitutional and strike it down, or it can simply declare it unconstitutional without invalidating. The Supreme Court can be part of unconstitutional constitutional amendment discourse, as evident in the SCAD's decision annulling the NPCTG in the *13th Amendment Case* that ultimately led to the enactment of the 15th Amendment abolishing the system. The Court can also appear as a countervailing force against executive power vis-à-vis unconstitutional constitutional changes as was the case regarding the judicial restructuring part of the 8th Amendment. Moreover, the judiciary as a political

---

66 The matter was at some point dragged to the High Court Division, which in *Dr MA Salam v Bangladesh* (2009) 61 DLR (HCD) 737 held that any claim that Major Ziaur Rahman first declared independence of the country would be incompatible with the Proclamation of Independence of 1971.

entity may be motivated by the self-interest of preserving its power within the governance structure.[67] Indeed, like in India, the Supreme Court in Bangladesh has used the doctrine of basic structure or UCA, along with the other tool of public interest litigation (PIL), as a "path" to judicial power.[68]

Political parties and elected branches of the government are also an important, probably the most important, factor in the political discourse of UCA. The executive branch is generally aware of what would or would not be an unconstitutional amendment. It nevertheless has decided to enact unconstitutional amendments, either to remain in power without any political resistance or to perpetuate power. In this process, the ruling party invariably and overwhelmingly sides with the executive. This scenario occurs particularly when the executive is autocratic or near autocratic or when parliament is dominated by a supermajority ruling party. In the case of the 8th Amendment, noted above, the amendments were first introduced extra-constitutionally by a dictator. A pliable parliament later formally enacted the 8th Amendment. In the case of the 15th Amendment, the executive turned out to be overweening and utilised all available constitutional means to achieve some unconstitutional changes through that Amendment. For example, it unduly influenced the parliamentary committee to discard a reform plan as regards the NPCTG system and to recommend its abolition instead. On the other hand, the executive-dominated parliament was quick in passing the Amendment Bill. As has already been noted, the Supreme Court played an active role in creating an a priori ground, by invalidating the NPCTG, for the legislative abolition of the system. The parliament and the executive government found justifications in that ground for de-constitutionalising the NPCTG.

11.6 Conclusions

As seen above, the politics of unconstitutional constitutional amendments in Bangladesh is inseparable from constitutional politics generally. In enacting what would in a normal constitutional sense be an unconstitutional amendment, the

---

67 In every decision annulling a constitutional amendment, the Supreme Court invoked the judicial independence principle. In other cases, too, it referred to the principle as an unamendable basic feature. See, for example, *Secretary, Ministry of Finance v Md. Masdar Hossain* (2000) 52 DLR (AD) 82; *BLAST v Bangladesh* (2010) 30 BLD (HCD) 194.

68 See Manoj Mate, 'Two Paths to Judicial Power: The Basic Structure Doctrine and the Public Interest Litigation in a Comparative Perspective' (2010) 12 San Diego Int'l L J 175. In the *16th Amendment Case (Bangladesh v Asaduzzaman Siddiqui* (2017) CLR (AD) (Spl) 1, judgment 3 July 2017), the SCAD used the doctrine to exert judicial supremacy, which is foiled by overt and covert unconstitutional attacks on the judiciary. In the aftermath of this decision, the then-Chief Justice SK Sinha was ingeniously forced, first, to flee the country and then to resign. See R Hoque and S Shamin, 'Bangladesh: The State of Liberal Democracy' in R Albert and others, *2017 Global Review of Constitutional Law* (Clough Center for the Study of Constitutional Democracy at Boston College 2018) 30. This case, a review of which is now pending before the SCAD, is beyond the scope of this chapter. But see Hoque (n 6).

ruling party and the government in power come together often to realise their narrow political interests, especially to have an undue electoral advantage. As such, the unconstitutional constitutional amendments are essentially exclusionary in decision-making.

This chapter shows that in some cases, the Supreme Court may turn out to be an active player in the politics of unconstitutional constitutional amendments. For example, the Court played varying roles in regard to the 8th and 15th Amendments: it stood against an unconstitutional amendment, refused to intervene when the amendment involved the sensitive issue of state religion, and laid the groundwork to enable the political branches to shun the NPCTG system arbitrarily, which had been chosen through a wider political consensus. This pattern of judicial behaviour is also discernible with respect to other constitutional amendments not covered in this chapter.

Beyond the judiciary, multiple political factors including the personal rivalries between the leaders of the major two parties and the conflict between the executive and the judiciary, which were beyond the scope of this chapter, are critical determinants in the politics of unconstitutional amendments. As reflected in the analyses of the 8th and 15th Amendments above, the people generally do influence, and are informed of, the politics surrounding an unconstitutional amendment. Undeniably, as is the case in any democracy, the politics of unconstitutional amendment in Bangladesh is deeply tied to diverse parameters of local (constitutional) politics. As a result, the concerned actors operate both cooperatively and against each other as regards unconstitutional amendments, depending on their self-interest.

Part IV
Commentaries

12 The power of judicial nullification in Asia and the world

*Richard Albert**

12.1 Introduction: The power of judicial nullification

Courts around the world have either asserted or exercised the power to nullify a constitutional amendment. Relying on this extraordinary power of judicial nullification, courts have sometimes prevented the ratification of an amendment even before political actors have proposed it and they have sometimes invalidated an amendment after its promulgation.[1] Yet the power of judicial nullification is not a global norm that all courts embrace. Many courts have rejected the legitimacy of the power of nullification, and have accordingly refused to exercise it unless the constitutional text expressly authorizes courts to review constitutional amendments.[2]

Much is known about this power of judicial nullification in the Americas and Europe. But much less is known about the existence, uses, and limits of this power in Africa and Asia. This book on the politics of unconstitutional amendments in Asia is therefore an opportunity to shine a light on the power of judicial nullification in the region. Surprisingly, the phenomenon of an unconstitutional amendment in Asia remains understudied despite its deep roots in the region. Scholars of constitutionalism know well that Indian courts have innovated and exercised this immense power of judicial nullification. Yet scholars around the world are relatively unaware of the region's other jurisdictional encounters with the possibility of an unconstitutional amendment. In this chapter, I situate the judicial nullification power in Asian countries within the larger global context, both to uncover the shared conceptual roots of this controversial power across borders and regions, and also to bring cases from Asia into conversation with

---

* I thank Rehan Abeyratne and Bùi Ngọc Sơn for inviting me to participate in the conference that has led to this important book on *The Law and Politics of Unconstitutional Constitutional Amendments in Asia*. I also thank Bonnie Leung for facilitating the program, and all conference attendees for their helpful comments on an earlier draft of this chapter.
1 For the most comprehensive study of this phenomenon, see Yaniv Roznai, *Unconstitutional Constitutional Amendments: The Limits of Amendment Powers* (OUP 2017).
2 See Richard Albert, Malkhaz Nakashidze, and Tarik Olcay, 'The Formalist Resistance of Unconstitutional Constitutional Amendments' (2019) 70 Hastings LJ 639.

DOI: 10.4324/9781003097099-12

cases from beyond. I begin by examining the pillars of the judicial nullification power, then I identify and illustrate six forms of judicial nullification in Asia and the world, and I close by turning to the future, to inquire into the next frontiers for the judicial nullification power as it continues to evolve in new directions.

12.2 The pillars of the judicial nullification power

The judicial power to nullify constitutional amendments has not yet taken root in all constitutional states nor it is likely to do so. Some constitutional states will remain inhospitable to the doctrine of unconstitutional constitutional amendment,[3] some judges on high courts around the world will recoil at the exercise of the extraordinary power to nullify an amendment,[4] and still other judges will reject the very idea that an amendment can be unconstitutional.[5] Nonetheless, the doctrine of unconstitutional constitutional amendment has migrated across jurisdictions and may continue to expand its reach, but for now it is far from achieving the status of a global norm.

12.2.1 A sword or a shield? Competing views of democracy

The idea of an unconstitutional amendment finds support or resistance in competing theories of democracy. On one view, the power of judicial nullification is an anti-democratic sword. Courts overstep their boundaries when they invalidate a constitutional amendment that has earned approval from the people or their representatives, or from both. Democracy here refers to governing on the basis of a popularly validated judgment made in the present moment. When a court exercises the extraordinary power of nullification, that is effectively a sword striking at the heart of democracy to the very core of collective movements in democratic self-governance.

The counterview is just as strongly rooted in democracy. Only here democracy is not understood as the ever-changing politics of the moment. Democracy is instead represented by the constitutional bargain made at the writing and ratification of the constitution. That is the highest expression of democracy, on this view, and that is what requires protection. As a result, when a court exercises its nullification power to invalidate an amendment, the court is defending the original constitution and its democratic foundations by protecting the constitution and its founding principles from attacks that would undermine the people's constitutional commitments. Here, then, the judicial nullification power is not an anti-democratic sword. It is a shield for democracy.

---

3 See, for example, Conseil constitutionnel [CC] [Constitutional Council] decision No. 62-20DC, Nov. 6, 1962, Rec. 27 (France).
4 See, for example, Leser v. Garnett, 258 U.S. 130 (1922) (United States).
5 See, for example, Saqartvelos Sakonstitucio Sasamartlo [Constitutional Court of Georgia] July 12, 2010, N2/2/486 (Georgia).

12.2.2 The theory of delegation

The best argument offered thus far to justify a court invalidating a constitutional amendment is anchored in the theory of constituent power, first articulated by Emmanuel Joseph Sieyès, a French political theorist whose principal interest was to build a theory to protect the essential right of the people to choose the meaning of their constitution and how it should change.[6] According to this theory of constituent power, only the people may create and, by its creation, legitimate a new constitution.[7] The people's representatives possess the considerably lesser power only to make changes to the constitution provided those changes are consistent with the structure and spirit of the people's constitution.[8] Any change more far-reaching than that – one that alters the core commitments of the constitution – must be authorized and therefore legitimated by the people themselves. For Sieyès, the people embody the constituent power, meaning the supreme body that constitutes all others. These other bodies – the constituted powers – are inferior to the people and their constituent power. These constituted powers include the legislature, the executive, and courts as well. The legal fiction of the theory of constituent power holds that these representative bodies of constituted powers are created, authorized, or regulated by the constitution, which in turn has been created by the people. The bottom line, then, is this: constituted powers are bound by the rules established in the constitution by the constituent power.

The democratic foundations of the doctrine of unconstitutional constitutional amendment begin now to come into focus. These foundations are anchored in the delegation theory of constitutional change. Given that the people have created the constitution and delegated to their representatives only the limited power to modify the constitution in ways that keep the constitution aligned with its original form and values, the constituted powers cannot make changes to the constitution authorized by the constituent power without doing violence to the expressed will of the people.[9] Only the people themselves exercising their constituent power may make such changes to the constitution. Seen in this light, where a court invalidates a constitutional amendment passed by the actors authorized by the constitution to make amendments, we can certainly describe this action as stifling a proximate form of democratic expression – the considered judgment of the amending actors. But this argument would miss the larger picture. The choice a court makes to invalidate an amendment that it believes violates the constitution is a vindication of the supreme democratic choice originally made by the people to create the constitution. On this view, what first seems to be an undemocratic arrogation of power by courts may instead appear to be a justifiable judicial intervention to protect the terms of the original bargain approved by the people.

---

6 See Emmanuel Joseph Sieyès, *Qu'est-ce que le Tiers-état?* (Éditions du Boucher 2002) (1789).
7 ibid 53.
8 ibid.
9 The most theoretically rich account of this idea of delegation appears in Roznai (n 1) 105–34.

12.3 Six forms of judicial nullification

So far we have canvassed the power of judicial nullification in broad terms mostly rooted in theory. It is now time to apply theory to practice, specifically to show how courts have deployed the power of judicial nullification when confronted with justiciable claims that a constitutional amendment is unconstitutional. Having studied the many uses of this extraordinary power, I have constructed six general categories of cases of judicial nullification of amendments. Each of these six categories is informed by a different approach to the question whether an amendment can be unconstitutional and ultimately declared by a court to be null and void. In what follows, I will explain and illustrate each of these six categories with reference to cases drawn principally from Asia in an effort to situate the richness of Asian experiences in the larger global context.

Before proceeding it is worth specifying when the power of judicial nullification is properly described as "extraordinary." It is extraordinary, and quite problematic, where the power is exercised in violation of a constitutional prohibition on its use or when it is exercised without express constitutional authorization, including where the constitution is silent on its authorization. The power of judicial nullification must be accepted as legitimate where the codified constitution expressly contemplates its use. The power is at its strongest where the constitution containing this authorization has been approved through a deliberative process of popular ratification.

12.3.1 Procedural irregularity

Judicial practice around the world reveals that courts have nullified constitutional amendments when, in the court's determination, an amendment has been passed in a procedurally irregular manner. The procedural irregularity that serves as the basis for nullifying the amendment concerns the adequacy of the process of voting to initiate, ratify, or promulgate an amendment. This first category of cases of judicial nullification is among the least controversial.

For instance, in Brazil, the Supreme Federal Tribunal has on more than one occasion identified procedural irregularities in a constitutional amendment. In 2007, the Court identified a procedural irregularity with an amendment that had been approved ten years prior but that was only then revealed to have failed to achieve the required supermajorities in the National Congress. Amending the Brazilian Constitutions requires 60 percent of each house of the National Congress to approve a proposal on two separate readings.[10] Constitutional Amendment n.19/1998 sought to modify the legal regime for the hiring and career development of civil servants, which is codified in Article 39 of the Brazilian Constitution. But the amendment had earned only 298 votes in the Chamber of Deputies on the first reading – fewer than the required 60 percent supermajority.

---

10 Constitution of Brazil, art 60, s 2.

Judicial nullification in Asia and the world 235

There are examples of procedural irregularity in Asia. One is evident in Thailand, as described in Khemthong Tonsakulrungruang's chapter in this volume, where the Constitutional Court nullified an amendment to create an elected Senate because the Speaker had rushed the parliamentary debate and a related vote.[11]

For another example of a procedural irregularity in Asia, we turn to Taiwan. In one case, the National Assembly adopted a set of amendments in 1999 that the Constitutional Court of Taiwan subsequently invalidated on both procedural and substantive grounds.[12] The constitutional challenge began when members of the Legislative Yuan filed a petition arguing that the amendment passed by the National Assembly – where votes had been cast in anonymous ballots in the second and third readings – violated the Constitution's amendment rules.[13] The petitioners argued also that there were irregularities in the vote because some of the amendment proposals had been defeated in the second reading but were still voted on again in the third.[14] The challengers raised other concerns, including that the amendment improperly extended term limits and also sowed confusion about their duration.[15] The Court held the amendment unconstitutional. Anonymous balloting, the Court explained, violated the principles of "openness and transparency" in the legislative process.[16] The Court moreover declared that the voting irregularities between second and third readings "contradict the fundamental nature of governing norms and order that form the very basis and existence of the Constitution, and are prohibited by the norms of constitutional democracy."[17] For the Court, it was paramount on all political actors to abide by the constitutional procedures for constitutional amendment: "The democratic constitutional process derived from these principles forms the foundation for the existence of the current Constitution and all [governmental] bodies installed hereunder must abide by this process."[18] A more detailed exposition of this case appears in Jiunn-rong Yeh's chapter in this volume.[19]

12.3.2 Subject-rule mismatch

The second category of cases points to the second reason why courts have nullified a constitutional amendment: a subject-rule mismatch. Where a constitution authorizes more than one procedure to amend the constitution, it is generally

---

11 See Khemthong Tonsakulrungruan, Chapter 9 in this volume.
12 See Constitutional Court of Taiwan, Constitutional Interpretation No. 499, 2000/3/24, online at: http://www.judicial.gov.tw/constitutionalcourt/en/p03_01.asp?expno=499.
13 ibid.
14 ibid.
15 ibid.
16 ibid.
17 ibid.
18 ibid.
19 See Jiunn-rong Yeh, Chapter 8 in this volume.

the case that these amendment procedures vary according to their difficulty and according also to the kinds of subjects those procedures may be deployed to amend. We often see this arrangement in constitutions that codify an escalating threshold of constitutional amendment, where there exists more than one procedure of constitutional amendment and where the threshold of agreement needed to ratify an amendment increases according to the importance of the constitutional rule to be amended.

For instance, the South African Constitution creates three amendment procedures, each linked to different parts and principles in the Constitution.[20] The lowest amendment threshold requires two-thirds approval in the National Assembly.[21] It is the Constitution's general amending formula and may be used to amend all parts and principles not specially assigned to a higher amendment threshold. The intermediate amendment threshold requires two-thirds approval in both the National Assembly and the National Council of Provinces.[22] This procedure must be used for any amendment to the Bill of Rights, the National Council of Provinces, or provincial rights and concerns.[23] The most exacting amendment procedure requires approval by three-quarters and two-thirds, respectively, in the National Assembly and the National Council of Provinces.[24] This onerous procedure must be used to amend the Constitution's statement of constitutional values and the highest amendment threshold itself.[25]

There is a consequence to this design. It raises the possibility that political actors may try to use an easier amendment procedure to amend part of the constitution that requires the use of a higher, more onerous procedure. We have seen this in many cases around the world, including in Ecuador. The question before the Ecuadorian Constitutional Court was which specific amendment procedure lawmakers should use to amend presidential term limits. Unsurprisingly, amendment opponents argued that the more rigorous procedure should be used, while amendment proponents preferred the easier route. The Constitutional Court ultimately ruled that the amendment could proceed under the less onerous procedure because it did not change the fundamental structure of the constitution.[26] One could imagine a similar constitutional controversy in an Asian country whose constitution codifies multiple amendment procedures. For instance, in Myanmar, the Constitution codifies two basic amendment procedures.[27] The default procedure requires approval from three-fourths of the bicameral legislature.[28] The other is expressly designated to amend matters of special importance in the

---

20 Constitution of South Africa, s 74.
21 ibid.
22 ibid.
23 ibid.
24 ibid.
25 ibid.
26 Dictamen No. 001-14-DRC-CC.
27 Constitution of Myanmar, ch XII.
28 ibid.

Constitution and is consequently harder to use because it combines the default procedures with a national referendum, making an amendment harder to accomplish.[29] A court, then, in Asia or elsewhere, could nullify an amendment made using what is deemed to be the wrong procedure.

12.3.3 Temporal limitations

The third category of cases where courts have nullified a constitutional amendment involves a violation of constitutionally specified durations of time. For instance, constitutional amendment rules often specify temporal limitations on when the constitution may be lawfully amended. One kind of temporal limitation is a safe harbor restriction, which prohibits political actors from making amendment proposals for a defined period of time. For example, a safe harbor may prohibit the introduction of a constitutional amendment for a certain number of years after the ratification of a new constitution, as in Cape Verde.[30] A safe harbor may alternatively limit the proposal of an amendment after a successful amendment of the constitution, as in Greece and Portugal.[31] Alternatively, a safe harbor may bar the reintroduction of a defeated amendment proposal until a defined period of time has elapsed, as we see in the Estonian Constitution.[32]

There are also deliberation requirements, which compel political actors to consider the merits of an amendment proposal within a predetermined interval or period of time. They come in two forms: ceilings and floors. The Costa Rican Constitution offers an example of a deliberation ceiling insofar as it requires a special commission to render advice on the proposed amendment within no more than 20 working days.[33] This is the upper limit for the commission to deliberate on the matter before the proposal proceeds through other steps. A court could nullify a promulgated amendment that had violated this temporal limitation. Conversely, the South Korean Constitution offers an example of a deliberation *floor*.[34] In order to formally amend the South Korean Constitution, the President must make an amendment proposal public for at least 20 days.[35] A deliberation floor like this one is the corollary of a deliberation ceiling. Rather than establishing an upper time limit for deliberating on an amendment proposal, a deliberation floor requires either political actors, the public, or both to consider an amendment proposal for a minimum duration. A South Korean court could read the deliberation floor in the Constitution as authorizing it to exercise the power of judicial nullification to invalidate an amendment that did not satisfy

29 ibid.
30 Constitution of Cape Verde, art 309.
31 Constitution of Greece, art 110; Constitution of Portugal, art 284.
32 Constitution of Estonia, s 168.
33 Constitution of Costa Rica, art 195.
34 Constitution of South Korea, art 129.
35 ibid.

this minimum deliberation requirement. This is the third category of uses of the nullification power.

12.3.4 Codified unamendability

Courts around the world have also exercised the power of judicial nullification in a fourth category of cases: when an amendment violates a codified unamendable rule. Codified unamendability refers to a textual rule prohibiting amendment, even where political actors could assemble the majorities needed to amend the rule, value, principle, structure, symbol, or institution that is protected against amendment. For instance, constitutions around the world designate various items as unamendable, including human dignity in Germany,[36] republicanism in France,[37] international law standards in Switzerland,[38] and the national flag in Turkey.[39] Constitutional designers can make virtually anything unamendable at the moment of constitutional creation.[40]

Consider the effect of unamendability in one specific instance. The Constitution of the Czech Republic codifies an unamendable rule protecting the "essential requirements for a democratic state governed by the rule of law."[41] This rule was put to the test when the Constitutional Court evaluated the constitutionality of an amendment that sought to shorten the term of the Chamber of Deputies.[42] The Court nullified the amendment, and with it the decision of the President to call new elections for the Chamber, on the basis of this codified unamendable rule. The amendment, in the Court's view, violated the fundamental prerequisites of democracy guaranteed by the Constitution.[43] The Court specified how the amendment would have changed an essential requirement for a democratic state: "That requirement is that the free competition among political forces be subject to the same rules, and, especially, to rules set in advance."[44] The Court made it clear that it had a duty to "protect the material focus of the constitutional order" when the Constitution is threatened by an improper amendment, as here, in the Court's view.[45]

---

36 Basic Law of Germany, art 1(1).
37 Constitution of France, art 89.
38 Constitution of Switzerland, art 194.
39 Constitution of Turkey, art 4.
40 Political actors might also seek to insert in the constitution an unamendable rule using the procedures of constitutional amendment. This would not be *prima facie* illegal or illegitimate, but it would require careful analysis of the context and procedure in order to evaluate the legality and legitimacy of such a change.
41 Constitution of the Czech Republic, art.9(2).
42 See *2009/09/10 – Pl. ÚS 27/09: Constitutional Act on Shortening the Term of Office of the Chamber of Deputies*, online at: https://www.usoud.cz/fileadmin/user_upload/ustavni _soud_www/Decisions/pdf/Pl%20US%2027-09.pdf.
43 ibid.
44 ibid.
45 ibid.

Several constitutions in Asia codify unamendable rules that could provide the predicate for a court to exercise the power of judicial nullification. For instance, the Cambodian Constitution expressly forbids amendments to the constitutional monarchy as well as to the system of liberal multiparty democracy,[46] and the Indonesian Constitution disallows amendments to the unitary form of the state.[47] In addition, the Nepalese Constitution bars amendments that violate "self-rule of Nepal, sovereignty, territorial integrity and sovereignty vested in people,"[48] while the Thai Constitution prohibits amendments changing the form of the state.[49] Courts in these Asian states could try to nullify amendments implicating these codified rules, as we have seen elsewhere.

12.3.5 Interpretive unamendability

Sometimes the unamendable rule may not appear anywhere in the constitutional text. This opens a fifth avenue for courts to exercise the power of judicial nullification. In these cases, the high court in a jurisdiction may believe that an unwritten norm is central to the polity, and it may apply that unwritten norm as a basis for nullifying a constitutional amendment. Rather than nullifying the amendment with reference to a codified unamendable rule, courts in this fifth category will nullify an amendment because it violates the court's own interpretation that some part or principle of the constitution is unamendable despite there being nothing codified in the constitution to that effect. It is a very controversial form of the power of judicial nullification, as Surya Deva suggests in his chapter for this volume, arguing that if a court exercises the power selectively and for self-serving purposes, the court risks weakening its own legitimacy.[50]

There are examples of the judicial nullification of amendments on the basis of this kind of interpretive unamendability. For example, the Supreme Court of Belize invalidated an amendment proposing to protect the power of the National Assembly to amend the Constitution with only limited judicial review.[51] The Court held that limiting its power to review the constitutionality of amendments would violate the basic structure of the Constitution, and those efforts were void.

The Court could point to no codified unamendable rule in the Constitution. The basis for the Court's decision was the preamble, whose values, the Court wrote, "have to be preserved for all times to come" and "cannot be amended out of existence."[52] For the Court, these special values include the rule of law, judicial review, the separation of powers, and "maintaining the balance and harmony of

---

46 Constitution of Cambodia, art 153.
47 Constitution of Indonesia, art 37.
48 Constitution of Nepal, art 274.
49 Constitution of Thailand, s 255.
50 See Surya Deva, Chapter 14 in this volume.
51 See British Caribbean Bank Limited v. Attorney General of Belize, Claim No. 597 of 2011 (2012).
52 ibid para 45.

the provisions of the Constitution."[53] Many of these values do not appear in the text of the Belizean Constitution's preamble. As the Court explained, they are unwritten values that must be inferred from the preamble and that are rooted in the spirit of the Constitution: "[E]ven though provisions of the Constitution can be amended, the National Assembly is not legally authorized to make any amendment to the Constitution that would remove or destroy any of the basic structures of the Constitution of Belize."[54] This was reason enough for the Court to nullify the amendment – even in the context of a constitutional text that codified no rule as unamendable.

Asian courts have exercised this power, too. The most prominent example comes from India, where the Supreme Court has nullified amendments that have violated a Court majority's interpretation of what constitutes the "basic structure" of the Constitution. In *Minerva Mills Ltd. v. Union of India*, the Court invoked the basic structure doctrine to nullify amendments to India's formal amendment rules.[55] The amendments had proposed to limit the Court's power to review constitutional amendments. The amendments declared that "no amendment of this Constitution ... shall be called in question in any court on any ground"[56] and that "for the removal of doubts, it is hereby declared that there shall be no limitation whatever on the constituent power of Parliament to amend by way of addition, variation or repeal the provisions of this Constitution under this article."[57] Nothing in the text of the Indian Constitution prohibited this amendment proposal – neither in the procedure used to propose it nor in the content it sought to introduce into the Constitution – yet the Court drew on its interpretation of the "basic structure" of the Constitution to reason that the proposed amendment should be nullified as unconstitutional. This doctrine has travelled from India to Malaysia, as H.P. Lee and Yvonne Tew explain in their chapter for this volume,[58] and may potentially travel to Pakistan, as Matthew Nelson suggests in his own chapter.[59] The doctrine may already exist in a peculiar form China, as Ryan Mitchell argues, insofar as some rules – namely those referring to *guoti* (or "state form") – could be treated as unrevisable through positive law.[60] Ridwanul Hoque highlights a potential pathology of the doctrine in Bangladesh: it may have grown to cover so much of the unwritten constitution that it effectively transforms what should be a theoretically amendable constitution into a practically unamendable text.[61]

---

53 ibid.
54 ibid.
55 1980 AIR 1789, 1981 SCR (1) 206, SCC (2) 591.
56 Constitution (Forty-second Amendment) Act, 1976, s 55.
57 ibid.
58 See HP Lee and Yvonne Tew, Chapter 5 in this volume.
59 See Matthew J Nelson, Chapter 6 in this volume.
60 See Ryan Mitchell, Chapter 3 in this volume.
61 See Ridwanul Hoque, 'The Politics of Unconstitutional Amendment in Bangladesh,' Chapter 11. Note that the Fifteenth Amendment to the Constitution of Bangladesh introduced a new unamendable rule in Article 7B.

12.3.6 Supranational constitutional restrictions

The last of six categories of instances in which courts have exercised the power of judicial nullification involves supra-constitutional rules. Where a country is a member of an international organization that has a charter of rules or practices, there may also be an adjudicatory body responsible for enforcing those rules and practices.[62] In the case of a signatory country amending its constitution in violation of this international charter, the adjudicatory body could find the amendment in conflict and therefore incompatible. For example, constitutional amendments in Nicaragua in 2004 and Togo in 2005 were found to violate the rules of regional multinational organizations.[63] In Asia, it is conceivable that a national high court or a supra-constitutional court could nullify a constitutional amendment where the amendment is held by the national or supra-constitutional court to violate the rules or practices of a charter to which the country is a signatory. Indeed, this is precisely the case in Vietnam; one scholar currently argues that the Vietnamese Constitution violates international human rights norms and is therefore unconstitutional.[64]

12.4 The next frontier of the judicial nullification power

We have thus far considered the judicial nullification power as applied to constitutional amendments. And if one accepts that the nullification power works as a shield for democracy – the claim that the judicial nullification power is an essential strategy to defend democracy – then the nullification power rests on strong theoretical foundations. On this view, the judicial power of nullification is consistent with democracy and moreover legitimate and indeed necessary.

12.4.1 An unconstitutional constitution?

But an important question nonetheless remains: what about using the judicial nullification power to invalidate an entire constitution, not just a mere amendment? Here I am not referring to a new constitution that masquerades as a constitutional amendment, a phenomenon I have identified as a constitutional dismemberment.[65] I am referring to the creation of a brand-new constitution that is subsequently scrutinized by a court for its constitutionality. That is the next frontier for the power of judicial nullification. And it is not too far off from

---

62 For an important discussion of this possibility, with insightful examples, see Yaniv Roznai, 'The Theory and Practice of "Supra-Constitutional" Limits on Constitutional Amendments' (2013) 62 International and Comparative Law Quarterly 557.
63 See Stephen J Schnably, 'Emerging International Law Constraints on Constitutional Structure and Revision: A Preliminary Appraisal' (2008) 62 University of Miami LR 417, 461–79.
64 For a discussion of this debate in Vietnam, see Bùi Ngọc Sơn, Chapter 4 in this volume.
65 See Richard Albert, 'Constitutional Amendment and Dismemberment' (2018) 43 Yale Journal of International Law 1.

242 *Richard Albert*

where we are today, as Bùi Ngọc Sơn shows in his discussion in this volume on the Vietnamese Constitution of 2013,[66] and as Mara Malagodi suggests about the Constituent Assembly in Nepal in this volume.[67]

Imagine, for instance, that a constitutional assembly is convened to write a new constitution. Further imagine that the assembly does indeed write a new constitution that is subsequently sent to the president for promulgation, as provided by the rules proposed by the constitutional assembly. Now imagine that someone challenges the new constitution on procedural grounds, arguing that the constitution should be sent to the people for ratification in a national referendum? Could a court – in Asia or elsewhere – hear the challenge and then rule on it, perhaps even going as far as validating the claim that a modern constitution requires popular ratification?

Imagine, alternatively, that the new constitution proposed by the constitutional assembly is inconsistent with the values of the current constitution to be replaced. Could the court intervene, either on its own or when presented a claim, to evaluate the substantive commitments in the new constitution and thereafter to exercise the power of judicial nullification if it determines that the new text does violence to a fundamental pre-constitutional value that inheres in the spirit of the country and its people? This scenario highlights serious questions about what courts should be able to do.

12.4.2 A challenge for scholars

There are limited examples in the world of courts issuing judgments on the constitutionality of an original constitution. The most prominent occurred in the context of South Africa's transformation from apartheid to democracy, when the court was authorized by the Constituent Assembly to review the proposed constitution for its conformity with a list of agreed-upon constitutional principles.[68] There also exists a recent example in Asia, specifically in Bangladesh, involving a court's invalidation of an amendment that had restored an original constitutional rule.[69] Yet neither of these cases quite reflects the full scope of the potential conflict: a full constitution held unconstitutional by a court, without the court being pre-authorized to exercise the extraordinary power of nullification. It has not happened yet, but it may only be a matter of time until it does. If one is comfortable with the judicial power of nullification for constitutional amendments, is there a principled distinction to be made that would exclude the nullification

---

66 Bùi Ngọc Sơn, Chapter 4 in this volume.
67 Mara Malagodi, Chapter 7 in this volume.
68 Certification of the Constitution of the Republic of South Africa, 1996, Case CCT 23/96 (Sept. 6, 1996).
69 See Po Jen Yap and Rehan Abeyratne, 'Judicial Self-Dealing and Unconstitutional Constitutional Amendments in South Asia' (2021) 19 International Journal of Constitutional Law 127; Ridwanul Hoque, 'Can the Court Invalidate an Original Provision of the Constitution' (2016) 2 University of Asia Pacific Journal of Law and Policy 13

of an entire constitution?[70] Scholars should turn their attention to this question sooner than later.

12.5 Conclusion: Bringing Asia into the global conversation

This volume makes an invaluable contribution to our understanding of the doctrine of unconstitutional constitutional amendments. Its focus on contextualizing the law and politics of the doctrine in Asian countries adds a much-needed regional perspective to the global conversation already underway about the role of courts in constitutional states. With the publication of this book, comparative analyses of the doctrine will be more global than before because Asian countries have not always been common reference points in the debate. Scholars of course refer to India, but to few other countries in the region. That should no longer happen, thanks to this important book.

In this chapter, I have explained and illustrated the six major categories of cases in which courts have deployed the doctrine of unconstitutional constitutional amendment to nullify a constitutional amendment. I have shown how this power of judicial nullification has been used in the context of a procedural irregularity, a subject-rule mismatch, a temporal violation, a codified unamendable rule, an uncodified unamendable norm, and a supranational restriction. I have drawn from cases around the world to situate Asian examples in each category in an effort to broaden the geographical references we commonly use to show how courts exercise the power of nullification.

These six categories of cases are meant to be illustrative, not exhaustive, of the grounds that courts in Asia and the world can invoke to nullify a constitutional amendment. There are of course momentous questions about the legitimacy of the judicial power of nullification lurking beneath each of these six categories. I leave those questions for another day, though I suspect that there are no easy answers, and that the best ones will acknowledge that the doctrine should not be seen as appropriate at all times for every jurisdiction. It is a contextual question whether a given constitutional state should authorize courts to exercise the extraordinary power of judicial nullification. All constitutional actors should be aware that there exist alternatives to invalidating constitutional amendments.[71]

---

70 I have explored this question in Richard Albert, 'Four Unconstitutional Constitutions and their Democratic Foundations' (2017) 50 Cornell International Law Journal 169.
71 For a discussion of alternatives, see Richard Albert, *Constitutional Amendments: Making, Breaking, and Changing Constitutions* (OUP 2019) 222–6.

13 Is the "basic structure doctrine" a basic structure doctrine?

Andrew Harding

13.1 Introduction: Concerning necessity and contingency

Let me first explain the purport of my apparently tautological title. By asking whether the "basic structure doctrine" is a basic structure doctrine, I am asking how *broadly applicable* is the basic structure doctrine (hereafter "BSD")? I recognise here that the BSD by no means exhausts the discussion of unconstitutional constitutional amendments, as is apparent from this volume as a whole. Nonetheless it is of fundamental importance. The question of the applicability of BSD appears to reduce to two possible positions.

The first is that BSD is a *necessary* phenomenon: it is an inevitable consequence of having *constitutional* and democratic government, as opposed to some other system of government. On this view a constitutional amendment could not survive the test of constitutionality if (at least on this but also possibly other grounds) it destroyed what we understand as a system based on the rule of law, in which the judiciary is independent and competent to rule on the constitutionality of laws and acts.[1] For example, a constitutional amendment that designated all judges as civil servants obedient to the command of the government[2] rather than the law, would, on this view, destroy the very essence of what we mean by "the constitution" and "constitutionalism." On this view, BSD would be a doctrine of the basic structure of potentially every constitution, embodying, that is, constitutionalism as we understand it – namely a system in which the constitution is law and secures adherence to the rule of law.

A second, quite different view, would be that BSD is not a necessary doctrine, but one that is *contingent* as a response to *particular local constitutional history* in certain cases. If, as argued in this chapter, the identification of BSD depends on

---

1 See, for example, *Liyanage v The Queen* [1967] AC 259, Privy Council; *Mohamed Faizal bin Sabtu v Public Prosecutor* [2012] 4 SLR 974, High Court, Singapore. One clear utility of the idea of a basic structure is that, distinct from limiting the power of constitutional amendment, it may provide a solid and useful basis for judicial review of ordinary legislation. This chapter is not addressed to basic structure in that (I suggest, rather obvious) sense.
2 If this seems unlikely, one could examine Indonesia's Judiciary Law of 1970, which had precisely such effect, although it was not framed as a constitutional amendment.

DOI: 10.4324/9781003097099-13

a view of the particular constitution, not constitutions in general, then it would not be a doctrine basic to constitutional structure per se.

Such is the dilemma I wish to attempt to resolve. I propose to call these two views, for simplicity's sake, the "necessary" and "contingent" views of BSD. The relevance of this question to a discussion of the politics of unconstitutional constitutional amendments[3] is clearly that, if the BSD is contingent as opposed to necessary, then its incidence and its content depend on the context in which the constitution is being interpreted. If on the other hand the BSD is necessary, then that would still be a doctrinal judgment having contextual impacts of which the judiciary would be unlikely to be unaware.

13.2 Further India: Kesavananda over time

Indulge me in stepping back in time to 1979, the year I first encountered the BSD through a reading of *Kesavananda*.[4] At that time, the BSD was under intense discussion by constitutional scholars, even those having no immediate interest in the fate of the Indian constitution. It was highly relevant that many constitutions across Asia had been heavily influenced by the Indian constitution, so that they represented a kind of "further India" in constitutional, as opposed to merely geographical, terms.[5] In retrospect, it seems as if constitutional lawyers spent as much time reading *Kesavananda* as they did speculating on its real meaning. In 1006 pages and 13 judgments[6] that split 7 to 6 in favour of BSD as the true interpretation of the Indian constitution, there was a great deal to speculate about. The speculation, which had taken six or seven years since the decision to circulate around the world, was very much about the nature of constitutional law itself. It drew into the discussion almost everything that was considered important – constitution-making and constituent power, the entrenchment of the constitution, constitutional amendments, the separation of powers, the nature of constitutional interpretation, the rule of law, fundamental rights,[7] the primacy of parliament or the extent of legislative power, and of course the politics of the judiciary. At a more prosaic level, the question was whether the Indian Supreme Court had indulged in a kind of Indian solipsism that could only be explained (and perhaps even then rather controversially, in the light of six dissenting judgments) in Indian terms; or whether they had stumbled upon something really profound that challenged us to question why the BSD was not applicable in all

---

3 As defined by Rehan Abeyratne and Ngoc Son Bui, Chapter 1 in this volume.
4 *Kesavananda Bharati v State of Kerala* (1973) 4 SCC 225.
5 H Clifford, *Further India: The Story of Exploration* (White Lotus Press 1990).
6 I had, and still have, the benefit of an elegantly edited 50-page redaction of the case by Professor S Jayakumar, but one still has to read the whole case to understand the arguments properly.
7 The case was and often still is referred to as "the fundamental rights" case, as opposed to "the basic structure" case.

cases, not just India's. Some were quick to dismiss it as the former, adverting to what they alleged to be the eccentric and idealistic nature of the Indian judiciary.[8]

Others viewed it more favourably as interesting and persuasive, but only in the Indian context. Others again viewed it as a kind of theory of everything that had been discovered in a single experiment. *Kesavananda* was, on this view, just about the most important case ever decided. But, let me emphasise, everybody was interested in how far this would go – did it have legs? The necessary or contingent nature of BSD was therefore implicated from the beginning of the debate.

Of course, as we now see from the very interesting and well-written chapters in this volume, BSD has in fact spread quite widely, having been discussed further in many other jurisdictions.[9] BSD can no longer be dismissed as a mirage on the horizon, an ambitious judicial coup d'état, or a kind of mishap in judicial understanding. It has circulated widely, as is evidenced in the present volume, and that cannot be ignored. But the question I address here is, how far can it properly go?

I argue that BSD is contingent, not necessary. I do not present here a detailed analysis of the cases in the relevant jurisdictions. That is expertly done in the various chapters in this volume. Rather, I offer a frame for thinking about the issue of transferability of the BSD. The question whether the BSD is "correct" is not, on my view, strictly an intelligible one, as its correctness cannot be judged at any level of generality. Indeed, the implication of discussing, as the papers here do, the *politics* of this issue, is that it is a matter of contingency rather than necessity. The politics, as politics go, cannot fail to differ across the globe even if constitutional law does not. Moreover, even if one assumed the inherent "correctness" of the BSD, this would still not answer the question, what is the precise content of that doctrine in this particular jurisdiction? To take an obvious example, the content of BSD would be different in a federal as opposed to a unitary jurisdiction. But if one examines the cases in Bangladesh, as Ridwanul Hoque does in this volume, one will see that even the particular structure of the judiciary is a contextual issue affecting the content of the BSD.[10] To take another example, Matthew Nelson, turning to the historical *contingencies* of basic structure jurisprudence in Pakistan, notes with specific reference to "religious issues" (for example, Article 62(1)(f)), that the role of "individual judges" and "the environment outside of the courtroom" was crucial.[11]

---

8 See, e.g., Ong Hock Thye J in *Karam Singh v Minister of Home Affairs* (1969) 2 MLJ 129, describing Indian judges as "indefatigable idealists." I should add that this statement was made before *Kesavanada*, but it reflected a common assumption after it, and was frequently quoted in that connection, portraying the BSD as the high watermark of Indian judicial activism.
9 Yaniv Roznai, *Unconstitutional Constitutional Amendments: The Limits of Amendment Powers* (OUP 2017), ch.2.
10 Ridwanul Hoque, Chapter 11 in this volume.
11 M Nelson, Chapter 6 in this volume.

A basic structure doctrine? 247

But 40 years after I published my first article, arguing for the applicability of the BSD in Malaysia,[12] the Malaysian courts appear to have come around to my view of the matter. In fact, they never completely closed the door on BSD, which in retrospect was, I think, a wise thing to do, not because the courts need decades to consider the applicability of the BSD, but because content may come to be seen in a different light over time as new cases are litigated.[13] However, the matter is still not completely clear, as is indicated in a recent Federal Court case, which overrules some previous cases on this point.[14] This indicates that the BSD, although broadly discussed since *Kesavananda*, is still, nearly 50 years later, a matter of great difficulty and controversy.

The discussion of breadth of applicability of the BSD also involves discussion of potential *restrictions* on its applicability. The discussion of Asian examples, with which I proceed, implies that Asian constitutional law and scholarship may add insights to be considered at the global level. Asia does not have to be a mere recipient or passive respondent; it can also be a major producer and analyser of general constitutional ideas.

On this topic of the BSD we now have a superb literature.[15] Yet, for several jurisdictions and types of constitutional order, we still lack careful and convincing analysis. Once we can figure out this issue of breadth consistently with the insights of this literature, we can decide how broadly applicable the BSD is. This is a decidedly important and (contrary perhaps to all appearances) very practical question. It decides whether a given court of final appeal or constitutional court can legitimately check the validity of a constitutional amendment against the

---

12 *Phang Chin Hock v Public Prosecutor* [1980] 1 MLJ 70; AJ Harding, 'The Death of a Doctrine? *Phang Chin Hock v Public Prosecutor*' (1979) 21 Malaya Law Review 365. The Malaysian case is discussed by HP Lee and Yvonne Tew, 'The Law and Politics of Unconstitutional Constitutional Amendments in Malaysia', chapter 5 this volume.
13 The literature on this matter is large. See further, HP Lee, ibid; Jaclyn Neo 'A Contextual Approach To Unconstitutional Constitutional Amendments: Judicial Power and The Basic Structure Doctrine in Malaysia' (2020) 15 (1) Asian Journal of Comparative Law 69 ; Yvonne Tew, *Constitutional Statecraft in Asian Courts* (OUP 2020); Wilson Tay, 'Basic Structure Revisited: The Case of *Seminyeh Jaya* and the Defence of Fundamental Constitutional Principles in Malaysia' (2019) 14 Asian Journal of Comparative Law 113; Muhammad Hassan and Johan Shamsuddin Bin Sabaruddin, 'An Induction of Basic Structure Doctrine in Malaysian Jurisprudence and Federal Constitution: An Overview' (2020) 26 JUUM 3; Low Hong Ping, 'The Doctrine of Unconstitutional Constitutional Amendments in Malaysia: In Search of Our Constitutional Identity' (2018) 45(2) JMCL 53. HP Lee, Richard Foo, and Amber Tan, 'Constitutional Change in Malaysia' (2019) 14(1) JCL 119, Yaniv Roznai, 'Constitutional Amendability and Unamendability in South-East Asia' (2019) Journal of Comparative Law 188.
14 The case is *Rovin Jotty v Lembaga Pencegahan Jenayah*, decided on 18 February 2021, Federal Court.
15 Most importantly, Roznai (n8); Sudhir Krishnaswamy, *Democracy and Constitutionalism in India: A Study of the Basic Structure Doctrine* (CUP 2009); Richard Albert, *Constitutional Amendments: Making, Breaking, and Changing Constitutions* (OUP 2019), 151ff. and for Asian cases and discussion, see Wen-chen Chang, Li-ann Thio, Kevin YL Tan, and Jiunn-rong Yeh, *Constitutionalism in Asia: Cases and Materials* (Hart Publishing 2014), 278ff.

248 *Andrew Harding*

implicit basic structure of the constitution, and rule it unconstitutional if it is deemed to destroy that basic structure. The BSD comes into play, one might say, when the chips are down, or when "constitutional hardball," as Mark Tushnet puts it,[16] is the order of the day, throwing into relief the politics of the judiciary and the nature of judicial power. When constitutions are under attack, the BSD becomes critical as a last bastion or shield for the judicial power. In many cases, these days, we find that constitutional order is not always assaulted from the outside as it repeatedly was in the 1960s and 1970s, when colonels simply binned or "suspended" the constitution. Sometimes it resembles the sick rose that is eaten from the inside by the insidious work of what David Landau calls "abusive constitutionalism."[17] In this sense, the scope of constitutional amendment becomes a really critical political question.

13.3 BSD in Singapore

Let me now explain more carefully, with reference to an argument about Singapore, what I mean by "contingent" as applied to the BSD. I offer a caveat here that the former Chief Justice of Singapore has argued that I am wrong in saying that BSD does not apply to Singapore's constitution.[18] If so, then that might be a good thing in the sense that it might lead to the entrenchment of important principles around rights and good governance and I would not cavil at such development. Or it might not. But in either event, we need to be satisfied that the BSD is plausibly applicable as a matter of convincing legal argument, not just that it is potentially appealing as a matter of judicial policy, which to my mind is another question. That question is I think much better settled by an eternity clause, as discussed by Silvia Suteu.[19] This may indeed be the ultimate fate of the BSD generally, as constitution makers become more aware of the currency of the BSD.

My argument arose from a narrative of Singapore's constitutional history, which goes like this.

Singapore had from 1958 a constitution as a self-governing British colony, which formed the basis of its State Constitution as a state of the Federation of Malaysia from 1963 to 1965. In 1965, Singapore left the Federation and its State Legislative Assembly, declaring itself the Parliament of a now independent republic, passed the Republic of Singapore Independence Act 1965. The Act declared the State Constitution (mutatis mutandis, obviously) as continuing to apply,

---

16 Mark Tushnet, 'Constitutional Hardball' (2004) 37 J. Marshall L. Rev. 523–53
17 David Landau, 'Abusive Constitutionalism' (2013) 49 UC Davis Law Review 189
18 Andrew Harding, 'Does the "Basic Structure Doctrine" Apply in Singapore's Constitution? An Inquiry into Some Fundamental Constitutional Norms', in J Neo (ed), *Constitutional Interpretation in Singapore: Theory and Practice* (Routledge 2017); Chan Sek Keong, 'Basic Structure and the Supremacy of the Singapore Constitution' (2017) 29 Singapore Academy of Law Journal 619. Singapore is not otherwise discussed in this volume.
19 Silvia Suteu, Chapter 14 in this volume.

together with some provisions of the Federal Constitution of Malaysia, such as those on fundamental rights and citizenship, on which the State Constitution was silent. From then until 1980, Singaporean lawyers had to look in at least three places to find "the constitution." There were a number of amending statutes passed in the meantime, two of which removed, and then later reinstated, the two-thirds' parliamentary majority requirement for a constitutional amendment. In 1980, Parliament then instructed the Attorney-General to consolidate the relevant documents into one document – the Constitution of the Republic of Singapore – simply by renumbering the provisions, and drafting amendments purely consequential on this renumbering or otherwise simply changing terms used to be consistent with Singapore's status as an independent republic.[20] Following that, the Constitution has been amended many times, sometimes in fundamental respects, as with the introduction of an executive presidency and innovations fundamentally altering the electoral system.[21] Thus, there was no point at which "the people" may be said to have considered what constitutional arrangements were appropriate. Indeed, quite the opposite occurred, as a new constitution was mooted in 1965, but never actually materialised.[22] Accordingly, my argument proceeded, there was no constitutional moment at which the constitution was entrenched, and in fact it is still referred to as a work in progress.[23]

A necessary premise here, in my view, is that for the BSD to apply there must be such a moment, and decisions affirming the applicability of the BSD do in fact refer extensively to constitutional history as an explanation and justification for applying BSD. If we go back, for example, to *Kesavananda* itself, we find it is riddled with statements assuming that there was a single and critical moment of constitution-making. At such a moment, "it was the common understanding that …"; action "could only be taken within the framework of the original document" or "the broad contours of the Preamble"; or that "fundamental rights were considered of such importance that …" or "placed on such a high pedestal that …," and so on.[24] There is also constant reference to the historical background and the intention of the constitution-makers;[25] and of course to the fact that unlimited power of amending the constitution given to parliament would elevate such

---

20 See A Harding, 'The 1980 Reprint of the Constitution of the Republic of Singapore. Old Wine in a New Bottle?' (1983) 23(1) Malaya Law Review 134
21 See Kevin YL Tan and Thio li-ann, *Constitutional Law in Malaysia and Singapore* (3rd ed, LexisNexis 2010), 420ff.
22 ibid., 73ff. Here the promised constitution is referred to as "the constitution that never was."
23 Lee Hsien Loong, *Singapore Parliamentary Debates, Official Report* (21 October 2008), vol 85, col 532.
24 Above n3, passim.
25 For more on this, see Surya Deva, Chapter 10 in this volume.

250 Andrew Harding

power to the status of constituent power.[26] As YV Chandrachud CJ, summing up the effect of *Kesavananda* in *Minerva Mills*, colourfully expressed it,

> The theme song of the majority decision in *Kesavananda Bharati* is: "Amend as you may even the solemn document which the founding fathers have committed to your care, for you know best the needs of your generation. But, the Constitution is a precious heritage; therefore, you cannot destroy its identity."

Somehow the former CJ of Singapore finds in the history of Singapore an implicit moment of some kind.[27] I do not myself, however, find one however hard I look or am keen to find it. The implication of this view is that the constitution would be entrenched purely by legislative action. It would also imply that the changes that have been made, some of which I have labelled fundamental, are either (implausibly) unconstitutional as destroying the basic structure, or await some kind of decisive endorsement as part of the permanent constitutional order. It follows naturally from this view that if, in the future, the people of Singapore were to "seal the deal" by appending their assent via some public-participation process or other mechanism, then the BSD might well be applicable. One problem with the former CJ's view is that if we say there is already an implicit moment of some kind, when did that moment occur, and which amendments are therefore not, in principle, caught by the BSD? To these questions there does not seem to be any convincing answer.

13.4 BSD and comparative law

From this case, I conclude that facts of constitutional history must point to some kind of popular or at least legitimated adoption of the constitution before the BSD can be regarded as salient. If it were otherwise, then a problem would arise in that a body, namely parliament, that is created by the constitution, could, without any limitation, destroy the very constitutional order on which its own existence depends. This argument is repeatedly used in justifying the BSD; but in my case study I argue it has no application in a case where parliament itself is the constitution-maker. A highly relevant consideration is whether parliament itself has the entire power to amend the constitution. This is not so in many cases, where, for example, a referendum or the assent of states, or other bodies, may be required to complete the process of constitutional amendment.[28] The fundamental point, and the beauty of the BSD, is that "the people" cannot act

---

26 *Kesavananda* contains so many such statements that it would be impossible to list even a tiny fraction. See, however, for acute analysis of this issue as handled in *Kesavananda* and otherwise, Krishnaswamy (n14) ch.1; and Sikri CJ's judgment in Kesavananda, at paras.89–90.
27 Chan Sek Keong (n 16).
28 For a table of amendment processes in Asia, see Chang et al. (n14) Table 4.3, at 257–8.

in vain by enacting a constitution that contains the worm of its own destruction, an unlimited amendment provision. They cannot have intended that the power of constitutional amendment could be used to destroy that which they had created. In this sense, the BSD only makes sense if it is in some sense an act of "The People."[29]

Another form of contingency here is, as I have suggested, the actual content of the basic structure itself, which will obviously differ from case to case. The fact that it differs considerably is to my mind evidence that the BSD itself must be contingent. If not, then what is it that a universal, necessary BSD as basic structure is aimed towards? It seems awkward and implausible to say that the BSD is always necessarily applicable, and yet the actual content of the basic structure so protected will differ considerably from case to case.

Let us take an example. Federalism may be part of the basic structure of the Indian, American, Pakistani, Malaysian, Australian, or Canadian constitutions; but it is not part of the constitution of the UK, the Philippines, Thailand, or Japan. Indeed, the nature of the constitutional order will be quite different according to whether the constitution is federal, and according to the way in which it is, or the process whereby it became, federal.

Similarly, Matthew Nelson in his paper discusses the possibility that Islam is part of the basic structure of Pakistan's constitution.[30] We could speculate, as the courts in Bangladesh and Malaysia have done, whether the same is true in those constitutional systems.[31] But it could hardly be true of Canada or Australia, nor is even the idea, that there has to be a religious principle of some kind at the base of the constitutional order, part of basic structure viewed generally. Some constitutions embrace secularism as a basic feature. This matter, like federalism, is purely dependent on contingency. In a similar vein, if the bill of rights in a constitution is part of the basic structure, it follows that a different set of rights will be entrenched in different cases; and if, as in Australia and Canada, there is no bill of fundamental rights in the constitution itself, then they cannot form part of the basic structure.

An even more difficult problem arises, however, with governmental structures. If the structure of government is part of the basic structure then it follows that this cannot be changed by an ordinary constitutional amendment that turns it into a different structure. For example, we could not turn a parliamentary into a presidential system or vice versa without adopting a completely new constitution. Nor could we turn a federal system into a unitary one, or vice versa. In fact, large numbers of Commonwealth states would on this view be unable to convert their system of government from a Westminster to a non-Westminster system, and would be stuck forever in a post-colonial constitutional trap unless

---

29 For an extended example, see Hahm Chaihark and Sung Ho Kim, *Making We the People: Democratic Constitutional Founding in Postwar Japan and South Korea* (CUP 2015), ch.1.
30 Nelson (n 11).
31 Hoque (n 10).

they jettisoned their constitutions completely.[32] But why should they have to do that? It seems quite implausible that they would, and in fact almost half of such Commonwealth states have done exactly what should be contrary to the BSD without anyone apparently imagining that this change was unconstitutional. Fundamentally, states are in my view entitled to change their system of government if they wish, and I see no strong policy consideration to the effect that they should not, assuming that the outcome is a democratic system of government. In terms of comparative constitutional systems, there are many ways in which they differ fundamentally; parliamentarism, presidentialism, and constitutional monarchy present just three possibilities that speak to basic structure. Of course, some such changes may be seen as good and others bad, and they will always be controversial. But to preclude the debate by saying that all such changes effected by constitutional amendment are by definition unconstitutional because they destroy the structure of the existing constitution seems almost perverse.

Now, there be may an exception here, in that perhaps a federation should not be allowed to abolish the rights of its constituent states without their consent: a proposition that seems axiomatic, although it has not always been observed. Conceivably, a federation should not alter its constitution in any manner detrimental to states or even a single state without the consent of all. Here, however, I am not sure that the answer lies in BSD, but rather it may lie in whatever "foedus" or treaty preceded the federal constitution, which is to say that this is a question that might well arise in international law rather than national constitutional law, which may or may not offer sufficient protection to a federal subject.[33] Of course, one way of dealing with this is for the argument to take the form of a clear constitutional rule or convention requiring consent of the federal subject/subjects to its/their rights being abolished or restricted.[34]

From this it seems to follow that in the BSD governmental structures need to be handled in a different manner from other issues such as the separation of judicial power or fundamental rights.

13.5 Constitutional amendment processes

Let me now turn to the body or bodies empowered to amend the constitution, and the delineation of provisions subject to this process.

Some constitutions expressly exempt some provisions from constitutional amendment. In this case of the eternity clause, the constitution defines its own basic structure, and nothing need be implied – indeed one could say that nothing ought to be or could be implied, because the constitution-makers have squarely

---

32 Kevin YL Tan and Thio Li-ann (n 17) ch.19.
33 Tom Ginsburg and Mila Versteeg, 'From Catalonia to California: Secession in Constitutional Law' (2019) 70 Alabama LR 923.
34 *Reference re Amendment of the Constitution of Canada* (Nos. 1,2 &3) (125 DLR 3d 1 1981), SC of Canada.

addressed the issue and drafted text that deals definitively with it. The German Basic Law goes further to say that the people can replace the entire constitution by an act of popular sovereignty.[35] This probably goes without saying, as no constitution is irreplaceable irrespective of whether it seeks to allow or prohibit such replacement.

Thus, while we may be justified in implying limitations on the power of constitutional amendment, going beyond the precise text where appropriate, we may not be justified in doing so where the constitution defines its own basic structure and delineates specifically how such basic structure may be amended. In this case, implied limitations, it appears, are inevitably precluded.

An example that springs to mind here is Myanmar's Constitution of 2008,[36] which contains two processes for constitutional amendment. The first is that a bill for amending the Constitution must be passed by more than 75% of the members of each house of parliament.[37] This applies to all provisions of the Constitution. The second is that a bill must be approved by a majority of the registered voters in a referendum, and this is applicable only to the most important provisions, as these are defined in the Constitution itself. This is an example of what has been referred to as "tiering" of constitutional amendment processes.[38] In this situation, I do not see how the BSD can have any application, because it would create large areas of ambiguity, and does not answer the question why we need to second-guess the constitution-makers' decision as to what is basic and what is not. We do not need to imply anything here, and such implication would fly in the face of, rather than interpret, the text. We would also be forced to conclude that there would be cases in which, say, 80% of the members of both houses and 75% of the voters agreed to an amendment, yet it might still be an unconstitutional amendment that violates the basic structure as determined by the courts – in this case the Constitutional Tribunal. This contradicts the very popular assent on which the BSD itself is based. Myanmar's constitution may, however, be argued not to be entrenched. Given the military coup of 1 February 2021, which was ostensibly an exercise of emergency powers pursuant to the Constitution, it seems likely that most people in Myanmar would be very happy for it not to be entrenched. It was subject to a 2008 referendum approving it, but prevailing opinion is that this

---

35 Preamble, and Articles 20, 79(3).
36 At the time of writing this constitution has been in effect eclipsed by the military coup of 1 February 2021 and the drafting of a Federal Democratic Union Charter by forces opposed to the military. Nonetheless, the 2008 Constitution is acknowledged as still in force by this Charter, albeit scheduled for abolition. But the general point made in the text is, I suggest, still valid.
37 It is worth noting that the military hold 25% of seats in both houses, so that any amendment requires, at least, one military supporter, even if all 75% of non-military members are in favour of the amendment. This degree of rigidity is almost unprecedented in constitutional law. See, further, M Crouch, *The Constitution of Myanmar: A Contextual Analysis* (Hart 2019), 167.
38 Abeyratne and Bui, Chapter 1 in this volume.

254 *Andrew Harding*

process was deeply flawed, and replacement of the 2008 Constitution is required and perhaps even likely to occur.[39]

It is hard to see how the BSD could plausibly be used to entrench such elements of the basic structure as praetorian provisions protecting the dominant role of the military. Such a position would run decidedly counter to every constitutional principle the BSD was invented to protect, and has been overwhelmingly rejected by the people of Myanmar in street protests since the coup. The reality is that in Myanmar, over ten years and for the time being, no constitutional amendment of any significance has been or is likely to pass, and that includes both ameliorative and destructive amendments.[40] Indeed, it is plausible that the unsuccessful attempts in 2013 and 2020 to amend the constitution may well have led to the coup, as the ruling party had received endorsement for change in the November 2020 election, and such change could only be to the detriment of the military power.

I conclude here that the BSD results from implication of basic structure and the manner of its protection, and must give way where the constitution expressly defines the basic structure and provides for the extent of its entrenchment. The BSD is especially problematical in such cases when provisions are protected by a referendum requirement. In the case of Singapore, for example, only one aspect of the constitution is protected in this way. Any bill restricting the sovereignty of Singapore must be approved in a referendum.[41] How could we apply the BSD to that most basic of all principles, the sovereignty itself of an independent republic? Clearly, we cannot do so in such a case, because provision is made for the people themselves to determine the issue.[42]

13.6 Uncodified constitutions

We can now turn to the odd cases of constitutions that are not codified, or "unwritten" constitutions as they are sometimes called. Are these subject to the BSD, and if so, how do we know what the BSD consists of, when there is no text into which we can add implication or use to explain the basic structure?

The UK, Israel, and New Zealand are well-known examples of this. From one point of view, not only does the BSD have no application, but the notion of constitutional amendment itself has no application either. Hence, the BSD has, so to speak, nothing of substance to which it could be attached. In these constitutions, we find that what corresponds to a constitutional amendment may simply

---

39 See A Harding (ed), *Constitutionalism and Legal Change in Myanmar* (Hart 2017); see (n 39).
40 Andrew Harding and Nyi Nyi Kyaw, 'Myanmar's Constitutional Impasse: The Constitutional Amendment Process in 2020', IConnect Blog, 12 November 2020.
41 Constitution of Singapore, Article 6. Cf., Mara Malagodi, Chapter 7 in this volume, for a similar provision in Nepal's 2015 Constitution (s.274(1)).
42 Indian sovereignty is, however, assumed as part of the basic structure of the Indian constitution; Kesavananda (n 4).

be a legislative act, so that the constitution is "uncontrolled."[43] Thus, it is a matter of opinion, not law, whether any piece of such legislation is a constitutional amendment. It remains of course a largely hypothetical question whether in such system the judges could strike down a statute for unconstitutionality. There are cases in the UK and in New Zealand that support such a proposition. The immediate answer might be in the negative, simply because there is no principle of constitutional supremacy in the absence of a codified constitution. Yet there are indications that such striking down might be possible on such grounds as that the law contradicts the "fundamental principles of the common law" (in the UK and New Zealand, at least), or is perhaps so fundamentally destructive of the rule of law as to be "unconstitutional," that is, not recognised as being consistent with the notion of "law" by the courts.[44]

Here one might indeed say that, although the BSD does not strictly have application, as we are not implying anything into any text, there is *in effect* a basic structure that is entrenched in some fashion and could be used to support judicial review of legislation. This could be seen as a translation of sorts of the BSD into the terms of a system that cannot, strictly speaking, make use of it. This a classic process in comparative law. We may note here that there is no constitutional "moment," but rather a gradual evolution of ideas that become in effect politically entrenched despite the absence of specific legal entrenchment. In the event of the striking down of a law as unconstitutional, such a system would have graduated or evolved into a different type of system – from parliamentary supremacy to an unusual form, perhaps, of constitutional supremacy.

A possibly analogous case is where there is a written constitution but that constitution is not entrenched. This might be because it just takes the form of an ordinary law and there is no special procedure different from ordinary legislation that is required to amend it. It would be uncontrolled in the sense indicated earlier. Or it may be that, as with Thailand, there have been so many constitutions that the currency is devalued, and no constitution is regarded as entrenched politically, even if it states that it is the supreme law, or even that some provisions are beyond the amending power or even a new constitution, to change.[45]

Analyses of Thai constitutions naturally then attempt to discover what it is that survives all constitution-making processes, finding the essence of Thai constitutionalism. This is often analysed in terms of what is called the "democratic regime with the king as head of state," a fundamental principle repeated in constitutions, especially preambles, since 1932, when the absolute monarchy was overthrown and the first constitution was drafted.[46] Here for basic structure we look, not to the constitution itself, but to what is fundamental and lasting, the golden thread

---

43 *McCawley v The King* [1920] AC 691, Privy Council.
44 See, e.g., *Jackson v Attorney-General* [2006] 1 AC 262, House of Lords.
45 On Thailand, see, further, Khemthong Tonsakulrungruang, Chapter 9 in this volume.
46 Andrew Harding and Peter Leyland, *The Constitutional System of Thailand: A Contextual Analysis* (Hart 2011), ch.1.

running through all constitutions. In other words, the position is, oddly, rather similar to those instances where there is *no* codified constitution, in that we look beyond the text to underlying social facts, or political, even quasi-religious, principles, even if the principles recognised in Bangkok are not the same as those recognised in London, or Tel-Aviv, or Wellington.

13.7 Conclusion

Let me conclude then with a brief summary of what I believe to be the proper breadth of the BSD, which I believe to be restricted in the several ways I have suggested.

First, the facts of constitution-making and entrenchment may or may not support the notion that the basic structure was, as a matter of implication, intended to be protected, and is accordingly beyond the power of the bodies ordinarily empowered to effect a constitutional amendment.

Second, we should be especially careful in implying the BSD in cases where some provisions are protected by a referendum requirement, as this is an exercise in popular sovereignty.

Third, the actual content of the basic structure varies from case to case, and we should be careful also in implying an intention to entrench a particular structure of government, as opposed to general principles such as the rule of law, judicial independence, and fundamental rights. Yet even these will take different forms in various cases.

Fourth, the BSD is not in principle applicable to unwritten constitutions and constitutions that are not entrenched. But this does not necessarily prevent judicial review of legislation in a way which is similar or analogous to BSD.

14 Eternity clauses as tools for exclusionary constitutional projects

Silvia Suteu

14.1 Introduction

There has been undoubted growth not just in scholarly interest in unamendability, but also in its judicial use around the world.[1] Courts from across the world have at least considered, if not fully embraced, doctrines of unconstitutional constitutional amendment, either in the form of enforcing a formal constitutional eternity clause or seeking to defend implicitly immutable constitutional principles and basic structures. This has happened not least in response to current variations of democratic backsliding and populist constitutional amendment abuse.[2] One underlying assumption underpinning this interest has been that unamendability will serve as democratic safeguard against the misuse of constitutional amendment procedures and can unmask concealed attempts at constitutional replacement or "dismemberment."[3]

In this chapter, I want to remind us that unamendability itself can be prone to abuse. Taking the constitutional politics surrounding unamendability seriously reveals it to be open to misuse and instrumentalised at the stage of constitutional drafting, as a consequence of dynamics in the constituent assembly or drafting body, or indeed later, when a basic structure doctrine may emerge. As we have long known about constitutional rigidity mechanisms in general, they will on balance serve to insulate elites and have been relied on to stifle much-needed

---

1 Yaniv Roznai, *Unconstitutional Constitutional Amendments, The Limits of Amendment Powers* (OUP 2017); Richard Albert, *Constitutional Amendments: Making, Breaking, and Changing Constitutions* (OUP 2019); Silvia Suteu, *Eternity Clauses in Democratic Constitutionalism* (OUP 2021).
2 Suteu (n 1), 152–9; Pietro Faraguna, 'Populism and Constitutional Amendment' in Giacomo Delledonne, Giuseppe Martinico, Matteo Monti, and Fabio Pacini (eds), *Italian Populism and Constitutional Law: Strategies, Conflicts and Dilemmas* (Palgrave Macmillan 2020); Tamar Hostovsky Brandes, 'International Law in Domestic Courts in an Era of Populism' (2019) 17(2) International Journal of Constitutional Law 576, 589–90; David Landau, 'Presidential Term Limits in Latin America: A Critical Analysis of the Migration of the Unconstitutional Constitutional Amendment Doctrine' (2018) 12(2) Law and Ethics of Human Rights 225.
3 Richard Albert, 'Constitutional Amendment and Dismemberment' (2018) 43 Yale Journal of International Law 1.

DOI: 10.4324/9781003097099-14

democratic change rather than protect against democratic erosion.[4] The Asian case studies so comprehensively covered in this volume, several of which I draw on in this chapter as well, amply show this ambivalence of unamendability.

I should clarify that I am not arguing that unamendability is *always* likely to be abused, whether by the political branches or the courts, and can never serve a positive defensive function. Mine is a reminder that this abuse can and does happen, and that the constitutional contexts where unamendability has most appeal – divided, post-conflict, fragile – are *also* the contexts most likely to result in the abuse of unamendability.[5] The paradox then is that it is precisely where most needed that unamendability may be most vulnerable, and most likely to provide cover for – rather than protect against – the erosion of democratic and rule of law safeguards. Such re-evaluations are beginning to be felt necessary more broadly. Scholars now acknowledge that we have been so focused on identifying and combatting abusive constitutionalism that we have ignored the possibility of abusive judicial review – of judicial intervention itself contributing to democratic backsliding rather than protecting from it.[6] This chapter can therefore be read as complementing this emerging literature that seeks to re-evaluate the functions and operation of constitutional unamendability.

My argument thus proceeds in three steps. First, by exploring the constitutional politics of constitution-making resulting in the adoption of eternity clauses, I find the latter often to be the products of intense political bargaining. Eternity clauses then become facilitators and guarantors of the hard-fought political pact, entrenching bargaining imbalances and exclusion rather than, or sometimes alongside, democratic, rule of law, and human rights guarantees. Second, I show that the entrenchment of majoritarian and exclusionary values and principles, including via eternity clauses and unamendability doctrines, is most likely to happen in fraught constitutional contexts: those that are divided, fragile, and affected by conflict. Third, I show how constitutional review of unamendability in such contexts may well exacerbate rather than help mitigate these problems.

I draw on a number of Asian case studies, especially Thailand, Nepal, India, and Bangladesh, as they help illustrate different varieties of my exclusionary unamendability thesis. Section 14.2 thus highlights the exclusionary potential of entrenching certain state characteristics – in the case of Thailand, monarchism and the role of the King as Head of State – and their propensity to lead to reduced avenues for democratic change. Section 14.3 looks at Nepal's case as one in which constitutional entrenchment and constitutional nationalism are intertwined and have been over various constitution-making iterations. Section 14.4

---

4 Melissa Schwartzberg, *Democracy and Legal Change* (CUP 2009).
5 For an earlier exploration of unamendability in post-conflict and post-authoritarian contexts, see Silvia Suteu, 'Eternity Clauses in Post-Conflict and Post-Authoritarian Constitution-Making' (2017a) 6 Global Constitutionalism 63.
6 Rosalind Dixon and David Landau, 'Abusive Judicial Review: Courts against Democracy' (2020) 53 UC Davis Law Review 1313; David Landau, 'Abusive Constitutionalism' (2013) 47 UC Davis Law Review 189.

Eternity clauses as tools 259

explores the rise of judicial turf protecting through recourse to unamendability, specifically invocations of judicial independence as part of basic structure doctrines in India and Bangladesh. While exclusionary unamendability is not a distinctly Asian problem by any means, the spread of unconstitutional constitutional amendment doctrines in the region over recent years makes it especially ripe for this type of analysis.

14.2 Fundamental state characteristics and undemocratic amendment: Thailand's unamendable monarchy

Reading constitutions as products of political bargaining is not new.[7] Constitution-making processes are not only enmeshed with political deal-making, they sometimes become *the* site of contestation and gamesmanship. The interplay between constitutions and constitutionalism, on the one hand, and political settlements, on the other, becomes especially evident during periods of transition. This is when "dilemmas of statecraft" are open for negotiation and mechanisms for conflict resolution become newly embedded into the constitutional and legal framework, with eternity clauses as one such repository.[8]

It is then not surprising to see these political bargaining dynamics and compromises reflected in the constitutional text, including in its provisions on constitutional courts and amendment. Political insurance theories developed around constitutional review have sought to understand why political actors involved in constitution-making processes would voluntarily accept limitations on their scope for action by independent courts.[9] Their explanation is that such court intervention acts as assurance to all sides in the event of loss of political office or political influence, as well as to prevent political persecution.[10] More recently, such theories have been applied beyond the constitution-making context to constitutional amendment.[11] Such analyses have tended to see constitutional review as a potential bulwark against constitutional amendments that seek to undo the original constitutional bargain. In other words, judicial intervention has been seen as a potential positive force in the face of attempts to remove the original

---

7 Jon Elster, 'Arguing and Bargaining in Two Constituent Assemblies' (2000) 2(2) University of Pennsylvania Journal of Constitutional Law 345.
8 Christine Bell, 'Bargaining on Constitutions – Political Settlements and Constitutional State-Building' (2017) 6(1) Global Constitutionalism 13.
9 Tom Ginsburg, *Judicial Review in New Democracies: Constitutional Courts in Asian Cases* (CUP 2003); Ran Hirschl, *Towards Juristocracy: The Origins and Consequences of the New Constitutionalism* (Harvard University Press 2007).
10 Tom Ginsburg and Rosalind Dixon, 'The Forms and Limits of Constitutions as Political Insurance' (2017) 15(4) International Journal of Constitutional Law 988.
11 Sergio Verdugo, 'The Fall of the Constitution's Political Insurance: How the Morales Regime Eliminated the Insurance of the 2009 Bolivian Constitution' (2019) 17(4) International Journal of Constitutional Law 1098 and Dante Gatmaytan, 'Judicial Review of Constitutional Amendments: The Insurance Theory in Post-Marcos Philippines' (2011) 1(1) Philippine Law and Society Review 74.

form of political insurance in the constitution, such as amendments to remove bicameralism or presidential term limits.

However, what has remained insufficiently appreciated is the extent to which the same bargaining dynamics in constitution-making may result in constitutional incoherence as well as exclusion in constitutional amendment rules generally, and eternity clauses specifically.[12] Post-conflict constitutions are especially prone to this type of incoherence, as hard-fought patchwork documents that often must facilitate state- and peace-building in contexts of weak institutional capacity.[13] The same is true for other constitutional contexts characterised by deep societal division and institutional weakness. As Stephen Gardbaum has argued about importing constitutional review (especially in its strong form) in such contexts, this may result in "unnecessary pressures and strains in an already difficult context."[14] The same should be asked about eternity clauses and, relatedly, the prospects of courts developing unconstitutional constitutional amendment doctrines.

As I have argued more extensively elsewhere, it can and does happen that inconsistent provisions are entrenched within the same constitution, including unamendable ones.[15] In fact, with eternity clauses often drafted as a key site of value pronouncements, we find them sometimes enshrining a commitment to democracy alongside authoritarian features, or a commitment to minority rights alongside the entrenchment of state characteristics that may serve to restrict these rights, such as an official religion or language. This seriously complicates readings of constitutional unamendability as a repository of constitutional identity.[16] What emerges is a picture not just of disharmony among and iterative contestation of constitutional values, but of textual entrenchment of exclusion that from the start blocks the possibility of correction through amendment.

This does not deny the positive role eternity clauses may play, both at the time of constitutional drafting – when they can themselves perform a political insurance role facilitating agreement on a final draft – and as textual hooks for an unconstitutional constitutional amendment doctrine developed later on – such as to prevent democratic backsliding and abusive constitutionalism. However, mine is a reminder that more often than appreciated, eternity clauses will not (just) be repositories of the lofty goods of constitutionalism such as democratic

---

12 For a similar argument applied to the Romanian Constitution and its eternity clause, see Silvia Suteu, 'The Multinational State That Wasn't: The Constitutional Definition of Romania as a National State' (2017b) 11(3) Vienna Journal on International Constitutional Law 413. Similarly on Israel, see Mazen Masri, 'Unamendability in Israel: A Critical Perspective' in Richard Albert and Bertil Emrah Oder (eds), *An Unamendable Constitution? Unamendability in Constitutional Democracies* (Springer 2018) 169.
13 Donald L Horowitz, 'Conciliatory Institutions and Constitutional Processes in Post-Conflict States' (2008) 49(4) William and Mary Law Review 1213. See also Joanne Wallis, *Constitution Making during State Building* (CUP 2014).
14 Stephen Gardbaum, 'Are Strong Constitutional Courts Always a Good Thing for New Democracies?' (2015) 53 Columbia Journal of Transnational Law 285, 289–90.
15 Suteu (n 1), 58–9, 100–3.
16 Gary Jeffrey Jacobsohn, *Constitutional Identity* (Harvard University Press 2010).

Eternity clauses as tools 261

values, separation of powers guarantees, and rule of law principles. As negotiated and deeply political instruments, they are sometimes also sites of exclusion. Crucially, this happens within otherwise democratic, if imperfect, constitutional texts. Moreover, as will be shown in Section 14.4 below, certain institutional conditions need to obtain for judicial interventions in the name of unamendability to reinforce, rather than themselves undermine, democratic constitutionalism.

A good example to illustrate these points is that of Thailand, also discussed extensively in a chapter in this volume.[17] Thai constitutional politics reveal the problematic nature of otherwise seemingly innocuous eternity clauses. Successive Thai constitutions have proclaimed themselves democratic but have at the same time rendered the monarchical form of the state and the role of the King as the Head of the State unamendable, all in a volatile context characterised by frequent coups.[18] Section 255 of Thailand's 2017 Constitution thus prohibits "an amendment to the Constitution which amounts to changing the democratic regime of government with the King as Head of State or changing the form of the State." Its origins rest in the 1997 Thai Constitution, which otherwise introduced many elements of liberal democracy including a long bill of rights and constitutional review. A product of political bargaining, the eternity clause must be understood as seeking to protect so-called "Thai-style democracy," which not only entrenches the monarchy but also positions the military as "guardian of the crown" and the judiciary as the "faithful accomplice" of Thai-style democracy.[19]

The Thai eternity clause has been relied on as a formal ground to block repeated attempts to reform the system and actually correct the undemocratic constitutional foundations of the constitution. The Constitutional Court has repeatedly stated that it sees itself as the guardian of the constitution and the rule of law with powers to review amendments, even without a mandate to do so in the constitutional text.[20] The Court struck down a series of amendments to the 2007 Constitution on both procedural and substantive grounds, including an attempt to reintroduce the directly elected senate.[21] Invoking counter-majoritarian and rule of law considerations, the Court thus brought in an unelected senate among the list of unamendable elements of the Thai Constitution. The Court thus developed its own, counter-majoritarian understanding of democracy, which it then deployed to protect the purported original spirit of the constitution. In so doing, it blocked

---

17 Khemthong Tonsakulrungruang, Chapter 9 in this volume. See also Bui Ngoc Son, 'Politics of Unconstitutional Constitutional Amendments: The Case of Thailand' in Henning Glaser (ed), *Identity and Change–The Basic Structure in Asian Constitutional Orders* (Nomos forthcoming).
18 See generally, Eugenie Merieau, *Buddhist Constitutionalism in Thailand: When Rājadhammā Supersedes the Constitution* (Hart 2021); Andrew Harding and Peter Leyland, *The Constitutional System of Thailand: A Contextual Analysis* (Hart 2011) 1–37.
19 Tonsakulrungruang (n 7).
20 Const Ct Decision 1/2557 (2014).
21 Const Ct Decision 15-18/2556 (2013).

constitutional change that would have rendered the constitution more rather than less democratic.

Thailand's example therefore raises questions about what happens to justifications of unamendability when we are dealing with unamendable constitutional norms that may not be democratic. Should courts embrace doctrines of unconstitutional constitutional amendment when the amendments themselves are more democratic than the original constitution they try to change? The preservative logic of unamendability does not lead to easy answers in such contexts. As the chapter on Thailand in this volume also shows with respect to recent amendment attempts, the usual narrative of amendments potentially weakening democratic commitments does not hold for Thailand. Instead, as the author argues:

> In this case, the roles are reversed. The amendments represent the people's will to challenge the authoritarian legacy in the 2007 Constitution but the Constitutional Court's invocation of unamendability thwarted that will and entrenched authoritarianism, an abuse to liberal democratic constitutionalism indeed.[22]

One could retort that Thailand's case is less edifying because its constitution could be classified as undemocratic overall, so that unamendability in this context should not be taken as instructive.[23] However, as I argue in the next section, these types of constitutions are precisely where unamendability is most needed and most often found. It is in contexts where democracy is new, fragile, and contested that the "lock on the door" function of unamendability[24] – whether enshrined in an eternity clause or a basic structure doctrine – becomes most salient. It is precisely in hybrid or contested democratic contexts that unamendability is paradoxically most needed and most prone to abuse. Indeed, one of the most often cited examples of unamendability in action, Turkey, similarly originated in a post-coup constitution whose democratic pedigree has always been dubious.[25]

---

22 Tonsakulrungruang (n 7).
23 Or, more generally, that Thai political and constitutional instability are due to borrowing from Western constitutionalism. Merieau (2021) disputes this, showing the root of this instability lies in precisely the indigenous Thai understanding of constitutionalism and of the Thai monarchy. See also Eugenie Merieau, 'Buddhist Constitutionalism in Thailand: When Rājadhammā Supersedes the Constitution' (2018) 13(2) Asian Journal of Comparative Law 283, 298–303.
24 Roznai (n 1), 133–4.
25 Ersin Kalaycıoğlu, '*Kulturkampf* in Turkey: The Constitutional Referendum of 12 September 2010' (2012) 17(1) South European Society and Politics 1, 5. On Turkey's eternity clause and the recent constitutional reform in Turkey, see Oya Yegen, 'Debating Unamendability: Deadlock in Turkey's Constitution-Making Process' in Richard Albert and Bertil Emrah Oder (eds), *An Unamendable Constitution? Unamendability in Constitutional Democracies* (Springer 2018) 281.

Others that could be added to this list, such as Bangladesh, are discussed elsewhere in this very volume.[26]

Moreover, it is again precisely in such contexts that another oft-repeated claim – that unamendability is merely a brake and cannot stop a renewed constitution-making process where this is deemed necessary – is similarly problematic. The Thai example shows that an imperfect constitution may be hugely difficult to amend, with risks of instability that make amendment rather than replacement the only avenue realistically open. In such instances, the constitutional politics of unamendability reveal the true viability of the road to constitutional revolution.

14.3 Eternity clauses and minority exclusion: Unamendable constitutional nationalism in Nepal

Unamendability will play out differently in contexts that are divided, fragile, and conflict-affected, just as all constitutional institutions will, counting also the constitutional courts enforcing it.[27] Paradoxically, of course, these are also the contexts most in need of unamendability's purported defensive and state-building promise. These are the constitutional settings where constitutional democracy is still a work in progress and as such needs shoring up, including via legal and constitutional means. Typically, part of that apparatus will encompass strong commitments to human rights, some version of judicial review, and increasingly, a formal eternity clause.[28]

However, again a more holistic interpretation of these constitutional commitments presents a more complicated picture, including of eternity clauses. This can be illustrated by challenging three prominent assumptions often found in understandings of constitution-making processes generally, and of unamendability specifically. The first is an assumption that the constitution-making process will give rise to a more or less consensual outcome, that allows us then to speak of the adopted constitution as an expression of a single, unified, and pacified constituent power.[29] As the embodiment of the will of the people, eternity clauses are therefore not only important symbolic statements, but also to be enforced and

---

26 On Bangladesh's Article 7A as an "anti-coup protective clause," see Ridwanul Hoque, 'Eternal Provisions in the Constitution of Bangladesh: A Constitution Once and for All?' in Richard Albert and Bertil Emrah Oder (eds), *An Unamendable Constitution? Unamendability in Constitutional Democracies* (Springer 2018) 195, 218 and the same author's Chapter 11 in this volume.
27 For a more extensive analysis of unamendability in post-conflict constitutions, see Suteu (n 1), 48–82.
28 Suteu (n 1), 55–8; Christine Bell, *Peace Agreements and Human Rights* (Oxford University Press 2003) 200.
29 Vicki Jackson, '"Constituent Power" or Degrees of Legitimacy?' (2018) 12(3) Vienna Journal of International Constitutional Law 319; Zoran Oklopcic, 'Constitutional Theory and Cognitive Estrangement: Beyond Revolutions, Amendments and Constitutional Moments' in Richard Albert, Xenophon Contiades, and Alkmene Fotiadou (eds), *The Foundations and Traditions of Constitutional Amendment* (Hart 2017) 51, 60.

operationalised against attempts at constitutional change. In reality, more often than not, this is not the case: not only do deep divisions and cleavages persist during constitution-making, but whose will, exactly, gets enshrined may not be obvious or indeed desirable. This may be the will of dominant political elites; of the winning side following a conflict; and, given the growing internationalisation of constitution-making, of external actors with varying degrees of influence over domestic politics.[30]

A second assumption is that democratic pluralism and peaceful electoral competition will quickly become the norm, whereas in many fragile, divided, and conflict-affected contexts, single-party dominance or electoral volatility are often the reality instead. This then is reflected not just in political forces' ability to abuse the amendment procedure, but also in their capacity to entrench their grasp on power, including through the courts. The same dominance risks being embedded in the constitutional text itself where these forces are able to pursue their political goals during the constitution-making process as well. For example, Maoist openness to multiparty democracy during Nepal's conflict went largely ignored by a government seeking to end the conflict with the former's military defeat.[31] Even where some degree of power-sharing is sought, this may be done instrumentally and without key elites such as the military relinquishing their dominance, as was the case in Myanmar.[32]

Finally, I have already mentioned a third assumption in the previous section: one of constitutional coherence and of a pacified constitutional identity, the latter instantiated in amendment rules and eternity clauses among other sites in the constitutional text.[33] The messy reality of constitutional politics around constitution-making, including deal-making and the possibility of domination by one set of forces seeking to entrench their position, cannot escape unamendable provisions. Thus, they are not always the constitutional ordering mechanism they are supposed to be, at the top of a neat constitutional hierarchy, and also do not always or only enshrine uncontested values and core principles of liberal constitutionalism. The most blatant example of this in a post-conflict context are constitutionalised amnesties and immunities for past coup and wartime leaders, which have on occasion been "eternalised."[34]

We could briefly return to Thailand's example here. The 2007 Thai Constitution was contested by democratic forces in the country as the result of the 2006 coup, but nevertheless embraced by many as necessary "to get the country going."[35]

30 On the latter, see Suteu (n 1), 163–78.
31 Madurika Rasaratnam and Mara Malagodi, 'Eyes Wide Shut: Persistent Conflict and Liberal Peace-building in Nepal and Sri Lanka' (2012) 12(3) Conflict, Security and Development 299.
32 Aurel Croissan and Jil Kamerling, 'Why Do Military Regimes Institutionalize? Constitution-Making and Elections as Political Survival Strategy in Myanmar' (2013) 21(2) Asian Journal of Political Science 105.
33 Another such site typically cited are constitutional preambles. See Suteu (n 1), 98–100.
34 ibid, 77–81.
35 Tonsakulrungruang (n 7).

The hope was to be able to draft a truly "popular" constitution later. The relatively low bar for constitutional amendment initially set in the constitution would have been reassuring in this sense. This reminds us that constitution-making is a creature of compromise, and drafting decisions must be seen diachronically. Rather than a single, easily identifiable constituent moment encapsulating a constituent will (including via an eternity clause), constitution-making often reflects a concatenation of decisions, some express in the draft, others not, and of expectations, some of permanence and some of change.[36] The Thai Constitutional Court's invocation of original constituent power to block the 2013 constitutional amendment that would have restored a fully-elected senate, seen in its broader constitutional political context, therefore becomes problematic. Such arguments would be even more disputable regarding the 2017 Constitution, which was adopted only once new king Vajiralongkorn's demand for recognition of his power to intervene in politics was enshrined in the draft, post-referendum approval. "Whose will does this constitution represent?",[37] indeed.

Another instructive example here would be that of Nepal. The 2015 Constitution of Nepal contains a doubly entrenched eternity clause. Article 274(1) declares: "This Constitution shall not be amended in way that contravenes with self-rule of Nepal, sovereignty, territorial integrity and sovereignty vested in people." Article 274(2) then protects the former from amendment. Such double unamendability is rarer but not unheard of, with the case of Honduras's eternity clause – which on top of double entrenchment also contained criminal sanctions for even proposing prohibited constitutional amendments – perhaps most known.[38] The Nepalese eternity clause can only be fully understood in context, one that stretches back decades given the country's constitutional instability, as well as holistically, in conjunction with other constitutional provisions on sovereignty, territory, and minority rights. It is only then that its exclusionary potential is revealed.

The 2015 Constitution was the culmination of a protracted constitution-making process. Emerging after three decades of monarchic autocracy, the country's 1990 Constitution was meant to pave the way to democracy and guarantee fundamental rights.[39] A decade-long civil war between 1996 and 2006 led to the abrogation of the 1990 Constitution in 2007, replaced by an Interim Constitution that was meant to be quickly superseded by a new draft prepared by a constituent assembly.[40] The 240-year-old Hindu monarchy was also abolished in 2008. The new constitution was to remove the hegemony of the upper caste communities that had been entrenched in the 1990 document, as well as to finally achieve

---

36 Another example here is that of the Indian Constitution, whose drafters had expected it to be subject to amendment and improvement over time.
37 Tonsakulrungruang (n 7).
38 Landau (n 6).
39 Mara Malagodi, *Constitutional Nationalism and Legal Exclusion: Equality, Identity Politics, and Democracy in Nepal (1990–2007)* (Oxford University Press 2013).
40 ibid, 6.

social justice and the political inclusion of previously marginalised groups and communities.[41] It was also to seal the transition to a secular federal republic.[42] Despite repeated extensions, this first constituent process (2008–12) collapsed.[43] The current constitution is the result of a second constituent process operating between 2013 and 2015.[44]

Nepal's is thus a case of non-linear constitutional negotiations, as well as illustrating the difficulties of pursuing peace-building alongside constitution-building.[45] Its 2015 Constitution has been the object of significant contestation, which helps contextualise the otherwise innocuous-seeming constitutional eternity clause. One core locus of contestation has been citizenship. Previous progress on allowing the passing of citizenship along matrilineal lines was reversed in the 2015 Constitution.[46] The latter contains exclusionary citizenship provisions that constrain Nepali women's ability to pass on their citizenship to their children (Part 2 of the Constitution). This choice, in spite of years of protest and mobilisation by the women's movement, is steeped in fears over the "Indianization" of Nepal via frequent cross-border marriages between Madhesi women and Indian men in the Terai region.[47] In other words, a sovereigntist territorial logic permeates gendered citizenship arrangements that perpetuate exclusion and discrimination.

Another focal point of contestation has been the constitutionalisation of federalism in the new constitution (Preamble and Article 4(1)). Federalism was first introduced in Nepal in 2007 in its interim constitution following mass protests,

---

41 Yash Ghai, 'Ethnic Identity, Participation and Social Justice: A Constitution for New Nepal?' (2011) 18(3) International Journal on Minority and Group Rights 309 and Malagodi (n 38).
42 Mara Malagodi, 'The End of a National Monarchy: Nepal's Recent Constitutional Transition from Hindu Kingdom to Secular Federal Republic' (2011) Studies in Ethnicity and Nationalism 234.
43 For a discussion of dynamics within that first constituent process, including the significant interventions of the Nepalese Supreme Court, see Mara Malagodi's Chapter 7 in this volume.
44 For a perspective on the two constituent processes in Nepal from the point of view of public participation, see Abrak Saati, 'Participatory Constitution-Building in Nepal – A Comparison of the 2008–2012 and the 2013–2015 Process' (2017) 10 (4) Journal of Politics and Law 29.
45 Rohan Edrisinha, 'Challenges of Post Peace Agreement Constitution Making: Some Lessons from Nepal' (2017) 9(3) Journal of Human Rights Practice 436; Bell (n 27).
46 "Progress" in this context is relative. The 1990 Constitution had included exclusionary provisions on matrilineal citizenship transfer, but constitutional litigation and the silence of the post-2007 interim constitution allowed for some advances in this area. See Mara Malagodi, 'Challenges and Opportunities of Gender Equality Litigation in Nepal' (2018) 16(2) International Journal of Constitutional Law 527, 546–8.
47 ibid; Barbara Grossman-Thompson and Dannah Dennis, 'Citizenship in the Name of the Mother: Nationalism, Social Exclusion, and Gender in Contemporary Nepal' (2017) 25(4) Positions: Asia Critique 795.

and has from the onset been enmeshed with identity politics.[48] During negotiations in the second constituent assembly, opinion was divided between those looking to federalism as a vehicle to secure the inclusion of previously marginalised communities and those fearing it would destabilise and, in its ethnic form, Balkanise Nepalese society.[49] Protests surrounding federal demands continued throughout the workings of the assembly, which only managed to fast-track its drafting in the aftermath of the 2015 earthquakes.[50] The compromise eventually reached set up three levels of government – federal, provincial, and local – and, faced with continued protests and amendments tabled before the draft had even been ratified, actually named and demarcated the federal units.[51]

As Yaniv Roznai and I have shown elsewhere, eternity clauses regarding territory – such as declaring territorial integrity unamendable, as Article 274(1) of Nepal's Constitution also does – can be ambiguous and unenforceable.[52] However, they do typically indicate deep anxieties about the constitutional self-definition of the state and adopt a defensive stance towards perceived infringements on sovereignty from either within or without. I have also argued elsewhere that these types of eternity clauses often also entrench a nation-state logic and that, rather than remaining symbolic statements of state sovereignty, can be and have been enforced judicially to block constitutional overhaul.[53]

The legal continuities of constitutional nationalism in Nepal mean that an ethnocultural notion of the nation, initially transposed into the 1990 constitutional settlement, continues to permeate the constitutional system.[54] The 2015 Constitution has not only not quelled contestation, especially around the state's federal features and citizenship, but contestation has continued and now

---

48 Though as Malagodi has argued, that earlier constitutionalisation was meant to appease these demands without leading to change in practice and "Nepal remained *de facto* a unitary state." Mara Malagodi, '"Godot Has Arrived!" Federal Restructuring in Nepal' in George Anderson and Sujit Choudhry (eds), *Territory and Power in Constitutional Transitions* (OUP 2019) 161, 168.
49 ibid, 172.
50 ibid, 176 and Michael Hutt, 'Before the Dust Settled: Is Nepal's 2015 Settlement a Seismic Constitution?' (2020) 20(3) Conflict, Security and Development 379.
51 See fuller discussion of why "the federal question" was the single most contentious issue throughout Nepal's post-2007 constitutional negotiations in Mara Malagodi, 'The Rejection of Constitutional Incrementalism in Nepal's Federalisation' (2018) 46 Federal Law Review 521 and Rohan Edrisinha, 'Debating Federalism in Sri Lanka and Nepal' in Mark Tushnet and Madhav Khosla (eds), *Unstable Constitutionalism Law and Politics in South Asia* (CUP 2015) 291.
52 Yaniv Roznai and Silvia Suteu, 'The Eternal Territory? The Crimean Crisis and Ukraine's Territorial Integrity as an Unamendable Constitutional Principle' (2015) 16(3) German Law Journal 542.
53 Silvia Suteu, 'The Multinational State That Wasn't: The Constitutional Definition of Romania as a National State' (2017b) 11(3) Vienna Journal on International Constitutional Law 413.
54 Malagodi (n 38).

268 *Silvia Suteu*

plays out in the arena of constitutional amendment. The Madhesi community in particular is fighting for greater constitutional recognition and inclusion, as well as for more proportionate representation in parliament. As a consequence, the constitution was amended in January 2016, a mere four months after its ratification, to respond to some of these demands.[55] However, because the amendment had failed to address their core demand of a fresh demarcation of provincial boundaries, the Madhesi parties walked out of the vote on the bill. In June 2020, a second amendment was passed, enshrining in the constitution a new map to be used in the Coat of Arms of Nepal.[56] The new map depicts three regions, disputed with India, as part of Nepalese territory. The amendment bill was certified by Nepal's President as not trespassing against the eternity clause and signed into law in spite of India's objections that it amounted to an "artificial enlargement" of national borders.[57] Other as yet unsuccessful attempts at constitutional amendment include pushing for recognition of linguistic diversity, remedying the discriminatory citizenship rules, and again increasing the proportional representation of the Madhesi community.[58] Crucially then, these dynamics persist in spite of the eternity clause. There have even been calls to amend Article 274 itself, insofar as it is perceived to hinder the revision of provincial boundaries.[59]

14.4 Basic structure doctrines and judicial turf protection: Unamendable judicial supremacy in judicial appointments in India

Much ink has been spilled describing the emergence, evolution, and transnational migration of India's basic structure doctrine.[60] The doctrine is premised on the idea of implicit rather than explicit constitutional unamendability, whereby even

---

55 Constitution of Nepal (First Amendment 2072) Bill. Articles 42, 84, and 286 were then amended to guarantee to the Madhesi community the right to participate in state bodies and the legislature on the basis of the principle of proportional inclusion and to increase the number of parliamentary seats allocated to the southern region.
56 Constitution of Nepal (First Amendment 2072) Bill.
57 'Nepal's President Signs Bill to Redraw Map Incorporating 3 Indian Areas' *The Week* (18 June 2020), https://www.theweek.in/wire-updates/international/2020/06/18/fgn44-nepal-map-president.html.
58 'Nepali Congress Registers Its Own Constitution Amendment Bill' *Kathmandu Post* (3 June 2020), https://tkpo.st/2U4Zkfy.
59 Ram Kumar Kamat, 'FA Seeks Removal of Provisions of Article 274' *The Himalayan Times* (5 January 2017), https://thehimalayantimes.com/nepal/federal-alliance-seeks-removal-of-provisions-of-article-274.
60 See chapter by Surya Deva, Chapter 10 in this volume, and, *inter alia*, Madhav Khosla, 'Constitutional Amendment' in Sujit Choudhry, Madhav Khosla, and Pratap Bhanu Mehta (eds), *The Oxford Handbook of the Indian Constitution* (OUP 2016) 232; Sudhir Krishnaswamy, *Democracy and Constitutionalism in India* (OUP 2009); Pratap Bhanu Mehta, 'The Inner Conflict of Constitutionalism: Judicial Review and the "Basic Structure"' in Zoya Hasan, E Sridharan, and R Sudarshan, eds., *India's Living Constitution: Ideas, Practices, Controversies* (Permanent Black 2002) 179.

in the absence of a formal eternity clause in the constitutional text, an unamendable set of constitutional commitments is read into the constitution as forming its core or constitutional identity.[61] The basic structure doctrine has had a rich "career" since its early days in the *Kesavananda Bharati* case,[62] directly or indirectly influencing constitutional developments throughout the world and most notably in neighbouring Bangladesh and Pakistan,[63] and most recently in Malaysia and Singapore.[64] It has influenced constitutional debates and adjudication even where the doctrine has so far been rejected.[65]

Given this extensive scholarly activity on the Indian basic structure doctrine, only a brief account of one of its aspects will be highlighted here. Among the various elements the Indian Supreme Court has read into the constitutional basic structure has long been judicial independence. It is not the principle of judicial independence and its centrality to Indian constitutionalism that has been problematic, but the way in which the Indian Supreme Court has chosen to operationalise this principle in practice. The so-called *National Judicial Appointments Commission (NJAC)* or *Fourth Judges* case concerned a review of the Ninety-ninth Amendment to the Indian Constitution which sought to replace the collegium system of judicial appointments with an NJAC and thereby remove judicial supremacy in this arena.[66] The NJAC would retain as members the Chief Justice of India and two other senior justices, but would also include the union minister of law and justice, and two "eminent persons."[67] Two members could veto an appointment. The reform was meant to increase transparency and accountability in judicial appointments.[68]

The Indian Supreme Court struck down the amendment. It argued that by removing judicial supremacy in the judicial appointments process, the amendment

---

61 Jacobsohn (n 16). On implicit unamendability and unconstitutional constitutional amendment doctrines, see Suteu (n 1), 119–60 and Roznai (n 1), 39–70.
62 *Kesavananda Bharati v State of Kerala* (1973) 4 SCC 225.
63 On which see chapters by Ridwanul Hoque, Chapter 11 in this volume, and Matthew J. Nelson, Chapter 6 in this volume.
64 Jaclyn N Neo, 'A Contextual Approach to Unconstitutional Constitutional Amendments: Judicial Power and the Basic Structure Doctrine in Malaysia' (2020) 15 Asian Journal of Comparative Law 69; Yvonne Tew, *Constitutional Statecraft in Asian Courts* (OUP 2020). See also Chapter 5 by HP Lee and Yvonne Tew on Malaysia in this volume.
65 Gary J Jacobsohn and Shylashri Shankar, 'Constitutional Borrowing in South Asia: India, Sri Lanka, and Secular Constitutional Identity' in Sunil Khilnani, Vikram Raghavan, and Arun K Thiruvengadam (eds) *Comparative Constitutionalism in South Asia* (Oxford University Press 2014) 180.
66 *Supreme Court Advocates-on-Record Association v. Union of India*, (2016) 4 SCC 1.
67 The two eminent persons would be selected from a panel consisting of the Chief Justice, the prime minister, and the leader of the opposition in the Lok Sabha (the lower house of the Indian Parliament).
68 Po Jen Yap and Rehan Abeyratne, 'Judicial Self-Dealing and Unconstitutional Constitutional Amendments in South Asia' (2021) 19 International Journal of Constitutional Law 127; Rehan Abeyratne, 'Upholding Judicial Supremacy in India: The NJAC Judgment in Comparative Perspective' (2017) 49 George Washington International Law Review 569.

would undermine judicial independence and therefore the basic structure doctrine. The Court interpreted the constitutional duty of the Indian President to consult with senior justices in the judicial appointment process, enshrined in Article 124(2) of the Constitution, as implying a mandatory duty to follow that advice. The Court's concern with averting any political involvement in judicial appointments has been shown to contradict recent Indian constitutional realities: the President's cabinet had actually had the final say in the matter until this was changed via the Supreme Court's case law in 1993.[69]

Thus, the case operated a significant doctrinal and conceptual move from the uncontested protection of judicial independence as part of the basic structure to its equation with judicial supremacy in the judicial appointments procedure. Rehan Abeyratne has found that India is unique in affording such primacy to senior justices and that this system must be understood in the country's unique historical context.[70] Some readings of the *NJAC* case see it as less about judicial turf protection and more as an attempt to preserve the principle that parliamentary action remains subject to justification.[71] However, it is difficult to avoid the conclusion that the Indian Supreme Court sought to guard the status quo for institutional rather than principled reasons. As Surya Deva shows, the outcome has been a stalemate with both the executive and the judiciary claiming supremacy in the judicial appointments process.[72]

It is hard not to draw parallels to similar cases of basic structure doctrines being invoked to review changes to judicial appointments, as notably has happened in Bangladesh and Pakistan.[73] As Po Jen Yap and Rehan Abeyratne have argued, it may be possible to draw distinctions between these two cases and the Indian one, insofar as in the former two, judicial intervention can more plausibly be seen as a restoration of democratic control and removal of political influence over judicial appointments.[74]

However, similar interventions by constitutional courts reviewing and striking down changes to judicial appointments processes have also happened in constitutional systems less directly indebted to the basic structure doctrine and may be

---

69 Abeyratne (n 67), 611. In fact, it has been argued that the council system of judicial self-government is not only not the only institutional design option to ensure judicial independence, but may have unintended negative consequences. See David Kosar, *Perils of Judicial Self-Government in Transitional Societies* (CUP 2016) and Aida Torres Perez, 'Judicial Self-Government and Judicial Independence: The Political Capture of the General Council of the Judiciary in Spain' (2018) 19(7) German Law Journal 1769.
70 Abeyratne (n 67), 570.
71 Khosla (n 59), 245.
72 Deva (n 59).
73 *Bangladesh v. Asaduzzaman Siddiqui* (2017) Civil Appeal No. 6 of 2017 (AD) (Bangl.) and *Munir Hussain Bhatti v. Federation of Pakistan*, (2011) PLD (SC) 407 (Pak.). See discussion in Suteu (n 1), 147–51 and Yap and Abeyratne (n 57).
74 Yap and Abeyratne (n 67).

more worrying.[75] For example, in 2016, the Colombian Constitutional Court struck down constitutional amendments as against the constitutional replacement doctrine originally developed in the area of executive term limits.[76] It thereby struck down the newly created "Judicial Governance Council," with competences in the governance and administration of the judiciary, and the "Commission of *Aforados*," whose mandate includes prosecuting criminal and disciplinary offenses by senior justices. The amendments were found to contravene the principles of self-government of the judiciary, judicial independence, and the separation of powers. The political backlash was swift.[77] The doctrinal robustness of the court's intervention has also been challenged, given that the new institutions retained a diverse judicial membership and would have at least been plausible replacements for their predecessors.[78] As in the Indian case, the public policy justifications behind the reform included enhancing judicial accountability, transparency, and efficiency.

What these decisions illustrate is that our expectations of judicial interventions in the name of unamendability – in this case, of unamendable judicial independence principles – must be contextualised and even tempered. Understanding the basic structure doctrine and its progenies as protecting constitutionalism and democracy no longer suffices. The *NJAC* case and others like it remind us of the reality of judicial politics playing out in the constitutional arena. Apex courts will, under the best of circumstances, act as guardians of liberal constitutionalism, independent of political influence, and will exercise self-restraint in substantive review of amendments, only striking them down under the most exceptional circumstances. The Malaysian case law discussed elsewhere in this volume illustrates courts coming short of striking down constitutional amendments, but nevertheless making recourse to the basic structure doctrine to protect judicial review as an essential constitutional element.[79] However, the battles over judicial supremacy in judicial appointments highlight that courts also engage in "self-dealing" and deploy doctrinal means to protect their institutional self-interest.[80] This reality becomes even more complicated in situations of court capture and/or

---

75 Similar developments in Slovakia, where the Constitutional Court has also invalidated a new vetting procedure for judicial appointments in 2019, will not be covered here for reasons of space. See Decision PL. ÚS 21/2014 of the Slovak Constitutional Court and discussion in Suteu (2021), 150.
76 Decision C-285 of June 1, 2016 and Decision C-373 of July 13, 2016. See discussion in Mario Alberto Cajas-Sarria, 'Judicial Review of Constitutional Amendments in Colombia: A Political and Historical Perspective, 1955–2016' (2017) 5(3) The Theory and Practice of Legislation 245. On the Colombian constitutional replacement doctrine generally, see Carlos Bernal, 'Unconstitutional Constitutional Amendments in the Case Study of Colombia: An Analysis of the Justification and Meaning of the Constitutional Replacement Doctrine' (2013) 11(2) International Journal of Constitutional Law 339.
77 Cajas-Sarria (n 75), 267.
78 ibid, 267–8.
79 See HP Lee and Yvonne Tew, Chapter 5 in this volume.
80 Yap and Abeyratne (n 57).

institutional weakness, where such interests and the means to pursue them may even more overtly depart from doctrinal rigour and democratic constitutional principles.[81] My intention here has been narrower: to highlight the affinity between judicial turf protection and doctrines of constitutional unamendability. Unamendability can thus be deployed by courts as a veto power against perceived attempts to diminish their influence, even where the justification for the necessity of amendment strike down is tenuous at best.

14.5 Conclusion

Several conclusions emerge on the basis of the case studies discussed above and throughout this volume. The first is that studying the constitutional politics surrounding unamendability greatly enriches our understanding of the meaning, interpretation, and effects of constitutional eternity clauses and unconstitutional constitutional amendment doctrines. While this may at first glance seem obvious, it serves as a useful corrective to overly doctrinal readings of unamendability. It also serves as a warning against overly formalistic understandings, especially when it comes to textual eternity clauses. As the examples discussed here have shown, the text will only ever be one part of the story. It must be complemented by a contextual appreciation of the political bargains preceding and influencing constitution-making, as well as of the constitutional and political tugs of war that will ensue, including centred around unamendable provisions. Nepal's example is revealing here. The 2015 Nepalese Constitution and its eternity clause are fully understood only when looking back at the protracted process of constitution-making amidst complex patterns of interplay between constitutional nationalism and legal exclusion.

Moreover and relatedly, my analysis has also pointed to the need for holistic interpretation when assessing constitutional unamendability. Studying eternity clauses in isolation, not just of the broader constitutional and political context but also of the broader constitutional architecture, risks obscuring subtle details about how an eternity clause or unamendability doctrine interacts with other elements of the constitutional set-up. The example of Thailand is a case in point here. Its entrenchment of the monarchy only reveals its true meaning when the interconnectedness of the monarch, military, and courts is appreciated. This institutional edifice must be contextualised further by understanding the specificities of "Thai-style democracy" and its various iterations.

Finally, I would emphasise the need to adopt a longitudinal view when reconstructing the evolution of unconstitutional constitutional amendment doctrines. Contrary to the lawyerly impulse to focus on case-by-case developments, a longer term view will be conducive to a richer but also a more realistic assessment of the

---

81 For a discussion of such dynamics playing out in the Hungarian context of democratic backsliding, including through the development of a distorted doctrine of constitutional identity review, see Suteu (n 1), 152–9.

fate of eternity clauses and unamendability doctrines. As the Indian example shows with regard to the basic structure doctrine, understandings of unamendability will not necessarily develop linearly. We are increasingly seeing unconstitutional constitutional amendment doctrines deployed not in exceptional circumstances threatening the very core of democratic constitutionalism, but also as mechanisms of judicial turf protection and self-dealing. These developments may not negate the potential usefulness of unamendability as a stopgap against the erosion of democratic constitutionalism; they do demand heightened awareness of the delicate institutional dynamics that determine how courts operationalise unamendability over time.

My intention in this chapter is to issue a call for more caution about unreflectively and uncritically endorsing unamendability as a tool that reinforces democratic constitutionalism, especially at a time of ever-growing attacks on democracy. While eternity clauses and doctrines of implicit unamendability may serve useful defensive roles, we must also not look away from their "dark side" – whether in the form of textually enshrining constitutional exclusion and preventing democratic advances, or as a tool of unrestrained judicial self-empowerment. A thorough grounding in constitutional politics as advocated throughout this volume performs precisely this sobering function.

15 Why there?

Explanatory theories and institutional features behind unconstitutional constitutional amendments in Asia

*Yaniv Roznai**

15.1 Introduction: Unconstitutional constitutional amendments in a nutshell

The idea of unconstitutional constitutional amendments has taken a central role in global constitutionalism. Over the years, constitution-makers have increasingly imposed explicit limits on constitutional amendment procedures: while between 1789 and 1944, only 17% of world constitutions enacted in this period included unamendable provisions, between 1945 and 1988, 27% of world constitutions enacted in those years included such provisions, and out of the constitutions which were enacted between 1989 and 2015, more than half (54%) included unamendable provisions.[1] Unamendable provisions mostly refer to constitutional values, rules, and institutions that are considered the constitutional order's core values, in an attempt to preserve the core of the nation's constitutional identity – or the one which they aspire to.[2] Explicit unamendability is not merely declarative. In some countries, such as Brazil, Germany, and the Czech Republic, it is enforced through the exercise of substantive judicial review of constitutional amendments, ensuring their compatibility with the unamendable provisions.[3]

The fact that a constitution does not include explicit unamendability does not necessarily mean that the constitutional amendment power is absolute and that all the parts of the constitution are amendable. Constitutional courts around the world have recognized a core of basic constitutional principles which should be regarded as implicitly unamendable. The most famous example is the Indian one, where in *Kesavananda Bharati v. State of Kerala* (1973), the Indian Supreme Court held that the power of the parliament "to amend the constitution does not

---

* I thank Bùi Ngọc Sơn and Rehan Abeyratne for inviting me to participate in this project, and the participants in the conference for their comments.
1 Yaniv Roznai, *Unconstitutional Constitutional Amendments – The Limits of Amendment Powers* (OUP 2017) 20–1. On the origins, differentiation, and migration of unamendable provisions, see Michael Hein, 'Entrenchment Clauses in the History of Modern Constitutionalism' (2018) 86(3–4) Legal History Review 434.
2 Roznai (n 1), mainly chapter 2.
3 Roznai (n 1), mainly chapter 8.

DOI: 10.4324/9781003097099-15

include the power to alter the basic structure, or framework of the constitution so as to change its identity,"[4] as it is "a precious heritage,"[5] creating what has come to be known as the "basic structure doctrine" (or BSD).[6]

The BSD migrated into neighboring and other states, and was applied, in various forms and variations, in courts in Bangladesh, Pakistan, Uganda, Kenya, Taiwan, Colombia, Peru, Belize, and Slovakia. In these countries, courts declared that some basic features, fundamental principles, or material core of the constitution are so imperative to the constitutional order and its identity that they are beyond the amendment power even without any explicit limitations.[7]

Where courts enforce implied or explicit limitations on constitutional amendments, they regard themselves as "guardians of the constitution" and its core values.[8] Of course, while in some countries the doctrine has been adopted, in other countries courts have rejected their authority to substantively review amendments on various grounds.[9]

So, unamendability and the unconstitutional constitutional amendment doctrine have their manifestations in Latin America,[10] Europe,[11] and – as this book elaborates – also in Asia.[12] This book indeed focuses on the latter region, where important developments both in jurisprudence and constitutional politics have been occurring. This chapter seeks to provide an explanatory theory behind the doctrine of unconstitutional constitutional amendments in Asia.

Elsewhere, I have elaborated on the constitutional theory behind the doctrine. I have claimed that the constitutional amendment power is a delegated legal competence which acts in trust and is therefore limited both explicitly and implicitly. Firstly, it must obey those explicit conditions stipulated in the constitution. Secondly, the body which holds the constitutional amendment power in trust cannot use it in order to destroy the constitution from which its authority derives. The amendment power is the internal method that the constitution

---

4 *Kesavananda Bharati v. State of Kerala*, AIR 1973 SC 1461.
5 Justice Chandrachud in *Minerva Mills, Ltd. V. Union of India*, AIR 1980 SC 1789, 1798.
6 Much has been written about this doctrine. See, for example, Sudhir Krishnaswamy, *Democracy and Constitutionalism in India: A Study of the Basic Structure Doctrine* (OUP 2010).
7 Roznai (n 1), mainly chapter 3.
8 See, for example, Rory O'Connell, 'Guardians of the Constitution: Unconstitutional Constitutional Norms' (1999) 4 Journal of Civil Liberties 48; Gábor Halmai, 'Unconstitutional Constitutional Amendments: Constitutional Courts as Guardians of the Constitution?' (2012) 19(2) Constellations 182.
9 Richard Albert, Malkhaz Nakashidze, and Tarik Olcay, 'The Formalist Resistance of Unconstitutional Constitutional Amendments' (2019) 70 Hastings LJ 639.
10 Yaniv Roznai, 'Constitutional Unamendability in Latin America Gone Wrong?', in Richard Albert, Carlos Bernal, and Juliano Zaiden Benvindo (eds), *Constitutional Change and Transformation in Latin America* (Hart Publishing 2019) 93.
11 Lech Garlicki and Yaniv Roznai, 'Introduction: Constitutional Unamendability in Europe' (2019) 21(3) European Journal of Law Reform 217–25.
12 Yaniv Roznai, 'Constitutional Amendability and Unamendability in South-East Asia' (2019) Journal of Comparative Law 188.

provides for its self-preservation. By destroying the constitution, the delegated amending power undermines its own raison d'être. To amend the constitution as to destroy it and create a new constitution would be *ultra vires*. Also, since every constitution consists of a set of basic principles and features, which determine the totality of the constitutional order and make up the "spirit of the constitution" and its identity, the constitutional amendment power cannot be used to destroy the basic principles of the constitution. The alteration of the constitution's core results in the collapse of the entire constitution and its replacement by another – but this is for the people's primary constituent power, not the delegated organs, to decide via a proper channel of higher-level democratic participation and deliberations. And finally, like any governmental organ, the amending authority – acting as trustee of the people – cannot abuse its powers and must act in good faith.[13] Accordingly, when courts enforce limitations on constitutional amendments, they ensure that the amendment power does not exceed its authority, thereby protecting popular sovereignty and the vertical separation of powers between the primary constitution-making power and the secondary constitutional amendment power.[14]

In this chapter, I do not repeat the abovementioned theoretical framework, but – as the focus of this book is on the politics of unconstitutional constitutional amendments – I wish to provide some explanatory remarks on this issue. In Section 15.2, I list various explanatory theories that can explain why courts have intervened in various constitutional amendments in Asia. These theories are not mutually exclusive but reinforcing. In Section 15.3, I provide a brief look to another jurisdiction in Asia – Israel – and to some of the recent debates on the applicability of the BSD in Israeli constitutional law. In Section 15.4, I elaborate on the institutional features that can explain why doctrines such as the BSD are necessary in certain countries. Section 15.5 concludes.

15.2 Explanatory theories

15.2.1 Crowin's higher law

The first theory that comes to mind is Corwin's "higher law background" of American constitutional law.[15] According to this notion, there is a certain "common right and reason" that guides the common law, which is, according to Corwin "something fundamental, something permanent; it is higher law."[16] Of course, the idea of higher law can receive a local, and not necessarily universal, understanding and application.

---

13 Roznai (n 1), chapters 4–6.
14 Roznai (n 1), chapter 7.
15 Edward S Corwin, 'The "Higher Law" Background of American Constitutional Law' (1929) 42(3) Harvard LR 365.
16 ibid 370.

And accordingly, in China, Ryan Mitchell tells us, there is the notion of *guoti* (literally "state form") – a basic constitutional structure of the state. The polity's structure is theoretically unchangeable, in the sense that it reflects pre-legal social realities.[17] As Richard Kay noted, "The fundamental principles of [a] society ... are not the products of the law. They determine what the law is."[18] Arguably, in every society there can be pre-legal principles that may limit even formal constitutional law. Often, like in Germany, this supra-constitutional notion is constitutionalized within the document.[19] In Nepal, the Constitution of 2015 includes in Art. 274(1) an unamendable provision according to which no amendment may violate the constitution's basic structure by contravening Nepal's independence, self-rule, territorial integrity, or the principle of popular sovereignty.[20] But very often the fundamental limits on positive law are not explicitly provided. In Vietnam, as we understand from Bui Ngoc Son, it was not a formal constitutional unamendability but rather a political or constructive unamendability,[21] according to which political limits to constitutional amendments protect "core norms of constitutional socialism" in a way that the core identity of the socialist regime remains unchanged even in the face a new constitution.[22] In Japan, the postwar Constitution of 1947 is based on three principles that form the pillars of the entire constitutional order: popular sovereignty, fundamental human rights, and pacifism, pillars that are so important for what the constitution means that – according to the dominant constitutional theory – they are beyond the formal amendment power.[23] The clearest manifestation is the aforementioned Indian BSD – the idea that certain inherent values and characteristics are so important to what the polity means that they are formally unchangeable.[24] And similarly, consider the Pakistani Supreme Court's approach, according to which any constitutional amendment must not violate the salient features or basic form of Pakistan's Constitution – the parliamentary form of government blended with Islamic provisions.[25]

All these examples are akin to Carl Schmitt's absolute substantive constitution, or Constantin Mortati's "Material Constitution." For Schmitt,

> the authority "to amend the constitution" ... means that other constitutional provisions can substitute for individual or multiple ones. They may do

---

17 Ryan Mitchell, Chapter 3 in this volume.
18 Richard S Kay, 'Comparative Constitutional Fundamentals' (1991) 6 Connecticut Journal of International Law 445, 466.
19 Otto Bachof, *Verfassungswidrige Verfassungsnormen?* (JCB Mohr 1951) 29–57.
20 Mara Malagodi, Chapter 7 in this volume.
21 The concept of "constructive unamendability" is taken from Richard Albert, *Constitutional Amendments: Making, Breaking, and Changing Constitutions* (OUP 2019) 158.
22 Bui Ngoc Son, Chapter 4 in this volume.
23 See Koichi Nakano, Chapter 2 in this volume.
24 Surya Deva, Chapter 10 in this volume.
25 *District Bar Association Rawalpindi v Federation of Pakistan*, PLD 2015 SC 401; see Matthew J Nelson, Chapter 6 in this volume.

so, however, only under the presupposition that the identity and continuity of the constitution as an entirety is preserved.[26]

According to Mortati, the formal constitution can change but only so far as the substantial form of the state and its ideological presuppositions are respected.[27] These two theories highly resemble the BSD that seeks to preserve the core constitutional identity even from formal amendments.

15.2.2 Ely's democracy and distrust

About 40 years ago, John Hart Ely published his influential *Democracy and Distrust*.[28] Briefly put, Ely presented a "participation-oriented, representation reinforcing"[29] theory of judicial review that focuses on failures in the political process. Particularly, Ely claimed that judicial review is required and legitimate in two circumstances in which the political process cannot be trusted: where incumbent officials are blocking the channels of political change, and where the majority is systematically disadvantaging a minority because of hostility or prejudice.[30]

While Ely's theory was tailored to conditions in the United States, a political process theory of judicial review is extremely relevant and can be applied to constitutional law and courts around the world.[31] Consider Taiwan's Interpretation 499 concerning the extension of the term of the legislature.[32] In this Interpretation, the Fifth Amendment of 1999 was invalidated on procedural and substantive grounds.[33] According to the Taiwan Constitutional Court, an amendment process requires openness and transparency as the fundamental elements to facilitate democratic deliberation and rational communication. Yet, as the Court observed, the procedural requirements were not fulfilled by the National Assembly during the reading sessions of the fifth constitutional revision. Among these various procedural flaws, the use of secret ballots was considered manifest and gross and had already undermined the legitimacy and validity of the fifth constitutional revision. The Court condemned the application of secret balloting in the amendment

---

26 Carl Schmitt, *Constitutional Theory* (Jeffrey Seitzer tr., Duke University Press 2008) 150.
27 Constantino Mortati, *Law Constituzione In Senso Materiale* (Giuffré, 1998, or. ed. 1940) 35. See Marco Goldoni and Tarik Olcay, 'The Material Study of Constitutional Change', in Xenophon Contiades and Alkmene Fotiadou (eds.), *Routledge Handbook of Comparative Constitutional Change* (Routledge 2020).
28 John Hart Ely, *Democracy and Distrust: A Theory of Judicial Review* (Harvard University Press 1980).
29 ibid 87.
30 ibid 103.
31 See Stephen Gardbaum, 'Comparative Political Process Theory' (2020) 18(4) International Journal of Constitutional Law 1429.
32 J.Y. Interpretation No. 499 (2000). See generally David S Law and Hsiang-Yang Hsieh, 'Judicial Review of Constitutional Amendments: Taiwan', in David S Law (ed.), *Constitutionalism in Context* (Cambridge University Press 2021) (forthcoming).
33 Jiunn-rong Yeh, Chapter 8 in this volume.

process as a clear violation of the principle of openness and transparency. The Court further examined the substantive matter of the disputed constitutional amendments, holding that some contradicted constitutional provisions that are "integral to the essential nature of the Constitution." By applying the theory, the Court struck down both proportional-appointment and term-extension clauses due to their inconsistency with the essential provisions of the Constitution – the principles of democratic republic, popular sovereignty, protection of rights, and separation of powers. As Yeh mentions, "by denying the necessity of extending the fixed term of the National Assembly, the Court considered such extension as the betrayal to the people, which should be deemed inconsistent with the principle of popular sovereignty."[34] Yeh notes that "As the monopolistic institution to approve constitutional amendments, the National Assembly abused its power for 'rent-seeking' tradeoffs to gain its own political interests."[35]

One can rather easily apply Ely's theory in this case. The paradox at the heart of Interpretation 499, Yeh writes, is "whether the self-interested National Assembly would be willing to reduce its own political interests by exercising its monopolistic amendment power."[36] So, the court faced a "discredited National Assembly that seeks to expand powers and collect political gains in every round of constitutional revision."[37] There was public dissatisfaction that "arose as the clear reflection of distrust in the politics of constitutional amendment."[38] Democracy and distrust were at the basis of this judicial decision that was aimed at correcting failures in the political process. In retrospect, David KC Huang and Nigel NT Li wrote that

> It is no exaggeration to say that the hard work of at least three generations brought an end to the Chinese political tradition of lifelong tenure. The Interpretation set a milestone marking Taiwan's progress towards democratisation and constitutionalisation, because no politician in this country dares to extend his or her term of office from that point onward.[39]

So, in many aspects, the judicial review of constitutional amendments can assist in protecting democracy.[40]

---

34 ibid.
35 ibid.
36 ibid.
37 ibid.
38 ibid.
39 David KC Huang and Nigel NT Li, 'Unconstitutional Constitutional Amendment in Taiwan: A Retrospective Analysis of Judicial Yuan Interpretation No. 499' (2020) 15 University of Pennsylvania Asian LR 427.
40 See Yaniv Roznai, 'Who Will Save the Redheads? Towards an Anti-Bully Theory of Judicial Review and Protection of Democracy' (2020–1) 29(2) William and Mary Bill of Rights Journal 327.

Or consider Thailand, as Khemthong Tonsakulrungruang elaborates in his chapter. In its judgment, the Constitutional Court was warning that, despite the principle of a rule by majority, democracy forbade the majority from abusing its superior status to harass the minority, turning into the tyranny of majority which calls for judicial intervention.[41] Further, the Court held that "power must be exercised with righteousness, independence, and honesty, for the collective benefit of all Thais, without conflict of interest, abuse of power, or total monopoly of politics," and that "a political body is not allowed to abuse any law to support its unduly gain."[42] While the application of Ely's theory to the Thai example seems inadequate, as the court was preventing the legislature from becoming a more democratic body, these judicial statements during a substantive judicial review of constitutional amendments allude to the notion that courts should intervene when there is a failure in the political process in the sense of tyranny of a minority or abuse of political authority.

Finally, judicial intervention to prevent political process abuse can also be seen in Nepal, where under the 2007 Interim Constitution, the Supreme Court limited the ability of the Constituent Assembly to adopt amendments that would extend its own term.[43] When the Supreme Court issued, in 2011, an order according to which: "if the Constituent Assembly was to fail to promulgate the new constitution within the next six months, its term would automatically expire after those six months,"[44] it acted to prevent a failure in the political process. "Constitution making is not an exercise that can continue indefinitely without a fresh electoral mandate," Former Chief Justice Kalyan Shrestha later explained in an interview with Mara Malagodi. The Supreme Court claimed, "[T]he Constituent Assembly ought to answer to the People and respond to their aspirations by finalising the new constitution."[45] This was a democracy-enhancing intervention.

15.2.3 *Ginsburg's political and policy insurance*

Tom Ginsburg famously showed how judicial review is more likely to be instituted when constitution-makers predict losing power after constitutional adoption or revision, as the judiciary can protect the drafters' values that they might not be able to maintain through the political process. Judicial review, in this sense, is a type of political or policy insurance through which constitution-drafters can

---

41 Const Ct Decision 15-18/2556 (2013) 20, cited in Khemthong Tonsakulrungruang, Chapter 9 in this volume.
42 Const Ct Decision 1/2557 (2014) 11-12, cited in Tonsakulrungruang (n 41).
43 Malagodi (n 20). Malagodi describes how on 25 May 2011, a five-judge bench of the Supreme Court ruled that the 8th Amendment extending the term of the Constituent Assembly for one year was unconstitutional, yet did not issue an order of invalidation because the decision was delivered just three days before the expiry of the extended term.
44 *Adv. Bharat Mani Jangam and Adv. Bal Krishna Neupane v. Prime Minister and Cabinet Office et al.* Writ N. 068-WS-0014; see Malagodi (n 20).
45 Malagodi (n 20).

protect their future political interests.[46] Constitutional unamendability, mainly explicit, and its judicial enforcement can be another useful insurance tool.

In Nepal, for example, the 1990 Constitution included an unamendable provision (Art. 116) prohibiting amendments contrary to the "spirit of the Preamble." The idea, as Malagodi elaborates, was to preserve the constitutional monarchy and multiparty democracy, which were at the core of the political compromise leading to the constitution.[47] This provided a dual insurance: "the King endeavoured to prevent a republican turn, while on the other hand, the political parties sought to preclude a return to monarchical absolutism."[48]

In Thailand, meanwhile, constitutional amendments cannot overthrow the democratic regime with the king as the head of the state. Because the king is considered "the core of Thai political arrangement," as Tonsakulrungruang explains, the constitution protects with the most extreme rigidity – unamendability – the idea that Thailand is and must remain a democratic kingdom.[49] And this Thai-style democracy with the king as the head of the state was repeated often by the Constitutional Court. Arguably, even under the 1997 Constitution that provided a more liberal model of democracy with a Constitutional Court with a long list of rights, an unamendable provision was inserted, which is a type of insurance, in case of political loss. As Tonsakulrungruang notes:

> The judiciary and the army are two modern institutions founded by King Chulalongkorn over a century ago during the modernization of the Siamese Kingdom. Both remain unchanged ever since ... The two institutions therefore are the bastions of conservative royalists. They were part of a vast network of the king's allies.[50]

While such unamendability could not block a completely new constitution-making process, it could hinder such a process, as already occurred when the Constitutional Court held that the 2007 constitution, adopted by a referendum, could not be replaced through the ordinary legislative powers of parliament; rather, it required a referendum.[51]

---

46 Tom Ginsburg, *Judicial Review in New Democracies – Constitutional Courts in Asian Cases* (CUP 2009). See also Rosalind Dixon and Tom Ginsburg, 'The Forms and Limits of Constitutions as Political Insurance' (2017) 15(4) International Journal of Constitutional Law 988.
47 Malagodi (n 20).
48 Malagodi (n 20). See also Mara Malagodi, *Constitutional Nationalism and Legal Exclusion in Nepal* (OUP 2013) 126, 172.
49 Tonsakulrungruang (n 20).
50 Tonsakulrungruang (n 20).
51 Const. Ct. Decision 18-22/2555 (2012), cited in Tonsakulrungruang (n 20).

15.2.4 Hirschl's hegemonic preservation

Ran Hirschl's hegemonic preservation theory offers a complementary political account to Ginsburg on judicialization. According to Hirschl, elites who foresee themselves losing power establish constitutional review as a strategy for preserving some of their substantive values by placing them outside the realm of ordinary law-making.[52] A twist to Hirschl's theory arises when courts use the BSD to preserve their own powers.

Indeed, there seems to be an increasing trend in global constitutionalism of courts applying the BSD to invalidate constitutional amendments aiming to affect judicial review, the structure of the judicial system, or the ways in which judges are appointed or removed. As Po Jen Yap and Rehan Abeyratne convincingly demonstrate, such constitutional amendments have recently been invalidated through BSD as violating unamendable principles as judicial independence or separation of powers.[53] In other words, various judicial cases developing or applying BSD serve to reinforce judicial supremacy or promote the courts' institutional self-interest, even if the amendments touching upon separation of powers or judicial independence are not necessary to protect against what David Landau terms abusive constitutionalism.[54]

For instance, in Pakistan, "judicial independence" with respect to judicial appointments was mentioned by the judiciary as another unamendable salient feature of the constitution.[55] In India, in *Supreme Court Advocates on Record Association v Union of India*,[56] the Supreme Court held that constitutional amendment that sought to replace the collegium system of judges' appointment with a National Judicial Appointment Commission violated judicial independence, which is part of the Constitution's basic structure. Prima facie, it appears that this decision does not offer a convincing explanation as to why judicial independence requires judges to have the final word on appointments.[57] Thus, the best explanatory theory is that the judgment was largely motivated by institutional self-interest: the Supreme Court was simply unwilling to relinquish its monopoly over appointments to the higher judiciary.[58]

Other places provide more examples. In Bangladesh, in its 1989 decision *Anwar Hossain Chowdhury v Bangladesh*,[59] the Supreme Court struck down part of the 8th Amendment that divided the Supreme Court's High Court

---

52 Ran Hirschl, *Toward Juristocracy* (HUP 2004).
53 Po Jen Yap and Rehan Abeyratne, 'Judicial Self-Dealing and Unconstitutional Constitutional Amendments in South Asia' (2021) 19(1) International Journal of Constitutional Law 127.
54 David Landau, 'Abusive Constitutionalism' (2013) 47 UC Davis LR 189.
55 *Nadeem Ahmed v Federation of Pakistan* (PLD 2010 SC 1165); Nelson (n 15).
56 (2016) 4 SCC 1; see Deva (n 16).
57 Rehan Abeyratne, 'Upholding Judicial Supremacy in India: The NJAC Judgment in Comparative Perspective' (2017) 49 George Washington International LR 569, 570, and generally 598–9.
58 ibid 613.
59 (1989) BLD (Special) 1.

Division into several regional permanent branches. Some, as Ridwanul Hoque remarks, argued "that the 8th Amendment decision reflected the Court's elitist mindset, and an 'invisible' compromise between the judiciary and the Dhaka-based elite lawyers."[60] In *Bangladesh v. Asaduzzaman Siddiqui* (2017),[61] the Supreme Court Appellate Division invalidated the Sixteenth Amendment, which made judges removable upon a presidential order supported by a two-thirds majority in parliament, rather than on the recommendation of a Supreme Judicial Council. In contrast with the Indian case, this Amendment would have vested the judicial removal power entirely in political hands. Accordingly, and considering the history of martial law and emergency rule in Bangladesh, this decision can be better justified.[62]

In Malaysia, HP Lee and Yvonne Tew elaborate how the basic structure doctrine has developed historically.[63] While in the past Malaysian courts were deferential to the government in light of the "dominant-party democracy,"[64] the 2018 elections in which the ruling Barisan National coalition lost an election for the first time not only brought a political transition but also opened the door for the strategic assertion of judicial power. As Yvonne Tew writes: "The Malaysian Federal Court's assertions of judicial power, which occurred even before the democratic transition in 2018, have become all the more relevant now."[65] This decline of political dominance allowed the Federal Court to defend and strengthen its authority, inter alia, by adopting the BSD in order to preserve its institutional power. Two recent Federal Court cases, *Seminyeh Jaya*[66] and *Indira Gandhi*,[67] invoke the BSD, and while neither invalidates a constitutional amendment, they powerfully assert that judicial power resides only in the civil courts. *Indira Gandhi* further declared that judicial independence and the separation of powers constitute part of the Constitution's basic structure.[68]

So, to conclude, Nelson is correct in his remark that "with reference to constitutional 'basic structure' ... judicial activism is also associated with broad *institutional* interests: judges encroach on parliament's constituent power to protect the interests of the judiciary."[69] This can be regarded as another type of hegemony preservation, this time emerging from the judicial hegemon itself. Of course, this is not to say that strong judicial protection, even through BSD, is unnecessary. Often, especially in the contest of populism and democratic erosion, an aggressive

---

60 Ridwanul Hoque, 'The Politics of Unconstitutional Amendment in Bangladesh', Chapter 11 in this volume, at n 24
61 Civil Appeal No. 6 of 2017 (AD).
62 Yap and Abeyratne (n 53).
63 HP Lee and Yvonne Tew, Chapter 5 in this volume
64 Po Jen Yap, *Courts and Democracies in Asia* (CUP 2017).
65 Yvonne Tew, *Constitutional Statecraft in Asian Courts* (OUP 2020) 154.
66 [2017] 3 MLJ 561.
67 [2018] 1 MLJ 545.
68 ibid at [42].
69 Nelson (n 15).

application of judicial power can be crucial for protecting judicial independence and – in turn – protecting other democratic institutions.[70]

15.3 Israeli debate and looking to Asia

On July 19, 2018, the Knesset (Israeli parliament) constituted The Basic Law: Israel – The Nation State of the Jewish People. This Basic Law was meant to be another "chapter" in the Israeli constitution – which is still in the making in light of the incremental constitution-making process – dealing with the nation's identity.[71] It establishes that Israel is the "national home of the Jewish people," and deals with state symbols like the flag and national anthem, the official language, national holidays, the Sabbath, Jerusalem as the capital, etc.[72]

Supporters of the Basic Law argue that it is mainly declarative and does not change the existing state of affairs. Opponents of the Basic Law claim that because it mentions neither the democratic character of the state nor the principle of equality, it alienates the non-Jewish minority in the state and aims to shift the balance in the "Jewish and Democratic" character of the state towards the former. Moreover, the provisions regarding the "exclusive" right to self-determination of the Jewish people (Art. 2), the decrease of the status of the Arab language from an official language to "a special status," and the provision according to which "The state views the development of Jewish settlement as a national value and will act to encourage and promote its establishment and consolidation" (Art. 7) are allegedly discriminatory towards non-Jews. On this basis, various petitions were submitted to the High Court of Justice (HCJ) against the Basic Law, and the HCJ held hearings before an extended bench of 11 judges.[73]

The challenges against the "constitutionality" of the Basic Law brought to the fore the question of whether the High Court of Justice possesses the power to review basic laws, which carry a constitutional status. One of the main speakers against the authority of the Court was the then-Minister of Justice Ayelet Shaked, who said that the arguments supporting the court's authority to review basic laws are dangerous and could bring down the fundamental system of government.

---

70 Yaniv Roznai and Tamar Hostovsky Brandes, 'Democratic Erosion, Populist Constitutionalism, and the Unconstitutional Constitutional Amendments Doctrine' (2020) 14(1) Law and Ethics of Human Rights 19.
71 On Israel's on-going constitutional process, see Adam Shinar, 'Accidental Constitutionalism: The Political Foundations and Implications of Israeli Constitution-Making', in Dennis Galligan and Mila Versteeg (eds.), *The Social and Political Foundations of Constitutions* (CUP 2013) 207; Gideon Sapir, *The Israeli Constitution: From Evolution to Revolution* (OUP 2018) 11–31.
72 See Suzie Navot, 'A New Chapter in Israel's "Constitution": Israel as the Nation State of the Jewish People' *VerfBlog* (27 July 2018), https://verfassungsblog.de/a-new-chapter-in-israels-constitution-israel-as-the-nation-state-of-the-jewish-people/
73 On July 8, 2021, the High Court of Jusitce rejected the petitions against the basic law, holding that it does not diminish the state's democratic features. See HCJ 5555/18 *Akram Hasson v. The Knesset*.

Supporters of judicial activism, she claimed, want Israel to be like Bangladesh, Colombia, Honduras, and India, where courts have the authority to repeal constitutional laws. "With all due respect, Israel has nothing to learn from them. Even as a joke, this has gone too far," Shaked said.[74] She also warned that if the High Court of Justice would strike down the highly contested Basic Law, this would be an "earthquake" and cause a war between the branches.[75] Her approach was supported by various public thinkers.[76] In contrast, others, such as the publisher of *Haaretz* newspaper, Amos Schocken, claimed that "the Basic Law on Israel as the Nation-State of the Jewish People must be declared an unconstitutional constitutional amendment that contravenes the basic values of the system, and it must be annulled."[77] Thus, the question of the court's authority to review basic laws and the applicability of the Indian BSD in Israel, is at the center of a heated public and academic debate. This discourse is far from being purely academic; it has clear dramatic practical implications, as the court is facing what seems like one of the most important judicial cases in its history.

Part of the debate in Israel surrounds the question whether the Indian BSD should be imported into Israel, and whether it is suitable for Israel to adopt the Indian jurisprudence on implied limits on the amendment power. India, as is well known, has been a great source of inspiration to the world through its BSD. As Dieter Conrad – "the man behind the 'basic structure' doctrine"[78] – noted, "in

---

74 Yehuda Shlezinger, 'Repealing Nation-State Law "Dangerous", Justice Minister Warns' *Israel Hayom* (10 October 2018), https://www.israelhayom.com/2018/10/10/repealing-nation-state-law-dangerous-justice-minister-warns/

75 'Shaked Warns of "Earthquake" if Israel's Top Court Quashes Nation-State Law' *i24NEWS* (6 August 2018), https://www.i24news.tv/en/news/israel/181123-180806-shaked-warns-of-earthquake-if-israel-s-top-court-quashes-nation-state-law

76 See, for example, Eugene Kontorovich, 'Basic Truths about the Basic Law' *Jerusalem Post* (12 August 2018), https://www.jpost.com/Opinion/Basic-truths-about-the-Basic-Law-564697: "any American constitutional lawyer would find the notion of an unconstitutional constitution ridiculous ... if [the Supreme Court] ... claims the authority to consider challenges to constitutional provisions, it will set itself up as a supreme authority that is above even Basic Law. This will put it above any checks and balances; it will be a true judicial coup"; Gadi Taub and Nissim Sofer claimed that while the use of the doctrine of "unconstitutional constitutional amendments" is common in struggling democracies such as India or authoritarian-like regimes as Turkey, it was rejected in old and established democracies that we want to resemble – the United States, France, Norway etc. A court's decision according to which it possesses the authority to review and invalidate basic laws, they hold, would be a usurpation of power and a "declaration of war on the legislative branch and the foundations of democracy." See Gadi Taub and Nissim Sofer, 'Constitutional Revolution 2.0' *Haaretz* (March 14, 2019), https://www.haaretz.co.il/opinions/.premium-1.7020948

77 Amos Schocken 'Annul the Nation-State Law' *Haaretz* (29 March 2019), https://www.haaretz.com/opinion/.premium-the-unconstitutional-basic-law-on-israel-as-the-nation-state-of-the-jewish-people-1.7066214

78 The BSD has migrated to Indian through Heidelberg University Professor Dietrich Conrad, who delivered a lecture at Banaras Hindu University in India on implied limitations on the amendment power which formed the basis for the acceptance of the doctrine in the Supreme Court of India. See AG Noorani, 'Sanctity of the Constitution: Dieter Conrad – The Man behind the "Basic Structure" Doctrine', in AG Noorani, *Constitutional Questions and Citi-*

286   *Yaniv Roznai*

this free trade of constitutional ideas the Indian Supreme Court has come to play the role of an exporter."[79]

The famous Indian jurisprudence on BSD also caught the eye of Aharon Barak, former president (Chief Justice) of the Israeli Supreme Court. It was reported that in 2004, when Aharon Barak was the president of the Israeli Supreme Court, he had a formal visit to India. After this visit, which Barak describes as a "dream coming true," Chief Justice Barak stated that he was "deeply impressed with the approach of the Indian Supreme Court that positioned various features of the Indian Constitution above constitutional amendments by Parliament."[80] The famous *Kesavananda* case was cited by President Barak in a 2006 judicial decision, concerning the relationship between basic laws and basic constitutional principles,[81] although in that case President Barak opined that there was no need to decide this question. *Kesavananda* was also cited by the Israeli Supreme Court in a more recent decision in which the Court issued a nullification notice to a temporary Basic Law that changed the annual budget rule to biennial one, for the fifth time in a row, by applying a doctrine of "misuse of constituent power."[82]

Aharon Barak also cites the Indian experience in his scholarly articles.[83] However, albeit looking at the Indian jurisprudence, Barak also explains the difficulty in applying the Indian BSD in Israel. In an academic article from 2011 (five years after his retirement), Barak explored the question of unconstitutional constitutional amendments in Israel, drawing from comparative experience. He argued that the Knesset's constituent authority is not unlimited. It is limited by supra-constitutional principles, yet these limitations are narrower than those accepted in comparative constitutional law because the constitution-making process in Israel is still on-going:

> Under the comprehensive and full meaning of this doctrine as it is accepted in comparative law, this question indeed has no place in Israel. The reason for this is that the concept of an "amendment" to the constitution is itself

---

zens' Rights: An Omnibus Comprising Constitutional Questions in India: The President, Parliament and the States and Citizens' Rights, Judges and State Accountability* (OUP 2005).
79 Dietrich Conrad, 'Basic Structure of the Constitution and Constitutional Principles' in SJ Sorabjee (ed.), *Law and Justice: An Anthology* (Universal Law Publishing 2003) 186.
80 Omer Carmon, 'Aharon Barak: The Indian Approach Positions Constitutional Features above Parliament's Constitutional Amendments' *News1* (22.02.2004), http://www.news1.co.il/Archive/001-D-40766-00.html
81 HCJ 6427/02 Movement for Quality Government v Knesset, 61(1) PD 619 (2005), para. 73 to President Barak's opinion.
82 HCJ 8260/16 Ramat Gan Academic Center of Law and Business v. Knesset (Sept. 6, 2017) (Isr.). For a review of this case, see Yaniv Roznai, 'Constitutional Paternalism: The Israeli Supreme Court as Guardian of the Knesset' (2018–19) 51(4) *Verfassung und Recht in Übersee* 415.
83 See, for example, Aharon Barak, 'Unconstitutional Constitutional Amendments' (2011) 44(3) *Israel LR* 321, n 27; Aharon Barak, 'On Constitutional Implications and Constitutional Structure' in David Dyzenhaus and Malcolm Thorburn (eds.), *Philosophical Foundations of Constitutional Law* (OUP 2016) 53, n 80.

problematic in Israel. The constitutional project in Israel is a work in progress. The mission has not yet been completed. The "whole" has not yet been completed, and in any case the arrangements for amending it have not yet been developed. In Israel, we have a process of enacting basic laws. From time to time, a new basic law is enacted in an area in which there was no previous basic law. From time to time, an amendment to an existing basic law is performed by enacting an amending basic law ... In my opinion, the Knesset is not omnipotent as regards the establishment of a new basic law or the amendment of an existing basic law. In both cases, the Knesset, as the constitutional assembly, must act within the framework of fundamental principles and fundamental values of the constitutional structure. It must act within the framework of the principle-based standards upon which Israel's Declaration of Independence and the entire constitutional project are based ... However, in Israel we are in the middle of a constitutional process, based on basic laws, which has not yet been completed. Even if one accepts the basic approach that there are restrictions on the establishment of a constitution in Israel or on the power to amend it, my opinion is that, as long as the project of enacting basic laws has not yet been completed, these restrictions operate in a narrower framework than is customary in comparative law.[84]

Put differently, it would be perplexing to adopt a basic structure doctrine *à la Kesavananda*, before there is a full structure of the constitution.[85] This notion was adopted by the Chief Justice of the Supreme Court, Esther Hayut, in a judgment regarding a formal constitutional amendment to the Basic Law regulating the Parliament – Basic Law: the Knesset, and amendment which allows the removal from the legislature of lawmakers whose actions constitute incitement to racism or support for an armed struggle against the state of Israel. Writing the court's opinion, Chief Justice Hayut wrote that although the amendment "seriously infringes basic rights," "it cannot be said that it contradicts the core of state's democratic identity." Citing Prof. Barak, President Hayut wrote that:

> For now, and considering the unfinished stage in which the Israeli constitutional enterprise is at, and especially as there are no established procedures for enacting and amending basic laws, there is a great difficulty in adopting a comprehensive doctrine concerning unconstitutional constitutional amendments such as we find in comparative law. It is worthy that the doctrine to be

---

84 See Barak, 'Unconstitutional Constitutional Amendments' (n 83).
85 In his chapter in this volume, Andrew Harding situates the Israeli case together with the New Zealand and UK examples of unwritten constitutions. Andrew Harding, Chapter 13 in this volume. I am unconvinced that the Israeli case is similar to those two, since Israel has explicit Basic Laws that – according to the jurisprudence of the Supreme Court – carry a constitutional status, and accordingly Israel has a constitution, though a still partial one. See Gary J Jacobsohn and Yaniv Roznai, *Constitutional Revolution* (Yale University Press 2020).

applied in this context in the Israel law ought to be set upon the completion of the basic law enterprise towards a full constitution.[86]

This statement is not a rejection of the idea of implied limits on the Knesset's constituent power; it is merely that the court did not see the need to examine the complex applicability of implied limits and left it undecided for that time.[87]

Indeed, it may very well be that in the upcoming judicial decision regarding the Nation State Basic Law, the question of such applicability may be answered. Indeed, throughout the debate concerning the Nation State Basic Law, references to the Indian BSD have made public appearances, when those advocating for the court's ability to review basic laws rely, among others, on the Indian experience – a comparison that those objecting to the Court's authority to review basic laws criticize as inappropriate.[88]

Barak's notion that a comprehensive doctrine as exists in India is inapplicable in Israel seems cogent. As Andrew Harding notes regarding the applicability of the doctrine in Singapore:

> There was no constitutional moment at which the constitution was entrenched, and in fact it is still referred to as a work in progress. A necessary premise here, in my view, is that for the BSD to apply there must be such a moment ... if, in the future, the people of Singapore were to "seal the deal" by appending their assent via some public-participation process or other mechanism, then the BSD might well be applicable.[89]

Supporters of the BSD claim that the parliament, created by the constitution, cannot destroy the very constitution from which it derives its existence. However, Harding claims, this argument "has no application in a case where parliament itself is the constitution-maker."[90] A similar argument can certainly be made regarding the Israeli on-going constitution-making process.

In contrast, however, this does not necessarily mean that the Knesset has an unlimited constituent power. Even though the constitution-making process is still on-going, this does not mean that there are no underlying basic principles – just as a building that is still in construction rests on certain foundational stones.[91]

---

86 HCJ 10214/16 MK Yousef Jabareen v. Knesset (27 May 2018), para. 25.
87 ibid.
88 Barak Kedem, 'Aharon Barak's Song of Praise to Indian Law' INN (14 October 2018), https://www.inn.co.il/Articles/Article.aspx/18234 (Hebrew)
89 Harding (n 85).
90 Harding (n 85).
91 One may compare this idea to the recent Miller 2 judgment of the UK Supreme Court. In this judgment, the Supreme Court stated that: "Although the United Kingdom does not have a single document entitled 'The Constitution', it nevertheless possesses a Constitution, established over the course of our history by common law, statutes, conventions and practice. Since it has not been codified, it has developed pragmatically, and remains sufficiently flexible to be capable of further development. Nevertheless, it includes numerous principles

Such core basic principles, which form the entire constitutional order, may be deemed as posing limits to constitutional change. In the recent judgment on the Nation State Basic Law, President Hayut wrote, "indeed, our constitutional structure is incomplete and it is quite possible that floors and branches will be added along the way, but these two pillars - the Jewish pillar and the democratic pillar - have long been placed in it. Denial of any of them leads to the collapse of the entire structure."

More recently, Barak developed a theory on the limits of the Knesset's constituent power. According to him, the interpretation of the Declaration of Independence establishes the "genetic code" of the Constituent Assembly, which is intended to establish a constitution that will realize the vision of the people and its creed. It is unauthorized to act contrary to the vision. Accordingly, even if one accepts the view that the Knesset possess constituent power, it is unauthorized to nullify the character of the state of Israel as a Jewish and democratic state.[92]

This focus on the Declaration of Independence is intriguing, from an Indian perspective, as it seems that in the Israeli context, the Declaration of Independence is playing a somewhat similar role to that which the constitutional preamble plays in the Indian basic structure doctrine.[93] If it is similar to a constitutional preamble, the Declaration of Independence provides clues to the Constitution's fundamental principles. This may support Barak's reliance on the Declaration of Independence. And in fact, it was suggested by Amnon Rubinstein and Liav Orgad that, when the Constitution is complete, the Declaration of Independence may function as the Preamble.[94]

The move to a limited constituent power would be dramatic indeed, yet not unthinkable. Indian jurisprudence was initially rooted in the British tradition, thereby rejecting the notion of implicit unamendability. However, this approach drastically changed. From a Diceyian notion of parliamentary sovereignty, Indian

---

of law, which are enforceable by the courts in the same way as other legal principles. In giving them effect, the courts have the responsibility of upholding the values and principles of our constitution and making them effective. It is their particular responsibility to determine the legal limits of the powers conferred on each branch of government, and to decide whether any exercise of power has transgressed those limits." See R (on the application of Miller) (Appellant) v The Prime Minister (Respondent) Cherry and others (Respondents) v Advocate General for Scotland (Appellant) (Scotland), [2019] UKSC 41, para. 39.

92 Aharon Barak, 'The Declaration of Independence and the Constituent Assembly' (2018) 11 Hukim – Journal on Legislation 9 (Hebrew).

93 See, for example, *Kesavananda Bharati v. State of Kerala*, AIR 1973 SC 1461, para. 620: "The basic structure of the Constitution is not a vague concept and the apprehensions ... that neither the citizen nor the Parliament would be able to understand it are unfounded. If the historical background, the Preamble, the entire scheme of the Constitution, the relevant provisions thereof including Article 368 are kept in mind there can be no difficulty in discerning [what] ... can be regarded as the basic elements of the constitutional structure." On the role of preambles in the unconstitutional constitutional amendment doctrine, see Roznai (n 1), 219.

94 On the constitutional roles of preambles in general, see Liav Orgad, 'The Preamble in Constitutional Interpretation' (2010) 8 International Journal of Constitutional Law 714.

jurisprudence shifted to a notion of a limited amendment power.[95] But we have much to learn from other Asian countries, and from the Global South more generally, as in many aspects, the Israeli constitutional order resembles jurisdictions in the Global South rather than the Global North.[96]

In the institutional conditions of Israel, as I have argued with Suzie Navot, implied limitations on constituent power are essential. Where the overly flexible legislative process is controlled by the government, and without a rigid constitution or political checks and balances, the only real balancing authority to the power of the majority is the Supreme Court. In Israel, the legislature holds a dual authority – legislative power and constituent power, with no procedural distinction. A Basic Law can be enacted without time delays and through an ordinary majority. And the Government de-facto controls the legislative process by strong coalition discipline. This composition causes the mingling of longer-term issues of constitutional planning with short-term interests of political power and raises the risk of misusing constituent power for short-term political interest or convenience. With a single chamber in the legislature, and the lack of procedural restrictions, the authority of the court to review basic laws is a central part of its ability to protect fundamental rights or the constitutional order.[97]

This leads us to the next section, in which I aim to argue that there are some institutional features that can explain why the basic structure doctrine developed in the Asian countries: features that are also applicable to the Israeli case.

15.4 Institutional explanations

Unamendability is a mechanism that aims to provide a block on legislative constitutional change mechanisms. It aims to protect against undermining the fundamental principles of the constitutional order and guard against abuse of power by the constituent power. However, the need to have this "lock on the door" should be analyzed in context and in light of other institutional and social factors. There are many such institutional features, but I shall highlight four factors that are crucial to my mind for understanding why BSD was developed in various cases and denied in others.

---

95 See Shivprasad Swaminathan, 'The Long Slumber of Dicey's Indian Monarch' (2016) 42(2) Commonwealth Law Bulletin 212.
96 In the Israeli judiciary as well as academia, Asian systems receive minor attention when conducting comparative analyses in public law, where the focus in mainly on the United States and Canada. See Margit Cohn, 'Comparative Public Law Research in Israel: A Gaze Westwards' (2019) 14 Asian Journal of Comparative Law 11–27.
97 Suzie Navot and Yaniv Roznai, 'From Supra-Constitutional Principles to the Misuse of Constituent Power in Israel' (2019) 21(3) European Journal of Law Reform 403.

15.4.1 Flexibility of the amendment process

Generally, the more difficult the amendment process is, the less there is a need for a doctrine of implied limits. The design itself provides various mechanisms of checks and balances on the amendment power. If the amendment process contains many complications, is time-consuming and includes temporal limitations, inclusive of various different bodies, or includes explicit unamendable provisions, there is less need for judicially created implied limitations. As Tomáš Ľalík writes concerning the Slovak Constitutional Court decision on unconstitutional constitutional amendments:

> It is very easy to amend the Slovak Constitution ... In the judgment ... the Constitutional Court recognised that flexibility was a problem when it noted that the existence of a substantive core meant that the Constitution was no longer helpless against the forces of a qualified majority of MPs and the possible misuse of the power to amend the Constitution. A victory in parliamentary elections was not tantamount to a coup d'état ... The discovery of a substantive core – the internal hierarchy within the text of the Constitution – shielded from constitutional amendment by the Constitutional Court, has augmented the rigidity of the text.[98]

This judicial protection of implied limitations, such as the BSD, becomes increasingly required in flexible constitutions that can be amended fairly easily. So, as HP Lee and Yvonne Tew show in Malaysia, the two-thirds majority required for constitutional amendments posed no constraint on the exercise of the power to amend the Constitution and the Constitution has been extensively amended.[99] And, as Tonsakulrungruang summarizes regarding Thailand, "the 2007 Constitution set a low bar for amending it but, through a series of decisions, the Constitutional Court significantly raised that bar," by creating a procedural distinction between constitutional amendment and constitutional replacement – the latter requiring a different and more inclusive and demanding process, and by creating implicit unamendability thereby making the amendment procedure extremely rigid through its judicial decisions.[100] As Landau and Bilchitz remark, "courts working in systems with flexible amendment rules but in contexts where there are powerful and unrestrained executives or political forces may feel pressure to police the use of the constitutional amendment rule itself."[101]

---

98 Tomáš Ľalík, 'The Slovak Constitutional Court on Unconstitutional Constitutional Amendment (PL. ÚS 21/2014)' (2020) 16(2) European Constitutional Law Review 328–43.
99 HP Lee and Yvonne Tew, Chapter 5 in this volume.
100 Tonsakulrungruang (n 41).
101 David Landau and David Bilchitz, 'The Evolution of the Separation of Powers in the Global South and Global North', in David Bilchitz and David Landau (eds.), *The Evolution of the Separation of Powers: Between the Global North and the Global North* (Cheltenham 2018) 1, 6.

The doctrine of unconstitutional constitutional amendments makes the amendment process more rigid and corrects, in a way, the problem of over-flexibility.

15.4.2 Party or executive dominance

Related to amendment flexibility is the question of party or executive dominance. Having a rigid two-thirds majority requirement for amendment is not of much use when the legislature is controlled by one party. For example, many African countries are ruled by dominant parties which have more than two-thirds of the seats in parliament. In such cases, the two-thirds majority requirement for amendments is not a major obstacle to amending the constitution. For example, in the 2005 Tanzanian elections, the ruling party occupied 77.8% of parliament's seats, easily overcoming the two-thirds requirement, which makes the Tanzanian Constitution very flexible in practice.[102]

When one party or the executive controls the amendment process, there is a heightened risk of abuse of the amendment process. Multiple parties or a weak executive are politically checked so there is less need for judicial involvement. And so, Lee and Tew write about Malaysia: "From independence in 1957 to 2018, the same ruling coalition ... had continuously dominated the political landscape for close to six decades."[103] This control over more than two-thirds of parliamentary seats, they elaborate, allowed for the constitutional amendment process to be utilized by the government and the ruling party to "maintain and increase its grip on power."[104] Even though the Federal Court in Malaysia in those years did not invalidate formal amendments, it "arguably left the door open to the possibility of future adoption [of the basic structure doctrine]."[105] And in Taiwan, as Yeh explains, one can explain the different approach of the court in JY Interpretation No. 499, in which an amendment was invalidated, and in JY Interpretation No. 721, which upheld an amendment, as follows. The former was an institutional check on the "notorious National Assembly" that had a monopoly and "could hardly be controlled by the mechanism of checks and balances,"[106] while in the latter case, the amendment was enacted also by the Legislative Yuan and passed through a more democratic and decentralized process.[107]

---

102 Charles M Fombad, 'Some Perspectives on Durability and Change under Modern African Constitutions' (2013) 11 International Journal of Constitutional Law 382, 403–4.
103 Lee and Tew (n 63).
104 ibid.; see also HP Lee, Richard Foo, and Amber Tan, 'Constitutional Change in Malaysia' (2019) 14(1) Journal of Comparative Law 119, 138.
105 Jaclyn Neo, 'Beyond Mortals? Constitutional Identity, Judicial Power, and the Evolution of the Basic Structure Doctrine in Malaysia' (2020) 15 Asian Journal of Comparative Law 69, 84.
106 Yeh (n 33).
107 Yeh (n 33).

15.4.3 Political-democratic-amendment culture

Years ago, Benjamin Akzin wrote that

> Among the countries which have whole-heartedly endeavoured to conform to the pattern of constitutionalism, there are two that have hitherto adhered to the British system and have not introduced a formal Constitution in the full sense of the word – New Zealand and Israel, though in the latter country the debate is still continuing. Possibly the British solution may suit New Zealand. For Israel, with its rather supercharged political climate, this writer would certainly recommend the added restraint of a formal Constitution.[108]

When the culture is that of "it's not done" – certain political actions are unthinkable and no one attempts to undermine the basic rules of the game – unamendability is less required. As Gert Jan Geertjes and Jefri Uzman showed, in politically enforced constitutions such as the UK or the Netherlands, there is a sense of "covert unamendability" according to which there is a constitutional convention, which may be enforced through disobedience of governmental branches, that certain constitutional arrangements shall not be abolished or significantly altered.[109]

When there is no stable political-democratic culture that respects the rules of the game, an external arbitrator – in the form of the judiciary – is important. I therefore agree with Silvia Suteu that unamendability is especially needed and

> most often found ... in contexts where democracy is new, fragile, and contested that the "lock on the door" function of unamendability – whether enshrined in an eternity clause or a basic structure doctrine – becomes most salient. It is precisely in hybrid or contested democratic contexts that unamendability is paradoxically most needed and most prone to abuse.[110]

In this respect, amendment culture is important. The rigid or flexible dimension usually focuses on the amendment procedure. Political scientists have attempted to measure constitutional rigidity by focusing on amendment rates and amendment procedures and hurdles.[111] Yet what may matter even more to the rigid-

---

108 Benjamin Akzin, 'The Place of the Constitution in the Modern State' 2(1) Israel LR (1967) 1, 8.
109 Gert Jan Geertjes and Jefri Uzman, 'Conventions of Unamendability; Unamendable Constitutional Law in (Two) Politically Enforced Constitutions' in Richard Albert and Bertil Emrah Oder (eds.), *An Unamendable Constitution? Unamendability in Constitutional Democracies* (Springer 2018) 89.
110 Silvia Suteu, Chapter 14 this volume.
111 See, for example, Arend Lijphart, *Patterns of Democracy* (2nd ed, Yale University Press 2010); Astrid Lorenz, 'How to Measure Constitutional Rigidity—Four Concepts and Two Alternatives' (2005) 17 Journal of Theoretical Politics 339; Donald S Lutz, 'Toward a Theory of Constitutional Amendment' (1994) 88 American Political Science Review 355.

ity or flexibility of a constitution than voting thresholds or temporal limits is the amendment culture in a constitutional tradition, meaning "the set of shared attitudes about the desirability of amendment, independent of the substantive issue under consideration and the degree of pressure for change."[112] In other words, constitutional rigidity is not merely institutional but also attitudinal and factual.[113] Take for example the UK which is considered a flexible constitution in light of the amendment procedure. Arguably, it is in fact a rigid constitution, and its rigidity stems from the constitutional culture, which obliges actors to show self-restraint in handling constitutional matters.[114] In Israel, for example, the amendment culture is not restrictive at all. In 2020 alone, 9 amendments to the basic laws were made and since 2013, 28 amendments have been made to the basic laws and 3 more new basic laws were enacted. In other words, Israel in recent years has had more constitutional changes than throughout the history of the US Constitution. Basic laws are sometimes amended in a day and a half. Many of the amendments are temporary and for specific circumstances.[115] In this context, implied limitations on the constituent authority to avoid misuse of powers seem almost inevitable.

15.4.4 *The existence or absence of effective supra-national institutions*

Finally, when a country is part of a strong regional mechanism, in which there are various political and legal machineries to ensure basic rules and values are respected, there is less of a need for a judicial development of a BSD as the various political actors are restrained in advance – a kind of a "chilling effect" – in trying to undermine constitutional fundamentals. Richard Albert thus correctly claims

> where a country is a member of an international organization that has a charter of rules or practices, there may also be an adjudicatory body responsible for enforcing those rules and practices. In the case of a signatory country amending its constitution in violation of this international charter,

---

112 Tom Ginsburg and James Melton, 'Does the Constitutional Amendment Rule Matter at All? Amendment Cultures and the Challenges of Measuring Amendment Difficulty' (2015) 13 International Journal of Constitutional Law 686, 699.
113 Xenophon Contiades and Alkmene Fotiadou, 'Models of Constitutional Change' in Xenophon Contiades (ed.), *Engineering Constitutional Change: A Comparative Perspective on Europe, Canada and the USA* (Routledge 2013) 417, 458–9.
114 Xenophon Contiades and Alkmene Fotiadou, 'The Determinants of Constitutional Amendability: Amendment Models or Amendment Culture?' (2016) 12 European Constitutional LR192.
115 See, for example, Nadav Dishon, 'Temporary Constitutional Amendments as a Means to Undermine the Democratic Order – Insights from the Israeli Experience' (2018) 51 Israel LR 389.

the adjudicatory body could find the amendment in conflict and therefore incompatible.[116]

Indeed, in various cases in Europe, America, and Africa, supra-national tribunals have held that they have the authority to review constitutional norms, and have even declared constitutional provisions as unconventional, in the sense that they violate international obligations and should be changed. And of course, supra-national organizations are increasingly involved in issues such as domestic constitutional change.[117] Such supra-national organizations and mechanisms provide another layer of protection and check on governmental powers, including on the constituent power.[118] In the absence of such supra-national observations and scrutiny, the need for domestic supervision is strengthened.

15.5 Conclusion

Various theories can explain the constitutional politics behind the adoption of unconstitutional constitutional amendment doctrines: the will to protect higher law, the aim to correct flaws in the political process and to enhance democracy, the will to make sure certain policies or ideologies are preserved by the judiciary, or the will of hegemons to preserve their powers. These can be mutually reinforcing theories behind judicial involvement in the amending process.

Of course, strategic theories are not enough. One must consider also the institutional and social context. When other rigid mechanisms of checks and balances and distribution of amending power exist, there will be less need for judicial intervention. I have listed four factors that influence the need to adopt judicial supervision of constitutional amendments in a given society: flexibility or rigidity of the amending process, party or executive dominance, the political-democratic-amendment culture, and the existence or absence of effective supra-national institutions.

If, as Surya Deva claims, the basic structure doctrine should be regarded as "a wider system of checks and balances in times with serious democratic deficits in all institutions of governance,"[119] then when analyzing its development, one should

---

116 Richard Albert, Chapter 12 in this volume.
117 See, for example, Stephan J Schnably, 'Emerging International Law Constraints on Constitutional Structure and Revision: A Preliminary Appraisal' (2007–8) 62 University of Miami LR 417, 422; David E Landau, 'Democratic Erosion and Constitution-Making Moments: The Role of International Law' (2017) 2 UC Irvine Journal of International, Transnational, and Comparative Law 87, 100–5; Tilmann Altwicker, 'Convention Rights as Minimum Constitutional Guarantees? The Conflict between Domestic Constitutional Law and the European Convention of Human Rights', in Armin von Bogdandy and Pál Sonnevend (eds.), *Constitutional Crisis in the European Constitutional Area Theory, Law and Politics in Hungary and Romania* (Hart 2015) chapter 13.
118 Yaniv Roznai, 'The Theory and Practice of "Supra-Constitutional" Limits on Constitutional Amendments' (2013) 62 International and Comparative Law Quarterly 557.
119 Deva (n 24).

also take into consideration other institutional vices that create veto points, checks and balances, or distribution of powers. He notes that in India, "Modi has accomplished a highly centralised and opaque model of decision making with almost no effective checks on powers from any source (internal or external to the executive)," and that in "such a scenario, the doctrine of basic structure should be relevant in controlling the propensity of the government to destroy the core constitutional values embodied in Indian Constitution."[120]

In light of Deva's approach, and returning to Israel, it is important to note that especially in the Israeli system of government, when basic laws are easily amended, where the legislature is composed of a single chamber, with government dominance in the legislation, there is a greater fear for abuse of constituent authority by the Knesset and an increasing justification for judicial review to impose limits.

---

120 ibid.

Index

Abe, S. 9, 23, 34, 36–37, 38, 45
Abeyratne, R. 202, 270, 282
Abhisit, V. 176
absolute constitution 47, 63
abstract review 23; *see also* judicial review
abusive constitutionalism 169, 182–185, 248, 258
Adhikari, B. 142, 143
Ahmed, K. 122, 128, 129
Akzin, B. 293
Albert, R. 5, 7, 13, 15, 68, 69, 80, 195, 294
Ali, Z. 95, 97
al-Mahmood, A. 114, 115
ameen 10, 111, 115, 125–127, 130, 132
amendment(s) 4, 102, 111, 252, 275–276; "benign constitutional violation" and 61–62; codified unamendability 238–239; to the Constitution of Bangladesh 211; under the Constitution of India 113–114; to the Constitution of Pakistan 115–116, 123, 124; under the Constitution of Thailand (2007) 172–173; constitutional treatment of in Nepal 140; deliberation ceiling/floor 237–238; under the Federal Constitution of Malaysia 88, 89–90, 91, 92, 93, 94, 105–108; under the "five power" constitutional system 52–53; flexibility of 291–292; formal 52, 189; *guoti* and 61, 64–65, 66; incremental model of 157, 159–162; informal 190, 191; interpretive unamendability 239–240; judicial nullification 231, 232, 233, 234; judicial power and 91–92; judicial review 87; of Malaysia's Land Acquisition Act 94–95; National Assembly and 160–161; under the People's Republic of China constitutional system 56, 60–61, 62, 63–64; procedural irregularity and 234–235; Provisional Constitution of the Republic of China (1912) 50, 51; public oversight 154; public scrutiny of 167; public sentiment towards 162; replacement and 169, 177, 181, 185, 187–188; royal assent and 106–108; self-interest of the ruling party and 211–212; subject-rule mismatch 235–237; supranational constitutional restrictions 241; temporal limitations 237–238; Thailand's constitutional drafting council (2012) 176–178; tiering 5–6, 253
Arato, A. 133
Armitage, R. 32
Article 96 Association 37
Aryal, O. P. 146
Aso, T. 37
Association of Scholars Opposed to the Security-Related Bills 42
Austin, G. 197
Awami League (AL) 20

Bangladesh 11, 12, 13, 18–19, 240; abolition of the caretaker government 219–224; basic structure doctrine (BSD) 210; Islam as state religion 218–219; non-party caretaker government (NPCTG) system 20, 212, 219, 220, 227; politics of unconstitutional amendment 212–214
Barak, A. 286, 288, 289

298 Index

basic structure doctrine (BSD) 10,
    12, 13, 16, 17, 19, 20, 87, 88, 91,
    92, 99–100, 109, 111, 112, 113,
    121–122, 123, 127, 130–131, 131,
    135, 140, 153, 190, 191, 209, 240,
    268, 269, 275, 283; applicability of
    244, 247; in Bangladesh 210–212;
    comparative law and 250–252;
    "contingent" view of 244–245, 246,
    248, 251; democracy and 196–198;
    governmental structure and 251–252;
    in India 194–198, 269–272; *Indira
    Gandhi Mutho v Pengarah Jabatan
    Agama Islam Perak and Others*
    97–99; informal amendment and
    203–208; Islam and 114–115; in
    Israel 285–288; *Kesavananda Bharati
    Sripadagalvaru v State of Kerala*
    245–248; *Maria Chin Abdullah v.
    Director-General of Immigration* 100–
    103; "necessary" view of 244; royal
    assent and 106–108; *Semenyih Jaya
    Sdn Bhd v Pentadbir Tanah Daerah
    Hulu Langat* 94–99; in Singapore
    248–250; uncodified constitutions
    and 254–256; *see also* institutional
    explanations for the development
    of BSD
"benign constitutional violation" 61–62
Beshara, C. J. 204–205
Bhatia, G. 206
Bhutto, B. 119, 124
Bilchitz, D. 291
Bluntschi, J. C. 48
Brazil 5, 234
Bùi, N. S. 9, 242
Bush, G. W. 33

cases: *Abdul Haque* 217; *Alma Nudo
    Atenza v Public Prosecutor* 10, 88,
    99–100, 104; *ami Ullah Baloch
    v Abdul Karim Nowsherwani*
    126; *Anwar Hossain Chowdhury
    v Bangladesh* 12, 210–211, 216,
    217, 218, 282–283; *Bangladesh v.
    Asaduzzaman Siddiqui* 283; *Bank
    of Oman Ltd v East Trading Co.
    Ltd.* 124; *District Bar Association
    Rawalpindi v Federation of Pakistan*
    111–112, 117, 120–122, 123,
    127, 131; *Fazlul Quader Chowdhry
    v Muhammad Abdul Haque* 113,
    113n7; *Federation of Pakistan v
    United Sugar Mills* 117; *First Judges*
    199, 200; *Fourth Judges* 7, 19, 194,
    201–202, 269–272; *Golak Nath
    v State of Punjab* 195–196; *The
    Government of the State of Kelantan
    v The Government of Malaya and
    Tunku Abdul Rahman Putra Al-Haj*
    91; *Hakim Khan v Government
    of Pakistan* 124, 125; *I.C. Golak
    Nath v State of Punjab* 113; *Imran
    Ahmed Khan Niazi* 126, 127; *Indira
    Gandhi Mutho v Pengarah Jabatan
    Agama Islam Perak and Others* 10,
    88, 97–99, 104, 109, 283; *Indira
    Nehru Gandhi v Raj Narain* 196;
    Irshad H. Khan v Parveen Ijaz 124;
    *Islamic Republic of Pakistan v Abdul
    Wali Khan* 117; *Kesavananda
    Bharati Sripadagalvaru v State of
    Kerala* 4, 12, 98, 113–114, 195,
    196, 198, 245–248, 249, 274–275,
    286; *Kuldip Nayar v Union of India*
    204; *Loh Kooi Choon v Government
    of Malaysia* 91; *M Saleem Ullah v
    Bangladesh* 220; *Mahmood Khan
    Achakzai v Federation of Pakistan*
    124–125; *Maria Chin* 10; *Maria
    Chin Abdullah v. Director-General
    of Immigration* 100–103, 104, 110;
    Minerva Mills Ltd v Union of India
    98, 116, 240; *Muhammad Abdul
    Haque v Fazlul Quader Chowdhury*
    213, 214; *Nadeem Ahmed v
    Federation of Pakistan* 112, 117;
    Phang Chin Hock v Public Prosecutor
    91; *Public Prosecutor v Dato' Yap
    Peng* 92; *Public Prosecutor v. Kok
    Wah Kuan* 93–94; *Qi Yuling* 59–60;
    Sajjan Singh v State of Rajasthan
    196; *Sami Ullah Baloch* 126–127;
    Sankari Prasad v Union of India 196;
    Second Judges 199, 200; *Semenyih
    Jaya Sdn Bhd v Pentadbir Tanah
    Daerah Hulu Langat* 10, 88, 94–99,
    97, 109; *Shankari Prasad v Union of
    India* 113, 114, 115; *Siravasa Rasiah*
    96; *Sunagawa* 27; *Supreme Court
    Advocates on Record Association v
    Union of India* 191, 193–194, 282;
    Third Judges 200, 202–203; *Zia-ur-
    Rahman v The State* 116–117
Chandrachud, C. 202
Chaudhry, I. M. 119, 120, 129

Chen, D. 62, 63, 64
China 8, 15, 45; "5-5" Constitution draft 52–53; Constitutional Outline by Imperial Order (1908) 48–49; *guoti* 9, 15; "New Democracy" 54; *see also guoti*; People's Republic of China (PRC)
Chinese People's Political Consultative Conference (CPPCC) 54–55
Choudhry, S. 208
codified unamendability 13, 238–239; *see also* judicial nullification
Cold War, Article 9 controversy during 25–28
collective self-defense 32, 36, 38, 39, 40, 41, 42, 43, 44
Colombia 7, 271
comparative law, basic structure doctrine (BSD) and 250–252
concrete review 23; *see also* judicial review
Constituent Assembly of Nepal 133
constituent power 4, 11, 14, 133, 169, 170, 181–182, 263; in Israel 288–290; judicial nullification and 233; *see also* democracy
constituted power 4, 233
Constitution of Bangladesh: 4th Amendment 215; 8th Amendment 210–211, 214–219; eternity clause in 225–226
Constitution of Brazil, Article 39 234–235
Constitution of Germany, Article 79(3) 3
Constitution of India 245–248; amendability of 189–190; Article 124 200; Article 368 113, 189, 189n2, 190; Article 370 19, 191, 205–206, 207, 208; Forty-Second Amendment 116; judicial review 113–114; Preamble 192; Twenty-Fourth Amendment 113
Constitution of Japan: Article 9 23, 24–25, 26–28, 29, 31, 32, 33, 34, 35, 36–37, 40, 44; Article 20 34; Article 96 26, 37
Constitution of Myanmar (2008) 253–254
Constitution of Nepal (1990) 136, 137, 281
Constitution of Nepal (2015) 13, 17, 17–18, 146, 148, 272; Article 274(1) 277; eternity clause 140, 265–268; *see also* Interim Constitution of Nepal (2007)
Constitution of Pakistan 214; Article 62(1)(f) 10, 111, 115, 126–127, 128–130; Article 175A 112, 121–122; Article 368(5) 116; Eighteenth Amendment 120; Eighth Amendment 115, 116, 118–119; Islam and 112; Islamic provisions 114–115, 127–130; judicial independence 112; Nineteenth Amendment 112, 122; Objectives Resolution 114–115, 118; Principles of Policy 114; Seventeenth Amendment 119; Thirteenth Amendment 119; Twenty-First Amendment 121
Constitution of South Africa 236
Constitution of Thailand (1997) 170–171, 175–176
Constitution of Thailand (2007) 12, 170, 171–173, 179, 180–181, 185, 264, 291
Constitution of Thailand (2017) 260
Constitution of the People's Republic of China (1954) 55; Preamble 55–56
Constitution of the People's Republic of China (1975) 56–57; "Four Big Freedoms" 57
Constitution of the People's Republic of China (1978) 57
Constitution of the People's Republic of China (1982) 58; amendment of 60–61, 62, 63–64; Article 1 59; Article 5 59; Article 11 58–59; Article 57 58; Article 62 58; Article 64 60
Constitution of the Republic of China (1946) 154, 154n3; Article 1 156; Article 27 158; "Fundamental National Policies" 53–54
Constitution of the Republic of Singapore 248–249
Constitution of the United States, Ninth Amendment 76
Constitution of Vietnam (2013) 9, 70, 71–72, 81, 82; amendment process 67; Article 3 76; Article 4 78–79; Article 12 75; Article 14 75–76; Hoàng's account of its unconstitutionality 73–75; human rights and 75–76; international law and 82; land ownership and 77–78; Objectives Resolution 124;

popular sovereignty and 78–80; as unconstitutional 69–70
Constitutional Court of Taiwan 168; J.Y. Interpretation No. 314 161; J.Y. Interpretation No. 342 161; J.Y. Interpretation No. 499 153, 155–156, 161–162; J.Y. Interpretation No. 721 167; political retaliation against 162–163; politicization of 163–164; popular sovereignty and 165–166
Constitutional Democracy Association (CDA) 39–40, 41
constitutional monarchy 47, 48, 51, 89; royal assent and 106–108; *see also* Japan; Malaysia; Thailand
Constitutional Outline by Imperial Order (1908) 48–49
constitutional politics 7, 133, 191, 257, 295; basic structure doctrine (BSD) and 192–198; in Malaysia 87, 108–109; Thailand 260; UCA as 14–20; unamendability 134
constitutional republic 51
constitutional supremacy, in Nepal 136–138, 148–149
constitutionalism 13, 17, 19, 42, 63, 87, 174, 175, 226, 244; abusive 169, 182–185, 248, 258; civic 165; in Japan 23–25; liberal 68, 81; popular 165; Thai 255–256; unconstitutional constitutions and 81–82
constitution-making process 245, 249, 256, 263, 272; bargaining dynamics of 259–260; Constituent Assembly of Nepal and 133; first Constituent Assembly of Nepal (CA1) 139; High Level Political Committee (HLPC) 139; post-conflict 260, 264; *see also* first Constituent Assembly of Nepal (CA1); second Constituent Assembly of Nepal (CA2)
constitutions 210; absolute 47, 63; amendment power 4–5; constituent power 4, 11; entrenchment 255, 256; essential features 113, 122–123, 124–125, 129; eternity clauses 3, 6, 13, 140, 149, 257, 272; interpretations 52–53; post-conflict 260, 262; relative 47; uncodified 254–256; unconstitutional 9, 241–242; *see also* amendment(s); basic structure doctrine (BSD); unamendability

constructive unamendability 15, 80
"contingent" view of BSD 244–245, 246, 248, 251
Corwin, E. 13, 274–276, 275
Cultural Revolution 56

Dam, T. S. 70–71
decisive model 11–12; *see also* Bangladesh; India; Taiwan; Thailand
deliberation ceiling/floor 237
democracy 13, 18–19, 112, 136, 179, 215; in Bangladesh 219, 225; basic structure doctrine (BSD) and 196–198, 244; judicial nullification and 232; Taisho 24; Thai-style 170, 173–174, 175, 182, 261
Democratic Party of Japan (DPJ) 31, 34, 35, 36
Deng, X. 57, 61
denotive model 10, 16, 135; *see also* Malaysia; Nepal; Pakistan
Deva, S. 12, 19, 239, 270, 295, 296
Dhungel, S. 141
dictatorship of the proletariat 56, 62
discursive model 8–9, 15, 16; *see also* China; Japan; Vietnam
Dixon, R. 6, 69, 82
doctrine of necessity 134, 141, 142, 145

Ecuador 236
Ely, J. H. 13; *Democracy and Distrust* 278
emergency powers, Malaysia and 105–108
Ershad, H. M. 215
eternity clause(s) 3, 6, 13, 15, 135, 153, 226, 257, 258, 259, 263, 272; in the Constitution of Bangladesh 225–226; in the Constitution of Nepal (2015) 140, 265–268; in the Constitution of Thailand (2017) 261–262
exclusionary unamendability 258
explanatory theories of unconstitutional constitutional amendments: Corwin's higher law 276–278; Ely's democracy and distrust 278–280; Ginsburg's political and policy insurance 280–281; Hirschl's hegemonic preservation 282–284

fazhi 60–61
Federal Constitution of Malaysia: amendment process 88, 89–90;

Article 4(1) 89, 96; Article 121(1) 88, 92, 93, 94–95, 98, 104; Article 150 105–106; Article 159 89; basic structure doctrine (BSD) and 94–99; Immigration Act 100; judicial review 97, 98, 103–104; royal assent as feature of 106–108
federalism 251, 252; in Nepal 266–267
first Constituent Assembly (CA1) 133, 134, 135, 138, 139, 150; aftermath of its dissolution 146–149; litigation over the dissolution of 140–146
formal amendment 52, 189; judicial appointments and 199–203

Gandhi, I. 97, 198
Gao, Q. 49, 62
Gardbaum, S. 260
Geertjes, G. 293
Germany 72, 253, 277
Ginsburg, T. 13, 172, 175, 280–281
Guidelines for US–Japan Defense Cooperation 32
Gulf War 28, 29
guoti 9, 15, 46, 47, 48–49, 51, 52, 65, 65n100, 66, 240, 277; Mao on 54; under the People's Republic of China constitutional system 64; in the PRC 59, 62, 63
Gyawali, C. K. 146

Hamid, A. 93
Harding, A. 13, 108, 288
Hasebe, Y. 42
Hatoyama, I. 25
Hayut, E. 287
hegemonic preservation theory 282
Higuchi, Y. 37
Hirschl, R. 13, 282
Hoàng, X. P. 9, 67, 68, 69–70, 80, 83; account of an unconstitutional constitution 73–75, 81, 82; constitutional writings 71–73; on human rights 75–76; on land ownership 77–78
Honduras 69, 82, 265
Hoque, R. 12, 13, 20, 246
Hosokawa, M. 29
Hossain, K. 216–217
Hua, G. 57
Huang, D. 279
human rights 25–26, 70, 72, 74, 83; under the Constitution of Vietnam

Index 301

(2013) 75–76; unconstitutional constitutions and 69

implicit unamendability 274–275
incremental model of constitutional reform 157, 159–162
India 6, 8, 10, 12, 18–19, 19, 111, 113, 135, 136, 231, 240; basic structure doctrine (BSD) 194–198; informal amendment 203–208; Jammu and Kashmir Reorganisation Act (2019) 191; judicial appointments 7, 199–203; judicial independence 269; National Judicial Appointment Commission (NJAC) 191, 194, 201, 203, 269–271; politics of legitimacy 192, 193, 194, 203; politics of supremacy 192–193, 194; President's Orders 206–207; unamendable judicial supremacy in judicial appointments 268–272
informal amendment 9, 23, 24–25, 44, 52, 190, 191, 203–208
institutional explanations for the development of BSD: existence or absence of effective supra-national institutions 294–295; flexibility of the amendment process 291–292; party or executive dominance 292; political-democratic-amendment culture 293–294
Interim Constitution of Nepal (2007) 17, 134, 135, 140, 149; 8th Amendment 141; Article 64 139, 144; Preamble 144
international law, unconstitutional constitutions and 82
interpretive unamendability 13, 239–240; *see also* judicial nullification
Islam 217, 251; *ameen* 115, 125–127, 130, 132; basic structure doctrine (BSD) and 114–115; Constitution of Pakistan and 112, 114, 116–117, 119–120; as essential feature of the Constitution of Pakistan 122–123, 129–130; as state religion of Bangladesh 218–219; *see also ameen*
Israel 276, 294, 296; Basic Law 284, 285; basic structure doctrine (BSD) 285–288; constituent power 288–289, 291; Declaration of Independence 289

Jangam, B. 144
Japan 8, 9, 15, 16; Basic Law on Education 34; Cabinet Legislation Bureau 24, 27, 29, 35, 36, 38, 41, 43; collective self-defense 32, 36, 38, 39, 40–42, 43; constitution reform debate 28–32; constitutionalism in 23–25; Counter-Terrorism Special Measures Law (2001) 33; Liberal Democratic Party (LDP) 27–28, 29, 30; National Security Council (NSC) 38, 41; Peacekeeping Operation (PKO) Law (1992) 28; Protection of the People Law (2004) 33; Self-Defense Force (SDF) 26, 32, 36; US-dependent security normalization 32–35
Japan Federation of Bar Associations (JFBA) 43
Jaran, P. 178
Jellinek, G. 52
Jiang, Z. 61
judicial activism 17, 44, 130, 134, 135, 140, 149, 150, 182–185, 193, 283, 285; of Taiwan's Constitutional Court 157–160
judicial appointments 120–122; in India 199–203, 268–272
judicial independence 18, 116, 199, 211, 217, 282; Indian 269–272; of the Supreme Court of Pakistan 112
Judicial Interpretation No. 499 11–12
judicial nullification 13, 231, 232, 234, 243; codified unamendability 238–239; constituent power and 233; democracy and 232; as "extraordinary" power 234; interpretive unamendability 239–240; procedural irregularity 234–235; subject-rule mismatch 235–237; supranational constitutional restrictions 241; temporal limitations 237–238
judicial reasoning on unconstitutionality 155
judicial review 15, 16, 18, 24, 87, 88, 97, 98, 99, 100, 110, 153, 154, 278, 278, 280–281; abstract 23; abusive 258; concrete 23; of the Constitution of India 113–114; of the Federal Constitution of Malaysia 100–102, 103–104, 105–106; Islam and 115, 116–117

Junejo, M. K. 119
J.Y. Interpretation No. 499 153, 164, 168, 278–279; judicial reasoning on unconstitutionality 155–156; popular sovereignty and 164–165, 166

Kamal, M. 216
Karki, S. 147
Kay, R. 277
Khan, G. I. 119
Khan, I. 130
Khwaja, J. S. 123
Kishi, N. 25, 28
Kobayashi, S. 37, 42
Koirala, S. 147
Koizume, J. 33, 34
kokutai 47–48
Komatsu, I. 38
Kramer, L. 165
Krishnaswamy, S. 197, 204

Laband, P. 52
L'alík, T. 291
land ownership, under the Constitution of Vietnam (2013) 77–78
Landau, D. 6, 7, 69, 82, 169, 248, 291
Lee, H. P. 10, 240, 283, 291, 292
Lee, T. 159
legal unamendability 80
Leghari, F. 119, 124
legitimacy: of the NPCTG system 222–223; politics of 12, 12, 190, 192, 194, 203
Li, N. 279
Liang, Q. 51
liberal constitutionalism 81
Liberal Democratic Party (LDP) 27–28, 29, 32, 34, 45; "new manifesto" 30
Lim, M. 101
locus standi 137

Maimun, T. 101
Malagodi, M. 11, 18, 242, 281
Malanjum, R. 10, 93, 95
Malaysia 8, 10, 16, 88; *Barisan Nasional* coalition 87, 90, 106–109; basic structure doctrine (BSD) in 94–99, 100–108, 247; constitutional politics in 87, 108–109; emergency powers 105–108; judicial power 91–92; Land Acquisition Act (1960) 94–95; Malaysia Act (1963) 91; National Security Council Act (2016)

106–107, 108; *Pakatan Harapan* coalition 109; Perikatan Nasional coalition 90, 105; Reid Commission 89; separation of powers 95–96, 97–99; *see also* Federal Constitution of Malaysia
Mao, Z. 57, 59, 62; on *guoti* 54
Masud, K. 128
Masuzoe, Y. 36
McElwain, K. M. 26
Mehta, P. B. 205
Meiji Constitution 24, 25; *see also* Constitution of Japan; Japan
Mitchell, R. 9, 277
Modi, N. 12, 19, 193, 198
Mohamad, M. 92
Mortarti, C. 277–278
Musharraf, P. 17, 119
Myanmar 236

Nakano, K. 9
Nariman, F. 197, 198, 208
National Council of Peace and Order (NCPO) 186–187
Navot, S. 290
"necessary" view of BSD 244–245
Nelson, M. 10, 11, 17, 240, 246, 251, 283
Nepal 10, 11, 13, 17–18, 133, 134, 138–139; basic structure doctrine (BSD) 140; constitutional supremacy in 136–138, 148–149; constitutional treatment of amendments 140; ethnic groups 137n10; federalism 266–267; High Level Political Committee (HLPC) 139; litigation over the dissolution of the CA1 140–146; People's War 136–137, 138; post-conflict constitution making 138–139, 149–150; pro-democracy movement 136; public interest litigation (PIL) 137, 144; unamendability of constitutional nationalism 263–268; *see also* first Constituent Assembly (CA1)
Neupane, B. 144
"New Democracy" 54
Ngo, B. C. 70–71
non-partisan caretaker government (NPCTG) 20
Nye, J. 32

Oder, B. E. 195
Ozawa, I. 28, 29, 35, 36, 38

pacifism 24; Article 9 of the Constitution of Japan and 25–28
Pakistan 10, 11, 16, 17, 111, 114, 213; judicial appointments 112, 120–122; *see also* Constitution of Pakistan
Pakistan Muslim League (PML-N) 119, 120, 127
Pakistan People's Party (PPP) 119, 120, 127
Pang, Y. 62
Peng, Z. 59, 62
People's Republic of China (PRC): "Anti-Rightist Movement" 56; Common Program 55; Cultural Revolution 56; dictatorship of the proletariat 56, 62; discussion groups 55; "Four Big Freedoms" 57; "Four Cardinal Principles" 7n68, 57, 58; "fundamental laws" 62–63, 64; Great Leap Forward 56; *guoti* 59, 60–63, 64, 65, 66; Reform and Opening Up 57, 58; rule of law and 58–59; Special Administrative Regions (SARs) 63
political parties 35, 136, 138, 139–140, 145, 162, 201; abuse of the amendment process 292; unconstitutional constitutional amendments (UCA) and 212, 227; *see also* constitutional politics
political question doctrine 138, 154
politics 7, 13, 28, 246; of legitimacy 12, 190, 192, 194, 203; of supremacy 12, 190, 192, 193; of unconstitutional constitutional amendments 212–214, 227; *see also* constitutional politics
popular sovereignty 140, 158; Constitutional Court of Taiwan and 165–166; Hoàng on 78–80; J.Y. Interpretation No. 499 and 164–165, 166
procedural irregularity 13, 234–235; *see also* judicial nullification
Provisional Constitution of the Republic of China (1912): amending 50; Article 2 50; Article 54 50
public interest litigation (PIL) 136, 137, 144, 193, 227; *see also* cases

Rabbani, R. 127–128, 130
Rahman, Z. 218
Ramachandran, R. 196–197
Rasool, S. 127
Regmi, K. R. 134, 141, 144, 146, 147

Index

relative constitution 47
Roznai, Y. 4, 13, 14, 69, 82, 197, 267
rule of law 99, 179, 180, 258; in the PRC 58–59

Saeed, A. 126
salient features doctrine 10, 11, 16
Samak, S. 176
San Francisco Peace Treaty 26
Sarit, T. 174
Sasada, E. 42
Schmitt, C. 4, 47, 52, 61, 63, 277–278
Schocken, A. 285
Science Council of Japan 42
Sebli, A. R. 100, 102, 103
second Constituent Assembly (CA2) 134, 147
secularism 127, 204, 218–219, 251; *see also* Islam
separation of powers 4, 16, 18, 49, 51, 70, 104, 110, 135, 146, 147, 179; Malaysia and 95–96, 97–98, 99, 100, 101; *see also* judicial review
Shah, N. H. 124
Shaked, A. 284–285
Shan, F. 64
Shapiro, M. 163–164
Sharif, N. 11, 111, 112, 119
Shikai, Y. 50
Shrestha, K. 145, 147, 280
Sieyès, E. J. 4, 233
Singapore 254; basic structure doctrine (BSD) in 248–250; Independence Act (1965) 248–249
Smend, R. 52
social contract 89
socialism 9; *guoti* and 64–65
socialist regimes, unamendability and 15
Somchai, W. 176
sovereignty 18, 25, 50, 72; popular 78–80, 140, 158, 164–165
Soviet Union 55
Staatsformenlehre 48
state form 48
Su, N. 161
subject-rule mismatch 13, 235–237; *see also* judicial nullification
Suchinda, K. 175
Sun, Y. 50, 158
supranational constitutional restrictions 13, 241; *see also* judicial nullification
Supreme Court Appellate Division (SCAD) 12–13, 20

Supreme Court of India 6–7
Supreme Court of Nepal 134, 135, 136, 137–138; aftermath of the dissolution of the CA1 146–149; cases on the extension of the CA1 term 142–146; judicial activism 149, 150
Supreme Court of Pakistan, judicial independence 112
Suteu, S. 6, 13, 135, 248, 293

Taisho Democracy 24, 44
Taiwan 8, 18–19, 168; electoral reform 167; incremental constitutional reform 157; judicial activism in 157–160; Judicial Interpretation No. 499 11–12, 164, 278–279, 292; National Assembly 154, 157, 160–161; National Assembly as sunset agency 158–159; presidential election and constitutional politics 159–160; public scrutiny of constitutional revision 167; public sentiment towards frequent constitutional amendments 162; Wild Lily Movement 160–161; *see also* Constitution of the Republic of China (1946); Constitutional Court of Taiwan
temporal limitations 13, 237–238; *see also* judicial nullification
term limits 9, 69
Tew, Y. 10, 240, 283, 291, 292
Thailand 8, 13, 18–19, 169, 170, 280; abusive constitutionalism 182–185; amendment rules 172; Black May 174–175; constituent power 177, 181–182; constitutional drafting council 176–178; coups 174; judicial activism 182–185; Phue Tai Party (PT) 176, 177; senatorial election (2013) 178–179; treaty-making procedure 179–181; unamendability of its monarchy 259–263
Thai-style democracy 173–174, 175; politics of unamendability and 182–185
Thaksin, S. 3, 19, 171, 175, 176, 178, 179, 183, 185
tiering 5–6, 253
Tonsakulrungruang, K. 12, 18–19, 280, 281, 291
Tripathi, P. K. 197
Tushnet, M. 248

unamendability 134, 135, 149, 156, 169, 170, 176, 182, 188, 190, 213, 257, 272; abuse of 258; codified 238–239; in communist regimes 15; of the Constitution of Bangladesh 225–226; of constitutional nationalism in Nepal 263–268; constructive 15, 80; implicit 274–275; informal 195; interpretive 239–240; of judicial supremacy in judicial appointments in India 268–272; legal 80; of Thailand's monarchy 259–263; Thai-style democracy and 182–185; unconstitutional constitutions and 80–81
uncodified constitutions 254–256
unconstitutional constitutional amendments (UCA) 4, 11, 13, 68, 87, 111, 132, 133, 149, 153, 154, 189, 191, 210, 226, 243, 257; 8th Amendment of the Constitution of Bangladesh 212, 214–219; 8th Amendment of the Interim Constitution of Nepal 141–142; 15th Amendment of the Constitution of Bangladesh 212, 219–224; basic structure doctrine (BSD) 10, 12, 16, 17, 19–20; constitution reform debate in Japan 28–32; constitutional design and 5; constitutional dismemberments and 5; as constitutional politics 14–20; decisive model 11–12, 18–19; democratic foundations of 233; denotive model 10, 16, 135; discursive model 8–9, 15, 16; essential features and 124–125; eternity clauses and 6; *guoti* 9, 15; implicit unamendability and 6–7; informal amendments 9, 24–25, 44; Islamic provisions 117, 118–120; Israel's Basic Law and 285; Judicial Interpretation No. 499 11–12; judicial rhetoric and 10; J.Y. Interpretation No. 499 155–156; models 11n41; politics of 212–214, 227; royal assent and 106–108; "salient features" doctrine 10–11; as theory 8; tiering and 5–6; *see also* basic structure doctrine (BSD); explanatory theories of unconstitutional constitutional amendments
unconstitutional constitutions 68, 69, 70, 72, 83; constitutionalism and 81–82; Hoàng on 73–75, 77–78; international law and 82; unamendability and 80–81
United Kingdom 72
United Nations (UN) 35
United States 5, 26, 45, 72; military alliance with Japan 32–35; "Reverse Course" policies 28
Universal Declaration of Human Rights, Article 17 78
Uribe, A. 7
US–Japan Joint Declaration on Security—Alliance for the 21st Century 32–33
US-Japan Security Treaty 26, 27, 28
Uzman, J. 293

Vietnam 8, 9, 15; Cùng Viet Hien Pháp ('Lets' Draw up the Constitution') 70–71; Hoàng's account of an unconstitutional constitution 73–75; intellectuals 67–68, 70; Petition 72 70; *see also* Constitution of Vietnam (2013)

Wang, C. 51
Winkler, C. G. 26
Wu, J.C.H. 52

Xiao, J. 63
Xu, K. 64

Yadav, R. B. 147
Yeh, J.-R. 11, 279
Yingluck, S. 169, 175, 176, 178, 179, 180, 181, 183, 185
Yuan, S. 51, 52

Zhang, J. 52, 53
zhengti/guoti dichotomy 46–47, 51, 63; *see also guoti*
Zhou, Y. 62
zhuquan 50
Zia-ul-Haq, M. 111, 114, 118, 128

Printed in the United States
by Baker & Taylor Publisher Services